Provincial Offences for Paralegals

SECOND EDITION

Jennifer Zubick

emond ▪ Toronto, Canada ▪ 2018

Emond Montgomery Publications Limited
60 Shaftesbury Avenue
Toronto ON M4T 1A3
http://www.emond.ca/highered

MIX
Paper from
responsible sources
FSC® C004071

Reprinted November 2019. Printed in Canada.

We acknowledge the financial support of the Government of Canada. Canadä

Unless otherwise noted, all forms and documents related to the *Provincial Offences Act* © Queen's Printer for Ontario, 2018. Excerpts from the *Paralegal Professional Conduct Guidelines* and *Paralegal Rules of Conduct* © The Law Society of Ontario (formerly Law Society of Upper Canada), 2017.

Vice president, publishing: Anthony Rezek
Publisher: Mike Thompson
Director, development and production: Kelly Dickson
Developmental editor: Sarah Fulton
Production supervisor: Laura Bast
Copy editor: Aliza Amlani

Permissions editor: Caitlin O'Brien
Typesetter: Cenveo® Publisher Services
Text designer: Tara Agnerian
Proofreader: Rebecca Russell
Indexer: Belle Wong
Cover image: Kinga/Shutterstock

Library and Archives Canada Cataloguing in Publication

Zubick, Jennifer, 1969-, author
Provincial offences for paralegals / Jennifer Zubick. — 2nd edition.

Includes text of the Provincial Offences Act (Ontario).
Includes index.
ISBN 978-1-77255-278-2 (softcover)

1. Contraventions (Criminal law)—Ontario—Textbooks.   2. Summary proceedings—Ontario—Textbooks.   I. Ontario. Provincial Offences Act.   II. Title.

KEO1175.Z83 2018   345.713'02   C2017-905788-X
KF9620.ZB3Z83 2018

Dedicated to my family ...
My immediate family,
my extended family, and
my friends that feel like family.

Brief Contents

Detailed Contents

1 An Overview of the Provincial Offences Act

2 Roles and Responsibilities

3 Procedural Streams

4 Classification of Offences

5 Your Client Has Been Charged

6 Helping Your Client Deal with Charges

7 Preparing for the Trial Date

8 Motions and Applications

9 What to Expect in the Courtroom

10 The Trial

11 Sentencing

12 Following Up with a Client

13 Reopenings and Appeals

14 Common Highway Traffic Act Offences

15 Other Common Acts

16 Administrative Monetary Penalties

Preface

The second edition of *Provincial Offences for Paralegals* is intended to introduce paralegal students to the fundamental concepts and procedures associated with provincial offences. My goal was to write this text in a practical yet straightforward and engaging manner. You will be guided through the different procedural streams and charging documents; the classification of offences and available defences; and the anatomy of a trial—including sentencing and appeals. Practice tips are added throughout the text to complement the subject-specific knowledge you will gain, offering invaluable advice that will help you to build and maintain your reputation as a professional in your future career. New to this edition, relevant cases are highlighted in Case in Point boxes, to demonstrate key points and to provide you with an understanding as to how the concepts are interpreted and applied by the courts.

Beginning with an overview of the *Provincial Offences Act* and a discussion of the roles and responsibilities of the key parties involved in the provincial offences system, *Provincial Offences for Paralegals*, 2nd Edition traces the process of a client being charged, arrested, and tried. It outlines the choices available to a paralegal at each stage, and describes the processes and techniques for entering pleas, filing motions and applications, preparing for trial, and interviewing and questioning witnesses. The principles of sentencing are discussed, and the steps that a paralegal should take following a satisfactory or an unsatisfactory outcome at trial are set out. The process and grounds for bringing an appeal are also discussed.

The text also offers coverage of common offences under the Highway Traffic Act, and provides an overview of selected sections from other key provincial legislation, including the *Compulsory Automobile Insurance Act, Liquor Licence Act, Environmental Protection Act, Occupational Health and Safety Act, Trespass to Property Act, Blind Persons' Rights Act, Dog Owners' Liability Act*, and relevant municipal legislation.

This text reflects the law and related forms as of October 2017. You are advised to consult the relevant court websites to access the current versions of the forms included here.

Acknowledgments

I would like to thank the team at Emond Publishing who helped me through every step of the revision and completion of this edition—specifically, Mike Thompson, Sarah Fulton May, Aliza Amlani, and Laura Bast. It was an absolute pleasure to work with the incredibly supportive Emond editing team. I also would like to express my appreciation for all of the contributions made by Steve Weir on the first edition of the text.

This edition would not have been possible if not for the support and understanding of friends and family. I would like to thank my students, past and present, from the Paralegal Education program at Humber College for helping me to realize the need for a text geared toward paralegals, and for appreciating the work that I do. I would like to thank my friends who tried to understand when I was busy writing, but were always willing to distract me when I needed it the most (especially Kim Morrison). I would also like to thank all of my law colleagues from Humber College, especially Samantha Callow, Jasteena Dhillon, and Reena Bauser, who were always willing to discuss various aspects of this text and offer their insight. As well, I would like to thank Carla Mariuz and Danijela Mikec from the City of Mississauga who were happy to share ideas and help with my inquiries.

Last but not least, I extend a very special thank you to my family for their ongoing support, patience, encouragement, and love. Thank you to my mom, and to my brothers Jay and Larry. And enormous gratitude to my husband José and my sons Gabe and Zack—as you already know, you are the inspiration and the motivation for everything that I do.

A Note from the Publisher

We wish to thank the following reviewers for their helpful suggestions and feedback on the previous edition as we developed this second edition: Anne Colterman, Algonquin College; Roumiana Moutafova, TriOS College; Nav K. Singh, law professor at various colleges and universities; Elizabeth Strutt-MacLeod, St. Clair College; and Domenic Zito, George Brown College.

Teaching supplements are also available for instructors who have adopted this book for their courses. For more information, please go to **emond.ca/POPL2** or contact your Emond representative.

About the Author

Jennifer Zubick received her Honours Bachelor of Arts degree in Psychology/Sociology from the University of Guelph; her Master of Arts degree in Sociology/Criminology from the University of Windsor; her Bachelor of Laws degree from the University of Windsor, Faculty of Law; and her Master of Laws degree in Alternative Dispute Resolution from Osgoode Hall Law School. She was called to the Ontario Bar in 2000. She has also co-authored another Emond publication, *ADR for Legal Professionals*. Jennifer is a full-time professor with Humber College and has been appointed as a Hearing Officer by the City of Mississauga and the City of Oshawa to adjudicate administrative penalty infractions. Her previous professional experience includes working as the Assistant Solicitor for the Town of Newmarket, a Policy Specialist for the Regional Municipality of York, a Mediator for the Information and Privacy Commission, a Roster Mediator for the Ontario Mandatory Mediation Program, and a Provincial Prosecutor for the Ministry of the Attorney General.

An Overview of the Provincial Offences Act

1

LEARNING OUTCOMES

After reading this chapter, you will understand

■ when and how the *Provincial Offences Act* is used;

■ the proper citation for the *Provincial Offences Act*;

■ which legislation is covered by the *Provincial Offences Act*;

■ the types of matters that are heard before the provincial offences court;

■ how the *Provincial Offences Act* is administered;

■ the difference between criminal and provincial offences;

■ the breakdown of the *Provincial Offences Act* and regulations; and

■ how the rules and regulations of the *Courts of Justice Act* apply to provincial offences.

Introduction

The *Provincial Offences Act*[1] (POA) is an Ontario statute that sets out the procedures for the administration and prosecution of charges laid under provincial statutes, municipal by-laws, and specific federal statutes. The POA is reproduced in Appendix A to this text.[2] The offences that follow the procedures of the POA are considered to be **regulatory offences**—meaning that laws have been enacted to regulate behaviour in society. For example, a stop sign regulates when drivers must bring vehicles to a halt. Committing a regulatory offence is typically considered to be a minor infraction or a social wrongdoing and is penalized accordingly. However, there are some more serious offences that have much harsher penalties, including substantial fines and the possibility of incarceration. For example, many of the offences in the *Liquor Licence Act*[3] carry a fine of up to $100,000 and the possibility of up to 12 months in jail for an individual who is charged, and a fine of up to $250,000 for a corporation that is charged. POA offences are also sometimes called **public welfare offences** because they are associated with laws that have been established to protect the well-being of the general public. For example, the *Smoke-Free Ontario Act*[4] was established in an effort to protect the public from the dangers of smoking.

An act under which a person is charged can be referred to as the **charging act**. The POA is seldom used to initiate charges and is considered to be more of a **procedural act** than a charging act. For example, a driver may be charged with speeding under the *Highway Traffic Act*[5] (the charging act) but would follow the procedures for responding to the speeding charge as set out in the *Provincial Offences Act* (the procedural act). However, the POA does contain seven sections that create procedure-related offences:

- Section 42: failure to appear in court,
- Section 75: breach of a probation order,
- Section 77: being party to an offence,
- Section 78: counselling an offence,
- Section 86: making a false statement,
- Section 91: contempt of court, and
- Section 99: publishing the identity of a young person.

It is much more common for paralegals to defend clients charged under a range of other statutes and by-laws than to defend clients charged with one of the offences

regulatory offences
offences that are a violation of laws that were enacted to regulate behaviour in society (also known as provincial offences)

public welfare offences
offences that are a violation of safety laws that were enacted to protect the public (also known as provincial offences)

charging act
a piece of legislation under which a person is charged (e.g., the *Highway Traffic Act*)

procedural act
a statute that sets out the procedures to be followed when dealing with an offence (e.g., the *Provincial Offences Act*)

---

1 RSO 1990, c P.33.

2 The POA is provided for your ease of reference when completing class activities and assigned questions. When representing a client you should always refer to the most current version of the POA.

3 RSO 1990, c L.19.

4 SO 1994, c 10.

5 RSO 1990, c H.8.

created by the POA. However, one of these POA offences could arise when representing a client on another charge. For example, an extreme outburst or inappropriate conduct by your client during a traffic trial could lead to the justice finding the defendant to be in contempt of court.

Proper Statutory Citation

As a primary source of law, the *Provincial Offences Act* must be cited using the proper statutory citation. The proper citation for the POA is:

Provincial Offences Act, RSO 1990, c P.33

- *Provincial Offences Act* = name of the statute
- RSO = the name of the statute series in which the Act appears (Revised Statutes of Ontario)
- 1990 = the year in which the statute was last published in a revised volume
- c = the chapter in which the statute appears
- P.33 = the letter "P" makes reference to the first letter of the name of the Act—"*Provincial Offences Act*" (not the page, paragraph, or part) and the number 33 indicates that the POA was the 33rd statute beginning with the letter "P" in the 1990 edition of the Revised Statutes of Ontario

Statutes Governed by the Provincial Offences Act

The offences under all provincial statutes are administered and prosecuted using the procedures set out in the POA. Examples of commonly prosecuted provincial statutes include: the *Highway Traffic Act, Compulsory Automobile Insurance Act,*[6] *Liquor Licence Act, Occupational Health and Safety Act,*[7] and *Environmental Protection Act.*[8]

The *Municipal Act, 2001,*[9] a provincial statute, creates the authority for municipalities (e.g., regions, cities, towns, townships) to enact by-laws that apply within their municipal boundaries. Infractions of these by-laws are also subject to the procedures set out in the POA.

A limited number of federal statutes are also governed by the procedures of the POA. Examples include: the *Canadian Environmental Protection Act,*[10] *Canada Shipping Act, 2001,*[11] and *Fisheries Act.*[12]

---

6 RSO 1990, c C.25.

7 RSO 1990, c O.1.

8 RSO 1990, c E.19.

9 SO 2001, c 25.

10 SC 1999, c 33.

11 SC 2001, c 26.

12 RSC 1985, c F-14.

PRACTICE TIP

When preparing to represent your clients, it is important to consult the procedures set out in the charging act as well as in the *Provincial Offences Act* (the procedural act). The charging act may contain provisions that override the procedures of the POA. For example, although the POA specifies that the general limitation period for laying a Part III charge is six months, one of the provisions in the *Compulsory Automobile Insurance Act* (CAIA) overrides this limitation period. Specifically, under the CAIA, proceedings may be commenced at any time within three years after the date of the offence if a driver was found operating a motor vehicle without insurance. The POA provides standard procedural information that applies in most situations to the majority of offences. However, if the charging act contains procedural information specific to the offence, the charging act provisions should be followed. If the charging act does not contain the required procedural information, look to the POA for the necessary information.

Common Charges

Traffic violations are the most common charges in the provincial offences system. Statistics compiled by the Ontario Court of Justice indicate that, across all of Ontario, 81.6 percent of provincial offence matters are charges under the *Highway Traffic Act*.[13] Of those traffic violations, the largest proportion is speeding. Other common traffic violations include: improper stop at stop sign, traffic light violations, distracted driving, failure to wear seat belt, and careless driving.

Parking offences can either be subject to the procedures set out in the POA or can follow a municipality's administrative penalty system (APS)[14] by-law, if such a by-law has been enacted. For a discussion of administrative penalties, see Chapter 16. Examples of common parking infractions include: parking in a fire route, failing to display parking permits, and parking at an expired meter.

By-laws vary from municipality to municipality. Behaviours that are regulated in one municipality might not be regulated in a neighbouring municipality. However, some of the by-law charges common in most municipalities involve parking offences, noise violations, licensing matters, and building permit violations.

Most environmental infractions, whether covered by municipal, provincial, or federal legislation, follow the procedures as set out in the POA.

---

13 Ontario Courts, *Provincial Offences Court Activity (Part I and Part III only), Charges Received/ Charges Disposed by Statute, Ontario Court of Justice Provincial Overview, January 2016 to December 2016*, online: <http://www.ontariocourts.ca/ocj/files/stats/poa/2016/2016-Q4-POA-Statute.pdf>.

14 Also known as administrative monetary penalty systems (AMPS).

PRACTICE TIP

Always review the actual wording of the charge(s) against each client. Reviewing the appropriate section(s) of the charging act will provide you with information you will need in preparing your defence and will help you to anticipate the prosecutor's case.

Comparison with Criminal Charges

Section 2 of the POA indicates that one of the purposes of the Act is to distinguish between provincial and criminal offences. In order to make such a distinction, when creating the POA it was necessary to establish procedures that were separate from the procedures used for criminal matters. The procedures that have been established for provincial offences are less restrictive and complex than criminal procedures, while still providing the opportunity for defendants to have their day in court.

Although provincial offences are sometimes called **quasi-criminal offences**, the offences are not considered to be criminal in nature. Provincial offences are often less serious than criminal offences, and a conviction does not result in a criminal record for the defendant. The offences are referred to as quasi-criminal because they do bear a resemblance to criminal matters (e.g., a defendant is charged for breaking a law) and because the procedure for dealing with some of the matters is similar to the criminal process (e.g., the defendant has the right to a trial and will be penalized if convicted).

Many people who consider themselves to be law-abiding citizens will find themselves in provincial offences court one day. For example, a driver could unintentionally make an improper turn while driving in an unfamiliar area. If a provincial offences officer witnesses this driving infraction, the driver may be charged. Theoretically, while the driver should be punished in some way for the wrongfulness of the act, he or she should not be punished to the same extent that criminal acts are punished. While there are some severe penalties under the POA, most are less severe than those under the *Criminal Code,*[15] and the defendant will not receive a criminal record if convicted.

> **quasi-criminal offences** offences that bear a resemblance to criminal matters because the procedure for dealing with them is similar to the criminal process (also known as provincial offences)

Administration of the Provincial Offences Act

Over the past decade, the attorney general has transferred most of the responsibility for administering the POA to the municipal level. Municipalities now have the responsibility for prosecuting all Part I and Part II matters, while the province has retained responsibility for the prosecution of Part III matters. Municipalities are also responsible for administering all of the provincial offences courts and collecting all fines under the Act.

---

15 RSC 1985, c C-46.

Breakdown of the Provincial Offences Act

The POA is divided into ten parts. Parts I, II, and III set out the procedures to commence proceedings for the different classifications of offences. Specifically, Part I deals with minor offences that are commenced using a Certificate of Offence, Part II focuses on the initiation of parking charges using a Certificate of Parking Infraction, and Part III involves commencing proceedings for more serious infractions by way of a document called an Information.

Parts IV through VIII contain general provisions that are applicable to Part I, Part II, and Part III hearings. Part IV deals with trials and sentencing in POA proceedings, while Part V provides miscellaneous additional information entitled "General Provisions," such as information about electronic copies, authorizing interpreters, and contempt of court. Part VI contains the special rules that apply if the defendant is a young person between the ages of 12 and 16, Part VII discusses appeals and reviews, and Part VIII sets out the rules and procedures relating to arrest, bail, and search warrants.

Part IX and Part X each deal with a specific issue that relates to the application and administration of the POA. Part IX deals with situations where another statute has authorized taking a proceeding before the Ontario Court of Justice or a justice for an order. Part X is specific to the municipal transfer agreements that provide municipalities with the authority to provide court administration and court support functions under the POA.

As mentioned, the full text of the POA is reproduced in Appendix A.

Provincial Offences Act Regulations

regulations
legislation that contains the rules or principles that are enacted under the authority of a statute

Regulations are the principles or rules that are enacted under the authority of a statute. At present, nine regulations are in force under the authority of the *Provincial Offences Act*.

1. *Certified Evidence*[16]—Explains which evidence can be considered as certified evidence.

---

16   O Reg 132/14.

2. *Costs*[17]—Sets out, in chart format, the costs that may be applicable under sections 60(2) and 60(1).

3. *Electronic Documents and Remote Meetings*[18]—Defines and sets out procedures for the use of electronic documents.

4. *Extensions of Prescribed Times*[19]—Permits the courts to extend time periods in the event of a mail strike.

5. *Fee for Late Payment of Fines*[20]—Establishes the administrative fee payable for fines in default.

6. *Forms*[21]—Provides information about provincial offences forms and sets out, in chart format, a table of forms.

7. *Parking Infractions*[22]—Provides specific information and designated forms to be used for parking infractions.

8. *Proceedings Commenced by Certificate of Offence*[23]—Prescribes format to be used for Certificates of Offence and other court forms, and provides the short-form wording that can be used on the Certificate of Offence.

9. *Victim Fine Surcharges*[24]—Sets out, in chart format, the victim fine surcharges that are added to every offence.

PRACTICE TIP

It is important to learn the content of the regulations as well as the content of the Act because the regulations will provide more specific information about designated topics. For example, the POA does not provide specific information about additional costs that are payable on conviction, but Regulation 945 sets out the various costs that may be added to a fine when there is a conviction.

Courts of Justice Act

The *Courts of Justice Act* (CJA)[25] is an Ontario statute. Together with its associated regulations, the CJA sets out the rules used for Ontario courts. Because provincial offences are dealt with in the Ontario Court of Justice and the Superior Court of Justice, it is important to understand the rules that apply to both of these courts.

---

17 RRO 1990, Reg 945. Reproduced in Appendix B to this text.

18 O Reg 67/12.

19 RRO 1990, Reg 946.

20 O Reg 679/92.

21 O Reg 108/11.

22 RRO 1990, Reg 949.

23 RRO 1990, Reg 950.

24 O Reg 161/00.

25 RSO 1990, c C.43.

Two of the sections that apply to provincial offences matters are sections 38 and 39. These sections create the authority for the court and the justices. Specifically, section 38(2) of the CJA indicates that the Ontario Court of Justice has jurisdiction to perform any function assigned to it by or under the POA. Section 39 of the CJA grants power for a judge to preside in the Ontario Court of Justice and for a justice of the peace to preside in the Ontario Court of Justice in a proceeding under the POA.

In addition, the regulations to the CJA provide copies of some of the proper forms for provincial offences matters and set out the rules for proceedings and appeals. These regulations are listed below:

1. *Rules of the Ontario Court (Provincial Division) in Provincial Offences Proceedings*[26]—Prescribes various procedural matters such as the calculation of time, filings, delivery of notices, certificates and other documents, and the prescribed forms to be used.

2. *Rules of the Court of Appeal in Appeals under the Provincial Offences Act*[27]— Sets out the rules that govern appeals to the Court of Appeal.

3. *Rules of the Ontario Court (Provincial Division) in Appeals under Section 135 of the Provincial Offences Act*[28]—Sets out the rules that govern appeals in a Part I or II matter.

4. *Rules of the Ontario Court (General Division) and the Ontario Court (Provincial Division) in Appeals under Section 116 of the Provincial Offences Act*[29]— Sets out the rules govern appeals of Part III matters.

---

26   RRO 1990, Reg 200. Reproduced in Appendix B to this text.

27   O Reg 721/94.

28   O Reg 722/94.

29   O Reg 723/94.

KEY TERMS

charging act, 2
procedural act, 2
public welfare offences, 2
quasi-criminal offences, 5
regulations, 6
regulatory offences, 2

REVIEW QUESTIONS

Multiple Choice

1. Which of the following statutes sets out the procedures for pleading guilty to an insurance-related charge?

   a. *Highway Traffic Act.*

   b. *Insurance Protection Act.*

   c. *Provincial Offences Act.*

   d. *Compulsory Automobile Insurance Act.*

2. Which of the following statutes is considered to be a procedural act?

   a. *Highway Traffic Act.*

   b. *Liquor Licence Act.*

   c. *Dog Owners' Liability Act.*

   d. *Provincial Offences Act.*

3. Which of the follow statements is FALSE?

   a. A conviction on a provincial offence will result in a criminal record for the defendant.

   b. Provincial offences are sometimes called "quasi-criminal offences."

   c. Provincial offences have a separate set of procedures from criminal procedures.

   d. Most of the penalties for provincial offences are less severe than for criminal offences.

4. In the statutory citation *Provincial Offences Act,* RSO 1990, c P.33, what does "P.33" refer to?

   a. Page 33.

   b. Paragraph 33.

   c. Part 33.

   d. The 33rd statute listed in the P volume of the RSO.

5. What does Part VI of the *Provincial Offences Act* deal with?

   a. Trials and sentencing.

   b. Appeals and reviews.

   c. Arrest, bail, and search warrants.

   d. Special rules that apply if the defendant is a young person.

6. Where would you look to find the proper procedures for appealing a traffic conviction?

   a. *Highway Traffic Act.*

   b. *Provincial Offences Act.*

   c. *Courts of Justice Act.*

   d. The charging document.

7. Where would you look to find the full text wording of the charging section for a stop sign offence?

   a. *Highway Traffic Act.*

   b. *Provincial Offences Act.*

   c. *Courts of Justice Act.*

   d. The charging document.

8. Which statute establishes the authority for a justice of the peace to preside over traffic matters?

   a. *Courts of Justice Act.*

   b. *Provincial Offences Act.*

   c. *Criminal Code.*

   d. *Highway Traffic Act.*

9. What type of information does O Reg 67/12 contain?

   a. Establishes the administrative fee payable for fines in default.

   b. The short-form wording that can be used on the Certificate of Offence.

   c. Defines and sets out the procedures for the use of electronic documents.

   d. Sets out victim fine surcharges that are added to every offence.

10. Which of the following is an offence in the *Provincial Offences Act*?
    a. Improper stop at intersection.
    b. Fail to surrender insurance.
    c. Breach of a probation order.
    d. Parking at an expired meter.
    e. Stunt driving.

11. Which branch of government is responsible for collecting the fines under the *Provincial Offences Act*?
    a. Municipal government.
    b. Provincial government.
    c. Federal government.
    d. Different branches of government for different parts of the POA.

Short Answer

1. Would the *Provincial Offences Act*, RSO 1990, c P.33 apply to a person charged with speeding in British Columbia? Why or why not?

2. Explain why provincial offences are sometimes referred to as "quasi-criminal" offences.

3. Explain whether you would follow the provisions in the charging act or the procedural act (the POA) if they contain different procedural information.

4. Section 61 of the POA states that the maximum fine for a Part III offence is $5,000. However, the *Highway Traffic Act* indicates that the penalty for stunt driving, a Part III offence, can range from $2,000 to $10,000. Which maximum amount would apply and why?

5. When preparing for trial, which types of legislation should a paralegal consult?

Roles and Responsibilities

2

LEARNING OUTCOMES

After reading this chapter, you will understand

■ the various parties involved with provincial offences matters;

■ the duties and responsibilities of each of the parties; and

■ the proper way for a paralegal to address these parties.

Introduction

In order to understand how the provincial offences system works, it is necessary to understand the roles and responsibilities of the people who are involved with the administration and prosecution of provincial offences. This chapter will define and discuss the key players who are employed in the provincial offences field and provide a general overview of the functions they perform.

Defendant (Client)

defendant
has been charged with an offence under a statute governed by the *Provincial Offences Act*

There are several terms that are used to refer to a person who has been charged with an offence under a statute that is governed by the *Provincial Offences Act*.[1] The person charged is most commonly referred to as the **defendant** but may also be called the accused or the offender. If the defendant decides to hire a paralegal, the defendant becomes a "client" to the paralegal.

A properly retained paralegal is able to negotiate on a client's behalf and represent a client in provincial offences court proceedings. While in many cases a client does not need to be present for negotiations or the proceedings, it is crucial that the client remains involved throughout the process. A client must provide instructions to the paralegal to authorize settlement offers. In addition, he or she may be required to attend court as a witness in order to give evidence, and must assume all responsibility for paying court-imposed fines, surcharges, and costs.

The defendant may decide to represent himself or herself in court. In cases of self-representation, the justice is obliged to offer guidance to the defendant. Specifically, the justice has a duty to provide the required information and assistance to allow the defendant to make a full and proper defence to the charges before the court.

Provincial Offences Officer/Police Officer

police officer
has the authority to lay charges against a defendant

provincial offences officer
has the authority to lay charges against a defendant for specific types of provincial offences (includes a police officer)

Provincial offences officers and police officers have the authority to lay charges against a defendant. Section 1(1) of the POA provides definitions for a **police officer** and for a **provincial offences officer**:

"police officer" means a chief of police or other police officer but does not include a special constable or by-law enforcement officer.

"provincial offences officer" means
    (a) a police officer;
    (b) a constable appointed pursuant to any Act;
    (c) a municipal law enforcement officer referred to in subsection 101(4) of the *Municipal Act, 2001*[2] or in subsection 79(1) of the *City of Toronto Act, 2006*[3] while in the discharge of his or her duties;

---

1 RSO 1990, c P.33.

2 SO 2001, c 25.

3 SO 2006, c 11, Sch A.

(d) a by-law enforcement officer of any municipality or of any local board of any municipality, while in the discharge of his or her duties;

(e) an officer, employee, or agent of any municipality or of any local board of any municipality, whose responsibilities include the enforcement of a by-law, an Act or a regulation under an Act, while in the discharge of his or her duties; or

(f) a person designated under subsection (3).[4]

On the basis of these definitions, a "provincial offences officer" is a broad term that includes a police officer, municipal law enforcement officer, by-law enforcement officer, parking enforcement officer, and other designated individuals (e.g., provincial offences officers with provincial ministries, such as Ministry of Health and Long-Term Care, Ministry of Labour, Ministry of the Environment and Climate Change, and Ministry of Natural Resources and Forestry). By contrast, the term "police officer" is a very specific term that does not include other provincial offences officers. If a statute intends that an action be carried out only by a police officer, it will specifically use the term "police officer."

The provincial offences officer will investigate possible offences and, if appropriate, charge the defendant with an offence. If the defendant requests a trial, the officer will be notified to attend court. The officer is at court to provide support and information to the prosecutor, but it is not the officer's duty to negotiate a settlement with the defendant—negotiations are left to the prosecutor's discretion. If the matter proceeds to a trial, the officer can be called as a witness for the prosecution in order to provide evidence to support a conviction against the defendant.

Representative (Paralegal/Lawyer)

A **representative** is a lawyer or a paralegal who is authorized to represent a defendant in a proceeding under the POA. In accordance with section 1(1) of the POA, the definition of a representative is as follows:

> "representative" means, in respect of a proceeding to which this Act applies, a person authorized under the *Law Society Act* to represent a person in that proceeding.

The *Law Society Act*[5] authorizes both lawyers and paralegals to represent clients in legal proceedings. Lawyers and paralegals are required to meet educational requirements and complete an exam or exams in order to become a licensee of the Law Society of Ontario. The terms "barrister" and "solicitor" are sometimes used to refer to a lawyer. Terms that have been used to describe paralegals include "agent" or "court and tribunal agent."

representative
a lawyer or a paralegal who is authorized to represent a defendant in a proceeding under the POA

---

4 In accordance with s 1(3) of the POA, a minister of the Crown may designate in writing any person or class of persons as a provincial offences officer for the purposes of all or any class of offences.

5 RSO 1990, c L.8.

A legal representative is often hired to defend someone who has been charged with an offence. It is more common to see paralegals representing clients in provincial offences court than it is to see lawyers. However, lawyers will typically be retained if a client wants to appeal to the Court of Appeal or the Supreme Court of Canada because paralegals are permitted to handle appeals only in the Ontario Court of Justice. Both paralegals and clients must abide by rules of conduct that are enforced by the Law Society of Ontario.

Court Administration Staff

court administration staff
work within the courthouse providing information and performing various administrative duties

Court administration staff work in the courthouse providing information and performing various administrative duties. They serve an important role within provincial offences court. Their duties include: accepting payment of fines, scheduling trials, providing intake services, arranging for an officer's attendance at trial, requesting interpreters, and answering general inquiries about provincial offences.

While the court administration staff can provide information to defendants and their representatives, they are not in a position to provide legal advice or make court appearances on a defendant's behalf.

Court Clerk

court clerk
ensures POA proceedings run smoothly by providing assistance to the judge or justice

The **court clerk** ensures that POA proceedings run smoothly by providing assistance to the judge or justice. The clerk sits directly in front of the justice and faces the seating area of the courtroom. He or she wears a black robe, but does not wear a sash. A court clerk should be referred to as "Mister/Madam Clerk."

The court clerk will announce the justice's arrival in the courtroom and will commence and close the court proceedings. The clerk will also call the names of the defendants, administer oaths, arraign the defendants, record court proceedings, collect and itemize all exhibits used during a trial, and complete the necessary paperwork. As well, the clerk will ensure that courtroom protocol is followed at all times, often having to remind defendants and representatives of appropriate etiquette.

Court Security Officer

court security officer
special constables who have been appointed to assist with courthouse security and attend to specific incidents that may arise

Some provincial offences court locations employ **court security officers**. Court security officers are civilian members of a police services board who are appointed as "special constables" under section 53(2) of the *Police Services Act*.[6] Upon appointment, the powers of a police officer are conferred upon a special constable as is necessary to carry out the responsibilities of the job. Court security officers continually monitor all areas of the courthouse and attend to specific incidents when called into a courtroom.

---

6   RSO 1990, c P.15.

In some larger municipalities, court security officers screen everyone entering the courthouse using a metal detector, and search all bags and belongings being brought into court facilities.

Prosecutor (Crown)

A **prosecutor** is an agent of the attorney general who prosecutes the charges against the defendant, and is sometimes referred to as "the Crown." According to section 1(1) of the POA, the definition of a prosecutor is as follows:

> "prosecutor" means the Attorney General or, where the Attorney General does not intervene, means the person who issues a certificate or lays an information and includes an agent acting on behalf of either of them.

While prosecutors are agents of the Ministry of the Attorney General, some prosecutors will be employed by a municipality and others will be employed by another branch of the Ontario government (e.g., Ministry of the Environment and Climate Change). If the municipality has entered into a municipal transfer agreement with the province in accordance with Part X of the POA, the municipal prosecutors can take responsibility for the prosecution of designated matters. Currently, many municipal prosecutors conduct the prosecutions for Part I and Part II provincial offences charges, while provincial prosecutors conduct the prosecution for Part III matters. It is not a requirement for prosecutors in provincial offences court to be lawyers. In fact, most prosecutors are graduates from a paralegal diploma program at a community college.

The prosecutor's office duties include: preparing cases, evaluating charges, reviewing statements, interviewing witnesses, assessing the admissibility of evidence, researching case law, ensuring evidence has been collected, and providing disclosure to defendants (e.g., officer's notes, accident report).

At court, a prosecutor will participate in plea negotiations and resolution discussions with the defendant, and, if necessary, present a case to the justice as to why there is sufficient evidence to support a conviction.

According to Rule 4.01(5.1) of the *Paralegal Rules of Conduct*:[7]

> When acting as a prosecutor, a paralegal shall act for the public and the administration of justice resolutely and honourably within the limits of the law while treating the tribunal with candour, fairness, courtesy, and respect.

As such, the prosecutor's role is to assist with the administration of justice, act as an agent of the court, and ensure that proceedings are fair and ethical. A prosecutor should not be concerned about "winning" or "losing," but with ensuring that justice is served.

prosecutor
an agent of the attorney general who prosecutes the charges against the defendant

---

7 *Paralegal Rules of Conduct* (Toronto: Law Society of Ontario, 2007), online: <http://www.lsuc.on.ca/paralegal-conduct-rules>.

The Justice

A justice presides over provincial offences proceedings. The Ontario Court of Justice is composed of provincially appointed judges and justices of the peace. Section 1(1) of the POA provides definitions for a judge and for a justice:

"judge" means a provincial judge;

"justice" means a provincial judge or a justice of the peace.

On the basis of these definitions, a "justice" is a broad term that includes a provincial judge or a justice of the peace. By contrast, "judge" is a very specific term that refers only to a judge.

PRACTICE TIP

It is important to look at the wording in the statute. If it is intended to apply to only a judge, the statute will specify "judge." If the section could also apply to a justice of the peace, the term "justice" will be used.

Justice of the Peace

A justice of the peace is sometimes referred to as a JP. However, "JP" is an informal term that should never be used in a professional setting. A justice of the peace, who wears a black robe with white neck tabs and a green sash across the chest, should be addressed as "Your Worship."

A **justice of the peace** is part of a lay bench whose members are not required to have legal training or experience in the justice system. Historically, there were no formal requirements to become a justice of the peace because such appointments were political. However, the *Access to Justice Act, 2006*[8] changed the appointment process to include an application and interview, leading to an appointment by an advisory committee. Applicants for a justice of the peace position must have completed a degree or diploma and have at least 10 years of full-time work experience, not necessarily related to the law. As a result, justices of the peace have varied backgrounds, including a wide range of educational, business, and volunteer experiences.

The powers, duties, and jurisdiction of a justice of the peace are established in case law and by statute. The two main areas of jurisdiction for justices of the peace are criminal law pursuant to the *Criminal Code* and provincial offences under the POA. Justices of the peace deal with virtually all trial-level provincial offences decisions, including municipal by-law matters. Justices of the peace are also responsible for denying or issuing an Information and applications (e.g., summons or warrant), accepting guilty pleas, and presiding at trials to give a verdict.

justice of the peace
a magistrate who presides over proceedings in provincial offences court

---

8 SO 2006, c 21–Bill 14.

In the criminal courts, justices of the peace have jurisdiction to hold bail hearings, grant search warrants, and preside over some criminal hearings. They are responsible for issuing or denying information documents, summonses, warrants (including search warrants) and for other matters of the criminal process.

Provincial Court Judge

A **provincial court judge** also wears a black robe, but can be distinguished by a red sash across the chest. A judge should be referred to as "Your Honour."

Provincial judges decide some of the more serious provincial offences cases. The charging act will specify if a judge is to preside over the matter. As well, provincial judges hear all provincial offences appeals. Provincial judges are appointed by the lieutenant governor in council on the recommendation of the attorney general. The qualifications of a provincial court judge are set out in section 42(2) of the *Courts of Justice Act*.[9] Specifically, provincial court judges must have been a member of the bar (i.e., a lawyer) of one of the provinces or territories of Canada for at least ten years.

provincial court judge
a lawyer who has been appointed a judge and typically presides over more serious provincial offences cases and appeals

Court Interpreter

In accordance with section 14 of the *Canadian Charter of Rights and Freedoms*, Part I of the *Constitution Act, 1982*:[10]

> A party or witness in any proceedings who does not understand or speak the language in which the proceedings are conducted or who is deaf has the right to the assistance of an interpreter.

And with section 125(2)(a) of the *Courts of Justice Act*:

> [H]earings in courts shall be conducted in the English language and evidence adduced in a language other than English shall be interpreted into the English language.

Therefore, if a defendant does not understand or speak English, a **court interpreter** can be provided if requested. Court interpreters provide translation services on a freelance basis but must apply to the Ministry of the Attorney General in order to appear on the roster of accredited court interpreters. Court interpreters must translate exactly what has been stated.

Court interpreters provide services in many different languages, including sign language. The defendant (or defendant's representative) must request the interpreter in advance, typically at least four weeks before the trial date. The defendant (or defendant's representative) must complete a Notice of Intention to Appear (NIA) and indicate the desired language of interpretation. Alternatively, an Interpreter Request form can be used after the NIA has been filed. The court administration staff will be

court interpreter
provides translation services to defendants who do not speak English

---

9 RSO 1990, c C.43.

10 RSC 1985, App II, No 44.

responsible for ensuring an interpreter is present. The services of a court interpreter are provided at no cost to a defendant or witness.

Section 84 of the POA indicates that a judge or justice "may authorize a person to act as interpreter in a proceeding before the justice [judge] where the person swears the prescribed oath and, in the opinion of the justice [judge], is competent." This allows some discretion on the part of the justice to allow non-accredited individuals to act as interpreters.

Interpreters are required to swear the oath set out in section 27 of the *Rules of the Ontario Court (Provincial Division) in Provincial Offences Proceedings.*[11]

Witnesses

witness
has first-hand knowledge about the matter being prosecuted

Witnesses have first-hand knowledge about the matter being prosecuted. The provincial offences officer who laid the charges against the defendant will typically be called as a witness by the prosecutor. There may also be civilian witnesses who are willing to testify at trial for the prosecution.

The main witness for the defence is usually the defendant. Other defence witnesses may include individuals who were with the defendant at the time of the alleged offence or civilian witnesses.

If a witness refuses to attend the trial, he or she can be summoned for trial. The person wishing to summon the witness must appear before a justice of the peace and swear the summons. If the justice is satisfied that the witness will provide material evidence, the summons will be issued and must be served by a provincial offences officer pursuant to section 26 of the POA. In accordance with section 60(2) of the POA, witnesses can recover costs and fees associated with attendance at court, as set out in Regulation 945, *Costs*.

---

11   RRO 1990, Reg 200.

KEY TERMS

REVIEW QUESTIONS

Multiple Choice

1. Which of the following statements is TRUE with regard to representation at trial?

    a. Defendants must be represented by a paralegal or lawyer to have a trial.

    b. Defendants can be self-represented at trial.

    c. A defendant must be represented for Part III trials.

    d. Upon request, the court will appoint a legal representative for Part III trials.

2. Which of the following job descriptions would require an applicant to have a background as a lawyer?

    a. Justice of the peace.

    b. Prosecutor.

    c. Judge.

    d. Both a and c.

3. Which of the following officers is NOT classified as a provincial offences officer?

    a. By-law officer.

    b. Police officer.

    c. Parking enforcement officer.

    d. They are all considered to be provincial offences officers.

4. Which of the following tasks is NOT a responsibility of a provincial offences officer?

    a. Charges the defendant with an offence.

    b. Serves the offence notice on a defendant.

    c. Engages in plea negotiations with the defendant immediately prior to trial.

    d. Provides support and information to the prosecutor.

5. Which of the following people would wear a black robe, but no sash in the courtroom?

    a. Justice of the peace.

    b. Judge.

    c. Court clerk.

    d. Prosecutor.

6. To whom does the title "Justice" refer?

    a. Justice of the peace.

    b. Provincial court judge.

    c. Prosecutor.

    d. Both a and b.

7. Which of the following statements is FALSE with regard to court-provided interpreters in the provincial offences courts?

    a. Interpreters provide translation services on a freelance basis.

    b. Defendants must provide their own interpreter.

    c. Interpreters provide services in many different languages, including sign language.

    d. The justice has discretion to allow non-accredited individuals to act as interpreters.

Short Answer

1. You walk into a courtroom and see a justice wearing a black gown and a red sash across the chest. What is this person's role and how will you address this individual?

2. Which forms can be used to request a court interpreter?

3. What are the two main areas of jurisdiction for a justice of the peace?

4. What is the procedure for compelling a witness to attend a trial?

5. Describe the duties of a court clerk.

Procedural Streams

3

LEARNING OUTCOMES

After reading this chapter, you will understand

■ the different procedural streams and charging documents under Parts I, II, and III of the *Provincial Offences Act*;

■ the framework for fines, service, and limitation periods for each procedural stream; and

■ where to find additional information about commencing proceedings and procedural requirements.

Introduction

The first three parts of the *Provincial Offences Act*[1] (POA) govern the commencement of proceedings for various provincial offences. Part I of the POA deals with minor offences and Part II with parking offences, while Part III sets out the procedure for the more serious offences that are prosecuted under the POA. These groupings are referred to as the **procedural streams**.

procedural stream
a category under which an offence can be classified that then determines the procedure for dealing with the charge throughout the provincial offences system

Part I Offences

Part I of the POA deals with the majority of minor offences, such as speeding, drinking in public, trespassing, and other infractions. Part I offences have a prescribed corresponding set fine. Only a provincial offences officer may commence a proceeding under Part I by completing, signing, and then filing a certificate of offence (see Figure 3.1).

Charging Document

While most people simply refer to the charging document as a "ticket," there are multiple copies of the document with proper names and specific requirements for each. Historically, tickets were handwritten by officers, but it is becoming more common for tickets to be prepared electronically using a mobile device.

For handwritten ticketing, the officer's ticket book usually contains up to 25 ticket sets that are sequentially numbered. Each ticket set will have the **certificate of offence** on top followed by a carbon copy called the **offence notice**[2] and additional copies that are used for administrative and record-keeping purposes. The ticket book will usually also have several loose pages at the back that are not attached to any of the ticket sets called a **summons**.[3] If the officer chooses to issue a summons, the officer will insert it in the ticket set so that it becomes a carbon copy of the certificate.

certificate of offence
a certificate of a violation prepared by an officer under Part I of the POA and filed with the court to commence proceedings

offence notice
a document served on the defendant to inform him/her of the charges (commonly called a "ticket")

summons
a document issued to a defendant requiring attendance in court

For electronic ticketing, the portable ticketing device produces multiple copies of the required information in the necessary formats for the officer, defendant, enforcement agency, and the court.

Regardless of which system is used, officers are required to fill in the certificate of offence so that it is "complete and regular on its face," meaning that it must have all of the necessary information about the officer, the defendant, and the charges. The copy that is served on the defendant is the offence notice or summons and the copy that is filed with the court is the certificate of offence. The proper format for the certificate of offence is set out in section 2(1) of O Reg 108/11 under the POA (see Form 1 in Figure 3.1).

---

1   RSO 1990, c P.33.

2   Historically, the offence notice was coloured yellow. However, electronic ticketing will usually produce a white copy, and other colours (e.g., green) have been used in recent years for the handwritten copies.

3   A summons used for Part I offences is usually coloured pink.

Figure 3.1 Certificate of Offence Under Part I of the POA

ICON Location Code *Code d'emplacement du RIII*	Offence number *Numéro d'infraction*

Form 1, *Provincial Offences Act*, Ontario Court of Justice, O. Reg. 108/11
Formulaire 1, Loi sur les infractions provinciales, *Cour de justice de l'Ontario, Règl. de l'Ont. 108/11*

Certificate of Offence
Procès-verbal d'infraction

I, _____ ,
Je soussigné(e)   (print name / *nom en lettres moulées*)

believe and certify that on the day of   Y / A   M / M   D / J   Time / *heure*
crois et atteste que le | 2 | 0 | | | | | | | | | | M

Name _____
Nom   (family / *nom de famille*)

_____
(given / *prénom*)   (initials / *initiales*)

Address _____
Adresse   (number and street / *numéro et nom de la rue*)

_____
(municipality / *municipalité*)   (P.O. / *C.P.*)   (province)   (postal code / *code postal*)

Driver's licence no. / *N° de permis de conduire*   Juris / *Aut. Lég.*

| | | | | | | | | | |

Birth date / *Date de naissance* Y / A M / M D / J	Sex / *Sexe*	Motor vehicle involved / *Véhicule impliqué* ☐ N / *N*	Collision involved / *Collision* ☐ Y / *O*	Witnesses / *Témoins* ☐ Y / *O*

At _____
À   (municipality / *municipalité*)

Did commit the offence of _____
A commis l'infraction de

_____

contrary to _____ sect. _____
contrairement à   *l'art.*

Plate no. *N° de la plaque d'immatriculation*	Juris *Aut. Lég.*	Commercial *Utilitaire* ☐ Y / *O*	CVOR *IUVU* ☐ Y / *O*	NSC *CNS* ☐ Y / *O*	Code

CVOR No. - NSC No. / *N° de l'IUVU - N° du CNS*
| | | | | | | | | | | | |

And I further certify that I served an offence notice   ☐ Or other service date of:
personally upon the person charged on the offence date.   *Autre date de signification, le :*
J'atteste également qu'à la date de l'infraction, j'ai signifié, en
mains propres, un avis d'infraction à la personne accusée.   _____

Signature of issuing Provincial Offences Officer *Signature de l'agent des infractions provinciale*	Officer No. *N° de l'agent*	Platoon *Peloton*	Unit *Unité*

Set fine of *Amende fixée de* $ $	**Total payable** **Montant total exigible** $ $	Total payable includes set fine, applicable victim fine surcharge and costs. / *Le montant total exigible comprend l'amende fixée, la suramende compensatoire applicable et les frais.*

Summons issued. You are   Y / A   M / M   D / J   Time / *heure*
required to appear in court on | 2 | 0 | | | | | | | | | | | M
Assignation. *Vous êtes*   Ct. room / *Salle*   at the Ontario Court of Justice POA Office at / *à la Cour*
tenu(e) de comparaître devant   *d'audience*   *de justice de l'Ontario, Bureau des infractions provinciales au*
le tribunal le

Deemed not to dispute charge under s. 9(1)(a) of the *Provincial Offences Act*. Set fine imposed. / *Réputé ne pas*
contester l'accusation aux termes de l'alinéa 9 (1) (a) de la Loi sur les infractions provinciales. Amende fixée imposée.

                                        Y / A   M / M   D / J
_____ | 2 | 0 | | | | | |
          Justice / *Juge*

Form / *Formulaire* 1 (November 2, 2011 / *2 novembre 2011*)

Set Fines

set fine
the amount of monetary penalty determined by the chief justice of the Ontario Court of Justice for an offence under Part I or Part II

The term "set fine" refers to the amount of the predetermined monetary penalty as established by the chief justice. The **set fine** is a fixed amount, and does not include costs, the victim fine surcharge, and added fees. The set fine amount for an **offence** under Part I is included on the offence notice in a box near the bottom labelled "set fine." This is the amount that is prescribed for an out-of-court guilty plea to the charge. If a summons is served on the defendant, there will be no specified set fine and no opportunity for an out-of-court guilty plea.

offence
a violation of a piece of legislation, or of a regulation or a by-law made under a piece of legislation

For most offences, especially those under provincial statutes, the government ministry or other body that administers the legislation applies to the chief justice for approval on the set fine for offences. Officers cannot issue a fine that is different than the set fine. If the officer believes a higher fine may be warranted, the officer must serve the defendant with a summons to appear in **court** to allow the justice to determine the appropriate fine.

court
the Ontario Court of Justice, which includes the provincial offences court

Municipalities have broad authority to enact their own fines, including escalating fines for by-laws. In the past, municipalities had to apply to the regional senior justice for approval on short-form wordings and corresponding set fines for by-law matters.

If a matter proceeds to court for a trial, the set fine does not apply and the penalty provisions of the POA or the charging act prevail. The maximum fine for a conviction on a Part I offence is $1,000, unless otherwise stated in the charging act.

Short-Form Wordings

The term "short-form wording" refers to approved language used to describe an offence on a Part I charging document. The short-form wording, as established by the chief justice, provides the defendant with written notice of which offence they are alleged to have committed. For example, section 134 of the *Highway Traffic Act*[4] deals with officers directing traffic. The full text of that section is quite lengthy and describes situations when an officer may be required to direct traffic and the need for drivers to obey, but the approved short-form wording is simply "disobey officer directing traffic."

> ### PRACTICE TIP
>
> Approved set fines and short-form wordings can be found on the Ontario Court of Justice website[5] and are updated when the chief justice approves changes. Paralegals should regularly check this website in order to be aware of any changes.

Proper Service

In the majority of cases under Part I, a provincial offences officer will personally serve the defendant with an offence notice or a summons by handing it to the defendant

---

4   RSO 1990, c H.8.

5   *Ontario Court of Justice, Set Fines I of the Provincial Offences Act*, online: <http://www.ontariocourts.ca/ocj/how-do-i/set-fines/set-fines-i/>.

at the time and place of the offence. However, under section 3(3) of the POA, an officer has up to 30 days from the date of the offence to issue and personally serve an offence notice or summons on the defendant. This allows time for an officer to further investigate the need for charges to be laid.

Service is usually simple. Most often, the issuing officer who completed the certificate of offence gives the offence notice or summons to the defendant and signs the certification area on the certificate to indicate when and how service was completed. In cases where it was not served at the time of the offence, the officer will have to specify the date of service. Section 3(6) of the POA allows the offence notice or summons to be served by a person other than the provincial offences officer who issued the certificate of offence. In such cases, the serving officer must complete an affidavit of service.

It is sufficient under Part I for an officer to certify that service has taken place, and he or she would not normally be asked to testify in court to establish proper service.

PRACTICE TIP

It is important for paralegals to ensure that service of an offence notice or summons on a client complied with the POA. For Part I offences, an officer may not leave the charging document with someone other than the defendant. However, there may be an exception to the general rule if a defendant attempts to evade service.

CASE IN POINT

Personal Service of an Offence Notice

City of London v (Leslie) Erdesz, 2009 CanLII 10394, [2009] OJ No 1008 (SC).

Facts

A provincial offences officer attended at the defendant's residence to issue four charges. Prior to writing up the tickets, he spoke to the defendant and explained that the purpose of the visit was to lay the charges. As the officer walked to his vehicle to fill out the tickets, the defendant went inside his house. After he had completed the notices, the officer knocked at the front door and when it was not answered, left the offence notices in the defendant's mailbox.

At trial, the defendant took the position that there was improper service of the offence notices since the POA requires personal service. The prosecutor took the position that by filing the offence notices and then appearing in court the defendant had attorned to the jurisdiction of the court. The justice agreed with the defendant that he had not been personally served and ordered a stay of the charges.

The City of London brought an application for an order of mandamus (an order that would require the provincial offences court to proceed with the trial of four offences).

Relevant Issue

Personal Service of an Offence Notice

Decision

Failure to serve personally is an irregularity only. The purpose of personal service is to give notice so that the defendant is made is aware of the charges. Since the defendant had responded to the notices and appeared in court, the court drew the inference that the defendant did get the documents and was aware of the charges. Application was granted.

> ## PRACTICE TIP
>
> If your client is a young person, the special provisions in Part VI of the POA apply. In accordance with section 95, a young person must receive a summons to appear in court. An offence notice cannot be used. In addition, a copy of the summons must be delivered to the parent of the young person. Paralegals should check to make sure these special provisions have been followed when representing a young person.

Limitation Periods

limitation period
the time allowed for an officer to lay a charge against a defendant

The **limitation period** is the time within which an officer is authorized to lay a charge against a defendant. For Part I offences, this is a two-stage calculation. Under section 3(3) of the POA, the officer is required to serve the defendant with the offence notice or summons within 30 days of the date of the alleged offence. However, service of the offence notice alone is not sufficient to commence a proceeding. In accordance with section 4 of the POA, the certificate of offence must be filed in court as soon as possible, but no later than seven days after service has taken place. The court administration office will not accept the certificate if the officer attempts to file it past the deadline, and the charge will be considered abandoned. In rare instances where the certificate may have been accepted *in error* by the court administration office, a paralegal could either request that the prosecutor withdraw the charge or bring a motion to have it quashed. Paralegals should caution their clients that even if the officer has missed the time frame for filing, the officer still has the option to re-lay the charge if it is still within the 30-day time frame for service (or within six months if the officer decides to lay it as a Part III charge).

> ## PRACTICE TIP
>
> Regulation 200 of the *Courts of Justice Act*[6] provides the framework for calculating the limitation period. To calculate the service time frame, add 30 days to the date of the offence (in other words, for an offence that occurs on March 1, the officer must serve the defendant by March 31). To calculate the filing time frame, exclude the date of service, and if the last day for filing is a holiday (Saturday, Sunday, or a statutory holiday), it is extended to the first business day following the holiday.

Part II Offences

Part II of the *Provincial Offences Act* deals with parking infractions.[7] Most drivers who run afoul of regulatory requirements and are charged as a result have improperly used a vehicle, violating rules for stopping, standing, or parking. Most parking infractions are created by municipal by-laws and carry a monetary fine.

---

6 RSO 1990, c C.43.

7 Many municipalities in Ontario have established (or are in the process of establishing) administrative penalty by-laws in order to deal with parking tickets outside of the POA. See Chapter 16 for a discussion of administrative penalties.

Charging Document

The charging document for Part II is a **certificate of parking infraction**. Similar to Part I charging documents, there are multiple copies required. The certificate copy is filed with the court, and the copy called the "parking infraction notice" (PIN) is served on the defendant (typically, the registered owner of the motor vehicle). Traditionally the PIN was a carbon copy of the certificate of parking infraction. However, in recent years most municipalities and other bodies have adopted technology to aid in the administration of parking enforcement. Many tickets are now computer-generated and printed by a mobile printer before being served on a driver (see Figure 3.2).

There is no provision to issue a summons to an individual under Part II.

certificate of parking infraction
a notice of a violation issued by an officer under Part II of the POA

Set Fines

Part II offences have approved set fines, similar to Part I. It is worth noting that victim fine surcharges are not added to parking infractions and that the amount of the set fine is indicated on the certificate of parking infraction. Some municipalities or other bodies have implemented reduced early payment amounts to encourage defendants to make payment.

Most set fines for Part II offences are established through municipalities' by-laws or the regional senior judge. The process of applying to the chief justice is used for very few parking infraction set fines, but the exceptions are found on the Ontario Court of Justice website.

> **PRACTICE TIP**
>
> In reviewing options with a client, it is important for paralegals to remember that the set fine for a Part I or Part II offence refers only to the out-of-court payment amount. If a trial takes place, the court may impose any fine in accordance with the POA; the set fine is only a guide, not a rule. As with Part I offences, Part II of the POA provides for a maximum fine of $1,000.

Proper Service

Service requirements for Part II are different from those for any other offence. Many parking infractions are observed in the absence of the person who has care and control of the vehicle. For example, the driver might not be present when a vehicle is parked at an expired meter. Section 15(4)(a) of the POA allows for service on the owner of the vehicle by affixing it to the vehicle in a conspicuous place—usually under a vehicle's windshield wiper blade. No one needs to be present at the vehicle for the PIN to be properly served, and once placed on the vehicle, the officer certifies service. Section 15(4)(b) of the POA allows for personal service of the person with care and control of the vehicle, and section 15(5) permits personal service of the operator. For example, if a driver was sitting in the vehicle while parked in a fire route, the provincial offences officer would likely serve the driver instead of affixing the PIN to the windshield.

Figure 3.2   Certificate of Parking Infraction Under Part II of the POA

Form 11, *Provincial Offences Act*, Ontario Court of Justice
Formulaire 11, Loi sur les infractions provinciales, Cour de justice de l'Ontario

Certificate of Parking Infraction
Procès-verbal d'infraction de stationnement

I, _____ ,
Je soussigné(e)   (Print name / *Nom en lettres moulées*)

believe from my personal knowledge and certify that on the _____ day of
crois, en me fondant sur me connaissance directe de faits, et atteste que le   *jour de*

_____ , 20 _____ , Time _____ | **M** |
                                        À (heure)

the owner (or operator) of the vehicle upon which was displayed the number plate:
le propriétaire de (ou l'utilisateur) du véhicule portant la plaque d'immatriculation suivante :

Plate No. / *N° de plaque d'immatriculation*	Province	Expiry Date *Date d'expiration* M / M Y / A

did commit the parking infraction of:
a commis l'infraction de stationnement de :

_____

_____

at   _____
à

_____
                                              (Municipality / *Municipalité*)

contrary to _____   sect. _____
contrairement à   *l'art.*

I further certify that I: **J'atteste en outré j'ai :**

A. served a parking infraction notice   ☐ A. *signifié un avis d'infraction de*
   on the owner of the vehicle   *stationnement au propriétaire de*
   identified herein by affixing it to the   *véhicule ci-identifié en apposant cet avis*
   vehicle in a conspicuous place at   *sur ce véhicule à un endroit bien en vue*
   the time of this alleged infraction or,   *au moment d'infraction reprochée ou;*

B. served a parking infraction notice   ☐ B. *signifié un avis d'infraction de*
   on the owner (or operator) of the   *stationnement au propriétaire (ou à*
   vehicle identified herein by   *utilisateur) du véhicule ci-identifié en*
   delivering it personally to the   *remettant cet avis en mains propres à*
   person having care and control (or   *la personne qui a la garde et le*
   operator) of the vehicle at the time   *contrôle (ou à utilisateur) du véhicule*
   of the alleged infraction.   *au moment de l'infraction reprochée.*

Signature of issuing Provincial Offences Officer *Signature de l'agent des infractions provinciale*	SET FINE *AMENDE FIXÉE*
	$ $
Officer No. / *N° de l'agent*	Unit / *Unité*

Complete only if operator Is charged / *Ne remplir que si l'utilisateur est inculpé*

Name of operator
Nom de l'utilisateur   (Last / *Nom*)   (First / *Prénom*)   (Middle / *Initiale*)

Address _____
Adresse

_____
         (Municipality / *Municipalité*)   (Province)   (Postal code / *Code postal*)

Driver's licence no. / *N° de permis de conduire*		
Birth date / *Date de naissance* Y / A M / M D / J	Sex / *Sexe*	Province

Form / *Formulaire* 11 (March 17, 2011 / *17 mars 2011*)

Unlike Part I, Part II requires immediate service of the PIN. There is no provision to serve a parking infraction notice at any time other than when the offence takes place. If service cannot comply with those requirements, officers may choose to lay a charge under Part III.

Section 15(6) requires the provincial offences officer to certify service by signing the certificate and specifying the date and method of service. Once service has been certified, the certificate shall be received in evidence and is considered to be proof of service.

Limitation Periods

There is no limitation period for service under Part II—or, to put it another way, the limitation period is immediate. Parking infraction notices must be served at the time of the offence based on the personal knowledge of the officer. Once served, however, several limitation periods or time calculations begin. The defendant (typically the registered owner of the vehicle) has 15 days to respond to the PIN.

If the defendant responds by paying the set fine, the matter is closed and no proceeding is commenced.

If the defendant does not pay the set fine within 15 days and no other response is made, a notice of impending conviction may be mailed to the owner providing an additional 15 days to respond. If there is no response after the additional 15 days, the defendant is deemed to not wish to dispute the charges. The municipality or other body can then follow the requirements under section 18.2 of the POA to request a conviction by filing a certificate requesting a conviction, provided this is done within 75 days of the date of offence. As well, the municipality or other body must certify that no payment has been received and no request for a trial has been filed.

The defendant also has the opportunity to request a trial within 15 days of service or within 15 days of the notice of impending conviction. In accordance with section 17 of the POA, if the defendant completes a Notice of Intention to Appear and requests a trial, the municipality or other body will have 75 days from the date of the offence to commence a proceeding by filing the certificate of parking infraction and evidence of ownership in the office of the court.

Part III Offences

The final procedural stream of the *Provincial Offences Act* is Part III, entitled Commencement of Proceeding by Information. The procedure of laying charges under Part III is very similar to the process of initiating a criminal proceeding.

Unlike simple and straightforward ticketing offences dealt with under Part I and Part II of the POA, Part III is commonly reserved for those offences that are complex or more serious in nature, or where the limitation periods under Part I or Part II have expired.

Charging Document

Section 22 of the POA indicates that defendants can be made aware that a proceeding under Part III has been commenced against them by being served with a summons (Form 104) (see Figure 3.3) prior to the provincial offences officer laying an

Figure 3.3   Summons to Defendant Before an Information Is Laid Under POA Section 22

Form 104	Courts of Justice Act
Formule 104	R.R.O. 1990 Reg. 200
	Loi sur les tribunaux judiciaires
	L.R.O. 1990, Règl. 200

SUMMONS TO DEFENDANT
SOMMATION ADRESSÉE AU DÉFENDEUR

Under Section 22 of the Provincial Offences Act
Aux termes de l'article 22 de la Loi sur les infractions provinciales

Ontario Court   *Cour de Justice*
of Justice   *de l'Ontario*
Province of Ontario   *Province de l'Ontario*

CD 000000

You are charged with the following offence
Vous êtes accusé(e) de l'infraction suivant

On the
Le _____ day of _____   yr *an 20* ____ at *à* _____   ☐ M

Name
Nom _____
Last/*Nom de famille*   First/*Prénom*   Middle/*Initiale*

Address
Adresse _____
Number and Street/*N° et rue*

At
À _____
Municipality/*Municipalité*   P.O./C.P.   Province   Postal Code/*Code postal*

_____
Municipality/*Municipalité*

Did commit the offence of
Vous avez commis l'infraction suivante _____

_____

Contrary to
Par dérogation à _____

Section
Article _____

Therefore you are commanded in Her Majesty's name to appear before the Ontario Court of Justice

À ces causes, au nom de Sa Majesté, vous êtes sommé(e) de comparaître devant la Cour de Justice de l'Ontario

At
À _____

_____

yr   at
an 20 ____ *à* _____   ☐ M

On the
Le _____ day of _____

Courtroom/*Salle d'audience* _____

and to appear thereafter as required by the court in order to be dealt with according to law.

et de comparaître par la suite chaque fois que le tribunal l'exigera de façon à ce que vous soyez jugé(e) selon la Loi.

Issued - *Émis*
this   *ce*
day of _____   yr *an 20* ____

_____
Signature of Provincial Offences Officer
Signature de l'agent d'infractions provinciales

Summons confirmed *Sommation confirmée* ☐	Summons cancelled *Sommation annulée* ☐

this _____ day of _____ yr 20 ____ by _____
le   *an*   *par*   A judge or justice of the peace in and for the Province of Ontario
Juge ou de paix dans et pour la province de l'Ontario

Driver's Licence No.	*N° du permis de conduire*		Class *Catégorie*	Cond *Restriction*
Sex *Sexe*	Birthdate *Date de naissance* D/J M Y/A	Registration No. *Numéro d'enregistrement*	Year *Année*	Province	Make *Marque*

Officer No. *Matricule de l'agent de police*	Unit *Groupe*

Defendant's Copy
Copie du défendeur

Note   This summons is issued under Part III of the Provincial Offences Act.
Cette sommation est émise aux termes de la partie III de la Loi sur les infractions provinciales.

information before a justice of the peace. This type of summons is similar to an appearance notice (Form 9) used in criminal proceedings, and allows a provincial offences officer to compel a defendant to attend court before the officer has appeared before a justice of the peace. Alternatively, section 24 of the POA provides that a summons (Form 106) could also be issued after the information is laid.

The summons itself is not the "charging" document. It simply advises the defendant that the officer has grounds to believe that an offence has been committed and that the defendant is required to attend court to answer to the charge. The information (Form 105) is the formal charging document for commencing proceedings under Part III of the POA (see Figure 3.4).

After a provincial offences officer has served a summons or if the officer decides to compel the defendant's attendance after the offence date, the officer must prepare and swear an information alleging the offence before a justice of the peace. Section 24 of the POA provides the procedure and framework for the laying and receiving of the information with respect to an offence.

As part of receiving the information, a justice of the peace may hear and consider evidence in the absence of the defendant in order to determine whether the case alleging the offence is made out (e.g., whether there is enough evidence to justify confirming/issuing a summons or issuing a warrant for arrest):

> 24(1) A justice who receives an information laid under section 23 shall consider the information and, where he or she considers it desirable to do so, hear and consider in the absence of the defendant the allegations of the informant and the evidence of witnesses and,
>> (a) where he or she considers that a case for so doing is made out,
>>> (i) confirm the summons served under section 22, if any,
>>> (ii) issue a summons in the prescribed form, or
>>> (iii) where the arrest is authorized by statute and where the allegations of the informant or the evidence satisfy the justice on reasonable and probable grounds that it is necessary in the public interest to do so, issue a warrant for the arrest of the defendant; or
>> (b) where he or she considers that a case for issuing process is not made out,
>>> (i) so endorse the information, and
>>> (ii) where a summons was served under section 22, cancel it and cause the defendant to be so notified.

If a summons has not yet been served and if the justice who receives the information is satisfied that the case has been made out, a Form 106 Summons will be issued and served on the defendant.

In many jurisdictions, the provincial offences officer who has investigated the offence and served the Form 104 summons is the same officer who completes and swears the information before a justice of the peace. However, the POA allows an information to be sworn by anyone. Some larger agencies rely on administrative staff to swear the formal information to keep officers free for service. Further, the swearing of an information is not limited to provincial offences officers or employees of administrative agencies. The language in section 23 of the POA indicates that *any person* may lay an information, meaning that it can be done by a private citizen.

Figure 3.4   Information Under Part III of the POA

INFORMATION
DÉNONCIATION

ONTARIO COURT OF JUSTICE
COUR DE JUSTICE DE L'ONTARIO
PROVINCE OF ONTARIO
PROVINCE DE L'ONTARIO

Under Section 23 of the *Provincial Offences Act*
En vertu de l'article 23 de la Loi sur les infractions provinciales

Form / *Formule* 105
Courts of Justice Act
Loi sur les tribunaux judiciaires
R.R.O / *R.R.O.* 1990 / O. Reg. / *Règl. de l'Ont.* 200

This is the information of
Dénonciation déposée par _____

of _____ , _____
de   (occupation / *profession*)

I have reasonable and probable grounds to believe and do believe that _____
J'ai des motifs raisonnables de croire et je crois effectivement que   (name / *nom*)

_____ on or about the _____ day of _____ , yr. 20___
                                        le ou vers le   *jour de*   *an*

at _____
à(au)   (location / *lieu*)

did commit the offence of
a commis l'infraction suivante :

contrary to _____   section _____
contrairement à(au)   *article*

_____
Signature of informant / *Signature du dénonciateur*

SUMMONS RETURNABLE / *SOMMATION À RAPPORTER*

Sworn before me
Déclaré sous serment devant moi

at _____   at _____
à(au)   *à(au)*

this _____ day of _____ , yr. 20___   on the _____ day of _____ , yr. 20___
ce   *jour de*   *an*   *le*   *jour de*   *an*

                                                                    at _____ .m., at _____
                                                                    à   *h, dans*   (courtroom / *salle d'audience*)

_____
Judge or Justice of the Peace in and for the Province of Ontario
Juge ou juge de paix dans et pour la province de l'Ontario

(Sec. / Art. 24) ☐   Summons for _____ , yr. 20___   Confirmed on _____ , yr. 20___
                          Sommation pour   *an*   *Confirmée le*   *an*   Justice of the Peace
                                                                                                              Juge de Paix

Date		

Pleads / *Plaidoyer* ☐ Guilty / *Coupable* ☐ Not Guilty / *Non coupable* ☐ Withdrawn / *Accusation(s) retirée(s)*
Found / *Décision*   ☐ Guilty / *Coupable* ☐ Not Guilty / *Non coupable* ☐ In Absentia / *Défaut de comparution*
                                                                              ☐ Sentence Suspended
                                                                                 Condamnation avec sursis

Fined $ _____ & $ _____   costs. Time to pay _____
Amende de $ *et* $ *pour les frais. Délai de paiement*

                                                          Date of Birth _____
                                                          Date de naissance   Day / *jour*   Mo. / *mois*   Yr. / *année*

Probation for
Période de probation de _____

Exhibits Filed
Pièces déposées
☐ Yes ☐ No
Oui   Non

Sentenced to imprisonment for
Peine d'emprisonnement de _____

_____
Judge or Justice of the Peace in and for the Province of Ontario
Juge ou juge de paix dans et pour la province de l'Ontario

FOR INFORMATION ON ACCESS
TO ONTARIO COURTS
FOR PERSONS WITH DISABILITIES, CALL
1-800-387-4456
TORONTO AREA **416-326-0111**

POUR PLUS DE RENSEIGNEMENTS SUR L'ACCÈS
DES PERSONNES HANDICAPÉES
AUX TRIBUNAUX DE L'ONTARIO, COMPOSEZ LE
1-800-387-4456
RÉGION DE TORONTO **416-326-0111**

POA 0001 CSD (rev. 11/03) (CD 001)

23(1) Any person who, on reasonable and probable grounds, believes that one or more persons have committed an offence, may lay an information in the prescribed form and under oath before a justice alleging the offence and the justice shall receive the information.

The person who lays the information is referred to as the **informant**.

informant
a person who commences a Part III proceeding against a defendant

Fines

In Part I and Part II, fines are established through the set fine procedure, but in Part III, there is no set fine or out-of-court settlement. The defendant cannot settle the case by paying an out-of-court amount. Instead, the fine for all Part III proceedings must be determined by a justice.

When determining a fine amount for Part III proceedings, it is important to look to the charging act for the offence. Many statutes provide their own penalty provisions (e.g., section 2(1)(b) of the *Trespass to Property Act* [8] provides a maximum fine of $10,000 for trespassing), but if a particular statute does not, the general penalty provisions found in section 61 of the POA apply and the maximum fine is $5,000.

Penalties for Part III matters are not limited to monetary fines. Other penalties may apply, including imprisonment and any specific penalties set out in the charging act for the relevant offence. For example, section 172 of the *Highway Traffic Act* deals with stunt driving and provides for licence suspension and vehicle impounding as additional penalties.

Proper Service

A Form 104 summons must be served at or near the place of the offence, and on the same date and at the same time that it occurred. The requirements for serving a summons before an information is laid are found in section 22 of the POA.

22. Where a provincial offences officer believes, on reasonable and probable grounds, that an offence has been committed by a person whom the officer finds at or near the place where the offence was committed, he or she may, before an information is laid, serve the person with a summons in the prescribed form.

Unlike a Part I notice or summons, which must be served personally on the defendant, or a Part II parking infraction notice, which must be served on the operator/owner of the vehicle, section 26(2) of the Act stipulates that a Part III summons can be served personally on the defendant, or can be left at the defendant's usual or last known place of residence with someone who appears to be at least 16 years of age.

Section 26(3) sets out the provisions for a provincial offences officer to serve the summons on persons who do not reside in Ontario:

26(3) Despite subsection (2), where the person to whom a summons is directed does not reside in Ontario, the summons shall be deemed to have been duly served seven days after it has been sent by registered mail to the person's last known or usual place of abode.

---

8 RSO 1990, c T.21.

There are also provisions in the Act for service on corporations:

26(4) Service of a summons on a corporation may be effected,

(a) in the case of a municipal corporation by,
(i) delivering the summons personally to the mayor, warden, reeve or other chief officer of the corporation, or to the clerk of the corporation, or
(ii) mailing the summons by registered mail to the municipal corporation at an address held out by it to be its address;
(b) in the case of any corporation, other than a municipal corporation, incorporated or continued by or under an Act by,
(i) delivering the summons personally to the manager, secretary or other executive officer of the corporation or person apparently in charge of a branch office of the corporation, or
(ii) mailing the summons by registered mail to the corporation at an address held out by it to be its address;
(c) in the case of [a] corporation not incorporated or continued by or under an Act by,
(i) a method provided under clause (b),
(ii) delivering the summons personally to the corporation's resident agent or agent for service or to any other representative of the corporation in Ontario, or
(iii) mailing the summons by registered mail to a person referred to in subclause (ii) or to an address outside Ontario, including outside Canada, held out by the corporation to be its address.

The most common method of establishing proof of service is for the provincial offences officer who has served the summons to complete and swear an affidavit of service, but the POA also allows a statement under oath or affirmation as proof of service.

It should be noticed that the information (Form 105) is not served on the defendant; instead it remains at the court. It is used to document every court appearance that the defendant makes on that matter.

Limitation Periods

When determining limitation periods, it is important to examine the charging act, but if a specific reference cannot be found, the general provisions of the POA will apply. Section 76 of the POA provides for a limitation period for offences under the Part III procedural stream. If no limitation period is stipulated under the legislation pertaining to the offence, a general limitation period of six months applies:

76(1) A proceeding shall not be commenced after the expiration of any limitation period prescribed by or under any Act for the offence or, where no limitation period is prescribed, after six months after the date on which the offence was, or is alleged to have been, committed.

(2) A limitation period may be extended by a justice with the consent of the defendant.

A limitation period prevents charges from being laid if too much time has passed since an offence occurred. It is important for the informant to establish the correct limitation period before commencing a proceeding.

PRACTICE TIP

It is essential to paralegals to understand the statutory framework of the limitation period and at what point the computation of time starts. You must determine if time should be computed starting at when the offence is committed or when the offence comes to the attention of an official, or if it is an offence that continues until it is remedied.

CASE IN POINT

Commencement of Limitation Period

R v Pickles, 2004 CanLII 60020, 237 DLR (4th) 568 (Ont CA)

Facts

A building contractor was hired to build a boathouse at a customer's cottage. The contractor went to the township's building department and was told that he would need to obtain approval from the Department of Fisheries and Oceans (DFO). When the DFO attended at the cottage, the contractor was advised that it would be difficult to obtain approval for a boathouse but that they could build a floating dock instead. The contractor built the dock without obtaining a building permit from the township. He was charged with the offence of building without a permit contrary to section 8(1) of the *Building Code Act, 1992*, SO 1992, c 23. The township discovered the dock 13 months after construction had finished and charges were laid against the contractor despite the *Building Code Act*'s one-year limitation period for that particular offence. The defendant took the position that the limitation period had lapsed for laying such a charge. The Crown's position was that the limitation clock should start to run when the township discovered the dock. At trial, the charge was dismissed on the basis of the limitation period. The trial decision was upheld on appeal in the Ontario Court of Justice.

The Crown appealed to the Ontario Court of Appeal.

Relevant Issue

Commencement of Limitation Period

Decision

The court agreed that the event that led to the charge was building the dock without a permit. Completion of the dock triggered the commencement of the limitation period. Therefore, laying the charge 13 months after the completion of the dock was outside of the prescribed limitation period. The appeal was dismissed.

KEY TERMS

REVIEW QUESTIONS

Multiple Choice

1. Who is permitted to serve an offence notice on the defendant?

    a. The provincial offences officer who observed the offence.

    b. Another provincial offences officer.

    c. A process server.

    d. a and b.

2. Who can lay an information before a justice of the peace to allege an offence has taken place?

    a. Provincial offences officer.

    b. Prosecutor.

    c. Court clerk.

    d. Any person.

3. Which of the following is a method of proper service for a parking infraction notice?

    a. Delivering the notice to the defendant at the time and place of the offence.

    b. Mailing the notice to the owner of the motor vehicle's last known address.

    c. Delivering the notice to the owner of the motor vehicle at his/her place of work or residence.

    d. Leaving the notice with someone at the defendant's usual or last known place of residence who appears to be at least 16 years of age.

4. What does the POA specify as the maximum fine for a Part I offence?

    a. $500.

    b. $1,000.

    c. $5,000

    d. The POA does not specify a maximum fine.

5. What does the POA specify as the maximum fine for a Part III offence?

    a. $5,000.

    b. $10,000.

    c. $50,000.

    d. The POA does not specify a maximum fine.

6. Within how many days of service of the offence notice does the officer have to file the certificate with the court?

    a. 7 days.

    b. 15 days.

    c. 30 days.

    d. The certificate is not filed with the court.

7. Who is permitted to serve a Part III summons on the defendant?

    a. Police officers only.

    b. Any provincial offences officer.

    c. Process server.

    d. Any person.

8. Maria, who lives in downtown Toronto, was charged under section 2(1)(a) of the *Compulsory Automobile Insurance Act* with operating a motor vehicle on a highway with no insurance. Which of the following would NOT constitute proper service of the Part III summons on Maria?

    a. Personally serving the summons to Maria at the time she was pulled over by the provincial offences officer.

    b. Mailing the summons to Maria's last known address.

    c. Personally serving the summons on Maria within six months of the offence.

    d. Leaving the summons with someone at Maria's usual or last known place of residence who appears to be at least 16 years of age.

9. For what purpose does the provincial offences officer sign the certificate?

   a. To identify him/herself as a provincial offences officer.

   b. To provide his/her contact information.

   c. To certify service on the defendant.

   d. The officer does not sign the certificate; it is signed by a justice.

Short Answer

1. What is the general limitation period for commencing a proceeding under Part III of the *Provincial Offences Act*?

2. In reviewing a case with your client, you need to ensure that there are no errors in service. What are the service requirements under Part I of the POA?

3. A summons under Part III could be served on someone other than the defendant. What are the service options under Part III?

4. Which section of the POA outlines service options on a corporation?

5. If the statute under which your client has been charged has no limitation period provisions, where is the limitation period found for service of a summons under Part III?

Scenario 1

On Monday, January 15, 20—, Kim was pulled over for sending a text message while driving contrary to section 78.1(1) of the *Highway Traffic Act*. While she was pulled over to the side of the road, the officer handed Kim an offence notice that had a set fine of $400 and had a written description of the charge as "Drive—handheld communication device."

1. Was this proper service? Why or why not?

2. What is the proper name of the document that will be filed with court office in order to commence proceedings in relation to this offence?

3. What is the final date that the officer can file the charging document with the court? Explain how you arrived at that date.

4. What would happen if the officer exceeds the time frame for filing?

5. Which procedural stream does this offence fall under? List three reasons why you know that it falls under that stream.

6. By which date will Kim have to make a decision about what she would like to do about this charge?

7. Is this the proper set fine and short form wording for this offence? Explain how you know.

Scenario 2

One evening in May, Mitchell parked his car at a meter and paid for two hours of parking before he went to meet some friends for dinner. Mitchell had lost track of time, but was relieved to return to his vehicle and see that there was no parking ticket. Unbeknownst to Mitchell, on his routine patrol of the area, By-law Officer Smidderson noticed the vehicle was parked at an expired meter and laid the charge under the relevant municipal parking by-law by leaving the parking infraction notice under the vehicle's windshield. Unfortunately, a prankster in the area had taken the notice off of Mitchell's car and thrown it in the garbage. A couple of weeks later Mitchell was shocked to receive a notice of impending conviction in the mail.

1. Was this proper service? Why or why not?

2. Mitchell wants to dispute service of the notice because he never saw it affixed to his vehicle. Does he have grounds to challenge service?

3. Which procedural stream does this infraction fall under? Explain.

4. Could Officer Smidderson have laid this charge under another procedural stream or by using a different process? Explain.

5. Instead of the scenario provided, assume that Mitchell arrived at the car as the officer was writing the ticket. He decided to get into his vehicle and leave the scene. Does this raise any issues relating to service?

Scenario 3

Stan was on his way to work early on a Monday morning. As he approached an intersection, the vehicle in front of him came to a sudden stop. Stan quickly glanced into his rear-view mirror and noticed that he had enough space to swerve into the next lane in order to avoid a collision. In doing so, he did cut off another vehicle, but at least he didn't cause an accident. Unfortunately, the other vehicle contained a police officer who had spilled his coffee all over himself when he was forced to brake so quickly in response to Stan's lane change. The officer was quite angry when he questioned Stan about his actions. He took down all of Stan's information and left the scene. Two months later, when Stan got home from work, his 15-year-old son told him that a police officer had come to the door and left a Form 106 Summons for Stan to appear in court. The officer had laid a charge of careless driving contrary to section 130 of the *Highway Traffic Act*.

1. Was this proper service? Why or why not?

2. Stan doesn't think that it was fair for the officer to wait so long to inform him of the charges. How long did the officer have to commence proceedings in this situation?

3. Which procedural stream does this offence fall under? List three reasons why you know that it falls under that stream.

4. Can Stan pay the set fine in order to resolve this matter outside of the courtroom? Explain.

Classification of Offences

4

LEARNING OUTCOMES

After reading this chapter, you will understand

■ the classification of regulatory offences (i.e., *mens rea*, strict liability, absolute liability); and

■ how the classification of offences has an impact on the roles of the prosecution and the defence.

Introduction

In the significant decision *R v Sault Ste Marie (City)*[1] the Supreme Court of Canada held that all regulatory (provincial) offences can be divided into three categories: *mens rea* offences, strict liability offences, and absolute liability offences. In delivering the decision of the court, Justice Dickson distinguished these categories as follows:

> I conclude, for the reasons which I have sought to express, that there are compelling grounds for the recognition of three categories of offences rather than the traditional two:
>
> 1. Offences in which *mens rea*, consisting of some positive state of mind such as intent, knowledge, or recklessness, must be proved by the prosecution either as an inference from the nature of the act committed, or by additional evidence.
> 2. Offences in which there is no necessity for the prosecution to prove the existence of *mens rea*; the doing of the prohibited act *prima facie* imports the offence, leaving it open to the accused to avoid liability by proving that he took all reasonable care. This involves consideration of what a reasonable man would have done in the circumstances. The defence will be available if the accused reasonably believed in a mistaken set of facts which, if true, would render the act or omission innocent, or if he took all reasonable steps to avoid the particular event. These offences may properly be called offences of strict liability. Mr. Justice Estey so referred to them in *Hickey*'s case.[2]
> 3. Offences of absolute liability where it is not open to the accused to exculpate himself by showing that he was free of fault.

The classification of an offence as *mens rea*, strict liability, or absolute liability provides the framework for the prosecution's case. Specifically, an offence's classification dictates what the prosecution will have to prove in order for a defendant to be convicted. Understanding the classification process is also key to the defence because it provides insight into how the prosecution will likely be proceeding, and it assists a paralegal in determining how to best defend a client against charges.

It is important to carefully examine the actual wording of the offence in the charging act when determining how it should be classified. It is also necessary to review existing case law for each offence to determine whether the classification has already been established by a court. The court's classification takes precedence over any interpretations that are made based on the wording of the offence.

mens rea **offence**
an offence for which the prosecution must prove that the defendant committed the illegal act and had a guilty mind (i.e., the knowledge, intent, or willingness to commit the act)

Mens Rea Offences

Mens rea—Latin for "guilty mind"—refers to the mental element of the offence, or the defendant's state of mind at the time of the offence. The wording of the offence will not actually state that it is a ***mens rea* offence**, but will instead use specific terminology

---

1   *R v Sault Ste Marie (City)*, [1978] 2 SCR 1299, 1978 CanLII 11, 40 CCC (2d) 353 at 1326-27; emphasis added.

2   *R v Hickey*, 1976 CanLII 663 (Ont SC).

to refer to the defendant's state of mind. For instance, such words as "intentionally," "knowledge," and "wilfully" suggest that the defendant was aware of his or her actions when the offence was committed. Most criminal offences are *mens rea* offences, but only a few provincial offences are classified in this manner.

When a charge is classified as a *mens rea* offence, the prosecution must prove, **beyond a reasonable doubt**, that the defendant committed the offence and possessed the necessary mental element at the time it took place.

Mens rea offences are considered to be more difficult for the prosecution to prove than either strict liability or absolute liability offences. The prosecution has to prove not only the defendant's wrongful actions, but also the defendant's thought process at the time of the offence. It is not easy to prove what another person was thinking at any point in time. In an effort to prove the mental element of the offence, the prosecution may rely upon admissions from the defendant, inferences from the defendant's behaviour, and other evidence that may be relevant to the situation.

An example of a *mens rea* offence is section 46(1)(a) of the *Gaming Control Act, 1992*,[3] which states:

> 46(1) Every person is guilty of an offence who,
> (a) knowingly furnishes false information in any application under this Act or in any statement or return required to be furnished under this Act or the regulations.

This is a *mens rea* offence because it refers to the defendant's knowledge at the time that the application was completed—specifically, the defendant's intent to provide false information on the application.

When dealing with a *mens rea* offence, the defence must either cast doubt on whether the defendant committed the illegal act or introduce evidence to raise a reasonable doubt about whether the actions were done intentionally, wilfully, or with knowledge. In the above example, the prosecution will attempt to prove that the defendant knew the information was false when he or she prepared the application but chose to include the false information anyway.

However, if the defendant had relied on information from another person and believed this information to be true, the defendant has not committed the mental element of the offence (i.e., it was not done knowingly). Although the prosecution may be able to prove that the defendant did complete the application with false information, there should not be a conviction because the action was not done knowingly.

Strict Liability Offences

In accordance with the Supreme Court of Canada's decision in *Levis (Ville) v Tetreault*,[4] most regulatory (provincial) offences are classified as **strict liability offences**. In fact, it is presumed that an offence is a strict liability offence unless the

beyond a reasonable doubt
a standard of proof where the prosecution must fully prove that the defendant committed the illegal act (to the extent that a reasonable person would not doubt that the act was committed)

strict liability offence
an offence for which the prosecution must prove that the defendant committed the illegal act; the defendant then has an opportunity to prove reasonableness or due diligence

---

3 SO 1992, c 24.

4 *Levis (Ville) v Tetreault*, 2006 SCC 12, [2006] 1 SCR 420.

wording suggests that it should be classified as a *mens rea* or an absolute liability offence, or a court has already decided how it is to be classified.

For a strict liability offence, the prosecution must only prove, beyond a reasonable doubt, that the defendant committed the offence. Unlike *mens rea* offences, the defendant's state of mind at the time of the offence is irrelevant.

Once the prosecution has proven that the defendant committed the offence, the **onus** switches to the defendant to provide a **due diligence** defence for his or her actions—specifically, that the defendant took all reasonable care to avoid committing the offence or was operating under a reasonable misapprehension of the relevant facts (i.e., mistake of fact).

The defence must prove due diligence on a **balance of probabilities**—a lower standard of proof than those instances when the prosecution must prove allegations beyond a reasonable doubt. That means the court must find that it was more likely than not that a defendant exercised due diligence in the circumstances. If due diligence is proven, the charges against the defendant will be dismissed and there will not be a conviction.

An example of a strict liability offence is failing to remain at the scene of an accident, contrary to section 200 of the *Highway Traffic Act*:[5]

> 200(1) Where an accident occurs on a highway, every person in charge of a vehicle or street car that is directly or indirectly involved in the accident shall,
>
>   (a) remain at or immediately return to the scene of the accident;
>
>   (b) render all possible assistance; and
>
>   (c) upon request, give in writing to anyone sustaining loss or injury or to any police officer or to any witness his or her name, address, driver's licence number and jurisdiction of issuance, motor vehicle liability insurance policy insurer and policy number, name and address of the registered owner of the vehicle and the vehicle permit number.

There is nothing in the wording of this offence to suggest that the prosecution must prove the defendant's state of mind (i.e., the words "intentionally," "wilfully," and "knowingly" are not included—see *mens rea* offences above). There is also no indication that due diligence cannot be used as a defence (see absolute liability offences below). Without such wording (and subject to a review of the case law), it can be presumed that it is a strict liability offence.

If the prosecution proves that the defendant left the scene of the accident, the defendant will have an opportunity to outline the steps that were taken to avoid leaving the scene or to explain how due diligence was exercised following the accident. The court will determine whether the defendant took all reasonable steps to remain at the scene.

Absolute Liability Offences

Absolute liability offences are those where the defendant is liable even if he or she was not at fault. The wording of the offence does not stipulate that it is an **absolute liability offence**, but it will often indicate that the defendant has no opportunity to

onus
the burden of proof or responsibility for proving that an allegation, exception, or defence should apply

due diligence
the standard of care that a reasonable person would be expected to apply to a specific situation

balance of probabilities
a standard of proof where an illegal act must be proven to be more likely than not to have occurred

absolute liability offence
an offence for which the prosecution must prove that the defendant committed the illegal act; the defendant has no opportunity to argue reasonableness or due diligence

---

5 RSO 1990, c H.8.

demonstrate reasonableness or due diligence. For instance, the terminology in the relevant section of the act may indicate that due diligence cannot be used as a defence, thereby making it an absolute liability offence.

The prosecution must prove, beyond a reasonable doubt, that the defendant committed the offence, but there is no need for the prosecution to prove the defendant's state of mind at the time of the offence. As well, the defendant is not given an opportunity to demonstrate due diligence or reasonable care.

Speeding, for example, is classified as an absolute liability offence. If the defendant did not realize that he or she was speeding because other vehicles were travelling at the same rate of speed, a conviction will still be entered if the prosecutor can prove that the defendant was driving at a rate of speed above the posted limit. Therefore, the defendant is absolutely liable for the offence. The defendant's state of mind (i.e., intention to speed or knowledge of the rate of speed) is irrelevant because this infraction is not classified as a *mens rea* offence. And because this is not a strict liability offence, the defendant does not have an opportunity to demonstrate due diligence (i.e., that it was reasonable to drive at the same speed as the other vehicles on the road).

An example of an absolute liability offence is section 84.1 of the *Highway Traffic Act*, which states:

> 84.1(1) Where a wheel becomes detached from a commercial motor vehicle, or from a vehicle being drawn by a commercial motor vehicle, while the commercial motor vehicle is on a highway, the operator of the commercial motor vehicle and the owner of the vehicle from which the wheel became detached are guilty of an offence. ...
>
> 84.1(5) It is not a defence to a charge under subsection (1) that the person exercised due diligence to avoid or prevent the detaching of the wheel.

In this example, subsection 5 clearly states that due diligence cannot be used as a defence. As a result, the defendant is absolutely liable even though reasonable steps may have been taken to prevent the wheel from detaching from the vehicle.

Absolute liability offences are generally considered the easiest for the prosecution to prove and the most difficult to defend against. Although due diligence cannot be argued by the defendant, some limited defences may apply in specific fact situations (e.g., involuntariness, causation, necessity).

For more information on defences, see the discussion in Chapter 11.

In *R v Sault Ste Marie (City)*,[6] Justice Dickson indicated that the following factors should be primary considerations in determining whether an offence is one of absolute liability:

1. The overall regulatory pattern adopted by the legislature.
2. The subject matter of the legislation.
3. The importance of the penalty.
4. The precision of the language used.

---

6 *Supra* note 1.

Charter Issues

An offence cannot be classified as absolute liability if a jail term is a possible penalty. In such cases, a jail sentence infringes on the defendant's life, liberty, and security of the person, contrary to section 7 of the *Canadian Charter of Rights and Freedoms*, because some opportunities for a defence are not available for absolute liability offences. As such, the section of the charging act in question would be deemed unconstitutional and may be **quashed**. In cases where an absolute liability offence can result in a jail sentence, the court can reclassify the offence as a strict liability offence, which gives the defendant the opportunity to demonstrate due diligence.

quash
to nullify or invalidate charges against the defendant such that the charges are thrown out of court

Classification/Reclassifications of Offences

The burden of proof rests with the party seeking to have the offence classified or reclassified. For instance, the defendant may want an offence to be classified as *mens rea* (because it is difficult for the prosecution to prove) or as strict liability (because it creates an opportunity to demonstrate due diligence). The defence would then be responsible for convincing the court that an offence should be classified/reclassified. The following case demonstrates how the classification of an offence can impact a defendant's ability to advance a defence.

CASE IN POINT

Classification of Offences

R v Kanda, 2008 ONCA 22, 88 OR (3d) 732.

Facts

The defendant was charged with driving while a passenger under 16 fails to properly wear a seat belt contrary to section 106(6) of the *Highway Traffic Act* [now section 106(4) of the HTA]. The defendant was driving his two sons, ages 12 and 8, to school when the officer noticed that one of the boys was leaning far forward in the vehicle. He pulled the vehicle over and discovered that the child was not wearing his seat belt. At trial, the defendant testified that he had ensured both of his children were properly buckled when they left the house and that he had not been not aware that one of his sons had unfastened the seat belt. However, the justice determined that the offence was classified as an absolute liability offence and therefore no due diligence defence was available. The defendant was convicted.

On appeal, the Ontario Court of Justice found that it was a strict liability offence and returned the matter to the trial justice to consider a due diligence defence.

The prosecution obtained leave to appeal to the Ontario Court of Appeal and the attorney general of Ontario obtained intervener status in order to determine the proper classification of this offence.

Relevant Issue

Classification of Offences

Decision

The Court of Appeal applied the framework established in *R v Sault Ste Marie*, [1978] 2 SCR 1299, 1978 CanLII 11, 40 CCC (2d) 353, to assess the subject matter, penalty, and precision of language for this offence. The court found the offence to be one of strict liability, for which a due diligence defence is available. The appeal was dismissed.

KEY TERMS

absolute liability offence, 42
balance of probabilities, 42
beyond a reasonable doubt, 41
due diligence, 42
mens rea offence, 40
onus, 42
quash, 44
strict liability offence, 41

REVIEW QUESTIONS

Multiple Choice

1. What is the most common classification for provincial offences?

   a. *Mens rea*.

   b. Strict liability.

   c. Absolute liability.

   d. Hybrid.

2. What is the standard of proof that applies when a defendant has the onus to demonstrate due diligence?

   a. Beyond a reasonable doubt.

   b. Balance of probabilities.

   c. Absolute certainty.

   d. More likely than not.

3. What is the standard of proof that applies when a prosecutor has the onus to demonstrate that the defendant committed the alleged offence?

   a. Beyond a reasonable doubt.

   b. Balance of probabilities.

   c. Absolute certainty.

   d. More likely than not.

4. For which type of offence does the onus switch to the defendant to demonstrate due diligence?

   a. *Mens rea*.

   b. Strict liability.

   c. Absolute liability.

   d. The onus switches for all types of offences.

5. For which type of offence is the defence required to prove the defendant's mental state?

   a. *Mens rea*.

   b. Strict liability.

   c. Absolute liability.

   d. The defence does not have to provide the defendant's mental state.

Short Answer

1. What does the prosecution have to prove to secure a conviction for an absolute liability offence?

2. What does the defendant have to prove to successfully defend against a strict liability offence?

3. What type of offence is "wilfully avoiding a police officer while being pursued"? How do you know?

4. For which type of offence must the prosecution prove that the defendant committed the offence beyond a reasonable doubt?

5. What does it mean if the description of an offence states that "anyone who knowingly falsifies a document is guilty of an offence ..."?

6. Name two ways that you can determine the classification of an offence.

7. Why is it important for a paralegal to know the classification of an offence?

8. Driving a vehicle without insurance is classified as a strict liability offence. How does this classification relate to your ability to prepare a client's defence?

Scenario

One day after school, Zack's mother asked him to ride his bike to the local store to pick up a few items. Zack was in a rush and was unable to find his bike helmet. His mother told him to go anyway, as long as he was extra careful. A police officer saw that Zack was riding his bike without a helmet and laid a charge under section 104 of the *Highway Traffic Act*.

Section 104 of the *Highway Traffic Act* reads:

104(2.1) No person shall ride or operate a bicycle on a highway unless the person is wearing a bicycle helmet that complies with the regulations and the chin strap of the helmet is securely fastened under the chin.

104(2.2) No parent or guardian of a person under sixteen years of age shall authorize or knowingly permit that person to ride a bicycle ... on a highway unless the person is wearing a bicycle helmet as required by subsection (2.1).

1. Assume Zack is 17 years old and was charged under section 104(2.1). Which type of offence would he face? How do you know?

2. Assume Zack is 14 years old and his mother was charged under section 104(2.2). Which type of offence would she face? How do you know?

Your Client Has Been Charged

5

LEARNING OUTCOMES

After reading this chapter, you will understand

■ some of the concerns and considerations for defendants charged with an offence;

■ a paralegal's role in advising clients and making decisions about how to proceed;

■ practical considerations for the intake interview and for dealing with your client throughout the process;

■ the requirements for arrest, with or without a warrant; and

■ the requirements for interim release (bail).

Introduction

As a paralegal, you will become accustomed to dealing with legal matters and making court appearances. After a few months of practice, you will likely start to lose the stress and anxiety that comes with appearing in court and will become more comfortable in the courtroom.

However, paralegals should keep in mind that for their clients, being charged with an offence can be difficult, stressful, or even embarrassing. It is important to try to see things from the client's perspective and make the process run as smoothly as possible for each and every client. You will need to take the time to explain all aspects of the charges and the process to your client, present options and recommendations, and ensure that the client provides full and complete instructions.

Intake Interview

The initial meeting with a client is an important step in understanding the case and building a defence. The information that you obtain during the intake interview will be critical in providing advice, conducting research, and representing your client's best interests.

Because many clients will be anxious about being charged with an offence, it is important that they feel comfortable in their discussions with a paralegal and that they receive the guidance and support they need. You should assure clients that any information that is disclosed will remain confidential and take the time to explain the process and their options.

When a client schedules an appointment to meet, ensure that copies of all relevant documentation are brought to the intake interview. When the client arrives for the meeting, you should verify the client's identity and make copies of the relevant documents for the file (i.e., driver's licence, proof of insurance, charging document, accident report). If the client comes to the office without an appointment, you may need to schedule a follow-up meeting to obtain the photocopies of relevant documents.

A defendant who consults a paralegal shortly after being charged should be instructed to make detailed notes of everything that occurred on the date that the charge was laid. This will help the defendant to collect his or her thoughts and recall some details that may otherwise have been forgotten. It will also provide the client with the option of using the notes to refresh his or her memory at trial—just as provincial offences officers can use their notes if they were made immediately after the incident.

Using notes at a trial may be helpful for those defendants who are nervous about testifying. However, the notes can be used only if they were made shortly after the incident because this is when the details will be recalled with the most accuracy. If there has been a delay before the notes were made, they will not be considered a reliable and accurate recollection of the incident.

The Law Society of Ontario provides a how-to brief on the steps to take when preparing a defence to the charge under the POA. The first step, Interview the Client, is reproduced in Figure 5.1.

Figure 5.1   Preparing a Defence to a Charge Under the *Provincial Offences Act*, Step One

 Interview the Client

- Carefully review all documentation provided to the client by the police.

- Gather all additional documentation relevant to the allegations that is in the possession of the client or potential witnesses.

- Obtain and review the process compelling your client's attendance at court.

- Obtain general background information from the client such as
    - name, date of birth, address and telephone number(s)
    - first language—request an interpreter if needed for the client or witness
    - marital status and names and ages of spouse and children
    - immigration status and resident history
    - education history and future plans
    - employment history and sources of income
    - ability to pay fine, including a surcharge
    - mental and/or physical health and treatment issues (if applicable)
    - criminal and/or provincial record of offences (or other relevant governmental record of misconduct), with explanations
    - bail, probation or other court or administrative orders or agreements in effect—with contact person to confirm compliance
    - outstanding charges
    - character references
    - other good character evidence (e.g., community work)

- Obtain details about the allegations against your client:
    - client's version of the allegations and evidence
    - details of any co-accused
    - names and contact information for all possible witnesses
    - steps taken to comply with the law (reasonable care, due diligence, etc.)
    - steps that could have been taken, with reasons for not doing so
    - whether the client or any other witness was impaired by alcohol or drugs
    - whether the client impeded the investigation
    - details of all contact with the authorities
    - details of the conduct of officers toward the client including any complaints with respect to treatment (consider relief under the *Canadian Charter of Rights and Freedoms*)
    - date, time and place of next court appearance
    - date, time and place of alleged offence

- Discuss the prospect of hiring a private investigator.
- Consider whether an expert such as an accident reconstructionist might be necessary.

Charging Document

charging document
the paperwork used to initiate charges against a defendant

At the first meeting with a client, you should carefully review the **charging document** and any other related paperwork, clarifying anything that requires a further explanation and checking for errors. Very few errors are considered to be "fatal," and most can be amended in court with the justice's approval. However, even **non-fatal errors** on the charging document (e.g., a misspelled name or incorrect plate number) should be raised in court because they can undermine the officer's credibility and make it more difficult for the prosecution to prove the case beyond a reasonable doubt. If there is a **fatal error** on the charging document (e.g., if the certificate of offence was not signed by the officer), you can bring a motion to quash the certificate or information. See Chapter 7 for a further discussion of errors.

non-fatal error
a mistake on a charging document that is not serious and will likely be amended in court

This is also an appropriate time to ensure that the proper charging document was used and properly served. As discussed in Chapter 3, to commence proceedings a defendant charged with a Part I offence must be personally served with an offence notice (or Part I summons); the owner/operator of a vehicle must be properly served with a notice of parking infraction for a Part II offence; and a defendant charged with a Part III offence must be personally served with a summons, or the summons must be left at the defendant's usual or last known place of residence with someone who appears to be at least 16 years of age.

fatal error
a serious mistake on a charging document that will result in the charges being withdrawn, dismissed, or stayed

Time Frames

Proper limitation periods and time frames must be followed by all parties dealing with provincial offences. As discussed in Chapter 3, for Part I matters, the offence notice or summons must be served within 30 days of the alleged offence, while for Part II matters, the parking infraction notice must be served at the time of the alleged infraction. The summons must be served within six months for alleged offences under Part III.

If service is to take place outside of these time frames, the defendant would have to consent to an extension of the limitation period. Most defendants would not agree to extend the limitation period for service because it means that they would be charged with an offence when the prescribed time for laying charges has lapsed.

If there is an issue concerning proper service within the limitation period, the defence can challenge the jurisdiction of the court to hear the matter, and ask the prosecutor to withdraw the charges or bring a motion to quash the charging document.

If it is a Part I matter, the defendant must make a choice on how to respond to the charges within 15 days of being served. For Part II matters, there is also a 15-day response time, but defendants are given an additional 15 days to respond after being mailed a notice of impending conviction.

Rules of the Ontario Court (Provincial Division) in Provincial Offences Proceedings[1] of the *Courts of Justice Act* ("POA Rules;" See Appendix B at the end of this text) section 11(1) states: "The clerk of the court shall not accept for filing a certificate of offence more than seven days after the day on which the offence notice or summons was served unless the time is extended by the court."

Therefore, provincial offences officers must ensure that their notices are filed within seven days or the matter will be considered abandoned. If a defendant pays the set fine listed on the offence notice and the certificate is not subsequently filed with the court, the POA Rules, section 19 requires the money to be refunded to the defendant.

The time it takes for a matter to be scheduled for trial will vary depending on whether the charge falls under Part I, Part II, or Part III, and where the jurisdiction is located in the province (e.g., some courts may experience a backlog, causing a longer wait for trial dates). In accordance with section 11(b) of the *Canadian Charter of Rights and Freedoms*,[2] a trial must be held without unreasonable delay. A trial scheduled within 11 or 12 months is typically seen as reasonable in terms of time frame. The time the defendant takes to select an option for a Part I offence is subtracted from the total time it takes for a case to go to trial. Any further delays by the defendant (e.g., requesting an adjournment) are not factored into the length of time it takes for a trial to be scheduled.

All days referred to in the POA are calendar days, not business days, as specified in the POA Rules, section 4. The regulation further specifies that:

1. The time shall be calculated by excluding the first day and including the last day of the period.

2. Where a period of less than six days is prescribed, a Saturday or holiday[3] shall not be reckoned.

3. Where the last day of the period of time falls on a Saturday or a holiday, the day next following that is not a Saturday or a holiday shall be deemed to be the last day of the period.

4. Where the days are expressed to be clear days or where the term "at least" is added, the time shall be calculated by excluding both the first day and the last day of the period.

Options/Possible Outcomes/Risks

As a paralegal, you should present each client with the options, explain the possible outcomes and risks associated with each option, and make recommendations. However, your client will make the final decision on how to respond to a charge. Although

---

1 RRO 1990, Reg 200.

2 *Canadian Charter of Rights and Freedoms*, Part I of the *Constitution Act, 1982*, being Schedule B to the *Canada Act 1982* (UK), 1982 c 11.

3 Note: the term "holiday" includes Sundays and statutory holidays.

a paralegal will know the law and procedure, only the client will fully appreciate the personal and/or professional impact that such a decision will have, and is therefore in the best position to make a decision.

This is not to suggest that the client will dictate every decision on the file. Although the client will be responsible for significant decisions, the paralegal should be entrusted to make any decisions that are necessary to meet the client's goals. This is recognized in the *Paralegal Professional Conduct Guidelines,* which states, "Subject to any specific instructions or agreement, the client does not direct every step taken in a matter. Many decisions made in carrying out the delivery of legal services are the responsibility of the paralegal, not the client, as they require the exercise of professional judgment. However, the paralegal and the client should agree on the specific client goals to be met as a result of the retainer" (paragraph 2 of Guideline 7).

The duty to present options, outcomes, and risks to your client is set out in Rule 3.02(2) of the *Paralegal Rules of Conduct,*[4] which states, "A paralegal shall be honest and candid when advising clients." This is further explained within paragraph 1 of Guideline 7 of the *Paralegal Professional Conduct Guidelines*:

> A paralegal has a duty of candour with the client on matters relevant to the retainer. A paralegal is required to inform the client of information known to the paralegal that may affect the interests of the client in the matter.

And also within the following excerpt from paragraph 2 of Guideline 7:

> A paralegal must honestly and candidly advise the client regarding the law and the client's options, possible outcomes and risks of his or her matter, so that the client is able to make informed decisions and give the paralegal appropriate instructions regarding the case. Fulfillment of this professional responsibility may require a difficult but necessary conversation with a client and/or delivery of bad news. It can be helpful for advice that is not well-received by the client to be given or confirmed by the paralegal in writing.

All clients should be fully informed of their options. It is easy to share good news and desirable outcomes with a client, but there may be a reluctance to share bad news. It is essential to properly document any advice given to a client, especially if the advice is not likely to be well received. You should confirm all advice in writing so that there is a paper trail in the file in case your actions are ever investigated.

Options for Part I: Offence Notice

A defendant who has been served with an offence notice has several options under the POA:

- *Payment Out of Court*: In accordance with section 8 of the POA, a defendant who does not wish to dispute the charge may plead guilty by paying the set fine (plus costs and surcharges). This is considered to be the payment-out-of-

---

4 *Paralegal Rules of Conduct*, Law Society of Ontario, online: <http://www.lsuc.on.ca/paralegal-conduct-rules>.

court option because it does not require a court appearance. Payment can be made in person, by mail, and over the telephone or Internet.

For more information on the options, outcomes, and risks associated with pleading guilty and making a payment out of court, see the discussion in Chapter 6.

- *Early Resolution Meeting with the Prosecutor*: Some jurisdictions offer the option of an Early Resolution Meeting with the Prosecutor under section 5.1 of the POA. By requesting an Early Resolution Meeting, the defendant will have an opportunity to meet informally with the prosecutor to discuss the possible resolution of the charge(s) without scheduling a trial date. It is worth noting that if the defendant lives more the 75km from the court house listed on the offence notice, the defendant can request for the meeting with the prosecutor to be conducted over the telephone.

For more information on the options, outcomes, and risks associated with attending an Early Resolution Meeting, see the discussion in Chapter 6.

- *Plea of Guilty with Submissions*: Section 7 of the POA provides the authority for a plea of **guilty with submissions**. This option is available for a jurisdiction that does not offer an Early Resolution Meeting under section 5.1 of the POA; a defendant who does not wish to dispute the charge but wants to make submissions (i.e., statements about the penalty or the amount of time to pay the fine) can attend at the time and place specified in the notice and appear before a justice. There is a common misconception that providing submissions means providing an explanation that could lead to the charge being dismissed or withdrawn, but that is not the case. A plea of guilty with submissions results in a finding of guilt by the court, but the submissions may bring a lower fine or additional time in which to pay.

guilty with submissions pleading guilty, but providing additional information on why the penalty should be reduced or the time for payment should be extended

For more information on the options, outcomes, and risks associated with pleading guilty with submissions, see the discussion in Chapter 6.

- *Notice of Intention to Appear to Dispute the Charge*: Sections 5 and 5.1 of the POA set out the procedure for a defendant to give notice of an intention to appear in court to enter a not guilty plea and have a trial. In accordance with section 5, notification can be given by completing the notice of intention to appear, found on the offence notice, or by completing the Notice of Intention to Appear (NIA) form[5]—see Figure 5.2, where this form is reproduced.

- *Failure to Respond*: A defendant who does not select an option within the 15-day time period has failed to respond. It is not usually considered to be an appropriate option and is not listed on the back of the offence notice, but some defendants will opt not to respond and others will fail to respond as an oversight.

A defendant who fails to respond will be "deemed to not wish to dispute" the charge. In accordance with section 9, the justice is required to examine the

---

5   O Reg 108/11: FORMS under the POA, Form 8.

Figure 5.2 Notice of Intention to Appear

NOTICE OF INTENTION TO APPEAR
AVIS D'INTENTION DE COMPARAÎTRE

ONTARIO COURT OF JUSTICE
COUR DE JUSTICE DE L'ONTARIO
PROVINCE OF ONTARIO
PROVINCE DE L'ONTARIO

Form / *Formulaire* 8
Provincial Offences Act
Loi sur les infractions provinciales

TAKE NOTICE THAT I, ______________________

VEUILLEZ PRENDRE AVIS QUE JE SOUSSIGNÉ(E), (defendant's name / *nom du défendeur/de la défenderesse*)

______ (current address / *adresse actuelle*) ______ (street / *rue*) ______ (apt. / *app.*)

______ (municipality / *municipalité*) ______ (province) ______ (postal code / *code postal*)

______ (offence number / *numéro de l'infraction*) ______ (offence date / *date de l'infraction*)

wish to give notice of my intention to appear in court to enter a plea of not guilty at the time and place set for the trial respecting the charge set out in the Offence Notice or Parking Infraction Notice.
désire donner avis de mon intention de comparaître devant le tribunal pour inscrire un plaidoyer de non-culpabilité à l'heure et au lieu prévus pour le procès en réponse à l'accusation énoncée dans l'avis d'infraction ou l'avis d'infraction de stationnement.

☐ I intend to appear in court to enter a plea at the time and place set for the trial and I wish that it be held in the English language.

☐ *J'ai l'intention de comparaître devant le tribunal pour inscrire un plaidoyer à l'heure et au lieu prévus pour le procès et je désire que le procès se déroule en français.*

I request a ______ language interpreter for the trial.
(leave blank if inapplicable)

Je demande l'aide d'un interprète en langue ______ *pour le procès.*
(*à remplir, s'il y a lieu*)

Note: If you **fail to notify** the court office of **address changes** you may not receive important notices *e.g.*, your Notice of Trial. You may be convicted in your absence if you do not attend the trial.

Remarque : *Si vous* ***omettez de prévenir*** *le greffe du tribunal de* ***tout changement d'adresse****, vous pourriez ne pas recevoir d'importants avis (p. ex., votre avis de procès). Vous pourriez être déclaré(e) coupable en votre absence si vous n'assistez pas au procès.*

______ Signature of defendant / *Signature du défendeur/de la défenderesse* ______ (date) ______ (telephone number / *numéro de téléphone*)

SOURCE: http://ontariocourtforms.on.ca/en/provincial-offences-act-forms/

certificate of offence to ensure that it is complete and regular on its face. If the certificate is found to be complete and regular on its face, the justice will enter a conviction. In many cases, a failure to respond is equivalent to the defendant agreeing to plead guilty.

However, there is a potential benefit to failing to respond. If there is an obvious error on the certificate, it will not be considered complete and regular on its face. Upon review by the justice, the certificate will then be quashed and there will not be a conviction. If the justice overlooks the error, in many cases the conviction can be appealed. It is interesting to note that if a similar error on the certificate was brought to the court's attention at trial, the certificate would likely be amended instead of quashed.

Options for Part I: Summons

A defendant who has been served with a Part I summons does not have as many options as someone who has been served with an offence notice.

Options are limited to entering a guilty plea, negotiating with the prosecutor, or pleading not guilty and having a trial. A defendant who has been summoned to court does not need to request a court date because the summons will specify the courtroom and the time and date of the trial. The officer has already decided that there will be a court date.

If a summons has been issued, attending court is mandatory, either personally or by way of a legal representative. If the defence does not appear for a court date after receiving a Part I summons, the court may issue an arrest warrant. Alternatively, the trial may proceed in the defendant's absence (***ex parte* trial**), and if the allegations are proven, a conviction will be entered.

ex parte **trial**
a trial held in the absence of the defendant or the defendant's representative

Options for Part II: Parking Infraction Notice

A defendant who has been served with a parking infraction notice has several options under the POA:

- *Payment Out of Court*: In accordance with section 16, a defendant who does not wish to dispute the charge may plead guilty by delivering the parking infraction notice and the set fine to the court office. In some jurisdictions, there is an early-payment amount specified on the notice to encourage defendants to pay the discounted fine instead of challenging the ticket.

- *Notice of Intention to Appear to Dispute the Charge*: Sections 17(1) and 18.1(1) allow a defendant who is served with a parking infraction notice or notice of impending conviction to give notice of intention to appear in court to enter a not guilty plea and have a trial by indicating this on the parking infraction notice and delivering the notice to a specified court.

- *Informal Negotiations*: Although not listed as an option on the parking infraction notice, some municipalities will allow defendants to engage in informal negotiations at the municipal office. A by-law officer or municipal employee may authorize a reduced payment (which amounts to a guilty plea and a conviction).

- *Failure to Respond*: A defendant who does not make a choice within 15 days is not automatically considered to have failed to respond. Because parking infraction notices are often served by affixing the document to the vehicle, there is no guarantee that the owner/operator of the vehicle actually received the notice on the date it was served, or that the owner/operator received it at all. Because of this, defendants may be given a further 15 days to make a choice. Typically, the defendant will be sent a notice of impending conviction pursuant to section 18(1) of the POA after the initial 15-day period has lapsed. If the defendant still does not respond to the notice within the additional 15 days, he or she will have failed to respond and a conviction will be entered. See Figure 5.3.

Figure 5.3   *Provincial Offences Act* Process for Part I, Part II, Part III Matters

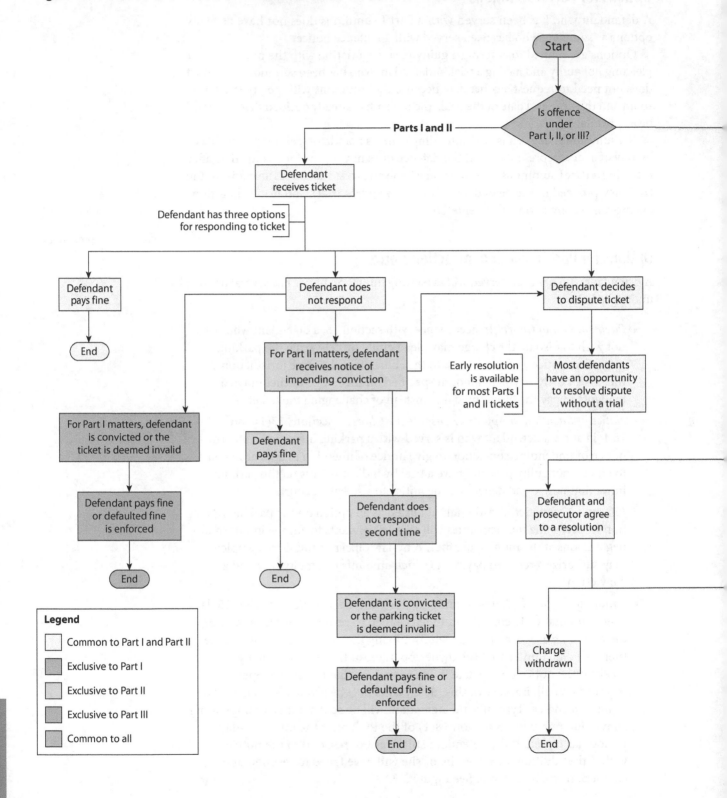

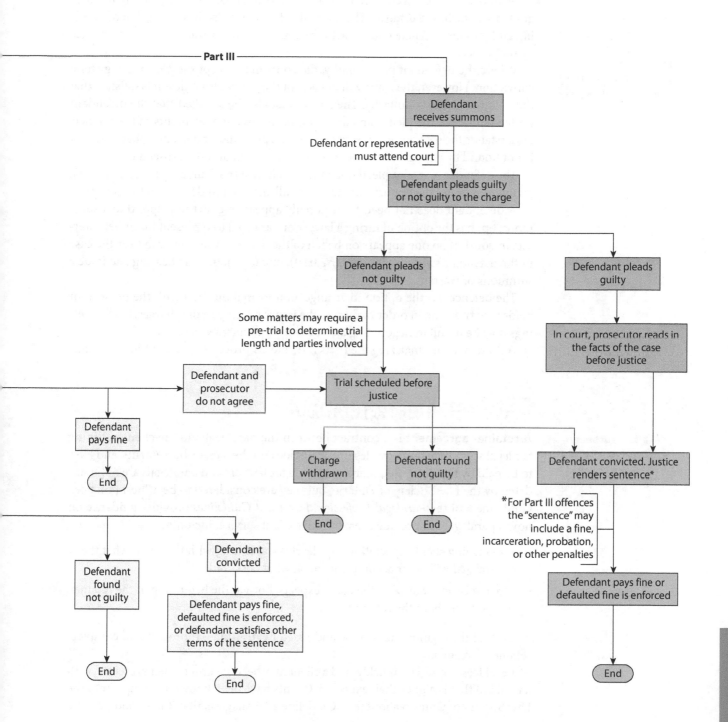

Options for Part III: Information

A defendant who has been served with a Part III summons must appear in court on the date specified on the summons. In court, the defendant has the option of pleading guilty or not guilty to the offence described in the charging document, pursuant to section 45. The prosecutor may also offer the defendant an opportunity to plead guilty to an **included offence**. Therefore, the defendant also has the option of pleading guilty to the alternate offence with the consent of the prosecutor and acceptance by the justice.

included offence
an alternative offence that still fits with the facts of the defendant's wrongful behaviour, but carries a lesser penalty

Where the defendant pleads guilty, the court may accept the plea and register a conviction. However, the court will not accept the guilty plea unless it is satisfied that the plea was made voluntarily. The court must also be satisfied that the defendant understands that the plea is an admission of the essential elements of the offence, understands the nature and consequences of the plea, and understands that the court is not bound by any agreement between the defendant and the prosecutor.

The defendant can also plead not guilty and have a trial pursuant to section 46(1), giving him or her the opportunity to make full answer and defence to the charges.

A defendant does not need to personally appear in court to respond to a summons, but has the option of hiring a lawyer or paralegal to represent his or her interests in court. If no one appears on behalf of the defence, the court can hear the case in the defendant's absence (an *ex parte* trial), or can adjourn the hearing and issue a summons or warrant.

The defence has the option to arrange an informal meeting with the prosecutor before the trial date in order to discuss the issues relating to the charges. Such meetings may be useful in negotiating a resolution or to narrow the issues.

A flow chart summarizing the Parts I, II, and III processes is set out in Figure 5.3.

Fees/Retainer Agreement

retainer agreement
an agreement for legal services between a licensee and a client

A **retainer agreement** is a contract between the paralegal and the client outlining the legal services that the paralegal will provide and the fees, disbursements, and HST to be paid by the client. Retainer agreements for lawyers and paralegals are not mandated by the Law Society of Ontario, but they are considered to be a "best practice." Guideline 6 of the *Paralegal Professional Conduct Guidelines* provides guidance on how a paralegal can provide more effective client service, including:

- managing client expectations by clearly establishing with the client what the paralegal will do or accomplish and at what cost, and
- being clear about what the client expects, both at the beginning of the retainer and throughout the retainer.

Both of these guidelines can be addressed by drafting a thorough and complete retainer agreement.

Legal fees can add up quickly, and a client may become upset when presented with a final bill that is higher than expected. Clients have been known to complain to the Law Society of Ontario about fees. Guideline 13.6 suggests that it is a good practice to discuss fees and disbursements before or within a reasonable time after commencing a representation. To ensure that there is no misunderstanding, this information should be provided or confirmed in writing.

For provincial offences matters, it is common practice to charge a flat fee and to collect a monetary retainer before the paralegal begins to work on the file. Like any other type of **monetary retainer**, the payment must be deposited into the paralegal's trust account, and cannot be transferred to the general account until the work has been completed and a statement of account or bill has been sent to the client.

Collecting a monetary retainer is a good practice for paralegals because it means that the client will not have to be tracked down to pay fees when the case is over. Collecting payment could be problematic if the matter was not resolved in the client's favour and the client is reluctant to pay. It also means that there is no confusion for the client about the amount of money being charged for the services being provided.

monetary retainer
a sum of money paid up front for legal services to be provided in the future

> **PRACTICE TIP**
>
> Fees vary for representation in provincial offences court. It is worth investigating the accepted rate in your jurisdiction to ensure that your fees are not set too low or too high in terms of what is considered to be fair and reasonable.

Special Considerations for Young Persons

Section 93 of the POA defines a young person as someone who is or, in the absence of evidence to the contrary, appears to be 12 years of age or older, but under the age of 16. Notice that this definition has a different upper limit from the age commonly prescribed by societal standards and in other legislation. It is also important to note that no one can be convicted of an offence if it was committed while he or she was under the age of 12.

Part VI of the POA provides special consideration and rules for young persons. Section 95 indicates that for Part I matters, a summons, not an offence notice, must be served on a young person. In addition, a copy of the summons must be delivered to the parent of the young person, pursuant to section 96. In many cases, this leads to the parent taking an interest in the proceedings against the young person.

When representing a young person, the paralegal must keep in mind that the young person is the client, not the person paying for legal services—often the parent. Because of this, special duties of confidentiality must be clarified. Fees can be discussed with the parent, but the retainer letter should establish who the client is, and therefore who will receive information about the case and who will provide instructions.

Because a young person is served with a summons instead of an offence notice, he or she does not have the option of making an out-of-court payment, even for a Part I offence. Under section 98 of the POA, a young person must be present in court for an entire trial, unless otherwise permitted by the court. That means a young person cannot avoid appearing in court by simply hiring a paralegal to deal with the matter on their behalf.

Where a young person fails to appear for a hearing despite being issued a summons, the court may adjourn the hearing and issue a summons to appear or an arrest warrant, pursuant to section 98(4) of the POA.

Some other special considerations for a young person relate to sentencing restrictions, arrest procedures, and provisions to prevent their identity from being published. When representing a young person, it is important to become knowledgeable about the rules in Part VI of the POA in order to fulfill your duty to your client.

Special Considerations If Your Client Has Been Arrested

Part VIII of the POA deals with arrest, bail, and warrants. Although the Act provides for the arrest of a defendant, with or without a warrant, most defendants charged with a provincial offence will not be arrested and will therefore not be required to attend a bail hearing.

Arrest with a Warrant

Section 24 of the POA gives a justice the authority to issue a warrant for the defendant's arrest at the time that the information is laid. Specifically, section 24(1)(a)(iii) states that where a justice "considers that a case for doing so is made out,"

> where the arrest is authorized by statute and where the allegations of the informant or the evidence satisfy the justice on reasonable and probable grounds that it is necessary in the public interest to do so, issue a warrant for the arrest of the defendant.

It is important to note that the POA does not provide a general power to arrest. Instead, it refers to authorization under the charging act, and the justice's reasonable and probable grounds to believe that it would be in the public interest to issue a warrant. After confirming such grounds through the allegations or evidence, the justice must complete Form 107 under the POA Rules in order to issue the warrant.

A warrant of arrest under section 24 must include the name or description of the defendant, and the offence, and order that the defendant be arrested immediately and brought before a justice. The warrant remains in force until it is executed by an officer.

Section 144 of the POA further clarifies the procedure for executing the arrest warrant. A police officer carries out a warrant by arresting the defendant, and the warrant applies only to a defendant in Ontario. It should be noted that the POA specifies that a warrant must be executed by a police officer, which means a provincial offences officer cannot carry out this duty. Upon arrest, the police officer must inform the defendant of the reason for arrest and produce the warrant, where feasible.

Arrest without a Warrant

A police officer may arrest someone without a warrant if the officer has reasonable and probable grounds to believe that a warrant is already in effect. Therefore, it is not always necessary for a police officer to possess a warrant.

It is possible in some situations for a person to be arrested without a warrant and by a civilian, not a police officer. In accordance with section 145 of the POA:

> Any person may arrest without warrant a person who he or she has reasonable and probable grounds to believe has committed an offence and is escaping from and freshly pursued by a police officer who has lawful authority to arrest that person, and, where the person who makes the arrest is not a police officer, shall forthwith deliver the person arrested to a police officer.

A civilian arrest without a warrant is authorized only if a person is believed to have committed an offence and is trying to escape from a police officer. Because this type of situation requires the police officer to have lawful authority to arrest that person, the charging act must indicate that an arrest can be made without a warrant for specified offences.

Interim Release

In most cases, a defendant who has been arrested will be released once served with a summons or offence notice. In fact, section 149 of the POA specifies that a defendant must be released by the arresting officer "as soon as is practicable" after being served. However, as specified in section 149, an officer does not have to release a defendant in cases where there are reasonable and probable grounds to believe that it is in the public interest to confirm the defendant's identity, to secure or preserve evidence, or to prevent an offence, and in cases where there is reason to believe that the defendant is not an Ontario resident and will not respond to a summons or offence notice.

If the defendant has been detained, the arresting officer is required under section 149(2) to escort him or her to the officer in charge at the police station. The officer in charge may release the defendant at this point if it is determined that the reasons for detaining the defendant no longer exist. In the case of a non-resident, the officer in charge may require bail to ensure the defendant's response to the charging document.

Bail Hearing

If a defendant has not been released by the arresting officer or the officer in charge, he or she must be brought before a justice within 24 hours for a bail hearing. The defendant then has an opportunity to plead guilty or undertake to appear at trial. In accordance with section 150 of the POA, the justice may release the defendant on an undertaking to appear at trial, unless the prosecutor can show cause as to why it is necessary to detain the defendant in order to ensure that he or she appears in court. A defendant who is being released may be required to enter into a **recognizance** to appear in court with or without a **surety**.

recognizance
an acknowledgment and agreement by the defendant that he or she will attend the next scheduled court appearance

surety
a person who agrees to be responsible for the defendant's appearance in court

> **PRACTICE TIP**
>
> Before a bail hearing, a paralegal should speak to the prosecutor in order to obtain disclosure about the offence, the reasons for detainment, and the possible need for a surety.

KEY TERMS

charging document, 50
ex parte trial, 55
fatal error, 50
guilty with submissions, 53
included offence, 58
monetary retainer, 59
non-fatal error, 50
recognizance, 61
retainer agreement, 58
surety, 61

REVIEW QUESTIONS

Multiple Choice

1. What is likely to happen if the defendant's last name is misspelled on the offence notice?

   a. It will be considered a fatal error and the charges will be withdrawn by the prosecutor as a result.

   b. The prosecutor will request an amendment to the certificate, which is likely to be granted since it is a non-fatal error.

   c. The prosecutor will request an amendment to the certificate, which is unlikely to be granted since it is a fatal error.

   d. The officer will be ordered to serve a revised offence notice.

2. In the case of errors on the charging document, when is it appropriate to bring a motion to quash?

   a. There must be a fatal error on the charging document.

   b. There must be a non-fatal error on the charging document.

   c. There must be both fatal and non-fatal errors on the charging document.

   d. A motion to quash is not related to errors on the charging document.

3. Which of the following statements is TRUE in relation to an adult's court appearance for Part III offences?

   a. The court will provide a paralegal or lawyer for the defendant.

   b. The defendant is required to hire a paralegal or lawyer.

   c. The defendant does not need to personally appear in court, but can instead hire a paralegal or lawyer.

   d. The defendant is required to appear in court, even if the defendant has hired a paralegal or lawyer.

4. Which of the following statements is true in relation to powers of arrest?

   a. The *Provincial Offences Act* provides a general power to arrest.

   b. In some cases, a civilian can arrest someone who is believed to have committed an offence and is trying to escape from police.

   c. A warrant of arrest under section 24 remains in force for 24 hours after it is issued.

   d. A warrant of arrest can be executed by any provincial offences officer.

Questions 5-7 deal with the following scenario:

Rebecca is a 15-year-old girl who was observed by a police officer to be consuming alcohol in a parking lot outside a movie theatre. The police issued a Part I Summons pursuant to section 31(2) of the Liquor Licence Act, *RSO 1990, c L.19 for having/consuming alcohol in a place other than a residence, a licensed premises, or a private place.*

5. Which of the following is an INCORRECT statement about the above scenario?

   a. Rebecca's parents must be notified.

   b. Rebecca cannot be convicted because she is younger than 16 years of age.

   c. Her identity cannot be published.

   d. All of the above are incorrect.

   e. None of the above are incorrect.

6. Rebecca's father retained a paralegal to represent her interests. Which of the following statements is correct?

   a. Rebecca will have to attend court because legal representation is not permitted for young persons.

   b. Her paralegal, but not Rebecca, must attend court.

   c. Both Rebecca and her paralegal will have to attend court.

   d. No one is required to attend court; Rebecca can just pay a fine.

7. When Rebecca's father retained the paralegal, he indicated that because he was paying the bill, he wants copies of all documents in the file. Does this raise any ethical issues for the paralegal?

   a. Yes, the paralegal's confidentiality requirements will not allow the disclosure of such information to anyone who is not a client.

   b. Yes, the paralegal cannot accept payment from anyone other than a client.

   c. No, a client is defined as the person who pays for services, so Rebecca's father is the client and is entitled to all documents.

   d. No, Rebecca and her father are joint clients and therefore are both entitled to all documents.

Short Answer

1. What will happen if a defendant does not respond within 15 days of receiving a parking infraction notice?

2. What will happen, in most cases, if a defendant does not respond within 15 days of receiving an offence notice?

3. What will happen, in most cases, if the defendant fails to appear at a trial after submitting a Notice of Intention to Appear?

4. What will happen, in most cases, if the defendant fails to appear at a trial after being served with a summons?

5. Under what circumstances will a defendant not be released on an undertaking during a bail hearing?

Scenario 1

Gabe was pulled over for driving 67km per hour in a 50km zone. When he was pulled over and asked for his licence he realized that he had forgotten his wallet at home. The officer issued an offence notice for "Speeding" contrary to section 128(1), and "Fail to Surrender Licence" contrary to section 33(1) of the *Highway Traffic Act*.

1. What are Gabe's options?

2. If Gabe does not want to dispute the charges but is still hoping to get a better deal, which option would be appropriate? Why would this option be appropriate for these charges?

3. If Gabe decides to request a trial date, how would he go about doing so?

Scenario 2

Recall the following scenario from Chapter 4:

One day after school, Zack's mother asked him to ride his bike to the local store to pick up a few items. Zack was in a rush and was unable to find his bike helmet. His mother told him to go anyway, as long as he was extra careful. A police officer saw that Zack was riding his bike without a helmet and charged him under section 104 of the *Highway Traffic Act*.

Section 104 of the *Highway Traffic Act* reads:

104(2.1) No person shall ride on or operate a bicycle on a highway unless the person is wearing a bicycle helmet that complies with the regulations and the chin strap of the helmet is securely fastened under the chin.

1. Assume Zack is 14 years old and was charged under section 104(2.1). Which charging document would be used? Explain.

2. Could Zack avoid having his parents find out by just paying the set fine in this case? Why or why not?

3. Would the situation be different if Zack was 11 years old?

4. Would the situation be different if Zack was 16 years old?

Scenario 3

Toby was charged with driving his vehicle without insurance contrary to section 2(1)(a) of the *Compulsory Automobile Insurance Act*. He was served with a Part III summons to appear in court on June 25, 20—.

1. Since Toby did not have a good reason for driving without insurance, he decided to skip his court date. What is the procedure for dealing with a defendant's non-attendance for a Part III matter?

Helping Your Client Deal with Charges

6

LEARNING OUTCOMES

After reading this chapter, you will understand

- the options and outcomes in making a guilty plea;
- criteria that must be met in order for the court to accept a guilty plea;
- consequences of a guilty plea;
- the process of requesting a trial; and
- the defendant's options, risks, and outcomes once a trial has been requested.

Introduction

After you have set out the possible options, your client will have to decide how he or she would like to deal with the charge(s). As a paralegal, you can help your client to weigh the pros and cons of each option, but the ultimate choice must be theirs.

If your client is considering pleading guilty, options are available concerning when and how the guilty plea will take place. A guilty plea can occur either in or out of court, depending on the circumstances. After discussing the options relating to a guilty plea, it is important to advise your client of the consequences of a conviction.

If your client does not want to plead guilty, the next step is to request a trial date. Requesting a trial date is only an option for Part I matters (without a summons) and those that fall under Part II. A Part I or Part III summons already includes a date and time for trial, so the defendant does not have the option or the responsibility of making such a request.

A defendant who does not want to plead guilty can give notice of his or her intention to appear in court to enter a not guilty plea and have a trial. In accordance with sections 5 and 17, the proper indication can be made on the back of the offence notice or parking infraction notice, or by completing Form 8, a **Notice of Intention to Appear** (NIA) (see Figure 5.2 in Chapter 5).

A second option for a defendant who does not want to plead guilty is to request a meeting with the prosecutor, as per the procedures set out in section 5.1 of the POA. The court clerk will then set a meeting date and location and give notice of the date to the defendant.

Notice of Intention to Appear
Form 8, used for the defendant to request a trial

If Your Client Wants to Plead Guilty

A guilty plea means that the defendant accepts responsibility for the offence and that he or she has given up the right to a trial. Upon entering a guilty plea, there will be a conviction.

On their website, the Law Society of Ontario provides a how-to brief on the steps to take when preparing a defence to charge under the POA. In Step 6, Attend the Trial/Enter a Guilty Plea, the Law Society suggests:

> If the client chooses to enter a guilty plea, obtain clear unequivocal written instructions outlining the aspects of the plea comprehension hearing including but not limited to possible penalties, ancillary orders, the right to have a trial, admission of essential elements of the offence, admission of mitigating and aggravating facts, voluntariness of the plea, an understanding that even a joint submission is subject to the approval of the presiding judge or justice, etc.

A guilty plea can take place at different stages of the proceedings.

Out-of-Court Payment

In accordance with sections 8 and 16 of the POA, a defendant who does not wish to dispute the charge may plead guilty by paying the set fine (plus costs and a victim fine surcharge). This is called the payment-out-of-court option because it does not require a court appearance. Most jurisdictions have several methods for paying a fine, including by mail, in person, by telephone, and online payments.

Making an out-of-court payment is considered to be an admission of guilt, and the defendant will be convicted of the offence. This option may be desirable for someone who is in need of closure or certainty, who wants to accept responsibility for their actions, or who does not want to invest additional time and money in the case. However, it is not always the best option because the defendant will have to pay the full set fine. By waiting until a later stage in the proceedings, the defendant may be able to request a reduced fine or even have the charge amended to a lesser included offence.

Early Resolution Meeting with the Prosecutor

For Part I offences, a defendant who does not necessarily want to have a trial, but also does not want to plead guilty to the original charge(s), can consider arranging a meeting with the prosecutor pursuant to section 5.1 of the POA, if offered in that municipality. This has been historically referred to as a first-attendance meeting and allows for out-of-court negotiations.

During the meeting, the prosecutor will sometimes offer to amend a charge in exchange for a guilty plea. The prosecutor may suggest an included charge, which would result in a lower fine or fewer **demerit points**, in the case of a driving offence. If a defendant accepts the prosecutor's offer, he or she will appear before a justice sitting in court and plead guilty to the amended charge. At this point, the defendant and the prosecutor will have the opportunity to give submissions regarding the sentence. The justice has discretion to impose the set fine or any other fine that is permitted by law.

demerit points
a penalty administered by the Ministry of Transportation for driving offences

It is important to note that since the justice is not limited to imposing the set fine or a lesser fine, a defendant who chooses this option could end up paying a fine that is higher than the set fine, up to the maximum allowed under the POA or the charging act. However, in most cases, a guilty plea before a trial date is considered to be a **mitigating factor**, and it is unlikely that the justice would increase the fine.

This option may be desirable for a defendant who is not interested in having a trial, but hopes to reach a more desirable outcome. However, there is no guarantee that the prosecutor would be willing to reduce the fine or offer a lesser included charge. In addition to the potential benefit of negotiating a better deal, a resolution meeting would save on legal fees and the amount of time invested for the defendant.

mitigating factor
favourable information about a defendant that is presented to a justice after conviction which may lead to a lesser penalty

On the other hand, one of the drawbacks of pleading guilty at a resolution meeting is that disclosure would not yet be available—meaning that the defendant wouldn't have had the chance to review the case against him or her before entering a plea. It should also be noted that a defendant who misses an early resolution meeting will be deemed to not wish to dispute the charge and the prosecutor will ask the justice to enter a conviction.

If the defendant does not request an early resolution meeting with the prosecutor, there will typically be an opportunity to speak with the prosecutor immediately before the trial. At this point, it is still possible to see charges substituted in exchange for a guilty plea.

PRACTICE TIP

Before meeting with the prosecutor, review the charging act to get a sense of offences that could be considered included offences. Look for those that carry a lower fine or fewer demerit points. If you are not satisfied with the offer made by the prosecution, you might suggest alternate charges that may put your client in a better position.

Plea of Guilty with Submissions

Section 7 of the POA provides the authority for a plea of guilty with submissions for Part I offences. In jurisdictions without resolution meetings, a defendant who does not wish to dispute the charge can enter a guilty plea and still have the opportunity to make submissions to a justice on the penalty. Although section 7 specifically states that the submissions relate to the penalty, defendants are often under the misconception that if they provide an explanation as to why they committed the offence, the charges will be withdrawn or dismissed. A defendant's submissions may result in a lower fine or additional time to pay, but if the guilty plea is accepted, it will result in a conviction.

Under section 7, the justice has discretion to impose the set fine or a lesser fine, but cannot impose a fine that is higher than the set fine. A defendant will not risk having to pay more by pleading guilty with submissions than if he or she had made an out-of-court payment, and may actually end up paying less.

Defendants seeking a lesser fine often submit that their finances are strained as a result of unemployment, being in school, maternity leave, or child support payments, for example. Some defendants are willing to pay the full amount but are just not able to do so within the prescribed 15-day time limit, and are requesting an extension of time to pay the fine.

Because this option is also considered to be an admission of guilt, it will result in a conviction and carry the normal penalties that follow such an outcome. This option may be desirable for a defendant who is not interested in fighting the charges, but who hopes to receive a break on the penalty. It also provides a sense of closure and certainty, and allows a matter to be resolved quickly. But, as with the resolution meeting, there is no opportunity to review disclosure before entering a plea.

Pleading Guilty at Trial

Sometimes a defendant who requested a trial date intending to dispute the charges changes his or her mind by the time the trial date arrives. At this point, the defendant is not required to follow through with a trial, and still has an opportunity to plead guilty to the original charges or to amended charges as negotiated with the prosecutor. At this stage, the set fine is considered to be only persuasive (used as a guideline), so the justice has discretion to impose another amount.

This option may be desirable to a defendant who was initially unsure of how to handle the matter, and needed more time to consider the options and make an appropriate decision. One additional benefit for the defendant is that it prolongs the due date for any fine that will be payable. Some defendants may also use this as a delay tactic to prolong the appearance of demerit points on the driving record for *Highway Traffic Act*[1] convictions.

Procedure for Pleading Guilty

The procedure for pleading guilty depends on the stage in the proceedings when the plea is entered. If the defendant makes an out-of-court payment of the set fine, it is considered to be a guilty plea and a conviction is registered as soon as the fine is paid.

Different jurisdictions have varied procedures concerning a meeting with the prosecutor. For Part I matters, once the option is selected to request a meeting, a time and place will be sent to the defendant. For Part III matters, inquiries should be made at individual court offices about procedures for meeting with the prosecutor.

In order to plead guilty with submissions, the defendant must attend court and appear before a justice. The guilty plea is put on the record and the defendant may then make submissions on the penalty. In this case, the defendant is usually given time to pay the fine (i.e., the statutory 15 days, or longer if specified by the justice).

To plead guilty at trial, the defendant must complete the Notice of Intention to Appear form (see this form in Figure 5.2 in Chapter 5), attend at the scheduled trial date, and enter a plea.

With the exception of cases where voluntary payment is made of the set fine, the justice can exercise discretion on whether to accept the defendant's guilty plea. Pursuant to section 45(3) of the POA, the justice may accept a guilty plea only if he or she is satisfied that the defendant:

(a) is making the plea voluntarily;
(b) understands that the plea is an admission of the essential elements of the offence;
(c) understands the nature and consequences of the plea; and
(d) understands that the court is not bound by any agreement made between the defendant and the prosecutor.

Consequences of a Guilty Plea

Regardless of when the defendant pleads guilty, the result is the same: the defendant has admitted that he or she committed the offence, has given up the right to a trial, and is aware that there will be a finding of guilt and a conviction.

For Parts I and III matters, a conviction means the defendant must pay a fine, plus **costs** and a **victim fine surcharge**. For Part II matters, a conviction results in a fine and costs, but no victim fine surcharge. Other than in cases when the payment-out-of-court option is chosen by the defendant or when the defendant pleads guilty with submissions, the set fine is only persuasive. The justice has discretion to impose a fine that is higher than the set fine.

For driving-related offences, a guilty plea means that the Ministry of Transportation will be notified and the conviction will be registered on the defendant's driving record for three years from the date of the conviction. If demerit points are

costs
a fee added to a court-imposed penalty

victim fine surcharge
a fee added to a court-imposed penalty that is then transferred to a special fund to assist victims of crime

---

1 RSO 1990, c H.8.

associated with the offence, they will remain on the defendant's record for two years from the date of the offence. Demerit points are applicable to *Highway Traffic Act* offences and are automatically imposed by the Ministry of Transportation, not by the court. It is beyond the jurisdiction of the provincial offences officer, prosecutor, or justice to remove the points. The only way to remove or decrease the number of demerit points is to plead guilty to an included charge that carries no points or a lower number of points.

With any driving-related conviction, there is also a risk that the defendant's insurance premiums will increase, but that is a private matter for the defendant to discuss with an insurer. Each insurance company has its own policies and procedures for premium increases. Any insurance rate increase is determined by the insurer, not the court or the Ministry.

If the charges are related to a motor vehicle accident, there is a possibility that the conviction will be used against the defendant if a civil lawsuit is commenced. Because this can have serious implications for the defendant, paralegals should try to determine the likelihood of a civil action being filed against the defendant.

If Your Client Does Not Want to Plead Guilty

A defendant who does not want to plead guilty will have to request a trial in order to move the matter on to the next stage. Having a trial scheduled does not necessarily mean that the matter will go to trial—there are additional steps and options that may be appropriate for your client as his or her matter moves toward the trial date.

Notice of Intention to Appear

The Notice of Intention to Appear (NIA), or Form 8, can be used for Part I or Part II matters to allow the defendant to request a trial date (see this form in Figure 5.2).

In many jurisdictions, this form is copied on yellow paper and is available from court offices. However, a growing number of municipalities are posting the forms online, and so not all NIA forms will be on yellow paper.

The NIA must include the defendant's correct name and address, even if the offence notice contained an error. The defendant may also use this form to request a trial in English or French, or to request an interpreter who can provide translation services for another language.

In accordance with section 125(2) of the *Courts of Justice Act*,[2] evidence presented in a language other than English must be interpreted into English. Therefore, if your client or a witness does not speak or understand English adequately, an interpreter should be considered. For Part I and Part II matters, the interpreter can be requested by checking the appropriate box on the NIA or by using an interpreter request form, but for Part III matters an interpreter request form would be used.

Once an interpreter has been requested, the court administrative staff will make the arrangements for a qualified interpreter to attend court and to translate as needed, at no charge to the defendant or witnesses. Family members and friends do not

---

2 RSO 1990, c C.43.

typically act as interpreters, but in some cases can be approved by the justice. If the interpreter fails to attend court, the prosecutor may decide to withdraw the charges or request an adjournment to another date.

Notice of Trial

For Part I matters, section 5(5) and section 5.1(11) state that the court clerk shall, as soon as is practicable, give notice to the defendant and prosecutor of the time and place of the trial. The authority for the requirement to give notice for parking infractions under Part II is contained in section 17(4).

The notice will be sent to the address listed on the NIA or the offence notice or parking infraction notice. It is important to ensure that the address is correct and that the court is notified if there is an address change.

Notice of trial is not necessary for a Part I or Part III summons because the defendant received the details of the trial, including the date, time, and courtroom, when served with the summons.

Options, Outcomes, and Risks

A defendant who requests a trial date may take further steps and has additional options beyond having a trial.

Seek Disclosure

Because the defendant's decision must be made within 15 days of being served, there is not enough time to obtain **disclosure** from the prosecution and make an informed choice on how to proceed with the matter. By giving notice of an intention to appear, the defendant has an opportunity to request and obtain disclosure from the prosecution. After reviewing any documents that are disclosed, the defendant may be able to determine whether the case is strong enough to proceed to trial. If disclosure is not requested prior to the trial date, the defendant may want to ask for an adjournment in order to obtain disclosure. However, such a request is subject to the justice's approval and is not always granted.

disclosure
documentation that the prosecutor will be relying on to prove the charges against the defendant

Negotiate with the Prosecutor

The defendant will typically have an opportunity to negotiate with the prosecutor or show required documentation to the prosecutor either immediately before trial or at a scheduled meeting with the prosecutor. The negotiations may lead to the charges being withdrawn, a lesser charge being offered in exchange for a guilty plea, or an agreement with the prosecutor regarding submissions on the penalty. A lesser charge may be considered to be an included offence pursuant to section 55 of the POA.

The best-case scenario for the defendant would be to have the charges withdrawn. This may occur if they are considered to be "paper charges"—for example, if the defendant was a licensed driver at the time of the offence, but had unintentionally left his or her driver's licence at home. The prosecutor has the discretion to withdraw the charge if proof is shown that the driver has a licence. Another example is a charge that stems from the need for an auto repair, such as a broken headlight. If the defendant has a receipt from a mechanic showing that the repair was carried out within a reasonable time, the prosecutor may be willing to withdraw the charge.

PRACTICE TIP

Arrive at court 20 to 30 minutes before the scheduled time in order to speak to the prosecutor. This will ensure that the prosecutor has sufficient time to consider your client's charges before court commences.

Plead Guilty

A defendant who has changed his or her mind and decided to plead guilty can still do so at this stage.

For more information on guilty pleas, see the discussion earlier in this chapter.

Ensure Officer's Attendance

Requesting a trial date gives the defendant a chance to ensure that the officer attends the trial. Occasionally, there may be a reason for an officer not to attend court, such as being called to another police matter or being scheduled for annual leave or training. In many cases, the prosecution will withdraw the charges because the case would be difficult to prove without the officer's evidence. It is worth noting that the prosecutor has the option of requesting an adjournment. However, section 49(3) states that the court shall not adjourn a Part I or Part II trial to allow the provincial offences officer who completed the certificate to attend court, unless the court is satisfied that it is required by the interests of justice.

PRACTICE TIP

Do not assume that an officer will not be attending court just because you do not see him or her in the courtroom. Some officers will arrive after court has already started. When you check in with the prosecutor, ask whether the officer has already checked in and, if not, whether the prosecutor is anticipating the officer's attendance.

---

institutional delay
the amount of time it takes for a matter to get to trial, minus any delay that was caused by the defendant

Unreasonable Delay

Requesting a trial date allows the defendant to ensure that the trial is scheduled without unreasonable delay. Case law has established that an unreasonable **institutional delay** is contrary to section 11(b) of the *Canadian Charter of Rights and Freedoms*.[3] If a motion for unreasonable delay is successful, the proper remedy is for the proceedings to be stayed by the justice. **Staying the proceedings** means that the prosecution of the offence has been halted and there will not be a conviction entered against the defendant.

> **staying the proceedings**
> the prosecution of the offence has been halted and a conviction will not be entered against the defendant

For more information on motions brought under the *Canadian Charter of Rights and Freedoms*, see the discussion in Chapter 8.

CASE IN POINT

Calculation of Unreasonable Delay

R v Jordan, 2016 SCC 27.

Facts

The accused, Jordan, was arrested and charged with various drug offences in December 2008. Over the next 49.5 months he proceeded through the various procedural stages of the criminal justice system, including a bail hearing, preliminary inquiry, and ultimately several months of trial dates.

At the start of his trial, Jordan had brought an 11(b) Charter application for a stay of proceedings due to unreasonable delay. The trial judge found that the delay was not unreasonable and therefore the application was dismissed and he was convicted. His appeal to the British Columbia Court of Appeal was dismissed because Jordan had not suffered significant prejudice as required by the framework set out in *R v Morin*, [1992] 1 SCR 771, 1992 CanLII 89. Jordan appealed to the Supreme Court of Canada.

Relevant Issue

Calculation of Unreasonable Delay

Decision

When Jordan brought an appeal to the Supreme Court of Canada, the panel indicated that the framework established

in *R v Morin*, *supra*, relied too heavily on the notion of prejudice and didn't encourage the parties to attempt to prevent delays. As such, they established a new framework, based on a ceiling beyond which delay is presumptively unreasonable. The presumptive ceiling is set at 18 months for cases going to trial in the provincial court, and at 30 months for cases going to trial in the superior court (or cases going to trial in the provincial court after a preliminary inquiry), unless there are exceptional circumstances to justify the delay. Below the presumptive ceiling, the burden is on the defence to show that the delay is unreasonable. The appeal was allowed, the convictions were set aside, and a stay of proceedings was entered.

Commentary

This is a highly significant case because it completely revised the framework to determine if there has been an unreasonable delay (prior to this decision, the framework as set out in *R v Morin*, *supra*, had been the binding precedent). Suggested reading: *R v Morin*, *supra*.

Seek an Adjournment

A defendant who has been given a court date can attempt to **adjourn** the matter to a new date. The motion to adjourn can be brought with or without notice. However, it can be risky to request an adjournment without notice because there is no guarantee that the motion will be granted, and the defendant may have to proceed to trial on the original court date.

> **adjourn**
> put the trial over to a new date

---

3 *Canadian Charter of Rights and Freedoms*, Part I of the *Constitution Act, 1982*, being Schedule B to the *Canada Act 1982* (UK), 1982, c 11.

Adjournments are often sought in order to retain a lawyer or paralegal. They are also commonly requested in order to allow a defendant to ask for and review disclosure materials.

For more information on motions for adjournment, see the discussion in Chapter 8.

Trial

Requesting a trial date provides the option of having a trial. Sometimes the defence will opt not to call witnesses or enter evidence at trial, but will instead use the proceedings to ensure that the prosecution proves all elements of the offence. Other times, both the prosecution and defence will call witnesses, and the justice will consider the evidence and render a decision.

A trial brings the possibility that the defendant will be successful and charges will be dismissed, which means there will not be a conviction. However, there is also the possibility that the defendant will be convicted. Upon conviction at trial, the justice has the opportunity to determine the sentence. It is worth noting that at this point, the set fine for Part I and Part II offences is only persuasive, and the justice has discretion to raise or lower the fine. If it is a driving-related offence, a conviction also leads to a driving record with the Ministry of Transportation, the possibility of demerit points, and a potential increase in insurance premiums.

Choosing a trial may be appropriate for someone who wants to keep his or her options open but does not necessarily need to resolve the matter quickly.

Failure to Appear

A defendant who requests a trial date and has been given notice of the trial but does not attend court on that date will be deemed to not wish to dispute the charge. This is considered a failure to appear at trial, as set out in sections 9.1 and 18.4 of the POA. The justice is still required to examine the certificate of offence to ensure that it is complete and regular on its face. If the certificate is complete and regular on its face, the justice will enter a conviction in the defendant's absence and impose the set fine for the offence. In most cases, failing to appear is equivalent to a defendant indicating a desire to plead guilty.

However, there is a unique situation where the defence may intentionally decide not to appear on a Part I or Part II matter so that the certificate will be examined by the justice. If the justice notices an error on the certificate, it will not be considered complete and regular on its face. In this case, the certificate will be quashed and there will not be a conviction. It is interesting to note that if a similar error on the certificate were raised at trial, the document would likely be amended. Although there is a risk that the justice may miss the error, failing to appear at trial is an option if there is an obvious error on the certificate.

In cases where a defendant fails to appear for a Part III matter or for a Part I summons, an *ex parte* trial will take place, where the court will hear the prosecution's case. If the prosecutor is able to prove all elements of the offence, a conviction will be entered. Alternatively, instead of an *ex parte* trial, the justice has the discretion to adjourn the hearing and issue a summons to appear or issue an arrest warrant for the defendant.

Special Considerations for Out-of-Jurisdiction Matters

Provincial offences matters are heard and determined by the Ontario Court of Justice (and in special circumstances in the Superior Court of Justice) in the county or district in which the offence occurred.

As a paralegal, if a defendant wants to retain you to defend a matter that is out of your local jurisdiction, or possibly even out of the province or country, you should consider several factors, including whether it would be cost effective for the defendant. Travel and accommodations, plus the fee for representation, may exceed any fines and consequences from a conviction. As well, Ontario is presently the only place in Canada or the United States that regulates paralegals allowing them to act independently as paid legal representatives in court.

It may be more appropriate to refer the matter to a legal representative who practises in the jurisdiction where the charges were laid.

KEY TERMS

REVIEW QUESTIONS

Multiple Choice

1. What does a plea of "guilty with submissions" mean?

   a. Charges may be dismissed against a defendant if he or she provides a good explanation for committing the offence.

   b. The defendant will have the opportunity to give submissions as to penalty.

   c. The defendant wants to dispute the charge.

   d. The prosecution's standard of proof is reduced to "balance of probabilities."

2. Which type of fine does the justice have to administer when the defendant pleads guilty at trial?

   a. A fine higher than the set fine.

   b. A fine lower than the set fine.

   c. The set fine is binding.

   d. Justice has discretion regarding the fine as long it is within the statutory range.

3. Who has the responsibility to administer demerit points?

   a. The police officer.

   b. The justice.

   c. The prosecutor.

   d. The Ministry of Transportation.

4. How long do demerit points stay on a driver's record?

   a. Two years from the date of the conviction.

   b. Two years from the date of the offence.

   c. Three years from the date of the conviction.

   d. Three years from the date of the offence.

5. How long do convictions stay on a driver's record?

   a. Two years from the date of the conviction.

   b. Two years from the date of the offence.

   c. Three years from the date of the conviction.

   d. Three years from the date of the offence.

6. Under what circumstances is a motion guaranteed to be granted?

   a. If it is first court appearance.

   b. If request is for the purpose of requesting and reviewing disclosure.

   c. If defendant has hired a legal representative.

   d. There is no guarantee that a motion will be granted.

7. If a matter proceeds to trial, which effect does the set fine have if the defendant is convicted?

   a. It is the minimum fine that can be awarded.

   b. It is used as a guideline, but it is not binding.

   c. It is the binding penalty upon conviction.

   d. The set fine cannot be revealed once a matter proceeds to trial.

8. What will happen, in many cases, if the officer is not present at trial for a Part I offence?

   a. The prosecutor will request an adjournment.

   b. Trial will proceed in officer's absence.

   c. Charges against the defendant will be withdrawn.

   d. The officer will be contacted and asked to attend trial immediately.

Short Answer

1. What possible submissions may a defendant make when requesting a lesser fine?

2. How are demerit points imposed?

3. How does a conviction affect a defendant's driving record?

4. How does a driving conviction affect how much a defendant pays for auto insurance?

5. What are two ways to request a trial date for a Part I matter?

6. Why is an NIA not used for Part III matters?

7. How are "paper charges" usually handled by the prosecutor?

8. What will happen if the defendant or the defendant's representative fails to appear at trial for a Part III matter?

9. What is likely to happen if an officer does not attend the court date? What else could happen in this situation?

Scenario 1

Luke, a self-represented defendant, indicates that he would like to plead guilty with submissions. In his submissions to the court, he explains that he should not be convicted of a speeding charge because he was hurrying to get to the hospital after receiving a phone call from his son's school that his son had been injured on the playground.

1. Would it be proper for the justice to convict Luke in this case? Explain.

2. Luke tells the justice that he is willing to pay the fine, but he would like the demerit points associated with the offence to be removed. Do you think the justice will remove the points in this case?

3. What should Luke do in this case?

Scenario 2

Sean did not attend his careless driving trial because his paralegal told him the wrong date. Although neither Sean nor his paralegal attended court, Sean was not convicted and the certificate was quashed.

1. Explain how it is possible that the certificate was quashed and Sean was not convicted.

2. A careless driving charge can be brought under Part I or Part III. How do we know that Sean was charged under Part I?

3. Assume that the certificate was complete and regular on its face. What would happen if Sean did not attend his trial?

Preparing for the Trial Date

7

LEARNING OUTCOMES

After reading this chapter, you will understand

- ◼ the steps that should be taken to prepare for the trial date;

- ◼ the purpose of and procedure for requesting disclosure;

- ◼ how to summon a witness to court; and

- ◼ how to request an interpreter if your client or witness does not speak or understand English.

Introduction

Once a Notice of Intention to Appear has been filed with the court, you should immediately start preparing for the upcoming trial—even before a trial date has been assigned by the court.

Network

If you have not handled a particular type of offence in the past, it can be worthwhile to speak to other paralegals who have experience with such an offence or who have seen the charge successfully defended in court. Your contacts may have ideas, information, and expertise to offer, so send a message to your paralegal contacts to see whether any of them are willing to share information. Rule 3.01 of the *Paralegal Rules of Conduct* requires any services undertaken on a client's behalf to be performed to the standard of a competent paralegal. Further, the Rules require a paralegal to recognize when he or she lacks competence and when to decline to act, collaborate with another licensee, or take the steps to gain competence. Your network of paralegals can be especially helpful with collaboration and gaining competence.

> **PRACTICE TIP**
>
> Always try to share your ideas, information, and expertise with your network of contacts when asked. Other paralegals may be more willing to return the favour when you need assistance.

Becoming a member of a paralegal association, such as the Ontario Paralegal Association, provides networking opportunities and mentoring for newly licensed paralegals. Whether the networking is through conferences, meetings, or online discussions, you will have a chance to meet and communicate with other paralegals throughout Ontario.

The Law Society of Ontario requires paralegals to complete at least 12 hours of continuing professional development each year. This includes at least three "Professionalism Hours" (topics related to professional responsibility, ethics, or practice management), and the remaining hours focus on substantive or procedural law, or related skills. Programs, seminars, and conferences offered by the Law Society of Ontario and other organizations bring paralegals together to learn as well as network with one another.

One of the best ways to meet new paralegals and learn how to defend various offences is to sit in court and observe. This cannot be emphasized enough. Watching other paralegals in court will allow you to pick up some helpful tips and techniques, and gain an understanding of effective defence strategies. You will also have an opportunity to talk to other paralegals during breaks in the proceedings.

Review the Charging Act

The charging act—the act under which your client has been charged—can provide important guidance on how to defend a charge in court. Although it is critical to review the section under which your client has been charged, it is also beneficial to review related sections and subsections of the act that may describe penalties, possible defences, and exceptions to the charge.

Penalty provisions are often found near the charging sections in a statute, although the exact placement of these provisions varies from statute to statute and section to section. In some cases, the penalties are in the same section as the offence, while in others, the provisions are listed in a section or subsection that follows the charging section. In still other cases, the penalties are included at the end of a part to the act or, possibly, at the end of the entire act. Because the penalties are not listed in a consistent place for all offences in all acts, it is especially important to seek out the penalty provisions by reviewing all related sections and subsections.

The charging act also contains important information about the classification of an offence. It is a good idea to refer to the relevant section of the charging act in order to examine the wording of the offence. This will help to establish whether the offence is *mens rea*, strict liability, or absolute liability. It is necessary to understand the classification in order to prepare a full answer and defence to the charges. However, you cannot rely on the wording of the offence alone because the court may have interpreted the classification differently. Also, a previous classification may have been reclassified on appeal. Therefore, you should also review the relevant case law to determine the offence's current classification.

In some cases, the related sections and subsections of an act will describe which defences will or will not be accepted for that particular charge. For example, section 2(2) of the *Trespass to Property Act*[1] indicates, "It is a defence to a charge under subsection (1) in respect of premises that is land that the person charged reasonably believed that he or she had title to or an interest in the land that entitled him or her to do the act complained of." This subsection explains that a possible defence to a trespassing charge is a belief by the defendant that he or she owned the land. Another example appears in section 84.1 of the *Highway Traffic Act*,[2] which deals with a situation when a wheel detaches from a commercial motor vehicle. Subsection 84.1(5) specifically removes a potential defence, stating, "It is not a defence … that the person exercised due diligence to avoid or prevent the detaching of the wheel." This wording clearly shows the intention of the act to designate this as an absolute liability offence.

---

1 RSO 1990, c T.21.

2 RSO 1990, c H.8.

Information about exceptions can also be found in the related sections and subsections. There are often exceptions or situations where an act that is usually prohibited is actually permitted. If one of these exceptions is relevant, the burden of proof is on the defence to show that the exception applies to the defendant on a balance of probabilities. For example, under section 106 of the *Highway Traffic Act*, it is an offence to drive a vehicle while not wearing a seat belt. However, subsection (6) provides a list of several situations when a driver is not required to wear a seat belt, such as when he or she has a medical certificate. If your client recently had an injury or surgery, his or her doctor may have provided a medical certificate verifying the situation and confirming that the client is unable to wear a seat belt. In such a case, producing the medical certificate in court should result in the charges being withdrawn or dismissed.

A thorough review of the charging act will also help to prepare you for any negotiations that may take place with the prosecutor, either at an Early Resolution Meeting or immediately prior to trial. When reviewing the charging act, you should search for alternate offences that are related to your client's charge. With your client's fact situation in mind, consider whether any of the alternate charges could be considered as an included offence. Specifically, consider whether your client's fact situation could fit with any of the other offences listed in the act. Make a list of all other offences that could apply and then conduct further research regarding the applicable penalties for each of the alternate charges. With your client's approval, you may want to suggest a guilty plea to one of the alternate charges when meeting with the prosecutor. For example, drivers are frequently charged with careless driving contrary to section 130 of the *Highway Traffic Act* because the broad wording of the offence encompasses a wide range of driving behaviours. For example, careless driving behaviours can range from a driver who tries to multi-task by shaving while driving on a long commute to a driver who accidentally smashes his or her vehicle through a storefront window. However, even when it is laid as a Part I offence, careless driving carries a set fine of $400 and six demerit points. Depending on the facts of the offence, you may be able to negotiate it down to an included offence that carries a lesser fine and fewer demerit points. As an example, a careless driving charge is often laid when there has been a motor vehicle collision. Depending on the facts of case, other wrongful driving behaviours may also be related to the collision and can be used in negotiations with the prosecutor. As an example, "fail to turn to the left to avoid a collision" relates to a driver who didn't do something he or she should have done. Since it carries a lesser fine ($85) and only two demerit points, it would put your client in a better position than a careless driving conviction.

A review of the regulations accompanying the charging act may provide additional information that is relevant to your client's situation. For example, Regulation 339/94 of the *Highway Traffic Act* lists the number of demerit points for various driving offences. This will help you to understand the impact that a conviction will have on your client. Be sure to ask your client about his or her driving record, the number of points that are registered on his or her record, and when the points will be removed. Knowing this information in advance allows you to be fully prepared and able to represent your client's best interests when entering into negotiations with the prosecutor.

PRACTICE TIP

Not all clients will be entirely truthful about their driving record, or they may not remember specific details about previous convictions. Consider ordering a Driver's Abstract from the Ministry of Transportation so that you will have a full and detailed statement of your client's driving record. There are several different types of abstracts that are available, and they can be ordered online at <https://www.ontario.ca/page/order-drivers-record>. Most types of uncertified abstracts can be obtained for $12, while the certified abstracts can be obtained for $18 (at the time of publication).

Review Procedural Act and Relevant Regulations

Paralegals should review the procedures as set out in the POA. As well, it is important to review the regulations made under the POA and the CJA, in particular, the *Rules of the Ontario Court (Provincial Division) in Provincial Offences Proceedings*[3] (POA Rules, reproduced in Appendix B), which sets out the applicable rules and required forms to be used.

Determine the Elements of the Offence

The **elements of the offence** are the items that have to be proven by the prosecution to secure a conviction. In order to determine the elements of the offence, you will look to the actual wording of the charging section of the charging act, and consider each and every word in the section.

For example, section 144(15) of the *Highway Traffic Act* states, "Every driver approaching a traffic control signal showing a circular amber indication and facing the indication shall stop his or her vehicle if he or she can do so safely, otherwise he or she may proceed with caution."

The elements of the offence that must be proven by the prosecutor (i.e., the evidence that the prosecutor's witnesses will have to provide) include:

- the defendant was the driver;
- the defendant was driving a vehicle;
- there was a traffic control signal showing an amber indication;
- the defendant approached the traffic control signal;
- the defendant did not stop at the traffic control signal; and
- it would have been safe for the defendant to stop, or the defendant did not proceed through the intersection with caution.

When preparing for trial, making a list of the elements of the offence will help you to anticipate the prosecutor's evidence. Listen carefully as the prosecution presents

elements of the offence
the items that have to be proven by the prosecutor to secure a conviction

---

3 RRO 1990, Reg 200.

the case against your client. If the prosecution does not prove all elements of the offence, the defendant can bring a motion for a non-suit or can raise the elements that were not proven during closing statements in order to raise a reasonable doubt. For example, if the prosecutor called the officer as a witness and the officer neglected to mention the colour of the indication on the traffic control signal, there may be grounds to bring a motion for a non-suit.

Look for Errors on the Charging Document

A paralegal should always review the charging document for errors. A common misconception is that if there is an error on the charging document, the charges will be withdrawn. However, that is rarely the case. In fact, there would have to be a fatal error on the charging document for the charges to be withdrawn or quashed. Most errors are not considered fatal, and in many cases the court will amend the charges at trial. Section 34 of the POA gives the court the authority to amend the information or certificate at any stage in the proceeding if there has been an error.

Minor errors on a charging document are quite common, so it is worthwhile to review the document for errors and to consider the effect that this will have in court. Minor mistakes, such as a misspelled name or address, or an incorrect digit or letter in the licence plate, will be considered non-fatal errors and amended in court. However, even minor errors on a charging document can raise a reasonable doubt as to whether there should be a conviction. If you find more significant errors that interfere with your client's ability to prepare full answer and defence to the charge, you will want to consider bringing a motion to quash the charging document. However, be prepared for the prosecution to oppose your motion and bring a countermotion for an amendment pursuant to section 34.

For more information on quashing the charging document, see the discussion in Chapter 8.

Section 34(4) of the POA sets out what the court must consider when deciding whether to amend the charging document. Specifically, the court will consider the evidence that has been given, the circumstances of the case, whether the defendant has been misled or prejudiced, and whether the amendment can be made without causing injustice. If your client has been misled to the extent that he or she was unable to prepare a full answer and defence to the charges, or if you feel that there has been prejudice or injustice to your client, you may want to consider arguing against the prosecutor's amendment request.

If the court agrees to amend the charging document, the existence of the errors will still undermine the officer's credibility, raising questions about the overall investigation. You will want to summarize the errors in your closing statement so that the court can consider whether there is reasonable doubt about your client's guilt in the charges before the court.

As stated earlier, very few errors are considered to be "fatal," but there are a few that will justify quashing the charging document. Some examples include:

- The proper offence date and date of service must be written on the charging document. A document that contains an incomplete or incorrect date, or where the date is missing altogether, will likely be quashed. The correct dates are important because certain timelines take effect on these dates. For example, an offence notice must be served on the defendant within 30 days of the offence date for a Part I offence, and the defendant has 15 days from the date of service to respond. If the charging document contains incorrect dates, the timelines will be affected.

- Although a spelling error in the defendant's name is not fatal, that would not be the case if the name is missing altogether. The prosecution would have difficulty proving that the person before the court is the same person who committed the offence because the document does not specify who committed the offence.

- The charging document must specify where the offence took place to ensure that it was properly filed in the court that has jurisdiction for that location.

- The officer's signature is necessary in order to certify the allegations and to verify that an offence notice was served upon the defendant for a Part I offence. Without the signature, there is no proof of service. However, it is essential that the certificate of offence copy is signed by the officer, but it is not essential that the offence notice copy is signed. If you notice that the officer's signature is missing from the defendant's copy, arrive for trial early and ask the court clerk if you can review the certificate copy to verify that it was signed by the officer.

In some cases, if the set fine or the total payable is incorrect it can be considered a fatal error, which will result in the certificate being quashed. In order for this to take place, the defendant would have to opt to "fail to respond" within the 15-day period that he or she is given to make a decision. This causes the certificate to be reviewed by a justice as part of the default judgment process or "deemed to not wish to dispute" docket. At this stage, the justice does not have the jurisdiction to amend the certificate and would be forced to quash it. By contrast, if the error is raised at the trial stage, the justice has the authority under section 34(1) to make amendments to the certificate (e.g., fixing the set fine) instead of quashing the certificate.

CASE IN POINT

Dealing with Certificate Errors During Default Proceedings

London (City) v Young, 2008 ONCA 429

Facts

This case involved multiple defendants (with a total of 16 certificates) who did not respond to their offence notices within the required 15-day period. Since each of these notices contained an error in the set fine, the certificates were quashed as part of the default judgment process (set out in section 9.1 of the POA) as they were not "complete and regular on their face." On appeal to the Ontario Court of Appeal, the city took the position that the justice should have amended the errors during the default proceeding instead of quashing the certificates.

Relevant Issue

Dealing with Certificate Errors During Default Proceedings

Decision

The Court of Appeal determined that the set fine is one of the components of the certificate of offence that must be accurate in order for the certificate to be complete and regular on its face. Further, the court indicated that a justice has no jurisdiction to amend a defective certificate at the default judgment stage and that it was proper for the justice to quash the certificates because of the incorrect set fine. As such, the Court of Appeal dismissed the appeal.

Conduct Research

Changes to the law and new interpretations of charging sections occur every day in our courts, which means paralegals must continually research the law for updates and binding precedents. This can be a challenge for a busy paralegal who is trying to run an office and make court appearances. Fortunately, resources are available that allow paralegals to stay up to date with any changes to the law that affect provincial offences matters.

Belonging to a paralegal organization can be invaluable for sharing information and discussing new cases. Some organizations have regular meetings that allow for discussions, while others post relevant information on their websites or provide an online discussion area for their members. Electronic mailing lists are available for discussing case law and asking questions.

The annual volumes of the *Annotated Ontario Provincial Offences Act* and the *Annotated Ontario Highway Traffic Act* are indispensable because they list the leading cases for every section of the statutes. The amount of time saved is certainly worth the cost of purchasing a new volume each year.

Legal encyclopedias, textbooks, and articles can also refer you to the leading cases on a topic. Electronic finding tools, such as Lexis Advance Quicklaw and the Canadian Abridgment Case Digests, can help you to search for relevant case law. Other resources that may be useful in finding and updating cases include CanLII, Law-Source, and BestCase.

Part of your research may also include attending at the scene of the offence with your client or another witness. Depending on the circumstances, it may be appropriate to take photographs, videos, measurements, or speak to other people in the area. However, any evidence collected at the scene should be collected by the defendant or witness so that it can form part of his or her testimony at trial (e.g., the person who took the photograph is the only one who can speak about it and have it entered into evidence at trial).

Request Disclosure

A defendant is entitled to know the case against him or her. When a defendant intends to plead not guilty, section 46(2) of the POA indicates that he or she is entitled to make full answer and defence to the charges that have been laid. In order to do this, the paralegal should request and review copies of the evidence that the prosecutor will be using in the case. This is known as requesting disclosure and there is no charge to make the request or receive the documentation. When the defence makes a request for disclosure, the prosecutor must provide any information that is in his or her possession and that will be relied on to prosecute the defendant. It is worth noting that the disclosure obligations are one-sided: while the prosecutor must give the defendant all relevant documents, the defendant does not have a reciprocal duty to disclose information to the prosecutor that will be used to defend against the charges.

Paralegals should submit a request for disclosure as soon as the defendant receives notice of trial. It may take several weeks, or even months, for full compliance. The earlier that disclosure is requested, the more likely you will receive the relevant documents before the trial date. The defence can write a letter to request disclosure or can use a form that is available at the prosecution office or, in some cases, online. Since it is not a standardized form, each prosecution office will provide its own version of the disclosure request form and its own procedure for making the request. After the form is completed, it can be faxed, submitted online, or delivered to the office, in accordance with the disclosure procedures of that prosecution office.

PRACTICE TIP

Obtain confirmation that your disclosure request has been received. If sending it by fax or submitting online, print off the confirmation page to verify that it has been sent. If dropping it off in person, bring a second copy to the court office and ensure that it is stamped and initialled by the court administration staff. If the disclosure request is not fulfilled, you will be able to prove that it was properly submitted and be in a good position to request an appropriate remedy, such as a stay of the proceedings, an adjournment, and/or an order for the production of the disclosure documents.

Each court has its own procedure for forwarding the disclosure documents. Some courts will fax or mail the documents, while others will request that the documents be picked up. When you receive the disclosure documents, arrange to meet with your client so that you will be able to review the documents together and discuss and interpret the contents.

You can expect the disclosure to include a copy of the notes that the police officer made at the time of the alleged offence. It is useful for the defendant to see the notes because the officer may use them to refresh his or her memory at the trial. The amount of detail in the notes varies from officer to officer: some provide specific details, while others write only one or two lines. Other documents in the disclosure package may include a copy of an accident report, witness statements, photos of the vehicle, or a disc with the officer's video recording of the offence (e.g., the cruiser's video of a vehicle proceeding through a stop sign).

When reviewing the documents, consider whether anything may be missing. If you think that is the case, submit another written request for disclosure and specify what you are seeking. If you have made repeated requests and still not received disclosure by the trial date, you will have an opportunity to pursue a remedy.

CASE IN POINT

Prosecution's Duty to Disclose Relevant Information to the Defence

R v Stinchcombe, [1991] 3 SCR 326

Facts

The accused, Stinchcombe, was a lawyer who was charged with the criminal offences of breach of trust, theft, and fraud. At the preliminary inquiry, Stinchcombe's former secretary was called as a Crown witness, but her evidence supported the defence's position. Prior to trial, the same witness gave a tape-recorded statement to an RCMP officer and, during trial, a written statement to another police officer. The Crown opted not to call her as a witness at trial. When the defence requested disclosure, they were denied access to the contents of these statements.

The trial proceeded and the accused was convicted of breach of trust and fraud (the theft charges received conditional stays). On appeal, the Court of Appeal affirmed the convictions without giving reasons. Stinchcombe appealed to the Supreme Court of Canada.

Relevant Issue

Prosecution's Duty to Disclose Relevant Information to the Defence

Decision

The Supreme Court affirmed that in order for a defendant to be able to make full answer and defence to charges, the defendant is entitled to receive disclosure from the Crown (this is also applicable to disclosure for provincial offences). The fruits of the investigation are the property of the public to ensure that justice is served and not the property of the Crown. Such disclosure must take place before the accused chooses his mode or trial or makes a plea. The Supreme Court allowed the appeal and ordered a new trial for Stinchcombe.

When disclosure has been requested but not provided, some prosecutors will automatically withdraw the charges. If that is not the case, the defence can seek an adjournment and request that the justice order production of the disclosure documents as a remedy. But it is difficult to justify such a remedy if the defendant or the defendant's legal representative is partly responsible for the non-disclosure (e.g., if disclosure was not requested in a timely fashion before the trial date, or if the disclosure request form was incorrectly filled out or missing important information).

A stay of proceedings is another remedy that is used in exceptional circumstances. If there have been repeated requests for disclosure and the disclosure has not been provided, the justice may grant a stay of proceedings as an appropriate remedy.

Consider Witnesses

When preparing for trial, you need to consider who your witnesses will be. They could include people who were present at the scene and involved in some way with the defendant, such as passengers in a car, or someone who witnessed the incident but was not directly involved. Some witnesses will volunteer to attend court, but others will need to be compelled to testify through a summons.

Section 39 of the POA provides the authority to issue a summons to witnesses to attend the trial. In order to compel a witness to attend court, the person requiring the witness must appear before a justice and swear the "summons to witness." The justice may ask for detailed reasons as to why this witness should be compelled to attend court. The summons will be granted if the justice is satisfied that the witness has material evidence to offer at trial. The summons will require the witness to attend court to give evidence, and can also specify that the witness bring anything that has been itemized in the summons. The summons is to be served on the witness by a provincial offences officer, in accordance with section 26(2) of the POA.

> **PRACTICE TIP**
>
> Issuing a summons for a witness to appear in court is always a good practice. In addition to compelling the witness's attendance at court, a summons could assist the witness in arranging time off work or school because it provides a documented reason for absence. As well, if for any reason the witness fails to attend court, you will be in a better position to request an adjournment because proper procedures were followed to compel the witness's attendance at court.

Consider the Need for an Interpreter

In accordance with section 125(2)(a) of the *Courts of Justice Act*,[4] evidence given in a language other than English must be interpreted into English. Therefore, if your client or one of your witnesses does not speak or understand English adequately, you should consider the need for an interpreter. For Part I and Part II matters, an interpreter can be requested by checking the appropriate box on the Notice of Intention to Appear. For Part III matters, an interpreter can be requested at the first court appearance when the trial date is set.

If the need for an interpreter arises after the Notice of Intention to Appear has been filed or after the first court appearance, an Interpreter Request form is available from the court and can still be completed. Once an interpreter has been requested, the court administrative staff will make the arrangements for an interpreter to attend court and to translate as needed. If the interpreter has been properly requested yet does not attend court, the prosecutor may withdraw the charge(s) or request an adjournment.

Consider Any Necessary Motions and Charter Applications

As you prepare for trial, you should consider whether it is necessary to bring any motions, either with or without notice. As well, if you feel that your client's rights under the *Canadian Charter of Rights and Freedoms*[5] have been breached or that the law under which your client has been charged is unconstitutional, you will need to prepare a notice of constitutional question and ensure that it is properly served.

---

4 RSO 1990, c C.43.

5 Part I of the *Constitution Act, 1982*, being Schedule B to the *Canada Act 1982* (UK), 1982, c 11.

CASE IN POINT

Unconstitutional Classification of Charging Section

R v Raham, 2010 ONCA 206

Facts

As she was driving on a highway, the defendant, Raham, sped up to pass a truck. Her rate of speed was measured by a police officer as 131km/hr in an 80km/hr zone. Raham was charged with stunt driving contrary to section 172 of the *Highway Traffic Act*. At trial, the defendant took the position that, as an absolute liability offence that carried the possibility of imprisonment, the offence was contrary to section 7 of the Charter. However, the trial justice interpreted the offence as one of strict liability and convicted the defendant. Raham appealed to the Ontario Court of Justice on the basis that the justice had erred in finding that the section was constitutional. The appeal judge agreed with the defendant and held that the stunt driving law was unconstitutional. The attorney general's office brought an appeal to the Court of Appeal of Ontario.

Relevant Issue

Unconstitutional Classification of Charging Section

Decision

The Court of Appeal unanimously determined that the appeal judge had erred in classifying stunt driving as an absolute liability offence. As such, the acquittal was set aside. The panel agreed that stunt driving should be classified as a strict liability offence, which provides the opportunity for a defendant to advance a due diligence defence. As such, the appeal was allowed, the acquittal was set aside, and a new trial was ordered for Raham.

For more information on the types of motions or applications and the required procedures, see the discussion in Chapter 8.

Consult with Client

The most important person in any proceeding is your client. Clients often complain about a lack of communication or poor communication from their legal representatives, so be sure to update your client on a regular basis about the work that has been done on his or her file. No matter how busy your practice becomes, it is essential to take the time to consult with your client. It is also important to remember that your client is the ultimate decision-maker for any significant decisions on a file, so you must obtain their instructions and consent before taking any steps on the case.

Consider whether your client should testify at the trial. Some of your clients will likely want to take the stand, but others may not feel comfortable. You may also have clients who would not make a good witness. If your client is going to testify, you can assist by reviewing the evidence and preparing him or her for cross-examination. If your client is not going to take the stand, explain how this will limit your ability to defend the matter (e.g., he or she will not be able to offer evidence to dispute the prosecution's evidence, and the defence will rely on raising doubt as to whether prosecution has proven all elements of the offence).

As a paralegal, you will become accustomed to going to court and will start to feel comfortable in this environment. However, most of your clients will never feel comfortable going to court and may rely on you for additional support and guidance both prior to the trial date and when appearing in court.

KEY TERM

elements of the offence, 83

REVIEW QUESTIONS

Multiple Choice

1. Where are the penalty provisions contained in a statute?

    a. In the same section as the offence.

    b. At the end of the statute.

    c. At the beginning of the statute.

    d. Varies by statute and section.

2. When he was on his way to see his doctor, Zanab was charged with failing to wear his seat belt contrary to section 106(2) of the *Highway Traffic Act*. Zanab recently underwent abdominal surgery and was told by his surgeon to drive only to and from medical appointments. The surgeon further advised that he should not risk wearing a seat belt when driving. Zanab tried to explain this to the officer, but did not have proof with him at the time. At the court date, Zanab produced a certificate from his doctor. Who has the burden of proof to demonstrate that the exception applies in this case?

    a. Prosecutor.

    b. Defence.

    c. Justice.

    d. Either a or b.

3. Under which circumstances will a summons to witness be granted?

    a. If the justice is satisfied that the witness has material evidence to offer at trial.

    b. Upon submission of any request by the defence.

    c. Only if the witness refuses to attend upon verbal request.

    d. If the trial date is less than two weeks away.

Short Answer

1. Explain how to request an interpreter for Part I and Part II matters and for Part III matters.

2. Outline some examples of fatal errors.

3. What will the court consider if the prosecution has requested an amendment to the charging document?

4. According to section 144(18) of the *Highway Traffic Act*, "Every driver approaching a traffic control signal showing a circular red indication and facing the indication shall stop his or her vehicle and shall not proceed until a green indication is shown." List the specific elements of this offence that would have to be proven by the prosecution.

5. Using Appendix C, what is the correct set fine for an offence under section 144(18) of the *Highway Traffic Act*?

6. Patrick was charged with careless driving contrary to section 130 of the *Highway Traffic Act* after he was involved in a minor rear-end collision. This offence has a set fine of $400 and has 6 demerit points. Using Appendix C and Appendix D, find an included offence that could result in a lesser penalty for Patrick.

Scenario 1

To celebrate their recent engagement, Val and Curtis had a special brunch complete with champagne and orange juice at Val's mother's house. When they were ready to leave, Val's mom insisted that she take the remaining full bottles of champagne and one bottle that was half full. Val couldn't get the cork back in the bottle, so she carefully propped it between her knees for the drive home. They were pulled over on the way home and Curtis was charged with driving a motor vehicle with an unsealed container of liquor contrary to section 32(1) of the *Liquor Licence Act*. After the officer left, they noticed that he forgot to sign the offence notice.

1. Does the missing signature mean that this charge will be thrown out of court? Explain.

2. Are there demerit points associated with this charge? How do you know?

3. Curtis faxed in a disclosure request one week before his trial date. Did he follow proper procedure?

Scenario 2

Alison has a very busy paralegal practice. In preparing her client's case, she requested disclosure from the prosecution in a timely fashion, but it was never provided. Unfortunately, a key defence witness who had guaranteed his attendance did not show up for the trial.

1. How should Alison deal with this situation?

2. If Alison decides to summons the witness to a new trial date, what will she have to prove to the court in order to get the summons to witness?

3. What remedy should Alison seek if an adjournment is granted but disclosure is still not provided by the new trial date?

Motions and Applications

8

LEARNING OUTCOMES

After reading this chapter, you will understand

- the procedures and process involved in bringing a motion under the *Provincial Offences Act*;

- the legal framework for motions;

- the most common motions brought in the provincial offences court; and

- the procedure to bring a Charter application.

Introduction

While the POA is meant to provide a streamlined process and allow matters to proceed on their merits by limiting technical challenges or objections, it is still important to understand the rules and procedures and when it is best to introduce a motion or application—and when to avoid doing so. Knowing when it is not a good time to bring a motion or application comes with experience and practice, and there are some general suggestions to guide your judgment. Essentially, anything that requires a justice to make an interpretation or decision prior to trial, and in some cases during trial, will be dealt with by way of a motion or application.

Legal Framework for Motions

moving party
the party who brings a motion

responding party
the party who does not initiate the motion but will have an opportunity to respond to it

pre-trial motion
a motion brought with notice in advance of the trial date

affidavit
a document sworn by a party to attest to the truthfulness of the statements within the document—often used in support of a motion

The rules governing applications and motions for provincial offences proceedings are set out in section 7 of Regulation 200 under the *Courts of Justice Act* (the "POA Rules").[1] The party bringing the motion is known as the applicant or the **moving party**, and the opposing party is referred to as the **responding party**. When initiating the motion as the moving party, particularly when requesting direction from the court or seeking an adjournment, it is to your advantage to demonstrate compliance with the rules.

In accordance with section 7(1) and section 7(2) of the POA Rules, in order to bring a motion or an application in advance of the trial date (also known as a **pre-trial motion**), a notice of motion/application form must be used (see Figure 8.1). The form is available from the provincial offences court administration office. Once the notice is prepared, it is then served on the opposing party (the defence would serve it on the prosecution and vice versa) and a copy is filed with the court. Sections 7(3) and 7(4) of the POA Rules indicate that the notice must be served on the opposing party at least three days before the motion is to be heard, and filed with the court at least two days before the date of the motion is to be heard. Given the time requirements, filing a notice as soon as is practicable is usually the best approach.

A notice of motion allows all parties to understand the issue and adequately prepare a response, and gives the court the opportunity to properly exercise its jurisdiction. It may or may not be the same justice who hears the pre-trial motion as the justice who presides at trial. Typically, the evidence to support a notice of motion filed by the defence is presented in the form of an **affidavit** (see Figure 8.2) from the defendant, but section 7(5) of the POA Rules indicates that evidence may also be given orally (with permission of the court) or in the form of a transcript of the examination of a witness.

Often a court will refuse to hear the merits of a motion when the rules have not been followed. Bringing a motion is a relatively straightforward process and only requires that a notice of motion be completed, usually with a corresponding affidavit sworn by your client. There are times it may be advisable to prepare a factum or book of authorities if the issue is complicated.

---

1 RSO 1990, c C.43.

Figure 8.1   Notice of Motion

NOTICE OF MOTION
AVIS DE MOTION

BETWEEN .... Prosecutor
ENTRE *Poursuivant*

and
et

.... Defendant
Défendeur

TAKE NOTICE that an application will be made by the ....
SACHEZ QU'UNE requête sera déposée par (Prosecutor/Defendant) / *(poursuivant/défendeur)*

on .... , yr. .... , before the Ontario Court of Justice
le *an* *devant la Cour de justice de l'Ontario*

at ....
á

in the following matter:
en ce qui concerne l'affaire suivant :

....

....

....

for an Order as follows:
pour une ordonnance comme suit :

....

....

....

....

....

And further take notice that in support of this application will be read the affidavit of ....
Sachez aussi qu'à l'appui de cette requête sera lu l'affidavit de

.... , and such other and further evidence as may be required.
ainsi que d'autres preuves qui s'avéreront nécessaires.

Dated this .... day of .... , yr. ....
Fait le *jour de* *an*

at ....
á

Signed ....
Signature

Address ....
Adresse

TO: / *Á :*
Prosecutor (or Defendant) and Clerk of the Court
Poursuivant (ou Défendeur) et au greffier de la Cour

DISTRIBUTION:

☐   Defendant/Prosecutor   ☐   Counsel for Defendant/Prosecutor   ☐   Agent for Defendant/Prosecutor
défendeur/poursuivant   *avocat du défendeur/poursuivant*   *mandataire du défendeur/poursuivant*

FOR INFORMATION ON ACCESS   POUR PLUS DE RENSEIGNEMENTS SUR L'ACCÈS
TO ONTARIO COURTS   DES PERSONNES HANDICAPÉES
FOR PERSONS WITH DISABILITIES, CALL   AUX TRIBUNAUX DE L'ONTARIO, COMPOSEZ LE
1-800-387-4456   **1-800-387-4456**
TORONTO AREA **416-326-0111**   RÉGION DE TORONTO **416-326-0111**

Figure 8.2   Affidavit

Ministry of the Attorney General	*Ministère du Procureur général*

GENERAL FORM FOR AFFIDAVIT
FORMULE GÉNÉRALE D'AFFIDAVIT

I, _____
Je / soussigné(e),

of
de _____

_____

make oath and say as follows:
déclare sous serment que: _____

_____

_____

_____

_____

_____

_____

_____

_____

_____

_____

_____

_____

_____

_____

_____

_____

_____

_____

_____

_____

_____

_____

_____
Signature

Sworn by the said _____
Déclaré sous serment par

before me, _____
devant moi

at _____
dans le/la

on the _____ day of _____ , yr. 20 ____
le   jour de   an

_____
(a commissioner, etc. / *commissaire, etc.*)

Common Motions

Section 7 of the POA Rules allows for any motion or application to be heard without notice, on consent, or where the court determines doing so would not be unjust. Whenever possible, it is best to follow the proper procedure and bring your motion or application with notice. However, it is quite common for motions in the provincial offences system to be brought without notice. For example, it would not be practical or possible to bring a pre-trial motion to adjourn when you learn the day before trial that your client will not be available to attend. As a general rule, the more serious the offence being prosecuted, the greater the likelihood that a pre-trial motion will be necessary.

Motion to Adjourn

A motion to adjourn is a request that the trial be moved to a different date. It is not uncommon for a motion to adjourn to be brought orally and without notice on the day scheduled for a trial by either the prosecutor or the defendant. However, if you know in advance that you or your client will not be able to proceed with the case on the trial date, you should follow the rules and complete a notice of motion so that it can be brought as a pre-trial motion. A defendant does not have a *right* to an adjournment, so he or she must be made aware that it is not uncommon for adjournments to be denied.

A motion to adjourn will be granted only if the moving party is successful in convincing the court that an adjournment is necessary under the circumstances. Be prepared to justify the reasons for the adjournment. For example, a defendant may be successful in getting an adjournment if he or she has retained a legal representative who is not available on the trial date. However, the defendant would have less chance of being granted the adjournment if it was revealed that the legal representative had been retained only on the day of the trial.

> **PRACTICE TIP**
>
> It is advisable to bring a motion to adjourn with notice well before the trial date. If the motion is not granted, you and your client will know that you will have to be ready to proceed on the scheduled trial date. If you were to bring a motion to adjourn without notice, you run the risk of being forced to proceed to trial unprepared if the motion is not granted.

It is worth noting that section 49(5) of the POA allows for an administrative adjournment of the first request for a new date for Part I and Part II matters:

Power of clerk to adjourn

> 49(5) The clerk of the court may, on behalf of the court, adjourn,
>   (a) the first trial date for a proceeding commenced under Part I or Part II to a date agreed to by the defendant and the prosecutor in a written agreement filed with the court; and

(b) any proceeding under this Act or any step in a proceeding under this Act, where no justice is able to attend in person, to a date chosen in accordance with the instructions of a justice.

This administrative procedure is typically available for minor offences that do not involve a motor vehicle collision. The required form can be obtained at the court office.

Motion for Further Disclosure

A common motion brought as a pre-trial motion is a request for further disclosure. Once a disclosure request has been submitted, most prosecutors recognize that providing timely and full disclosure improves procedural efficiency and will attempt to comply. However, sometimes further disclosure through a court order is required.

When reviewing your client's case and the materials provided by the prosecution, assess whether you believe the prosecution has withheld documents that you feel are relevant. If so, a motion for further disclosure would be appropriate.

In order to make full answer and defence to the charge, a defendant is entitled to know the evidence that will be used by the prosecution at trial. This right to make full answer and defence is set out in sections 7 and 11(d) of the *Canadian Charter of Rights and Freedoms*[2] and is further stated in section 46(2) of the POA.

The issue of bringing a motion before the court over disputed disclosure is not without jurisprudence in the provincial offences context. It should be noted that the trial justice has the authority to control which documents are relevant for disclosure. The Case in Point: *R v 1353837 Ontario Inc*, below, considers this issue.

CASE IN POINT

Control of Disclosure Process

R v 1353837 Ontario Inc, 2005 CanLII 4189 (Ont CA), 74 OR (3d) 401

Facts

The defendants were charged with fourteen *Building Code* violations under Part III of the POA. These included charges of obstruction and failure to comply. The defendant requested and received the initial disclosure, requested and received further disclosure, and then brought a pre-trial motion for further disclosure of 18 items. In response to the pretrial motion, the City complied with one item but filed an affidavit of the chief building inspector who indicated that all elements of the request for further disclosure were either irrelevant or had already been disclosed. The chief building inspector was not available for cross-examination. The justice considered the 18 items and ordered disclosure of three items, ruled that three were not relevant, accepted that the City had complied with eight items, and had already provided four items.

The defendant brought an application to the Superior Court to quash or set aside the justice's order. The reviewing justice granted the application to set aside the order, indicating that the refusal to cross-examine the building inspector was a denial of natural justice and therefore a jurisdictional error.

The City brought an appeal to the Court of Appeal. The panel determined that there was no jurisdictional error, set aside the decision of the Superior Court, and sent the matter back to a justice of the peace for trial.

Relevant Issue

Control of Disclosure Process

Decision

The court found that when disclosure disputes arise, trial justices have the right to control the disclosure process.

---

2   The *Constitution Act, 1982*, Schedule B to the *Canada Act 1982* (UK), 1982, c 11.

Motion for Particulars

A motion for particulars is brought when the defence would like additional information about the charges that were laid. With the vast array of agencies, police departments, other bodies, and informants that can commence proceedings under the POA, occasionally the circumstances of the case and the allegations concerning your client's conduct are unclear in the charging documents, particularly for Part III matters as they do not have established short form wording. It may be necessary in some circumstances to bring a motion for particulars with respect to the charge your client is facing. Section 35 of the POA provides the framework for a motion for particulars:

> 35. The court may, before or during trial, if it is satisfied that it is necessary for a fair trial, order that a particular, further describing any matter relevant to the proceeding, be furnished to the defendant.

Motion to Amend

A motion to amend is brought when the prosecution has become aware of an error on the charging document and makes a request that the court allow the error to be fixed. This type of motion is routinely granted for minor errors (e.g., spelling mistakes), but cannot be granted for fatal errors.

A motion to amend the certificate or information may be brought at any stage of a proceeding. Although bringing a motion to amend is largely a procedure carried out by the prosecution, having a good understanding of the jurisprudence and statutory requirements is key to ensuring that your client's rights are protected. Most of the precedent cases have favoured the POA's broad curative provisions and granted amendments as long as there was no prejudice to the defendant.

Section 34(1) of the POA provides the framework for motions to amend:

> 34(1) The court may, at any stage of the proceeding, amend the information or certificate as may be necessary if it appears that the information or certificate,
>
> > (a) fails to state or states defectively anything that is requisite to charge the offence;
> > (b) does not negative an exception that should be negatived; or
> > (c) is in any way defective in substance or in form.

In considering whether to grant the motion to amend, the court will consider the factors specified in section 34(4) of the POA, namely:

> (a) the evidence taken on the trial,
> (b) the circumstances of the case,
> (c) whether the defendant has been misled or prejudiced in the defendant's defence by a variance, error or omission; and
> (d) whether, having regard to the merits of the case, the proposed amendment can be made without injustice being done.

A motion to amend can be brought when the prosecution wants to have the defendant tried on the original rate of speed. This practice of "amending up" is addressed in the Case in Point: *York (Regional Municipality) v Winlow*, below.

CASE IN POINT

Amending Up to a Higher Rate of Speed

York (Regional Municipality) v Winlow, 2009 ONCA 643

Facts

The defendant was caught speeding on Highway 400 contrary to section 128 of the *Highway Traffic Act*.[3] The police officer who stopped him said that he was driving 30 kilometres per hour over the speed limit, but used discretion and charged him with speeding 15 kilometres per hour over the limit. The defendant requested a trial. At trial, the prosecutor sought an amendment back to the original rate of speed: 30 kilometres per hour over the limit instead of the amount specified on the certificate. The justice refused to amend the charge.

The prosecution appealed to the Ontario Court of Justice. The justice upheld the trial justice's decision and refused to amend the charge.

The prosecution then appealed to the Ontario Court of Appeal.

Relevant Issue

Amending Up to a Higher Rate of Speed

Decision

In this case, there was not enough evidence to support the amendment and the appeal was dismissed. However, of particular significance is the fact that the court ruled that the practice of amending up is permissible as long as there is no prejudice or injustice to an accused and the requirements of the *Provincial Offences Act* are met.

Motion to Quash

If you find that the charging document has serious defects apparent on its face, and you can successfully argue that an amendment or further particulars would not be appropriate in your case, you can bring a motion to quash under section 36(1) of the POA, prior to entering a plea to the charge. If successful, having charges quashed means that the charges against the defendant are thrown out of court and will not be further prosecuted. A motion to quash is often brought in opposition to the prosecution's motion to amend, but also could be brought on its own merits. Once a plea has been entered and the trial has commenced, you may bring a motion to quash only with permission of the court.

If the defence initiates a motion to quash, be prepared for the prosecution to bring a countermotion to amend the errors on the charging document. If the motion to amend is denied, it is likely that the motion to quash will be granted.

A motion to quash can be successful when the officer has failed to properly complete the charging document (e.g., when it contains a fatal error). Technical errors on the charging document that have resulted in the dismissal or quashing of charges include:

- the date of the offence is incorrect or missing;
- the defendant's name is missing;
- the charging officer's name is missing;
- the location of the offence is missing;

---

3 RSO 1990, c H.8.

- a description of the offence is missing;
- the offence indicated is unknown to law; and
- the offence notice was not served on the defendant within 30 days of the offence date or not filed with the court within seven days.

As a paralegal, it is important to rely on technical error arguments only when necessary and appropriate, given the nature of the case and the facts. Bringing a motion to quash based on frivolous technical errors will diminish your reputation and effectiveness. There is a time and a place for such motions, and knowing this comes with experience. These motions are by no means guaranteed, and proper preparation and oral argument are the keys to a successful outcome for the defence. The Case in Point: *York (Regional Municipality) v Wodood*, below, considers whether the provincial offences officer can make changes to the certificate after the notice has been served on the defendant.

CASE IN POINT

Amendments to the Certificate

York (Regional Municipality) v Wadood, 2017 ONCA 45

Facts

The defendant was charged with the offence of unsafe turn contrary to section 142(1) of the *Highway Traffic Act*. The certificate of offence contained all of the relevant information but did not indicate in which municipality the offence took place. Prior to filing it with the court, the officer added the words "City of Vaughan" to the certificate. The defendant requested a trial but did not appear on the trial date. The justice reviewed the certificate and found it to be "complete and regular" on its face and deemed the defendant did not wish to dispute the charge.

The defendant brought an appeal to Ontario Court of Justice. The justice acquitted the defendant, ruling that any changes to the certificate were made without authority and therefore were not permitted by the *Provincial Offences Act*.

The prosecution appealed to the Ontario Court of Appeal.

Relevant Issue

Amendments to the Certificate

Decision

The court found that the POA does not authorize such amendments, but also does not specifically prohibit the amendments. The nature of the amendment and the impact on the defendant would have to be considered for each case. An amendment would be allowed if it was simply a clerical order that did not cause the defendant to be misled or prejudiced. The appeal was allowed.

PRACTICE TIP

One of the best ways to ensure efficient advocacy for your client is to bring civility into your practice. Developing a rapport with court administrative staff and the prosecution will prove to be valuable when bringing motions and applications. It is also wise to consider consenting to prosecution motions that have been brought without notice (when doing so does not prejudice your client).

Motion for Non-Suit

A motion for non-suit—an example of a motion without notice—can be brought by the defence during the trial only at the conclusion of the prosecution's case. This is a rare motion and the standards for success are high. If the prosecution fails, through error or omission, to present evidence on all of the essential elements of the offence, you should be prepared to immediately introduce a motion for non-suit and request that the charges be dismissed.

The test for non-suit is rarely at issue. The test is simply: is there some evidence on each of the essential elements that could lead the trier of fact to properly convict? If the answer is yes, a motion for non-suit would not succeed. There is no weighing of the evidence at this stage. There is no risk to your client's case—unlike in the civil court system, where you would be prohibited from calling evidence if the motion failed. However, a motion for non-suit should be used only in the clearest of cases.

Motion for Joinder or Severance

Where there are multiple counts, informations, certificates, or defendants, section 38 of the POA allows for them to be tried together or separately. The framework for this is as follows:

> 38(1) The court may, before trial, where it is satisfied that the ends of justice so require, direct that separate counts, informations or certificates be tried together or that persons who are charged separately be tried together.
>
> (2) The court may, before or during the trial, where it is satisfied that the ends of justice so require, direct that separate counts, informations or certificates be tried separately or that persons who are charged jointly or being tried together be tried separately.

Depending on the particular facts of the case, there will be procedural advantages and disadvantages to consider in deciding whether to have two or more defendants tried together or separately. For example, in a situation where two drivers were drag racing and charged with stunt driving under section 172 of the *Highway Traffic Act*, it may be advantageous to have them tried together since each defendant is a non-compellable witness and cannot testify against the other defendant. If they were tried separately, one driver could be summoned to testify against the other driver.

Similarly, there can be procedural advantages and disadvantages to take into account when deciding whether to have two or more counts tried together or separately. For example, if a defendant is charged with careless driving, failure to wear a seat belt, and failure to surrender insurance, there is a risk that the justice will not consider each of these charges separately, but instead lump them together and find the defendant guilty of all charges. As well, in the case of multiple charges, the defendant may be willing to testify on one of the charges but not the others. Having them heard separately would allow the defence to make a distinct decision on how to proceed for each charge.

Motion to Stay the Proceeding

A motion to stay the proceeding should be brought if you feel that your client has been prejudiced in some way, for example, if there was a failure to provide disclosure or an abuse of process. The motion to stay will discontinue the prosecution and put it on a permanent hold (which is rarely recommenced). While a stay of proceedings is generally the relief sought for a Charter motion, there does not necessarily need to be a Charter breach in order to bring this type of motion.

Charter Motions

The *Canadian Charter of Rights and Freedoms* provides the framework for almost all of the legal procedures you will face in your career as a paralegal. This may include rights and remedies under the Charter, for example, the right to be free from unreasonable search and seizure under section 8. The most common Charter motion in the provincial offences setting involves delay and the protections afforded under section 11(b) of the Charter. Less frequent are motions to determine whether a section of a statute or regulation violates the *Constitution Act, 1982*.[4] Each case must be decided on its own facts and time frame.

From a practical standpoint, you need to be mindful of the time and effort needed to successfully bring a Charter motion and the evidence that is required. Bringing such a motion alleging a breach of your client's rights may be a strategic decision.

Proper research is essential in determining whether an actual breach has occurred, and even if one has, you still must weigh whether bringing a formal application to seek a remedy is appropriate. As a professional paralegal, you should avoid bringing "boilerplate" Charter motions for all cases that have taken an excessive amount of time to reach the trial stage. The majority of Charter issues have already been litigated, most before the Supreme Court of Canada, so searching for precedents prior to starting a Charter challenge is always in your client's best interest.

The legal framework for bringing a Charter motion is set out in section 109 of the *Courts of Justice Act*:

> 109(1) Notice of a constitutional question shall be served on the Attorney General of Canada and the Attorney General of Ontario in the following circumstances:
>
> 1. The constitutional validity or constitutional applicability of an Act of the Parliament of Canada or the Legislature, of a regulation or by-law made under such an Act or of a rule of common law is in question.
> 2. A remedy is claimed under subsection 24(1) of the *Canadian Charter of Rights and Freedoms* in relation to an act or omission of the Government of Canada or the Government of Ontario.

---

4 RSC 1985, app II, no 44.

In addition to serving the attorney general of Canada and the attorney general of Ontario, the notice of constitutional question (see Figure 8.3) must be served on the prosecution office at least 15 days before the trial date and must also be filed with the court.

Figure 8.3   Notice of Constitutional Question

PROVINCIAL OFFENCES FOR PARALEGALS

FORM 4F

Courts of Justice Act

NOTICE OF CONSTITUTIONAL QUESTION

(General heading)

NOTICE OF CONSTITUTIONAL QUESTION

The *(identify party)* intends to question the constitutional validity *(or* applicability*)* of *(identify the particular legislative provisions or the particular rule of common law) (or* to claim a remedy under subsection 24 (1) of the *Canadian Charter of Rights and Freedoms* in relation to an act or omission of the Government of Canada *(or* Ontario*))*.

The question is to be argued on *(day), (date)*, at *(time)*, at *(address of court house)*.

The following are the material facts giving rise to the constitutional question: *(Set out concisely the material facts that relate to the constitutional question. Where appropriate, attach pleadings or reasons for decision.)*

The following is the legal basis for the constitutional question: *(Set out concisely the legal basis for each question, identifying the nature of the constitutional principles to be argued.)*

(Date)   *(Name, address and telephone number of lawyer or party)*

TO   The Attorney General of Ontario *(as required by section 109 of the Courts of Justice Act)*
     Constitutional Law Branch
     4th floor
     720 Bay Street
     Toronto, Ontario M5G 2K1
     fax: (416) 326-4015

     The Attorney General of Canada *(as required by section 109 of the Courts of Justice Act)*
     Suite 3400, Exchange Tower
     Box 36, First Canadian Place
     Toronto, Ontario M5X 1K6
     fax: (416) 952-0298

     (or Justice Building
     234 Wellington Street
     Ottawa, Ontario K1A 0H8
     fax: (613) 954-1920*)*

     *(Names and addresses of lawyers
     for all other parties and of all
     other parties acting in person)*

(This notice must be served as soon as the circumstances requiring it become known and, in any event, at least 15 days before the question is to be argued, unless the court orders otherwise.)

RCP-E 4F (April 11, 2012)

As a legal representative, you are expected to know the requirements for notice. The likelihood of the court considering a Charter motion without proper notice under section 109 is almost non-existent. If the Charter breach comes to your attention only after the proceeding has commenced, it may be necessary to adjourn the matter to allow for notice to be served and a proper application to be brought forward to the court.

If you proceed with a Charter motion, it is advisable—in addition to the documentation for the notice of constitutional question—to prepare and file a proper factum setting out the legal issues, the precedent(s) on which you are relying, and affidavits from your client and any other witnesses, as applicable.

Some justices prefer to reserve their decision on a Charter motion until the case has been completed to allow them time to assess the evidentiary issues and the context of the prejudice against the defendant.

KEY TERMS

REVIEW QUESTIONS

Multiple Choice

1. Caleb was charged with a minor traffic offence. He would like to review the officer's notes so that he can be better prepared for his trial date. What is the proper way for him to make an initial request for disclosure?

   a. Bring a motion.

   b. Request it verbally from the officer.

   c. Phone the prosecution office and request it verbally.

   d. Complete a disclosure request form.

The following scenario applies to Questions 2-6:

Eden received a notice of trial in the mail. Her court date will take place close to two years after she was charged. She has heard that she likely has grounds to bring an 11(b) Charter motion and is also considering a motion for particulars.

2. Which of the following is the proper way for evidence to be provided in support of a motion for particulars?

   a. By affidavit.

   b. Orally, with permission from the court.

   c. By transcript of an examination of witness.

   d. These are all proper ways for evidence to be provided in support of a motion.

3. What document is used to give notice of an 11(b) Charter motion?

   a. Notice of motion.

   b. Notice of constitutional question.

   c. Notice of delay.

   d. Does not require notice. Can be brought without notice.

4. Which court would hear Eden's motions?

   a. Ontario Court of Justice.

   b. Superior Court of Justice.

   c. Court of Appeal.

   d. Supreme Court of Canada.

5. Which of the following will have to be served with notice of the 11(b) Charter motion?

   a. Court administration office.

   b. Justice.

   c. Prosecution.

   d. Court clerk.

6. What is the time frame requirement for serving an 11(b) Charter motion?

   a. It must be served 3 days before it is to be heard.

   b. It must be served 7 days before it is to be heard.

   c. It must be served 15 days before it is to be heard.

   d. It does not require service. It can be brought without notice.

7. For what purpose would a paralegal bring a motion for a non-suit?

   a. To obtain a new date for trial.

   b. To join two counts together.

   c. To separate counts.

   d. To challenge whether the prosecution has proven the essential elements of the offence.

8. Which of the following cannot be brought as a pre-trial motion?

   a. Motion for further disclosure.

   b. Motion to adjourn.

   c. Motion for a non-suit.

   d. They can all be brought as pre-trial motions.

9. The information served on your client was quite vague. What type of information should you bring to ensure that you are provided with the relevant details about the charges?

   a. Motion for further disclosure.

   b. Motion for particulars.

   c. Motion to adjourn.

   d. Motion for a non-suit.

10. At what stage can a justice grant the prosecution's motion to amend a charge?

   a. As a pre-trial motion.

   b. Before the defendant enters a plea.

   c. At the conclusion of the prosecution's case.

   d. At any stage of the proceeding.

Short Answer

1. What are the service and filing requirements for a notice of motion?

2. Who needs to be served with a notice of constitutional question?

3. What must a justice consider before determining whether to grant a motion to amend?

4. What should you look for when determining whether to bring a motion to quash?

5. What options are available if the prosecution is refusing to provide the disclosure you have requested?

6. List three ways a defendant can seek an adjournment.

Scenario

Habib was charged with careless driving contrary to section 130 of the *Highway Traffic Act*. He left a voice mail message on the court's general mailbox requesting disclosure, but did not get a reply or any of the documents that he requested.

1. Did Habib follow proper procedure for requesting disclosure? If not, what should he have done?

2. What is likely to happen if Habib attends court and asks the prosecutor to withdraw the charge since he did not receive disclosure?

3. What do you think Habib should do if the prosecutor does not withdraw the charge?

What to Expect in the Courtroom

9

LEARNING OUTCOMES

After reading this chapter, you will understand

- rules and etiquette in provincial offences courtrooms;

- the layout of provincial offences courtrooms;

- provincial offences procedures and the sequence of events; and

- what is involved in the arraignment of the defendant and entering a plea for your client.

Introduction

Rule 2 of the *Paralegal Rules of Conduct*[1] deals with professionalism and sets out the requirements for paralegals to conduct themselves with integrity and civility. Specifically, Rule 2.01(1) states that

> A paralegal has a duty to provide legal services and discharge all responsibilities to clients, tribunals, the public and other members of the legal professions honourably and with integrity.

Further, Rule 2.01(2) states,

> A paralegal has a duty to uphold the standards and reputation of the paralegal profession and to assist in the advancement of its goals, organizations and institutions.

These rules apply to a paralegal's conduct both outside and inside the courtroom. In court, maintaining the integrity of the profession means demonstrating appropriate behaviour, following all rules, displaying appropriate etiquette, showing respect for everyone within the justice system, and acting as a role model for everyone else in attendance. As such, this chapter will discuss appropriate behaviour in the courtroom.

Attending court can be intimidating and overwhelming for a newly licensed paralegal, who may not be aware of how a provincial offences courtroom is organized, as well as the procedures and the sequence of events that will take place. In order to make those initial court appearances less stressful, this chapter will also provide an overview of what to expect upon entering the courtroom.

Rules and Etiquette

Paralegals and everyone else attending court—from defendants and their representatives to witnesses and observers—are expected to abide by the rules and follow the norms of behaviour by displaying appropriate etiquette in the courtroom. Signs are typically posted at courtroom entrances to serve as a reminder of the rules.

Quiet in the Courtroom

While court is in session, everyone in the courtroom is expected to be quiet. Even whispering can be a distraction and is considered to be disrespectful. It is important to refrain from engaging in all side conversations, even with a client. If it is necessary to speak to a client, it would be more appropriate to discreetly leave the courtroom and have the conversation in the hallway.

---

1 Law Society of Ontario, *Paralegal Rules of Conduct* (1 October 2014), online: <http://www.lsuc.on.ca/paralegal-conduct-rules>.

Quiet in the courtroom also refers to the use of cellphones. Turning off a cellphone, rather than just using "vibrate" mode, is expected by the court. If vibrate mode is used, incoming calls can interfere with the court's intercom, and the vibration signal may be amplified through the speaker system. Smartphone alert systems, such as text notifications, should also be turned off while court is in session. You can be sure that the court clerk or the justice will remind or reprimand anyone who is not quiet in the courtroom. Such a reminder can be embarrassing for a paralegal and undermines his or her professionalism.

Recording Devices Prohibited

All recording devices are prohibited in the courtroom. Section 135(1) of the *Courts of Justice Act*[2] indicates that court hearings are open to the public; however, the proceedings cannot be recorded in any way. This prohibition includes cameras, video cameras, tape recorders, photo applications on cellphones, and all other recording devices. Unlike in the United States, television cameras and web cameras are rarely permitted to record Canadian court proceedings. With limited exceptions, section 136(1) of the *Courts of Justice Act* prohibits anyone from producing visual or aural representations of a court hearing.

In addition to the ban on recording devices in the courtroom, the *Paralegal Rules of Conduct* and the lawyer's *Rules of Professional Conduct* indicate that paralegals and lawyers cannot record a conversation with a client or other members of the profession without disclosing an intention to do so.

No Food or Beverages Allowed

Food or beverages may not be brought into the courtroom, and in some cases, you may be asked to refrain from chewing gum. In some instances, a pitcher of water and glasses may be set up at the front of the court. You are permitted to fill a glass and have a drink of water, but you should not arrive at court with your own beverage.

Pay Attention to the Proceedings

Provincial offences courts are open to the public, so there may be observers in the courtroom for any number of reasons. However, everyone in the courtroom is expected to pay attention to the proceedings. Disrespectful conduct, such as reading a magazine or newspaper, texting, chatting, or checking phone messages, will not be tolerated. Attention should always be focused on the matters at hand.

Dress Appropriately

Appropriate attire is expected in the courtroom. Although the courts do not specify what is considered appropriate, paralegals should be professionally dressed. In provincial offences court, most paralegals wear a business suit, with male paralegals also wearing a tie.

---

2 RSO 1990, c C.43.

Although clients do not have to be dressed professionally, they must be dressed neatly. Clients should be encouraged to dress in a tidy, conservative, and respectful manner, and avoid wearing jeans or printed T-shirts.

Everyone entering the courtroom will be required to remove sunglasses and hats (unless the hat is a religious head covering).

Punctuality

It is critical that paralegals and their clients arrive on time for their scheduled court appearance. Ideally, you should consider arriving 20 to 30 minutes early in order to allow for an opportunity to check in with the prosecutor, discuss how your client would like to proceed, and review any last-minute matters with your client. If you have multiple matters in the same courthouse but in different courtrooms, it is advisable to check in with the clerk and the prosecutor assigned to each of the courtrooms. If they are aware of a scheduling conflict, they may be able to accommodate when your matters will be heard.

Show Respect for the Justice

It is customary to show respect for the justice by standing when he or she enters or leaves the courtroom. You will be expected to remain standing until the justice sits down or the court clerk advises everyone to be seated. If it is necessary to leave the courtroom while court is in session, the appropriate practice is to wait until the justice is not speaking (ideally in between matters) before leaving. When entering or exiting the courtroom while court is in session, paralegals and lawyers are expected to stop at the door, pause, turn toward the justice, and bow slightly.

When your matter is called and you have been given an opportunity to speak, you show respect for the justice by standing up and facing him or her as you speak. Similarly, it is appropriate to stand when making an objection or questioning a witness.

Courtroom Layout

Most provincial offences courts are laid out in a very similar manner. The justice's bench is at the front and centre of the courtroom, slightly higher than the rest of the seating. The court clerk sits at a desk immediately in front of the justice. When a witness is called to testify, he or she is directed to the witness stand beside the justice's bench. All of these parties are facing the courtroom entrance.

The prosecution and defence tables are side by side, in front of the clerk's desk, facing the justice. Typically, the prosecutor will be at the table on the right and the defence will at the table on the left (viewed from the back of the courtroom), but there are certainly exceptions to that layout. Both tables have additional seating for witnesses, including provincial offences officers. Behind these tables is the public seating area for observers and for defendants, representatives, and witnesses who are waiting for their matters to proceed.

Provincial offences officers tend to sit in the public seating area, beside the prosecutor, or sometimes in additional seating provided along the sides of the courtroom.

Figure 9.1 shows a typical courtroom layout as found in provincial offences court.

Figure 9.1   Typical Provincial Offences Courtroom Layout

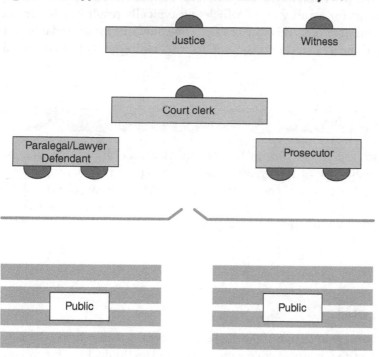

Checking in with the Prosecutor

The **docket** for all matters being heard in each **tier** will usually be posted just outside of the courtroom door. Before entering the courtroom, it is advisable to look at the docket to ensure your matters are listed for that courtroom on that date. By checking the docket, you will also be able to identify your client's case by line number. This will allow you to quickly and easily identify your matter when speaking to the prosecutor.

On arrival at the courtroom, paralegals should check in with the prosecutor. Legal representatives and defendants will typically do this by forming a line leading to the prosecutor's table. This process takes place on a first-come, first-served basis. Again, it is advisable that you arrive early enough to ensure that there is sufficient time to speak to the prosecutor and perhaps negotiate a resolution to the charges.

The prosecutor will expect you to identify the matter for which you have been retained (e.g., "Smith, line 14 on the docket") and will then ask how you would like to proceed. It is essential that you follow your client's instructions and inform the prosecutor if your client wishes to plead guilty or not guilty, or if an adjournment is being sought.

Because there will usually be a substantial number of matters on the docket, it is not possible for each and every defendant to have a trial. For example, in the Greater Toronto Area, it is not unusual to have 40 to 50 Part I matters scheduled within a 90-minute tier. The prosecutor also realizes that every matter cannot go

docket
the list of defendants scheduled for trial

tier
a court session over a specific period of time

to trial and will often offer a resolution to the matter, such as an included offence in exchange for a guilty plea—which will typically result in a lesser fine and/or fewer demerit points. This can be a desirable outcome for defendants, but it is important to ensure that clients consent before pleading guilty to an included offence.

> **PRACTICE TIP**
>
> Always be prepared for court. Thoroughly review your client's charge and the facts surrounding the offence, as well as the relevant charging act for any other related offences that may be consistent with your client's fact situation. If any of these offences carry a lesser fine and/or fewer demerit points, it may be appropriate to suggest the alternate offences to the prosecutor.

Typical Sequence

Prosecutors are in charge of the docket and have the authority to call matters in any order. They do not usually follow the order listed on the docket. One commonly used method of managing the docket is to first call matters that can be resolved quickly. This allows the courtroom to empty out somewhat and does not keep defendants waiting for any longer than is necessary. For example, it is common for a prosecutor to call **uncontested adjournments** or guilty pleas at the beginning of the court session because they can be dealt with quickly.

uncontested adjournment
a request by either the prosecution or the defence to move the trial to a new date which is being made with the consent of the other party

Most prosecutors will try not to unnecessarily inconvenience interpreters and civilian witnesses. Matters for which an interpreter is present will usually be called before other cases within the same resolution category. For example, guilty pleas with an interpreter would usually be called before guilty pleas with no interpreter, and trials with a civilian witness would commonly be called before trials that have only a police witness.

Some prosecutors will extend a professional courtesy to paralegals or lawyers in attendance. Recognizing that they may have matters in other courtrooms or other courthouses, prosecutors will sometimes be willing to call represented defendants before unrepresented defendants within the same resolution category.

> **PRACTICE TIP**
>
> If you find yourself in a situation where you are needed in two different courtrooms during the same court tier, mention this to the prosecutor. Some prosecutors may be willing to deal with your matter early in the proceedings, while others may be willing to have your matter **held down** until later in the tier or even to a different court tier. Most prosecutors will be willing to accommodate in some way.

held down
hearing a matter at a later time

When Your Client Is Called

When the prosecutor calls your client's name, you will stand up, move to the front of the courtroom, and stand at the defence table facing the clerk and the justice. You should then identify yourself as the paralegal who has been retained to represent the defendant. It is customary in provincial offences court to state your last name, your first initial, and your status—for example: "Good morning, Your Worship. My name is Jones, first initial B. I am a licensed paralegal retained to represent the defendant Smith in the matter before the court."

In most cases, the prosecutor will then inform the justice of the anticipated plea, request, or action. Specifically, the prosecutor may inform the justice of a request for an adjournment, a guilty plea (to the original or to an included charge), a plea of not guilty, a withdrawal of the charge, or a stay of the proceedings. If the request or action is an adjournment, withdrawal, or stay, the court clerk will collect the necessary information and complete the appropriate paperwork. In the event of a guilty or not guilty plea, the defendant will be arraigned.

The Arraignment and Plea

The **arraignment** takes place when the court clerk formally informs the defendant of the substance of the information or certificate, thereby helping the defendant to understand the charges before the court. A paralegal can be arraigned in place of a client, or a paralegal may choose to **waive arraignment**. By waiving arraignment, a paralegal is advising the court that it is not necessary to read out the charges.

Under the arraignment procedure, the clerk asks the defendant to state his or her name; reads out the charges; asks whether the defendant understands the charges; and asks how the defendant would like to plead to the charges. The defendant can choose to plead:

- guilty (conviction entered and defendant will be sentenced);
- guilty with submissions (conviction entered and defendant will be sentenced, but defendant has an opportunity to request a lesser fine or more time to pay);
- guilty to an included charge as specified by the prosecutor (conviction entered for included charge and defendant will be sentenced); or
- not guilty (a trial will be held).

In accordance with the conditions set out in section 45(3) of the POA,[3] the court may accept a guilty plea only if it is satisfied that the defendant is making the plea voluntarily and that the defendant understands that the plea is an admission of the essential elements of the offence, understands the nature and consequences of the plea, and understands that the court is not bound by any agreement made between the defendant and the prosecutor. The clerk or the justice will generally check to ensure that the defendant has made an informed choice and is aware of the consequences that will arise from the plea. If the justice does not accept the guilty plea, the defendant will likely have to proceed to trial or request an adjournment to a new date.

arraignment
the formal reading of the charges to the defendant or the defendant's representative in anticipation of a plea

waive arraignment
a legal representative tells the court clerk that it is not necessary to read the charges

---

3 RSO 1990, c P.33.

KEY TERMS

arraignment, 115
docket, 113
held down, 114
tier, 113
uncontested adjournment, 114
waive arraignment, 115

REVIEW QUESTIONS

Multiple Choice

1. Which of the following statements is true with regard to the arraignment of the defendant?

   a. Arraignment of the defendant occurs immediately before the trial and is handled by the same justice who will preside over the trial.

   b. Arraignment of the defendant occurs immediately before the trial and is handled by the court clerk.

   c. Arraignment of the defendant occurs immediately after the trial and is handled by the same justice who presided over the trial.

   d. Arraignment of the defendant occurs immediately after the trial and is handled by the court clerk.

2. What should you do when a justice enters the courtroom?

   a. Sit quietly.

   b. Stand up.

   c. Bow toward the justice.

   d. Approach the bench.

3. What are the rules regarding cellphones in the courtroom?

   a. Cellphones should be turned off in the courtroom.

   b. Cellphones can be turned to "vibrate" mode.

   c. Cellphones must not be brought into the courtroom at all.

   d. Cellphones are now permitted in court since they are recognized as a useful research tool.

4. What should you do when you enter or leave the courtroom?

   a. Recite the paralegal's oath.

   b. Pause and bow toward the justice.

   c. Announce your Law Society of Ontario identification number.

   d. Signal to the clerk that you are leaving.

5. Which of the following is true with regard to recording provincial offences proceedings?

   a. It is permissible to tape-record provincial offences proceedings.

   b. It is permissible to video-tape provincial offences proceedings.

   c. Paralegals can bring a motion to request permission to video- and tape-record proceedings.

   d. It is not permissible to video- or tape-record proceedings.

6. What is the proper way for a paralegal to state his/her name for the court?

   a. Robert Smith.

   b. R. Smith.

   c. Smith, Robert.

   d. Smith, first initial R.

7. What does it mean to waive arraignment?

   a. To tell the clerk you would like to plead guilty.

   b. To give up your right to a trial.

   c. To tell the clerk is it not necessary to read the charges.

   d. To give up your right to receive disclosure.

Short Answer

1. What is considered appropriate attire for a paralegal appearing in provincial offences court?

2. Where are you likely to find provincial offences officers sitting in the courtroom?

3. Explain the arraignment procedure.

4. Where can you find the docket for all matters in a specific court tier?

5. How do paralegals introduce themselves in court?

Scenario

Carol, an unrepresented defendant, arrived at the courtroom approximately 30 minutes after the court tier had begun. She rushed in the door and loudly apologized to everyone in the courtroom. As she hurried to find a seat, she spilled her coffee all over her Bon Jovi T-shirt. She finally took a seat beside the provincial offences officer, who was sitting beside the prosecutor. Carol started chatting with the officer to find out what she had missed. When she looked around the room, Carol recognized her neighbour in the witness box and started waving. She then took out her cellphone to send text messages to all of her friends about the neighbour's charges. Carol then played around with her phone in order to find the app that she could use to video-tape her neighbour's evidence.

1. List the rules and appropriate etiquette practices that were breached by Carol.

2. If Carol does not speak English and her interpreter is present so that she can enter a not guilty plea, when would the prosecution likely call her case?

   a. Before guilty pleas are heard.

   b. Before other not guilty pleas are heard when no interpreter is present.

   c. After other not guilty pleas are heard when no interpreter is present.

   d. Before uncontested adjournments.

   e. None of the above; Carol cannot use an interpreter to plead not guilty.

The Trial

10

LEARNING OUTCOMES

After reading this chapter, you will understand

- the components of a *Provincial Offences Act* trial;

- the framework for motions, evidentiary issues, and standards of proof;

- defences that may be relevant for provincial offences;

- witness considerations, questioning techniques, and evidence; and

- closing statements and the verdict.

Introduction

Although it may seem that the trial is the most important part of the legal process, it is typically the least likely outcome for the vast majority of charges. The other outcomes include a guilty plea to the original charge, a negotiation that leads to a guilty plea to an included offence, and numerous post-charge options and pre-trial issues that can prevent a matter from ever reaching trial. In 2015, over 88 percent of POA matters set for trial (313,000 of 355,000) were resolved on the trial date without a trial.[1] On average, roughly only 10 percent of the matters that are scheduled for trial will actually proceed to trial.

As a professional paralegal, it is crucial that you have the skills to advocate on behalf of your client. This means properly preparing yourself by reviewing every aspect of the case to ensure the best possible outcome for your client. Your client depends on you to provide candid and accurate advice, and sometimes that means achieving the best possible resolution without taking a case to a trial. But if having a trial is in your client's best interest, the greatest chance he or she will have for a positive outcome is for you to be thoroughly prepared.

Responding to a Motion Brought by the Prosecutor

As discussed in Chapter 8, several types of motions may be applicable. On the day of the trial, either the prosecution or the defence may bring a motion. Among other motions, paralegals should be prepared to respond in the event that the prosecution seeks a motion to adjourn or a motion to amend.

Motion to Adjourn

If the prosecution seeks a motion to adjourn, you will need to consider several factors as you prepare to respond (likely orally):

1. Did the prosecution provide you with prior notice?
2. Is the provincial offences officer present in court?
3. Is your client present?
4. Are there any witnesses?
5. Is the charge serious or straightforward?

There may be instances when it is in your client's best interest to consent to an adjournment request made by the prosecution, even when notice was not given. But if you are ready to proceed with the trial and if your witnesses are present, in many cases the court will turn down the prosecution's request for an adjournment. It is rare for the prosecution to be granted an adjournment because the officer was not in attendance.

---

1   Jeremy Griggs, MAG Modernization, "Provincial Offences Act Modernization" (16 August 2016), online: <https://www.amo.on.ca/AMO-PDFs/Events/16CONF/Proceedings/ConcurrentsB/POAGriggs20160816.aspx>.

Motion to Amend

If the prosecution seeks a motion to amend the certificate or information, you need to be prepared to respond by considering the following factors:

1. Did the prosecution provide you with prior notice?
2. Is the amendment designed to cure a defect in the certificate or information, or does it change the substance of the charge?
3. Is an adjournment necessary if the amendment is granted?
4. Is your client prejudiced by the requested amendment?
5. Is the amendment consistent with the administration of justice and the POA?

Minor amendments are regularly granted for POA matters, but you will certainly have an opportunity to speak to it if you feel that the motion should be refused, and you have the option to bring a motion to quash if you believe that the certificate is not complete and proper on its face and that the amendment would not be appropriate.

There are several other types of motions that, if applicable, could be presented prior to the trial commencing, including Charter applications, change of venue motions, and bias motions. If you are served with a motion in advance of the trial date you will have an opportunity to provide a written response, but motions without notice are responded to orally. It is therefore important to be familiar with the relevant jurisprudence and procedural sections of the POA as they relate to motions.

Court Orders

In some cases it may be appropriate for the prosecution or the defence to request that the justice order the public, or any member of the public, to be excluded from a hearing. This is set out in section 52(2) of the POA:

> 52(2) The court may exclude the public or any member of the public from a hearing where, in the opinion of the court, it is necessary to do so,
> > (a) for the maintenance of order in the courtroom;
> > (b) to protect the reputation of a minor; or
> > (c) to remove an influence that might affect the testimony of a witness.

This section is often relied upon in order to exclude witnesses from the courtroom, as their testimony can be influential upon other witnesses. An order to exclude witnesses means that a witness will not be in the courtroom to hear another witness's recollection of the events at issue and therefore helps to ensure that each witness maintains his or her own version of the events that took place. However, this does not apply to the defendant. Even with an order to exclude witnesses in place, the defendant is permitted to remain in the courtroom to hear testimony from all of the witnesses (unless the defendant has be removed from the courtroom due to misconduct or mental disorder pursuant to section 52(1)).

It may also be appropriate to request an order prohibiting the publication or broadcast of the identity of a minor, pursuant to section 52(3), if there is an indication that a member of the media is present in the courtroom.

Standard of Proof

standard of proof
the level of certainty needed to establish proof in a provincial offences trial; may apply to the level of certainty needed for the prosecution to obtain a conviction or the level of certainty for the defendant to exonerate himself or herself; can be beyond a reasonable doubt or on a balance of probabilities

The **standard of proof** for provincial offences is usually proof beyond a reasonable doubt. This standard of proof certainly applies to facts at issue, such as:

- the identity of the defendant;
- essential elements of the offence as charged; and
- the guilt of the defendant.

A defendant cannot be convicted of a provincial offence unless the justice is convinced beyond a reasonable doubt that the prosecution has proven all of the essential elements of the offence. This standard of proof requires close to absolute certainty.

Some other considerations for standards of proof are not directly related to the defendant's guilt or innocence. For example, when a defendant is charged with a strict liability offence, the prosecution must prove the essential elements of the offence *beyond a reasonable doubt*. The defendant will then have the opportunity to exonerate himself or herself by establishing mistake of fact or due diligence on a *balance of probabilities*.

The simplest way to describe the standard of a balance of probabilities is to imagine a measuring scale: whichever side tips the scale with the evidence establishes the case in their favour.

Burden of Proof

burden of proof
the responsibility for proving whether there should be a conviction; primarily rests with the prosecution for provincial offence matters

reverse-onus
the burden of proof shifts to the defendant to prove that he or she did not commit the offence

The **burden of proof** for establishing the defendant's guilt beyond a reasonable doubt rests with the prosecution. The prosecution must establish all of the essential elements of the offence as charged.

However, there are a few occasions when the burden of proof shifts to the defendant, who must prove that he or she did not commit the offence. This would include **reverse-onus** provisions in statutes, such as the "colour of right" defence in the *Trespass to Property Act*,[2] and Charter applications to establish prejudice, such as unreasonable delay under section 11(b).

In addition, the Ontario legislature has codified several examples in which the burden of proof lies with the defendant, as prescribed in section 47(3) of the POA:

> The burden of proving that an authorization, exception, exemption or qualification prescribed by law operates in favour of the defendant is on the defendant, and the prosecutor is not required, except by way of rebuttal, to prove that the authorization, exception, exemption or qualification does not operate in favour of the defendant, whether or not it is set out in the information.

Defences

In order to provide proper legal representation and identify any possible defences, you must first interview your client. During the interview, be sure to challenge your client's recollection and evidence after making note of his or her original account of the situation. If you believe you will be able to prove that your client did not commit the offence, the best defence may be to put your client on the stand to dispute the charges. However, in many cases the defendant does not take the stand, and this should be decided on a case-by-case basis.

For some provincial offences, the issue is not whether the client did or did not commit the act in question, but whether the client knew that he or she was prohibited from committing the act (i.e., a *mens rea* offence). Provincial offence law can be considered more complicated and nuanced than criminal law, which has clear lines of societal and moral boundaries.

For absolute liability offences, knowledge of the defendant's mental state is not required. The prosecution must prove only that the offence was committed for the court to register a conviction. By contrast, for strict liability offences, the prosecution must prove the offence was committed, and then the onus switches to the defence to demonstrate reasonableness.

Defences designed to question the act itself—for example, raising reasonable doubt as to whether the offence occurred at all—are used. It is important to pay attention to the fault element for all types of offences, ensuring that the prosecution has proven each element beyond a reasonable doubt. If the prosecution fails to do so, the best way to defend your client may be to bring a motion for non-suit.

Procedural and jurisdictional defences should also be considered. For example, was the charging document served within the limitation period, was the defendant properly served, are the charges properly documented as separate counts, and are they being heard in the proper jurisdiction? If the answer to any of these questions is no, there may be grounds to bring a motion to quash or a request to stay the proceedings.

There are several additional possible defences to provincial offence charges, including due diligence, necessity, causation, and involuntariness. However, it should be noted that with the exception of due diligence, these defences are not routinely used because it is difficult to meet the specific criteria and circumstances.

---

2   RSO 1990, c T.21.

Defence of Due Diligence

In the classic **defence of due diligence** or "reasonable precautions," the test laid out by the Supreme Court of Canada in *R v Sault Ste Marie (City)*[3] is still used today. The defence is available to an accused if, on a balance of probabilities, it is established that:

- the accused believed in a mistaken set of facts that, if true, would render the act or omission innocent; or
- the accused took all reasonable steps to avoid the particular event.

Under this test, the burden of establishing that due diligence was exercised falls on the defendant. In *R v Chapin*,[4] a case often cited in tandem with *R v Sault Ste Marie (City)*, Dickson J of the Supreme Court of Canada described the defence of due diligence as follows:

> An accused may absolve himself on proof that he took all the care which a reasonable man may have been expected to take in all the circumstances or, in other words, that he was in no way negligent.

There are many factors to consider when assessing the defence of due diligence. It is important to remember that due diligence is open for the defendant only on strict liability offences.

Defence of Necessity

To use the **defence of necessity**, the defendant must satisfy all of the following requirements, as described in *Perka v The Queen*.[5] The defendant must prove that:

- he or she needed to commit the act to avoid immediate peril;
- no other reasonable alternative existed;
- the harm caused by the defendant was less than the harm avoided; and
- he or she could not have foreseen the emergency.

As an example, a driver speeding on the highway to take his pregnant wife to the hospital would not likely meet the test for necessity. Most pregnancies do not result in immediate peril and are not viewed as emergencies. However, even if those requirements were met (e.g., a high-risk pregnancy and pre-term labour), there likely would have been reasonable alternatives, such as calling 911.

However, if, for example, a defendant had been camping in a remote area with no 911 service and a friend suffered an unexpected serious injury (e.g., fell into the fire, was attacked by a bear), the necessity defence may apply if the driver was speeding and there was no other way to get the friend to the hospital.

---

3 [1978] 2 SCR 1299, 85 DLR (3d) 161.

4 [1979] 2 SCR 121, 45 CCC (2d) 333.

5 [1984] 2 SCR 232 at 259, 14 CCC (3d) 385 at 404-5.

Defence of Causation

The term "causation" refers to the connection between the defendant's conduct and the outcome (the offence). The well-established "but-for test" examines whether the outcome would have occurred *but for* the conduct of the defendant. If there is not a direct link between the conduct and the offence, it may be appropriate to raise the **defence of causation**. For example, imagine a situation where the defendant stopped his or her vehicle an appropriate distance behind another vehicle but was rear-ended by a third vehicle that pushed him or her into the vehicle ahead. If the defendant was charged with following too close contrary to section 158 of the *Highway Traffic Act*,[6] the defendant may want to raise the defence of causation since it is questionable whether there is a direct link between the defendant's conduct and the outcome.

defence of causation
the defendant must show that there is no direct link between his or her conduct and the offence

Defence of Involuntariness

The defendant's actions must be voluntary and within the defendant's control. If the defendant's actions were involuntary, it may be appropriate to raise the **defence of involuntariness**. For example, if a passenger forcefully pulled the keys out of the ignition and caused the steering wheel to lock, the driver of the vehicle may be able to put forth the defence of involuntariness if charges were laid because the defendant's vehicle collided with another vehicle.

defence of involuntariness
the defendant must show that his or her actions were not voluntary and not within his or her control

Preparing Witnesses for Court

Many cases before the provincial offences court will have independent witnesses, outside of the charging officer and the defendant. It is important that you review disclosure materials for witness statements. The offence notice will have a box checked if there were witnesses present at the time of the offence.

In preparing for the trial, you need to decide which witnesses you will require, and consider whether a witness will testify for the prosecution or the defence. Neither party "owns" a witness. As a defence representative, you are allowed to interview any witness, including prosecution witnesses, and the prosecution may do the same.

If you are going to rely on the evidence of a defence witness, it is important to interview the witness before trial. This is an opportunity to assess the witness's credibility, review the evidence, and prepare him or her for court. You must ensure that the witness is able to recall his or her evidence and that it is consistent with prior statements. You cannot coach the witness or suggest what the evidence should be.

> **PRACTICE TIP**
>
> Proper witness preparation is crucial for a successful trial. But even with the best preparation, most witnesses are not experts, and they are nervous and anxious when they take the stand. Never ask a question if you do not know the answer or cannot adequately anticipate the response. Even with the best of intentions, a witness can become lost in the process, which can be very detrimental to your case.

---

6 RSO 1990, c H.8.

Presenting Evidence

Although courts rarely concern themselves with the question "What is evidence?" it is important for you, as part of your trial practice, to develop such an understanding. The law of evidence is vast, and this section provides only a primer on the areas you should consider when preparing for trial. Most courts adopt the definitions found in evidentiary texts when dealing with the question of evidence.

For example, *Phipson on Evidence*[7] states:

> Evidence, as used in judicial proceedings, has several meanings. The two main senses of the word are: first, the means, apart from argument and inference, whereby the court is informed as to the issues of fact as ascertained by the pleadings; secondly, the subject-matter of such means. The word is also used to denote that some fact may be admitted as proof and also in some cases that some fact has relevance to the issue of fact. In a real sense evidence is that which may be placed before the court in order that it may decide the issues of fact.

A simpler, less formal, and generally accepted definition of the term can be found in the introductory paragraph of *Cross on Evidence*:[8]

> The evidence of a fact is that which tends to prove it—something which may satisfy an inquirer of the fact's existence.

As a paralegal, there are several types of evidence that you will either tender or respond to during a trial:

1. *Real evidence*: This is evidence that is a tangible, physical object. Examples include videos or photographs, and items seized by the police, such as beer bottles or a weapon. The court can rely on this evidence to draw direct conclusions.

2. *Documentary evidence*: This is a very common form of evidence in regulatory trials. It refers to any written documents or records. Examples include government records, corporate search records, municipal tax records, and building permits.

---

7 Sidney Lovell Phipson et al, *Phipson on Evidence*, 13th ed (London: Sweet & Maxwell, 1982) at para 1-03.

8 Sir Rupert Cross & Colin Tapper, *Cross on Evidence*, 6th ed (London: Butterworths, 1985).

3. *Testimony*: This is the most common form of evidence in provincial offences trials, and takes the form of oral (*viva voce*) evidence of a witness made on the stand. Examples include the observations of the charging officer, an independent witness, or your client. It is often through oral testimony that the other types of evidence are adduced and then admitted.

PRACTICE TIP

The various formats that evidence can take are extensive. At a minimum, you should review the rules outlined in the *Provincial Offences Act*, the *Evidence Act*,[9] the *Courts of Justice Act*, and the related regulations to these Acts. If the prosecution attempts to introduce evidence that has not been previously disclosed, be prepared to object.

Expert Evidence

The more serious the offence, the more likely the defence will bring in an expert witness. In accordance with section 12 of the *Evidence Act*, a maximum of three **expert witnesses** are permitted, but it is relatively uncommon to have any experts testify for Part I and Part II matters. The following is an example of when to use an expert: if the defendant was charged after a serious motor vehicle collision that resulted in death or bodily injury, it may be appropriate to hire an accident reconstruction specialist to give opinions and beliefs about the circumstances surrounding the collision.

> **expert witness**
> a person who has specialized knowledge or experience that relates to the charges before the court

Voir Dire

In order to determine the admissibility of evidence, in some cases it will be necessary for the justice to hold a **voir dire**. If there is a need for a *voir dire*, the trial is halted, the party seeking to tender the evidence calls its witnesses first, and the witnesses are sworn in again. There is also an opportunity for cross-examination. The justice will make a decision on the *voir dire* and will apply the decision to the evidence in the original trial.

> **voir dire**
> a trial within a trial that is conducted to determine whether or not a specific element of evidence should be permitted

Officer's Notes

When the provincial offences officer is called as a witness, the prosecution will indicate to the justice that the officer would like to use his or her notes to refresh his or her memory when giving testimony. If you try to imagine the number of defendants that an officer would deal with through the course of their traffic investigations, it is clear why the officer would need a trigger to refresh his or her memory for an offence that took place several months prior to the trial date. While this is quite standard in a provincial offences trial, the defence does have an opportunity to see the notes and to object

---

9   RSO 1990, c E.23.

to the use of the notes, if appropriate. For example, if it is apparent that there have been additions or deletions to the notes, it may be appropriate to challenge their use.

Prosecutors will ask the provincial offences officer a series of questions, which usually include the following:

- Did you make any notes?
- When did you make the notes?
- Are they in your own handwriting?
- Have you made any additions, deletions, or alterations to these notes?
- Why do you wish to use the notes?
- Do you have an independent recollection of the event?

Statements Made at the Time of the Offence

In some cases, there may be an issue with a statement that was allegedly made to the provincial offences officer or person in the position of authority at the time of the offence. Specifically, there is a requirement that any such statements be made voluntarily. If the defence objects to the statement being used as evidence against the defendant because it was not made voluntarily, it will be necessary to move into a *voir dire*, as described above, to determine the admissibility of the evidence. In court, typical questions about statements made at the time of the offence will probe whether any promise or favour was made in return for a statement, whether the defendant was threatened in any way, and whether the provincial offences officer was in uniform.

Hearsay

hearsay
statements that have been made outside of court by someone other than the witness testifying on the stand

Witnesses can testify only about something that is within their personal knowledge or experience. Failure to do so will be considered **hearsay**. Since hearsay is second-hand information, it is generally not admissible in provincial offence trials.

In the criminal case, *R v Khelawon*,[10] Justice Charron provided the following explanation of hearsay evidence:

> The basic rule of evidence is that all relevant evidence is admissible. There are a number of exceptions to this basic rule. One of the main exceptions is the rule against hearsay: absent an exception, hearsay evidence is *not* admissible. Hearsay evidence is not excluded because it is irrelevant—there is no need for a special rule to exclude irrelevant evidence. Rather, as we shall see, it is the difficulty of testing hearsay evidence that underlies the exclusionary rule and, generally, the alleviation of this difficulty that forms the basis of the exceptions to the rule.

> In terms of exceptions, while an out-of-court admission by the defendant to another person would be considered hearsay, it is generally considered to be admissible. Furthermore, hearsay statements can be admitted in some cases if they are deemed to be necessary and reliable.

---

10   [2006] 2 SCR 787 at para 34.

The rules of hearsay apply equally to prosecution and defence witnesses. This fact may be significant in cases where more than one provincial offences officer dealt with the defendant. For example, if a defendant was waved down for speeding by one officer, but the charge was laid by another officer, both officers would have to be present at trial. One officer cannot provide evidence for the other because it would be considered hearsay.

Trial Sequence

A typical trial sequence starts with the prosecution calling witnesses. This is followed by the defence's turn to call witnesses, and the trial ultimately ends with the justice's verdict. The details of the trial sequence are outlined below.

Examination-in-Chief of Prosecution Witnesses

During the trial, the prosecution will present and question his or her witnesses first. This is known as the prosecution's **examination-in-chief**, which occurs when a party calls and questions its own witnesses. The prosecutor's goal is to bring out evidence from the witnesses that supports the prosecution's case. It is recommended that you make notes during the prosecution's examination-in-chief, pay attention to the witnesses' body language, and look for inconsistencies between the oral evidence and the disclosure provided by the prosecution. Witnesses for the prosecution include the provincial offences officer and any civilian witnesses who had given a statement at the time of the offence or can provide material evidence at trial.

> **examination-in-chief**
> the prosecution or defence questions its own witnesses at the trial

It is equally important to challenge the prosecution witnesses' evidence, where appropriate, and to try to persuade the witnesses to agree with your theory and statements in order to establish your client's defence. You have the right to object to improper or irrelevant questions raised by the prosecutor.

PRACTICE TIP

Establishing a rapport with a witness—even one who is hostile or unsympathetic— is also important. Avoid the appearance of harassing or getting upset with a witness, even if the evidence that might be obtained could be useful, because you may lose credibility and the message could be lost on the justice of the peace.

Cross-Examination of Prosecution Witnesses

At the conclusion of the examination-in-chief of each prosecution witness, the defence will have an opportunity to cross-examine. **Cross-examination** occurs when each side questions the opposing side's witnesses. The goal of cross-examination is to ask questions that challenge the truth, accuracy, or reliability of what has been stated. Cross-examining witnesses is one of the most important skills you need to acquire and perfect. During this process, you cannot give evidence on behalf of your

> **cross-examination**
> the prosecution or defence questions the opposing side's witnesses, following examination-in-chief

client, but you can make suggestions to the prosecution witnesses to see if they agree with your interpretation. You are permitted to seek permission from the justice to see the notes of any prosecution witness and to use the notes during cross examination.

The goals of cross-examination can be summarized as follows:

1. *Clarification*: After listening to the witness's testimony, it may be appropriate to clarify some of the evidence by asking questions that are beneficial to your client's position.

2. *Commitment to the evidence*: A witness must be committed to the evidence he or she provides to the court. Sometimes witnesses, knowingly or unknowingly, make contradictory statements that are vague on a question or fact. A paralegal must pursue an inconsistency in cases where the answer can be established in the client's favour. However, there will be times when it is best not to pursue an inconsistency with a witness if the answer may not serve your client's interest,

3. *Expose inadequate evidence*: Sometimes a witness's recollections may be less than perfect or an officer's notes may lack detail. This is an opportunity to persuade the justice to reduce the weighting that should be applied to the evidence.

4. *Confront false evidence*: There are times when it may be apparent that a witness may be lying. If you strongly believe that the evidence is false, you should not shy away from confronting the witness on the stand. However, there is a distinction between lack of credibility and outright lying. If uncertain, it may be enough to leave the trier of fact in doubt about the witness's credibility and move on.

> ### PRACTICE TIP
>
> You must always be mindful of the goals of cross-examination. If you are not asking questions to achieve one of these goals, you should stop asking questions and move on.

Re-Examination and Re-Cross-Examination of Prosecution Witnesses

After the cross-examination of a witness, the prosecutor will have an opportunity to re-examine the witness about anything new that was brought out in the cross-examination. This is also known as reply or rebuttal by the prosecution. Then the defence will then have an opportunity for re-cross-examination.

Prosecutor Closes Case

The examination-in-chief, cross-examination, re-examination, and re-cross-examination is repeated for every prosecution witness. After the prosecutor has finished calling all of his or her witnesses, the prosecutor will close the case, indicating that there is no more evidence to be presented.

At this stage, the defence should consider the evidence that was presented by the prosecution and whether they have proven all of the essential elements of the offence. If not, the defence may want to consider a motion for a non-suit. If the prosecution has proven the essential elements, there will now be an opportunity for the defence to start to call witnesses.

Defence Witnesses

After the prosecutor closes his or her case, the defence will then have the opportunity to call witnesses and conduct examination-in-chief in support of the defendant's case. This may include calling the defendant and any civilian witnesses who can offer material evidence.

The defendant does not have to take the stand. His or her right to remain silent is protected by the Charter. Keep in mind that if your client does take the stand they will be subject to the prosecutor's cross-examination. However, if you intend to rely on evidence such as documents, diagrams, or photographs, this evidence will have to be admitted into evidence through a witness.

As a paralegal, when conducting examination-in-chief of your own witnesses, including your client, you should inquire only into areas that will advance your client's interests. Being concise and clear will also be beneficial. Avoid asking questions that give the prosecution an opportunity to follow up with questions that may result in evidence detrimental to your client's position. For example, if you do not want the prosecution to ask questions about your client's past driving record, avoid raising the issue through your own questions.

Witnesses should be advised to listen carefully to questions from the prosecutor to try to understand the point that the prosecution is trying to make. They may pause momentarily to mentally compose a response before answering. Once they have answered a question they should be careful not to contradict themselves or change their answer. While it can be difficult to be subjected to cross-examination, the witness should remain calm and refrain from appearing defensive, keep answers short and to the point, and not offer more information than was asked.

The cross-examination, re-examination, and re-cross-examination processes described earlier will apply to any defence witnesses.

Closing Statements

When all witnesses have been called and examined, it is time for the prosecution and defence to provide closing statements. The closing statement provides the best opportunity to persuade the court to rule in favour of your client. If you decided to call witnesses in your client's defence, you will be required to make your closing statement first, giving the prosecution the final word. However, there are times when the justice of the peace will call on the prosecution first to sum up his or her case.

Preparing the closing statement begins as soon as you start working on a case. From the very beginning, you should be formulating ideas for structuring a persuasive and legally sound defence which will be reiterated in the closing statement. Those ideas are refined throughout the interview and case preparation (disclosure) phases of the case, as well as during the trial itself. The closing statement is perhaps the most important aspect of the trial, and, if done properly, can be an advocate's finest hour.

The elements of a strong, effective closing statement are set out below:

1. The closing statement allows you to explain the significance of the evidence and to offer reasons that support conclusions and inferences. It also gives you a chance to discuss credibility and the law, and to advocate on behalf of your client.

2. An effective closing statement presents a positive theory of the case in a clear, logical, and understandable fashion. It should incorporate the same theories that have been put forward throughout the trial.

3. The closing argument must not only engage the justice intellectually but have emotional appeal as well, because your goal is a dismissal of the charges.

4. You must emphasize why the court should rule in favour of your client. State the law and the weakness in the prosecution's case, and highlight your client's positive attributes. Strike a balance between quantity and quality.

The closing statement must only summarize what has been stated during the trial; it is not an opportunity to present fresh evidence.

PRACTICE TIP

It is important that you not read verbatim the notes for your closing statement. The justice will be watching you, so it is vital to establish eye contact. This is your last opportunity to sell your theory and version of the facts, and to convince the court of the soundness of your case. Be aware of the justice's facial expression and body language and be prepared to adapt if the justice appears confused by your statement.

The Verdict

verdict
the decision or ruling of the justice

After both parties have made their closing statements, the justice will review the evidence and provide a ruling, called the **verdict**. Depending on the complexity and length of the trial, the justice may give an oral ruling immediately or reserve judgment and provide oral or written reasons at a later date.

There is not much of an opportunity to offer any feedback or clarification when the justice is issuing a verdict. At this point, advocacy has no place, and your role is to make proper notes on the reasons provided in order to discuss with your client and to consider the appropriateness of an appeal.

PRACTICE TIP

If it is appropriate to ask the justice for clarification or to provide reasons, you must do so in a way that does not offend the court. Avoid using the phrase "with all due respect" and instead try "with the greatest of respect."

In many cases, you will receive an oral ruling immediately. If your client is found guilty, do not debate the verdict but put your efforts toward advocating for the best possible sentence for your client.

Regardless of the ruling, thank the court for its time. Civility and courtesy are always appropriate and in the best interests of the administration of justice.

KEY TERMS

burden of proof, 122
cross-examination, 129
defence of causation, 125
defence of due diligence, 124
defence of involuntariness, 125
defence of necessity, 124
examination-in-chief, 129
expert witness, 127
hearsay, 128
reverse-onus, 122
standard of proof, 122
verdict, 132
voir dire, 127

REVIEW QUESTIONS

Multiple Choice

1. What is the standard of proof that the prosecution has to meet in order to secure a conviction for a provincial offence?

   a. Balance of probabilities.

   b. Beyond a reasonable doubt.

   c. More likely than not.

   d. The standard fluctuates.

2. Which of the following explanations is most likely to result in an adjournment being granted?

   a. Defendant is not prepared to proceed.

   b. Prosecution is not prepared to proceed.

   c. The provincial offences officer has a conflict and is unable to attend.

   d. Defendant's paralegal has a conflict and is unable to attend.

3. Marina was charged with failure to remain at the scene of an accident. She was told by a paralegal that she would be able to raise the defence of due diligence. Which type of offence must failure to remain be in order for this defence to be available?

   a. A *mens rea* offence.

   b. A strict liability offence.

   c. An absolute liability offence.

   d. Any type of offence.

4. Marina has a photograph of the intersection where the collision took place. Which type of evidence is the photograph classified as?

   a. Real evidence.

   b. Documentary evidence.

   c. Testimony.

   d. Oral evidence.

5. What should you do when the justice delivers a verdict that you do not agree with?

   a. Ask the justice to reconsider the decision.

   b. Argue with the justice.

   c. State that you want to record to show that you do not agree.

   d. Politely accept the verdict and discuss possible next steps with your client.

Short Answer

1. What elements must the defendant establish in order to make out the defence of necessity?

2. Provide an example of a situation that could likely meet the test for necessity.

3. Describe four goals of cross-examination.

4. Define evidence and describe its purpose at trial.

5. You are representing your client at court on the day of trial and the prosecution brings a motion without notice to amend the certificate of offence. What factors should you consider before providing oral submissions in response?

6. What is the purpose of a court order to exclude the witnesses from a hearing?

7. What is a *voir dire*?

Scenario 1

You are representing your client on a charge of following too close under the *Highway Traffic Act*. At the outset of the trial, the prosecution advises you that it is bringing a motion to amend the charge to careless driving under the HTA. What submissions would you provide to oppose the prosecution's motion?

Scenario 2

You are representing a client who has received a parking ticket under a municipal by-law. After listening to the prosecutor question the issuing officer, you review your notes and are certain that the officer never mentioned the relevant by-law number or the motor vehicle's licence plate number. How would you deal with this oversight?

Scenario 3

Your client is on trial for a *Building Code* offence, in violation of a city by-law. The prosecutor advises you that the chief building official is ill and unable to attend court that day, and asks if you are willing to consent to an adjournment. How would you respond to the prosecutor's request?

Sentencing

11

LEARNING OUTCOMES

After reading this chapter, you will understand

■ the principles of sentencing;

■ the powers and restrictions of the court;

■ aggravating and mitigating factors;

■ set fines, costs, and victim fine surcharges; and

■ imprisonment and additional orders and penalties.

Introduction

Now that your client's guilt has been established, it may seem that the sentencing process requires the least amount of preparation. In fact, the sentencing stage is where you must put forth some of your strongest arguments on behalf of your client, and the outcome will ultimately have the greatest impact on your client's life.

In some situations a justice will adjourn sentencing to another date and conduct a full sentencing hearing where they may even allow evidence to be called, depending on the nature of the charge. In other situations, the justice may move directly to sentencing with little opportunity for you to provide input. There will be times when the range of sentence, and even the exact penalty, is prescribed by statute, so making arguments in such circumstances will often be of lesser value.

Purpose and Objective

Provincial offence laws ensure, among other things, that buildings are constructed properly, that workplaces are safe, and that drivers obey the rules of the road. It is in society's interest that individuals comply with such laws.

There should be consequences for someone who has plead guilty or has been found guilty of violating a regulatory law, and for most offences, a monetary fine is imposed. Several other sentencing options available to a justice are found in the *Provincial Offences Act*[1] and the charging act. Regardless of the sentencing options available, the court is guided by sentencing principles.

It is important to note that the court must give both the defendant, or his or her representative, and the prosecution an opportunity to make submissions on sentencing before rendering a decision. Section 57(1) of the POA provides the legal framework:

> 57(1) Where a defendant who appears is convicted of an offence, the court shall give the prosecutor and the defendant's representative an opportunity to make submissions as to sentence and, where the defendant has no representative, the court shall ask the defendant if he or she has anything to say before sentence is passed.

However, section 57(2) indicates that the omission to comply with subsection (1) does not affect the validity of the proceeding. In most cases, paralegals can expect to be asked to give submissions as to sentence on behalf of a client. Pursuant to section 57(3), the justice may ask questions about the defendant and his or her financial situation. While this information may help reduce the penalty, there is no obligation for the defence to respond to such inquiries.

A conviction on a provincial offence will not result in a criminal record; however, it should be noted that another record of sorts can be created following a conviction for a provincial offence. For example, driving convictions are tracked by the Ministry of Transportation, and the Ministry of Labour keeps a record of workplace safety violations.

---

1   RSO 1990, c P.33.

Principles of Sentencing

The same principles of sentencing apply to both provincial and criminal offences. Although not all criminal law principles are directly relevant to provincial offences, section 718 of the *Criminal Code*[2] provides a guide to sentencing principles and can be referred to for assistance.

> 718. The fundamental purpose of sentencing is to protect society and to contribute, along with crime prevention initiatives, to respect for the law and the maintenance of a just, peaceful and safe society by imposing just sanctions that have one or more of the following objectives:
>
> (a) to denounce unlawful conduct and the harm done to the victims or to the community that is caused by unlawful conduct;
>
> (b) to deter the offender and other persons from committing offences;
>
> (c) to separate offenders from society, where necessary;
>
> (d) to assist in rehabilitating offenders;
>
> (e) to provide reparations for harm done to victims or to the community; and
>
> (f) to promote a sense of responsibility in offenders, and acknowledgement of the harm done to victims or to the community.

This general-purpose provision of sentencing is framed by section 718.1 of the *Criminal Code*, which indicates that the sentence should be proportionate to the gravity of the offence and the degree of responsibility of the offender. This concept of **proportionality** is a key determinant of sentence for provincial offence matters. For example, a lesser sentence should be ordered for a minor offence whereby a defendant left his wallet at home by mistake and was unable to surrender his insurance card than for a more serious offence such as a defendant who has been driving without a valid insurance policy in place on an ongoing basis.

For the most part, the purpose of sentencing in provincial offences court focuses on **deterrence**, of which there are two types: specific and general.

- Specific deterrence focuses on the individual defendant and aims to deter that particular person from offending again.
- General deterrence aims to discourage others in society from committing that type of offence.

Deterrence, whether specific or general, is based on the assumption that potential offenders will consider the consequences of their actions and refrain from committing an offence. The court will usually place a greater emphasis on specific deterrence and the likelihood of future compliance going forward than on general deterrence.

proportionality
a principle in law that the penalty should be proportional to the offence that was committed

deterrence
a principle of sentencing intended to discourage a defendant from reoffending; specific and general are the two types of deterrence

Powers and Restrictions

To understand the powers and restrictions of the court, it is important to review the procedural stream under which the matter was commenced.

---

2   RSC 1985, c C-46.

- *Part I—Certificate of offence*: The court has the power to impose a fine of up to $1,000. A defendant may not be sent to jail or placed on probation.
- *Part II—Certificate of parking infraction*: The court has the power to impose a fine of up to $1,000. A defendant may not be sent to jail or placed on probation.
- *Part III—Information*: In accordance with section 61 of the POA, the maximum fine is $5,000, unless a higher fine has been established in the charging act. In addition, a broad range of sentencing options are available to the court, including imprisonment, probation, and other special orders. The POA and the charging act outline the appropriate range and sentencing options.

Aggravating and Mitigating Factors

The court will consider both aggravating and mitigating factors in determining what an appropriate sentence would be for the defendant.

In support of a harsher sentence for your client, the prosecution may ask the court to consider certain aggravating factors. These include:

- the conduct of your client during the offence;
- the conduct of your client during the court proceeding;
- public safety considerations;
- prevalence of the offence in the community; and
- previous convictions of your client.

In arguing for a more lenient sentence for your client, you may want to bring certain mitigating factors to the court's attention. These include:

- your client's ability to pay a fine (i.e., financial hardship);
- your client's driving record—if there have been no other convictions (for HTA offences, see note 8 below);
- the remorse that your client has shown for the offence, particularly for the impact it had on other parties;
- a sincere apology from your client to the court or other parties;
- the seriousness of the offence;
- the likelihood that your client will not reoffend; and
- other information about your client that may be relevant—for example, whether he or she is a student, single parent, recent immigrant, and so on.

It is worth noting that section 56 of the POA allows for the court to direct a probation officer to prepare a pre-sentence report in order to assist the court in imposing a sentence. The report may highlight some of the aforementioned aggravating and mitigating factors.

PRACTICE TIP

A thorough client interview is essential to gathering additional personal and financial information that you may be able to use to advocate for a more lenient sentence.

It is appropriate to provide the court with a concise description of your client's background and present circumstances to persuade the court to impose a sentence in the minimum range of the appropriate sentencing precedents.

Fines

A fine is the amount of money that a defendant will be ordered to pay within a specified time frame. For Parts I and II matters, the original charging document specifies a set fine. However, the term "set fine" may be misleading, suggesting that the stipulated amount is the fine that will always be imposed by the court. The set fine, however, is the amount a defendant will pay in an out-of-court settlement. If your client is convicted at trial, the amount of the fine may be specified in the charging act or be prescribed by the minimum and the maximum default amounts specified in the POA or in the charging act, whichever applies, and will be determined by the justice.

Although the court may be guided by the set fine when determining the penalty after a trial, it is not uncommon for a defendant to be ordered to pay an amount that is higher than the set fine. This should not be seen as punishment for having a trial, but as reflecting the fact that the justice was able to hear all of the evidence and more thoroughly assess the case. For offences where the charging act specifies particulars about the fine amount upon conviction, the justice will be bound by what is prescribed. The Case in Point: *R v O'Neill*, below, considers this issue.

CASE IN POINT

Set Fines at Trial

R v O'Neill, 2008 ONCJ 391

Facts

At trial, the defendant was convicted of speeding at a rate of 32km per hour above the posted speed limit. During sentencing, the prosecution sought a penalty higher than the set fine. The defendant's position was that an increased penalty would unjustly penalize him for having exercised his right to a trial.

Relevant Issue

Set Fines at Trial

Decision

The justice considered the jurisdiction of the court and the applicability of set fines. Upon reviewing the POA, case law and related materials, the justice indicated that he did not have lawful authority to create or read in a set fine for the trial sections of the POA. Therefore, the penalty provisions in the charging act and the general penalties in the POA apply at the trial stage, but the set fine does not exist as a sentencing option. Set fines are available only to defendants who settle out of court. Higher penalties are permitted at the trial stage.

Remember that in exceptional circumstances, under section 59(2) of the POA, the justice can impose a fine lower than the minimum or suspend the sentence. Specifically:

> 59(2) Although the provision that creates the penalty for an offence prescribes a minimum fine, where in the opinion of the court exceptional circumstances exist so that to impose the minimum fine would be unduly oppressive or otherwise not in the interests of justice, the court may impose a fine that is less than the minimum or suspend the sentence.

However, this is a very high standard to be met under section 59, and such relief is therefore not commonly granted. The Case in Point: *R ex rel City of Toronto v Doroz*, below, considers the use of suspended sentences for speeding offences at trial.

CASE IN POINT

Suspended Sentences at Trial

R ex rel City of Toronto v Doroz, 2011 ONCJ 281

Facts

The defendant was charged with speeding 57km/hr in a 40km/hr zone. After negotiating with the prosecutor, he agreed to plead guilty to the lesser speed of 50km/hr in a 40km/hr zone. During sentencing, the justice stated it's only fair and just for people to have a reasonable amount of reduction when they plead guilty. Since the justice indicated that she was unable to reduce below the set fine of $25 (see commentary re: *Winlow* below) she ordered a suspended sentence so the defendant would not have to pay a fine at all. The City of Toronto appealed to the Ontario Court of Justice on the basis that there was no authority for the justice to award a suspended sentence. The defendant did not take part in the appeal, and an *amicus curiae* was nominated to put forward a written response to the City's appeal. The *amicus* argued that a suspended sentence was a proper disposition by the trial justice.

Relevant Issue

Suspended Sentences at Trial

Decision

The judge considered the related provisions of the POA and relevant case law. He found that the imposition of a suspended sentence will be the exception and not the norm for speeding offences. While justices are permitted to impose suspended sentences in some cases, it was not appropriate to do so for this matter. Since the defendant did not take part in the appeal and since it would not be fair to impose a penalty at that stage, the appeal was dismissed.

Commentary

See also the *York (Regional Municipality) v Winlow*, 2009 ONCA 643 decision, in which the Ontario Court of Appeal unanimously held that there is no discretion to reduce the fines below the set fines for speeding offences.

There are times when a joint submission regarding sentence can be submitted by the prosecution and defence. This is most commonly done when there has been a guilty plea to an included offence. Despite the joint submission, the justice is not bound by any agreement made with the prosecution and has the ability to reject a joint submission if the justice feels that it is contrary to the public interest or would bring the administration of justice into disrepute.

Costs and Victim Fine Surcharge

Paying a fine will not be the only monetary amount that will be ordered against your client upon conviction. Regulation 945 made under the POA provides for *fixed costs* upon conviction, payable for the purposes of section 60(1)—see Table 11.1 below.

Table 11.1

1.	For service of offence notice or summons	$5.00
2.	Upon conviction under section 9 of the Act	$5.00
3.	Upon conviction under section 9.1 of the Act	$10.00
4.	Upon conviction under section 18 of the Act as it read on August 31, 1993	$3.75
5.	Upon conviction under subsection 18.2(6) of the Act	$16.00
6.	Upon conviction under section 18.4 of the Act	$12.75
7.	Upon conviction under subsection 54(1) of the Act	$30.00
8.	For service of a parking infraction notice issued other than under a municipal by-law	$3.75

Regulation 945 also provides that discretionary costs *may* be awarded under section 60(2) of the Act up to a maximum amount—see Table 11.2 below.

Table 11.2

1.	Fee for each witness for each day necessarily in attendance when trial scheduled	$6.00
2.	Travel expenses for each witness,	
	i. where witness resides in place where trial held	$2.50
	ii. where witness does not reside in place where trial held, a kilometre allowance as set out in Regulation 11 of the Revised Regulations of Ontario, 1990 entitled "Kilometre Allowances."	

Costs upon conviction under section 60(1) are fixed and are added to the fine by court administrative staff. By contrast, costs under section 60(2) are discretionary and are added only if ordered by the presiding justice. Even if a fine is not ordered by the court as part of the sentence, your client may still have to pay the section 60(1) costs if convicted.

In addition to fixed and discretionary costs, any defendant who is fined must pay a victim fine surcharge. Designed to assist victims of crime, the surcharge goes to a special fund, and the money is allocated to programs and services, such as Support-Link, Victim Support Line, Victim Crisis Assistance and Referral Services, and Victim/Witness Assistance Programs. Victim fine surcharges are added for Part I and Part III matters but are not added for Part II matters.

The fines and corresponding victim fine surcharges, reproduced in Table 11.3 below, are listed in the POA Regulation titled *Victim Fine Surcharges*.[3]

Table 11.3

COLUMN 1		COLUMN 2
Fine Range		Surcharge
$		$
0	– 50	10
51	– 75	15
76	– 100	20
101	– 150	25
151	– 200	35
201	– 250	50
251	– 300	60
301	– 350	75
351	– 400	85
401	– 450	95
451	– 500	110
501	– 1000	125
Over 1000		25% of actual fine

3 O Reg 161/00.

Time to Pay

Regardless of the amount of the fine your client is ordered to pay, the court is often willing to provide a reasonable amount of time in which to make payment. It is important that you be aware of your client's ability to pay a fine so as to be able to suggest a reasonable time frame to the court.

In the absence of any request for an extension of time to pay, fines are due 15 days after the court imposes sentence. Section 66 of the POA provides the framework for the time to pay and extensions:

66(1) A fine becomes due and payable fifteen days after its imposition.

(2) Where the court imposes a fine, the court shall ask the defendant if the defendant wishes an extension of the time for payment of the fine.

(3) Where the defendant requests an extension of the time for payment of the fine, the court may make such inquiries, on oath or affirmation or otherwise, of and concerning the defendant as the court considers desirable, but the defendant shall not be compelled to answer.

(4) Unless the court finds that the request for extension of time is not made in good faith or that the extension would likely be used to evade payment, the court shall extend the time for payment by ordering periodic payments or otherwise.

(5) Where a fine is imposed in the absence of the defendant, the clerk of the court shall give the defendant notice of the fine and its due date and of the defendant's right to make a motion for an extension of the time for payment under subsection (6).

(6) The defendant may, at any time by motion in the prescribed form filed in the office of the court, request an extension or further extension of time for payment of a fine and the motion shall be determined by a justice and the justice has the same powers in respect of the motion as the court has under subsections (3) and (4).

As indicated in section 66(6), defendants who would like time beyond the original amount of time for payment ordered by the court can complete Form 125 under the *Courts of Justice Act*, titled Motion for Extension of Time to Pay Fine (see Figure 11.1). This form is written in the first person and requires the defendant to fill in all of the information regarding the conviction (e.g., date and location of conviction, how much time was given to pay, how much has been paid, and details as to the inability to pay). In some jurisdictions the defendant may be required to appear before a justice in order to verbally explain the circumstances surrounding the request. The justice will then decide whether to grant or deny the application. If it is granted, the new due date will apply. If it is not granted, the defendant will have to abide by the original due date for the fine.

Figure 11.1   Form 125 under the *Courts of Justice Act*, titled Motion for Extension of Time to Pay Fine

MOTION FOR EXTENSION OF TIME TO PAY FINE
*REQUÊTE PRÉSENTÉE EN VUE D'OBTENIR UNE PROROGATION DU DÉLAI POUR
ACQUITTER LE PAIEMENT D'UNE AMENDE*

ONTARIO COURT OF JUSTICE
COUR DE JUSTICE DE L'ONTARIO
PROVINCE OF ONTARIO
PROVINCE DE L'ONTARIO

Under Subsection 66(6) of the *Provincial Offences Act*
Aux termes du paragraphe 66(6) de la Loi sure les infractions provinciales

Form / Formule 125
Courts of Justice Act
Loi sur les tribunaux judiciaires
R.R.O. / R.R.O. 1990
O. Reg. / *Régl. de l'Ont.* 200

Case / Offence Number:
Cas / Infraction _____

1. I,
    Je soussigné(e) _____   _____   _____

    (Family/Company / *Nom de famille / entreprise*)   (Given/*Prénom*)   (Initials/*Initiales*)

    Of
    de _____ _____ _____ _____ _____

    (Current address / *adresse actuelle*) (Street / *rue*) (Apt. / *app.*) (Municipality / *municipalité*) (Province) (Postal Code / *code postal*)

    was convicted in Ontario Court of Justice   At à Toronto *on le*
    ai été déclaré coupable devant la Cour de justice de l'Ontario   _____

    of the offence of   contrary to   section
    d'avoir commis l'infraction suivante _____ *par dérogation à* _____ *article* _____

    and was sentenced to pay a fine of $ (including cost and Victim Fine Surcharge).
    et j'ai été condamné à verser une amende de _____ *$ (y compris les frais et la suramende compensatoire).*

2. I was given   days/months to pay this amount.
    J'ai obtenu un délai de _____ *jours (ou mois) pour acquitter ce montant.*

3. I have paid $ in satisfaction of the above amount.
    J'ai versé _____ *$ pour qu'ils soient affectés au paiement du montant ci-dessus.*

4. I am unable to pay this amount within the time given for the payment for the following reasons:
    Il ne m'est pas possible d'acquitter le montant imposé dans le délai qui m'est accordé pour les raisons suivantes:

    _____

5. I hereby apply for an extension of time for payment until
    Je formule cette requête en vue d'obtenir une prorogation du délai de paiement jusqu'au _____

6. I am _____ years of age.   Driver's Licence No.:
    Je suis âgé de   *ans.*   *Numéro de permis de conduire*
                                                      _____ _____ _____

7. I am / *Je*
    (check one / *cochez l'un ou l'autre, selon le cas*)

    ○ employed. / *possède un emploi.*

    ○ unemployed. / *suis sans emploi.*

8. (check one / *cochez l'un ou l'autre, selon le cas*)
    ○ This is my first application for an extension.
       Je demande une prorogation du délai de paiement pour la première fois.

    ○ I previously obtained _____ extension(s) of time for payment, the last of
       J'ai déjà obtenu   *prorogation(s) du délai de paiement dont la dernière*

    which expired upon the   which will expire upon the
    s'est terminée le _____ *ou doit se terminer le* _____

Dated at TORONTO
Fait à

this _____ day of_____, yr. 20 ____   _____
ce   *jour de*   *an*   Signature

T (F) POA 0809 CSD (Dec 2013)

Default of Payment

A defendant who does not pay the fine within the prescribed time period is considered to be in default of payment and is subject to the civil enforcement of the fine. In accordance with section 68(1) of the POA, the clerk will complete a certificate with details of the fine and how much is owing. This certificate then acts as an enforcement order.

Additional steps, as set out in section 69 of the POA, may also be applicable. For example, the court may order suspension or non-renewal of any permit, licence, registration, or privilege. As well, the POA allows for other steps, such as a warrant requiring attendance before a justice to speak to the default of payment, a term of imprisonment, an extension of time to pay, or establishing a payment schedule. Further, section 69.1 provides the authority for reporting details about the defaulted fine to a consumer reporting agency, which can impact the defendant's credit rating.

Imprisonment

Imprisonment is available as a sentencing option only for charges that have been commenced by an information under Part III of the POA, and then only if the charging act provides for incarceration upon conviction. Typically, imprisonment is ordered only in situations where a lesser penalty would not be appropriate.

Several provincial statutes include imprisonment as a sentencing option, but a defendant is less likely to be sentenced to jail for a first-time conviction.

From the beginning of case preparation, it is important that you determine whether the prosecution will be seeking a jail term upon conviction. If the prosecution is considering a term of imprisonment, you may be well advised to request a pre-sentence report to assist the court in determining whether a jail sentence is appropriate in the circumstances.

Imprisonment provisions and conditions are found in sections 63 and 64 of the POA:

> 63(1) The term of imprisonment imposed by sentence shall, unless otherwise directed in the sentence, commence on the day on which the convicted person is taken into custody thereunder, but no time during which the convicted person is imprisoned or out on bail before sentence shall be reckoned as part of the term of imprisonment to which he or she is sentenced.
>
> (2) Where the court imposes imprisonment, the court may order custody to commence on a day not later than thirty days after the day of sentencing.
>
> 64. Where a person is subject to more than one term of imprisonment at the same time, the terms shall be served consecutively except in so far as the court has ordered a term to be served concurrently with any other term of imprisonment.

When imprisonment is a possibility, the court may consider pre-trial custody when determining the appropriate length of a sentence pursuant to sections 58 and 63(1). As well, the POA allows for terms of imprisonment less than 90 days to be served intermittently pursuant to section 72(1)(c), such as on weekends. This is an option that may be appropriate for to some clients.

PRACTICE TIP

Some defendants will be taken into custody immediately following their sentencing hearing. Clients should be advised of this possibility so that they can get their affairs in order (e.g., child care arrangements, arranging an absence from work, etc.).

Additional Orders and Penalties

probation order
a court order that places conditions on a defendant after conviction, often to control the defendant's movements and require certain action

While a **probation order** is the most common type of court order following a conviction, a justice may decide to make a prohibition order, as discussed below. As well, charging acts may specify additional penalties for specific offences.

Probation Orders

Probation is a penalty that can be ordered for convictions on offences, other than absolute liability offences, commenced by an information under Part III of the POA. It involves an established period of time during which the defendant must report to a responsible person designated by the court, be under the supervision of that person, and/or adhere to specific terms and conditions. Probation orders can be imposed for up to two years.

Section 72 of the POA indicates that the justice should consider the age, character, and background of the defendant, the nature of the offence, and circumstances of its commission. A probation order could be ordered in lieu of another sentence or in combination with another sentence. Pursuant to section 72(2) of the POA, the contents of a probation order are deemed to include conditions that:

> 72(2)(a) the defendant not commit the same or any related or similar offence, or any offence under a statute of Canada or Ontario or any other province of Canada that is punishable by imprisonment;
> (b) the defendant appear before the court as and when required; and
> (c) the defendant notify the court of any change in the defendant's address.

Within the probation order, the court may also require a defendant to satisfy any compensation or restitution that is required or authorized by an act or to perform community service. Section 73 indicates that the probation order comes into force on the date it was made or upon expiry of a sentence for imprisonment. As explained in section 74, a probation order can be changed, relieved, or terminated. In such case, the defendant must be made aware and be provided with a copy of the endorsed order.

If your client faces the possibility of incarceration or a high fine and you are concerned about his or her ability to comply, it may be in your client's best interest to suggest a term of probation for the court's consideration.

prohibition order
a court order that prohibits a defendant from engaging in activities that could lead to a repetition of the offence

Prohibition Orders

For Part III matters, some statutes authorize a **prohibition order** that is intended to prevent the recurrence of the offence or to counteract the behaviour of a defendant who may regard being fined simply as the cost of doing business (in violation of a municipal by-law). For example, section 67(3) of the *Planning Act*[4] states:

> Where a conviction is entered under subsection (1), in addition to any other remedy or any penalty provided by law, the court in which the conviction has been entered, and any court of competent jurisdiction thereafter, may make an order prohibiting the continuation or repetition of the offence by the person convicted.

Similar provisions are found in sections of the *Municipal Act, 2001*[5] and the *Building Code Act, 1992*.[6] Under a prohibition order, a defendant who further contravenes the by-law in question may face not only another charge under the by-law but also a contempt-of-court charge under the POA.

As a further example, section 5 of the *Dog Owner's Liability Act*[7] states:

> 5. When, in a proceeding under section 4, the court finds that the dog has bitten or attacked a person or domestic animal or that the dog's behaviour is such that the dog is a menace to the safety of persons or domestic animals, the court may make an order prohibiting the dog's owner from owning another dog during a specified period of time.

Additional Penalties in Charging Act

The charging act may set out specific additional penalties that are applicable. For driving-related convictions, demerit points are associated with a number of offences under the *Highway Traffic Act* (HTA).[8] These are not ordered by the court, but are imposed by the Ministry of Transportation. The justice does not have the authority to impose, waive, or reduce demerit points. As well, certain driving offences may have specified penalties, such as licence suspension with an increased term for licence suspension for reoffenders. For example, upon conviction, and in addition to fines and the possibility of imprisonment, stunt driving carries a licence suspension of up to two years for a first conviction and ten years for a subsequent conviction. In addition, section 210(1.1) of the HTA requires the registrar of Motor Vehicles to be notified of the conviction on an HTA matter and, pursuant to section 211(3), the court is required to forward the defendant's driver's licence to the registrar when a suspension is part of the penalty.

Another example of additional penalties specified within a charging act occurs in section 4 of the *Dog Owner's Liability Act*, which allows for specific penalties when a dog has bitten another animal or person. These specific penalties include that the dog be destroyed, or that the owner of the dog take measures for more effective control of the dog for purposes of public safety (e.g., confining the dog to its owner's property, restraining the dog by means of a leash or muzzle, and/or posting warning signs).

---

4 RSO 1990, c. P.13.

5 SO 2001, c 25.

6 SO 1992, c 23.

7 RSO 1990, c D.16.

8 RSO 1990, c H.8.

KEY TERMS

deterrence, 139
probation order, 148
prohibition order, 148
proportionality, 139

REVIEW QUESTIONS

Multiple Choice

1. Which of the following statements is true?

   a. The justice must accept a joint sentencing submission.

   b. The court is required to give the defendant an opportunity to be heard during the sentencing.

   c. The sentencing hearing must be within 30 days of the decision.

   d. A proceeding is not valid if the justice does not give the defendant an opportunity to speak during sentencing.

2. Which of the following would be an example of specific deterrence?

   a. As a result of her recent improper stop conviction and increased insurance rates, Lynne makes sure that she comes to a full and complete stop at every stop sign.

   b. Karen has started wearing her seat belt because she heard on the radio that the police in her area were doing a seat belt blitz.

   c. A muzzle order was put on his neighbour's dog for biting someone, so Aidan has stopped walking his dog in public parks.

   d. A group of high school students agreed to put phones away when driving after a speaker came to their school and spoke about the fatal accident he caused while texting.

3. For provincial offences, what does the purpose of sentencing tend to focus on?

   a. Rehabilitation.

   b. Punishment.

   c. Deterrence.

   d. Compensation.

4. Which of the following is true with regard to fines?

   a. The set fine is the amount that will always be ordered by the court upon conviction.

   b. If a fine is ordered by the court, it must always be paid immediately by the defendant.

   c. The court may order a defendant to pay a higher fine because of previous convictions.

   d. A set fine is prescribed for all offences within all three procedural streams.

Short Answer

1. For each procedural stream, identify the sentencing options available to the court.

2. Sentencing for provincial offences generally focuses on deterrence. What are the two types of deterrence? Provide a brief example of each.

3. If convicted, a defendant will often be ordered to pay a fine. In addition to a fine, what costs could a defendant be ordered to pay? How are these amounts determined?

4. List five examples of aggravating factors that a court may be asked to consider before sentencing a defendant.

5. List five examples of mitigating factors that a court may be asked to consider before sentencing a defendant.

6. Can a defendant be sent to jail for committing a provincial offence? Explain.

Scenario

You have been retained by Phong to represent him on his driving without insurance charge. He explained to you that his insurance had become so expensive because of several other driving convictions, but that he drove only three times every week in order to take his mother to the hospital for radiation treatment. In addition to looking after his sick mother, he is working three jobs to help raise his two younger brothers. When he was pulled over by the police officer, he panicked, knowing that he could go to jail if convicted, so he tried to run away from the police officer, but was caught and charged. He feels terrible about the incident, has apologized, and has provided character references from all three of his employers.

1. Identify three mitigating factors that you would raise if Phong was your client.

2. Identify three aggravating factors that you would expect the prosecution to raise.

3. Phong is concerned that he will be sent to jail and that there will be no one to take his mother to her medical treatments. What would you recommend in this case?

Following Up with a Client

LEARNING OUTCOMES

After reading this chapter, you will understand

- how to deal with satisfactory and unsatisfactory results;

- the need to inform a client of the consequences of conviction; and

- the steps to take when closing a file.

Introduction

After a court case is finished, a paralegal must still complete certain tasks and fulfill obligations to the client. When all work is complete, a paralegal will close the file and abide by specific requirements relating to the retention, storage, and destruction of the file.

Satisfactory/Unsatisfactory Results

conviction
a final decision by a justice that there is proof that the defendant committed the offence for which he or she was charged

There is some degree of risk associated with going to court. In many cases, paralegals will be able to obtain a satisfactory result through negotiation with the prosecution or success at trial. However, there will also be cases that produce a result that the client will view as an unsatisfactory result, namely a **conviction**.

Satisfactory Results

dismissed
a final decision by a justice that there is not enough evidence to support a conviction against the defendant

withdrawn
a decision by the prosecution to remove the charges against the defendant

If the charges against your client are **dismissed** or **withdrawn**, he or she should be satisfied with the outcome because there is no penalty and it is unlikely that further court action will take place (unless the prosecution files an appeal of the dismissal). Therefore, this would be an appropriate time to take steps to close the file.

If the charges against your client are stayed, this should also be considered a satisfactory result. But the client should be cautioned that, technically, a stay of proceedings means that they have been halted and could be recommenced by the prosecution. Since, it is quite rare for stayed proceedings to be recommenced, the file can now be closed.

Negotiating a guilty plea to an included (lesser) offence and agreeing with the prosecutor on sentencing submissions (such as a suspended sentence or the set fine) are also a satisfactory result. Clients who are most concerned about demerit points may be satisfied with an outcome that reduces or eliminates those points. Your client must provide instructions on what type of negotiated resolution would be suitable. If a resolution has been negotiated, the matter is complete and the file should be closed.

> ### PRACTICE TIP
>
> Whenever possible, try to turn a satisfied client into a source of referrals and repeat business. Think of ways to pass along your contact information (e.g., provide copies of your business card or a brochure) or to stay in touch with former clients (e.g., send out an email newsletter at regular intervals to advise of changes to relevant laws). You want to leave a good, lasting impression.

Unsatisfactory Results

Despite your preparation and strong advocacy skills, you may not always achieve a result that your client finds satisfactory. A client will usually consider a conviction to be an unsatisfactory result. Nevertheless, do not delay in discussing the results with your client.

Clients should be informed of their appeal rights and whether an appeal is recommended in their case. For more information on appeals, see the discussion in Chapter 13.

If a client has already gone through the appeal process, he or she should be made aware of further appeal rights (e.g., to the Ontario Court of Appeal and the Supreme Court of Canada), even though paralegals are permitted to appear only on the first level of appeals in the Ontario Court of Justice.

If the unsatisfactory result was achieved because of an error or omission on the part of the paralegal, the *Paralegal Rules of Conduct*[1] should be consulted for guidance. Specifically, Rule 3.02(21) and Rule 4.01(7) indicate that errors and omissions must be promptly disclosed and rectified whenever possible. Disclosure means that notice will have to be provided to your client and your insurer. As well, the client should be told to seek independent legal advice concerning any rights he or she may have arising from the error or omission (i.e., there may be grounds for a complaint or a claim against the paralegal). In some cases, there may be an opportunity to assist with rectifying an error. For example, if a paralegal missed a court date and the client was convicted as a result, the paralegal may be in a position to suggest that the defendant submit an application to reopen the case.

PRACTICE TIP

Many clients will be upset with a conviction. It is important that clients are made aware of the possibility of a conviction before the matter goes to trial so that they are not surprised.

Consequences of a Conviction

After sentencing, a client must be made aware of the consequences of a conviction. This includes informing the client of upcoming deadlines and time frames, such as when a fine is due or the duration of a licence suspension.

The consequences may vary depending on the penalties specified in the charging act. In some cases, the penalty may be a monetary fine, while in others, it may include demerit points, a licence suspension, and/or jail time. Some legislation authorizes additional penalties specifically related to the offence. For example, as discussed in Chapter 11, under the *Dog Owners' Liability Act*,[2] if a dog has injured a person or animal, the court may prohibit the owner from owning another dog for a specified period of time.

---

1   Law Society of Ontario, *Paralegal Rules of Conduct* (1 October 2014; amendments current to 2017), online: <https://www.lsuc.on.ca/paralegal-conduct-rules>.

2   RSO 1990, c D.16.

Closing the File

A file should be closed only after all matters relating to the file have been handled. Prior to closing any file, the paralegal should ensure that:

- all of the work that the paralegal was retained to complete has been completed;
- all undertakings have been satisfied;
- the paralegal has sent a full written report to the client, including any further action that may be recommended;
- the final account has been settled (i.e., any balance owing has been written off or no balance is remaining for the client in the trust account); and
- all documents and property have been returned to the client and the client has signed an acknowledgment that they have received the property (e.g., for *Provincial Offences Act* matters, this may include the original charging documents, the defendant's licence, photographs, and any other property in your possession).

PRACTICE TIP

Settling the account can be a challenge when dealing with clients, particularly those who have had an unsatisfactory result. For practical reasons, consider collecting a flat fee or retainer at the outset of a case in order to avoid trying to collect money from a disgruntled client. Paying a paralegal's bill may not be a top priority for a client who has just been ordered to pay a large fine or been sent to jail.

Prior to closing the files, a paralegal should take time to organize the contents of the file and remove any unnecessary or duplicated information. Paralegals may want to keep copies of any information that could be used as precedents for future matters. However, always take care to ensure that personal information is removed from any precedents or examples in order to preserve client confidentiality. Paralegals should also consider keeping draft copies of documents that would help to establish the history or progress of a matter.

Retention of Closed Files

In most cases, files must be kept for a minimum of seven years. In their practice management guidelines,[3] the Law Society of Ontario provides additional information and the following reasons for retaining client files after the file has been closed:

1. Defend Against Claims and Allegations of Misconduct: In accordance with the limitation periods set out in *The Limitations Act, 2002*,[4] the client has an

---

3   Law Society of Ontario, *Guide to Retention and Destruction of Closed Client Files, For Paralegals*, online: <http://www.lsuc.on.ca/with.aspx?id=2147499378#_TOC_250002>.

4   SO 2002, c 24, Sch B.

opportunity to make a claim against the paralegal well beyond the closure of the file. Specifically, clients may have up to 15 years after the date that an act or omission took place (or longer if minors or the mentally incapable are involved). Retaining the file will allow a paralegal to access the information that they may need to respond to a negligence action, breach of contract claim, or a complaint to the Law Society of Ontario.

2. Legal Requirements: A paralegal should retain client documents in order to assist the client to meet the statutory requirements of the *Income Tax Act*.[5]

3. Comply with Regulatory Requirements: The *Law Society Act*, By-Law 9[6] requires paralegals to maintain specific books or records as part of their law office accounting system. Trust accounting records or documents must be kept for ten years from the paralegal's most recent fiscal year end. All other accounting records or documents must be kept for six years from the paralegal's most recent fiscal year end.

4. Future Use: The paralegal may decide to retain the file for future use by the paralegal or may agree with the client to retain the file so that it is available for future use by the client.

While closed files are retained for a long period of time, they do not need to be retained indefinitely.

Storage of Closed Files

Closed files can be stored either at the paralegal's office on-site or in an off-site location, but they must be securely stored separately from active files. When deciding where to store closed files, consider a range of factors, including space requirements, cost of storage, preservation of client confidentiality, protection from damage or loss, and the ease at which a closed file can be retrieved. Some paralegal offices will opt to store their files electronically. If that is the case, keep a backup of the information and assess whether or not it would be appropriate to encrypt stored files. The Law Society of Ontario indicates that paralegals should be prepared to convert older electronic formats to new formats so that the content continues to be accessible and that they should include the file format of the documents on any list of electronic files in order to facilitate conversion of the document at a future date.[7]

Destruction of Closed Files

Upon closing a file, the paralegal should determine a file destruction date for each individual file and implement a system for keeping track of the destruction dates of all closed files (e.g., tickler system). As the date approaches it is advisable to review the file contents and determine if the destruction date stands as is, or if it should be extended. Paralegals should shred any documents that contain personal information in an effort to preserve client confidentiality.

---

5 RSC 1985, c 1 (5th Supp).

6 RSO 1990, c L.8, s 62(0.1).

7 Law Society of Ontario, *Guide to Retention and Destruction of Closed Client Files, For Paralegals*, online: <http://www.lsuc.on.ca/with.aspx?id=2147499378#_TOC_250002>.

KEY TERMS

conviction, 154
dismissed, 154
withdrawn, 154

REVIEW QUESTIONS

Multiple Choice

1. In most cases, how long must files be kept?

   a. Two years.

   b. Five years.

   c. Seven years.

   d. Ten years.

2. Which of the following would NOT be considered a satisfactory result for most clients?

   a. Charges dismissed.

   b. Charges withdrawn.

   c. Charges stayed.

   d. Conviction.

3. Which party is able to dismiss the charges against a defendant at trial?

   a. Prosecutor.

   b. Justice.

   c. Provincial offences officer.

   d. Court clerk.

4. What does it mean when charges have been "stayed" against a defendant?

   a. The prosecution of the offence has been halted.

   b. Once charges have been stayed they cannot be recommenced.

   c. There will still be a conviction, but no record for the defendant.

   d. There will still be a conviction, but the fine is waived.

5. What does it mean when charges against a defendant have been dismissed?

   a. The prosecution has decided to withdraw the charges.

   b. There was not enough evidence to support a conviction.

   c. There will still be a conviction, but no record for the defendant.

   d. There will still be a conviction, but the fine is waived.

6. Which of the following statements is FALSE about the storage of closed files?

   a. Closed files can be stored in a paralegal's office on-site.

   b. Closed files can be stored in an off-site location.

   c. Closed files should be stored at the client's place of residence.

   d. Closed files must be stored separately from active files.

Short Answer

1. What steps should be taken if a paralegal becomes aware of an error or omission on a file?

2. List three things a paralegal should do before closing a file.

3. Why is it important to retain closed files?

4. What are some considerations for a paralegal who would like to store files electronically?

Reopenings and Appeals

13

LEARNING OUTCOMES

After reading this chapter, you will understand

■ when a reopening is appropriate;

■ the procedure for requesting a reopening;

■ the difference between reopenings and appeals;

■ when an appeal is appropriate; and

■ the procedure for bringing an appeal.

Introduction

In cases where a defendant has been convicted, it may be appropriate to consider a reopening or an appeal of the decision, depending on the circumstances. Reopenings and appeals differ in their availability, procedure, and outcome. Both processes are a request for a provincial offences decision to be reconsidered in some way, but the processes are used in different circumstances. A reopening can be requested for Part I and Part II matters where the defendant has been convicted without a hearing if specific criteria is met. An appeal can be brought for all procedural streams if there are sufficient grounds to do so.

Reopenings

The purpose of a reopening is to provide a procedure for a defendant to request that the court strike out an existing conviction and order a new trial. If the defendant in a Part I or Part II matter has been convicted of an offence without a hearing, you as a paralegal can help your client to apply to strike out the conviction and essentially have the proceeding start over. The key criteria to distinguish a reopening from an appeal is that the defendant must have been convicted *without a hearing*.

There are a number of situations where a conviction without a hearing may occur, including:

- The defendant did not respond to the ticket within the 15-day time frame and, as a result, the defendant was convicted for failing to respond.
- The defendant's response appears to have been lost in the mail or misplaced by the courthouse and, as a result, the defendant was convicted for failing to respond.
- The defendant filed a notice of intention to appear and a court date was set, but the defendant did not receive the trial notice in the mail and was deemed to not wish to dispute the charges, and a conviction was entered in his or her absence.
- The defendant filed a notice of intention to appear and a court date was set, but the defendant did not attend court and was deemed to not wish to dispute the charges, and a conviction was entered in his or her absence.

Pursuant to sections 11 and 19(1) of the *Provincial Offences Act*,[1] a defendant who seeks a reopening may apply at the court office to have the conviction struck out within 15 days of becoming aware of the conviction. Note that the time frame is within 15 days of when the *defendant learned of the conviction*, not within 15 days of the actual conviction. This is because in a situation where the defendant was convicted without a hearing, he or she would not have been present in court and it might take some time before he or she learns of the conviction.

Most defendants will become aware of a conviction when they receive a notice from the court setting out the fine and the due date. However, there may be situations

---

1   RSO 1990, c P.33.

where the defendant does not receive notice of the conviction (e.g., if the defendant is having problems with mail delivery or has moved) and might not become aware of the conviction until he or she tries to renew a driver's licence or validation sticker and discovers the existence of the conviction and outstanding fines.

To apply for a reopening, the defendant must complete the affidavit in support of a request for reopening (Form 102 under Regulation 200 of the *Courts of Justice Act* ["POA Rules"]) (see Figure 13.1). Since this document takes the form of an affidavit, it must be in the name of the defendant, not the legal representative.

The defendant is required to provide a reason on the affidavit for not attending the hearing by choosing one of two options:

- explain why he or she was unable to appear at the hearing through no fault of the defendant's; or

- identify a notice or document relating to the offence that was not delivered to him or her.

The onus is on the defendant to prove that one of these criteria is applicable.

In the case of a defendant who was unable to appear through no fault of his or her own, a reason must be provided supporting that claim. For example, a defendant who had car trouble on the way to court or had hired a legal representative who did not attend the court date may be successful in suggesting that the absence was not his or her fault. However, a defendant who simply states that he or she forgot about the court date or slept in may be considered at fault and therefore have difficulty obtaining the reopening.

Alternatively, a defendant can identify a notice or document relating to the offence that was not delivered, including the notice of trial. In such a case, the defendant would not have known about the court date. However, it is important to keep in mind that a defendant is obligated to provide the court with an updated address. A defendant who does not properly inform the court of a new address contributes to the non-receipt of the notice or document and may have difficulty obtaining the reopening.

The statements made on Form 102 must be truthful and sworn before a commissioner of oaths. In accordance with section 1 of the *Commissioners for Taking Affidavits Act*[2] and paragraph 4.1 of subsection 1(1) of Ontario Regulations 386/12, paralegals are considered to be commissioners for taking affidavits in Ontario by virtue of their office and can therefore provide this service to clients.

A reference to section 86 of the POA is included at the bottom of the form. It states:

Every person who makes an assertion of fact in a statement or entry in a document or form for use under this Act knowing that the assertion is false is guilty of an offence and on conviction is liable to a fine of not more than $2,000.

This is included as a warning so that defendants are aware that there is a penalty for falsifying information or lying on the form.

---

2 RSO 1990, c C.17.

Figure 13.1   Affidavit in Support of a Request for Reopening

AFFIDAVIT IN SUPPORT OF A REQUEST FOR REOPENING
AFFIDAVIT À L'APPUI D'UNE DEMANDE DE RÉOUVERTURE

ONTARIO COURT OF JUSTICE
COUR DE JUSTICE DE L'ONTARIO
PROVINCE OF ONTARIO
PROVINCE DE L'ONTARIO

Under Section 11 or Subsection 19(1) of the *Provincial Offences Act,* or
Section 205.13 or Section 205.23 of the *Highway Traffic Act*
En vertu de l'article 11 ou du paragraphe 19(1) de la Loi sur les infractions
provinciales *ou de l'article 205.13 de l'article 205.23 du* Code de la route

Form/Formule 102
Courts of Justice Act
Loi sur les tribunaux judiciaires
O. Reg./Règl. de l'Ont. 200

I,*Je soussigné(e)* _____

(Family/Company / *Nom de famille/entreprise*)   (Given/*Prénom*)   (*Initials/Initiales*)

Of:*de* _____

Current address/*adresse actuelle*   Street/*rue*   Apt. / *app.*   Municipality/*municipalité*   Province   Postal Code/
code postal

make oath/affirm and say as follows:
déclare sous serment et affirme ce qui suit:

1. I was convicted without a hearing on   of the offence of
   J'ai été reconnu(e) coupable sans la tenue d'une audience le: _____   *de l'infraction de* _____

   contrary to   section
   contrairement à la(au) _____   *article* _____

2.   (a) I was unable to appear at my hearing through no fault of my own because:
            Je n'ai pu comparaître à mon audience, sans faute de ma part, parce que:

        _____
            (state reason/*donner la raison*)
        or/ou

        (b) a notice or document relating to the offence was not delivered to me, namely:
            un avis ou un document concernant l 'infraction ne m 'a pas été livré, notamment:

        _____
            (identify document/*préciser quel document*)

3.   The conviction first came to my attention on:
        J'ai pris connaissance de la déclaration de culpabilité pour la première fois: _____

Sworn/Affirmed before me at: _____
Fait sous serment/affirmé devant moi à:

This _____ day of _____ , yr. 20 _____
le   *jour de*   *an*

_____   _____
A Commissioner, etc./*Commissaire, etc.*   Signature of Defendant/*Signature du défendeur/de la défenderesse*

NOTE: Section 86 of the *Provincial Offences Act* provides:
Every person who makes an assertion of fact in a statement
or entry in a document or form for use under this Act
knowing that the assertion is false is guilty of an offence
and on conviction is liable to a fine of not more than $2,000.

REMARQUE: *Selon l'article 86 de la* Loi sur les infractions provinciales

« Est coupable d'une infraction et passible, sur déclaration de culpabilité,
d'une amende d'au plus 2 000 $, quiconque affirme un fit dans une
déclaration ou l'inscrit dans un document ou une formule dont la présent loi
prévoit l'usage, et sait que cette affirmation est fausse. »

FOR INFORMATION ON ACCESS
TO ONTARIO COURTS
FOR PERSONS WITH DISABILITIES, CALL
1-800-387-4456
TORONTO AREA **416-326-0111**

POUR PLUS DE
RENSEIGNEMENTS SUR
L'ACCÈS DES PERSONNES
HANDICAPÉES
AUX TRIBUNAUX DE L'ONTARIO,
COMPOSEZ LE
1-800-387-4456
RÉGION DE TORONTO
416-326-0111

T (F) POA0801 CSD (Nov 2013)

Source: https://www1.toronto.ca/City%20Of%20Toronto/Court%20Services/Files/pdf/Application%20for%20Reopening%20a%20Conviction%20on%20an%20Offence%20Notice%20_NonFillable.pdf

A defendant must file the request for a reopening in person, but the defendant is not required to pay the fine at this time. He or she should be made aware that the conviction will stay on the defendant's record pending the justice's decision. Once the reopening has been filed, the defendant will have to wait a few days for a justice to review the application and consider whether to reopen the matter. If the defendant's request is denied, the conviction remains. Although there is no opportunity to appeal the decision made on a reopening, the defendant could consider whether he or she has grounds to bring an appeal of the conviction and/or the sentence.

If the conviction is struck, the defendant will be given a certificate of striking out conviction signed by the justice (Form 103 under the POA Rules). See Figure 13.2. The defendant returns to the position he or she was in before the conviction, such that the conviction will be removed from the defendant's record and the defendant will then have the option of pleading guilty with submissions or completing a new notice of intention to appear to request a trial date. If a trial date is requested, the original options are still available to the defendant, including negotiating with the prosecutor, pleading guilty, or pleading not guilty.

While Part I and Part II matters can either be reopened or appealed, Part III matters cannot be reopened, only appealed. A reopening is available only if the defendant has been convicted without a hearing. However, for Part III matters it is not possible to have a conviction without a hearing because the court holds an *ex parte* trial if the

Figure 13.2 Certificate of Striking Out Conviction

Source: https://www.niagararegion.ca/living/provincial-offences/pdf/POA-0827-certificate-of-striking.pdf

defendant does not attend court. Even though the defendant is not present at the trial, an *ex parte* trial is still classified as a hearing, so a conviction during an *ex parte* trial would be a conviction *with* a hearing.

PRACTICE TIP

It is important to recognize that reopenings are not routinely granted to every defendant who submits an application. Paralegals should give careful consideration for the reason behind the defendant's conviction and should recommend applying for a reopening only if the defendant appears to meet the criteria.

Appeals

An appeal is a request for a higher court to review a decision made by a lower court. The appeal procedure allows wrongful decisions to be rectified and sets out a process that is fair and provides access to justice. Part VII of the POA and Ontario Regulations 722/94 and 723/94 set out the rules regarding appeals. Part I, Part II, and Part III matters can all be appealed, but the process, procedure, and rules differ slightly in the case of Part III matters. In all cases, pursuant to sections 116(1) and 135(1) of the POA, the prosecution, defence, or the attorney general (by way of intervention) may consider whether it would be appropriate and permissible to bring an appeal if dissatisfied with the decision or the sentence. As a paralegal, you should be prepared to explain the appeal process and possible outcomes to your client.

Subsection 6(2) of the Law Society of Ontario's *By-Law 4*[3] establishes the permitted areas of practice for paralegals. Specifically, the by-law allows paralegals to represent clients in proceedings before the Ontario Court of Justice under the POA. Because most appeals take place in the Ontario Court of Justice, paralegals are regularly able to represent clients on the first level of appeals. However, it should be noted that if the appeal is in the Superior Court of Justice, paralegals cannot appear because this is outside of the paralegal's permitted scope of practice.

Notice of Appeal

The notice of appeal form is available from the court office. In the notice of appeal, the **appellant** must state what is being appealed and the grounds for appeal. For example, the defendant may indicate that he or she is appealing the conviction on the grounds that it was a wrong decision on a question of law.

appellant
the party bringing an appeal, either the defence or the prosecution

Before filing a notice of appeal, the appellant must pay the fine in full. If the appeal is successful or if the fine is reduced on appeal, the payment will be refunded accordingly. An appellant who is unable or unwilling to pay the fine in advance can file a form called an application to file appeal without paying the fine (see Figure 13.3). If the application is granted, a judge will order a recognizance to appear on the appeal,

---

3   Law Society of Ontario, *By-Law 4* (1 May 2007), online: <https://www.lsuc.on.ca/uploadedFiles/By-Law-4-Licensing-02-23-17.pdf>.

Figure 13.3   Application to File Appeal without Paying the Fine

---

APPLICATION TO FILE APPEAL WITHOUT PAYING THE FINE
DEMANDE D'AUTORISATION D'INTERJETER APPEL SANS PAYER L'AMENDE

ONTARIO COURT OF JUSTICE   *Provincial Offences Act, s.111*
COUR DE JUSTICE DE L'ONTARIO   Loi sur les infractions provinciales, *s.111*
PROVINCE OF ONTARIO   (Part I, II and III)   Court File No. / *N° du dossier de la Cour*
PROVINCE DE L'ONTARIO   *(Partie I, II ou III)*

1.   I, ...
        Je soussigné(e),

        of ....,
        de   (Address/*Adresse*)

        was convicted in the Ontario Court of Justice at ....
        ai été déclaré(e) coupable par le juge siégeant à la Cour de justice de l'Ontario à

        on the .... day of ...., yr. ...., of the offence of
        le   *jour de*   *an*   *, d'avoir commis l'infraction suivante*

        ....

        ....

        contrary to .... section ....
        contrairement à   (statute or regulation/*loi ou règlement*)   *article*

        and was sentenced to pay a fine of $ .... (including applicable costs, fees, surcharges).
        et le tribunal m'a ordonné de payer une amende de $ *(y compris les dépens, frais, suramendes).*

2.   Reason for application:/*Motif de ma demande d'autorisation d'interjeter appel :*

        ....

        ....

        ....

        ....

I request a .... language interpreter.
Je demande les services d'un   (leave blank if inapplicable/*à remplir, le cas échéant*)   *interprète de langue*

Copies given to: ☐ Prosecutor (in person or by mail)   **Prosecutor's Date Stamp**
Copies remises à :   *Poursuivant(e) (en personne ou par la poste)*   (if given to prosecutor in person)
                                                                                                          Timbre dateur du(de la) poursuivant(e)
                                                                                                          (si remises en personne au (à la) poursuivant(e))

                                  ☐ Clerk of the court (in person)   **Court's Date Stamp**
                                      Greffier de la cour (en personne)   *Timbre dateur du tribunal*

_____   _____
     Signature of Defendant/*Signature du(de la) requérant(e)*   Date

Note: Section 111 of the *Provincial Offences Act* provides:

(1) A notice of appeal by a defendant shall not be accepted for filing if the defendant has not paid in full the fine imposed by the decision appealed from.

(2) A judge may waive compliance with subsection (1) and order that the appellant enter into a recognizance to appear on the appeal, and the recognizance shall be in such amount, with or without sureties, as the judge directs.

(3) A defendant may file an application to waive compliance with subsection (1) at the same time as the notice of appeal.

(4) The defendant shall give the prosecutor notice of any application to waive compliance with subsection (1) and the prosecutor shall have an opportunity to make submissions in the public interest in respect of the application.

For further information, please visit the website http://www.e-laws.gov.on.ca/index.html

Remarque : L'article 111 de la Loi sur les infractions provinciales se lit comme suit:

1) *l'avis d'appel d'un défenseur n'est pas accepté pour dépôt s'il n'a pas payé intégralement l'amende imposée par la décision portée en appel.*

2) *Un juge d'appel peut dispenser l'appelant de se conformer au paragraphe (1) et lui ordonner de consentir un engagement à comparaître en appel. Le juge décide du montant de l'engagement, avec ou sans caution.*

3) *Le défenseur peut déposer une demande de dispense de conformité au paragraphe (1) en même temps que l'avis d'appel.*

4) *Le défenseur donne avis au poursuivant de toute demande de dispense de conformité au paragraphe (1), auquel cas le poursuivant a la possibilité de présenter, dans l'intérêt public, des observations concernant la demande.*

Pour en savoir davantage, visitez le site Web http://www.e-laws.gov.on.ca/index.html

For Court Administration Use Only/Réservé à l'administration du tribunal

This matter will be heard on ...., 20 ...., at ....
L'audience de cette question aura lieu le   *, à*

Courtroom No. ....
Salle d'audience n°

Dated on the .... day of ...., 20 ....   _____
Fait le   *jour de*   Clerk of the court/*Greffier*

Source: https://www.niagararegion.ca/living/provincial-offences/pdf/Application-to-File-Appeal-without-paying-the-Fine-POA-0226.pdf which is an acknowledgment that the appellant is obligated to appear at the appeal and will pay a specified amount of money if he or she does not appear. The judge has discretion to determine the amount of the recognizance and to order it with or without a **surety**.

surety
a person who guarantees the appellant's attendance at the appeal

Upon filing the appeal, a conviction is not automatically stayed unless ordered by a judge, pursuant to section 112 of the POA. Some clients would want the conviction to be stayed pending the outcome of the appeal, so it is good practice to request a stay of the conviction. An additional step is recommended for *Highway Traffic Act* convictions. Convictions, demerit points, and suspensions are not automatically stayed for driving offences unless the registrar of Motor Vehicles is served with a copy of the notice of appeal. Under section 5 of Regulation 339/94 of the *Highway Traffic Act*,[4] if the registrar is served with notice of the appeal, the conviction, demerit points, and suspension shall not be entered on the driver's record. If the conviction, demerit points, and suspension have already been entered when notice is served, they will be removed.

Since an appeal is considered to be a review of a previous decision, the appeal judge will typically review only the evidence and oral arguments that were presented at trial. In rare circumstances an appeal judge may allow **fresh evidence** to be introduced at the appeal. It is advisable to inform the court and the prosecutor if your intention is to introduce fresh evidence. Be prepared for the judge to inquire about the evidence, whether it was available at trial/why it was not introduced at trial, and how you expect it will impact the outcome of your case.

fresh evidence
evidence that was not introduced at trial, but was attempted to be introduced at the appeal

It is rare for witnesses, including the provincial offences officer, to appear at the appeal hearing. Instead the justice will make a decision based on transcript, written submissions and, if needed, oral submissions.

Part I or Part II

A notice of appeal must be served on the opposing party and then filed with proof of service with the clerk of the court in order to commence an appeal for a Part I or Part II matter. The document that is used for an appellant to give notice is the notice of appeal, which is Form 1 under Regulation 722/94 of the *Courts of Justice Act* (see Figure 13.4).[5] The notice must state the reasons for the appeal and be filed within 30 days of the court's *decision*. Note that it is within 30 days of the decision, not within 30 days of *learning of* the decision. If more time is required to prepare the appeal, the defendant may apply for an extension pursuant to section 85 of the POA. This involves completing the form called an application for extension of time to appeal, which is available at the court office (see Figure 13.5). Transcripts or factums are not required for Part I and II appeals unless requested by the judge, but some defendants may decide to provide these documents anyway. The case to follow examines the use of transcripts on a Part I appeal.

After the notice of appeal has been filed, the court clerk will give notice to the parties of the time and place for hearing the appeal.

---

4   RSO 1990, c H.8.

5   RSO 1990, c C.43.

Figure 13.4 Notice of Appeal for Parts I and II Matters

NOTICE OF APPEAL UNDER SECTION 135 OF THE PROVINCIAL OFFENCES ACT
AVIS D'APPEL INTERJETÉ AUX TERMES DE L'ARTICLE 135 DE LA
LOI SUR LES INFRACTIONS PROVINCIALES

ONTARIO COURT OF JUSTICE *COUR DE JUSTICE DE L'ONTARIO* PROVINCE OF ONTARIO *PROVINCE DE L'ONTARIO*	Parts I and II of the *Provincial Offences Act* *Parties I et II de la* Loi sur les infractions provinciales	**Form/Formule 1** *Courts of Justice Act* Loi sur les tribunaux judiciaires O. Reg. / *Règl. de l'Ont.* 722/94

1. Ontario Court of Justice at
   Cour de justice de l'Ontario à

2. Appellant is:/*La partie appelante est:*
   ☐ Defendant   ☐ Prosecutor   ☐ Attorney General
      le défendeur (la défenderesse)   *le poursuivant*   *le procureur général*

3. Name of Appellant:
   Nom de l'appelant(e):

   Address for service:
   Domicile élu :

4. Counsel for Appellant: Name:
   Avocat(e) de l'appelant(e): Nom :

   Address for service:
   Domicile élu :

5. Name of Respondent *(if known)*:
   Nom de l'intimé(e) (s'il est connu):

   Address for service:
   Domicile élu :

6. Counsel for Respondent *(if known)*:
   Nom de l'avocat(e) de l'intimé(e) (s'il est connu) :

   Address for service:
   Domicile élu :

7. Decision of Ontario Court of Justice:/*Décision rendue par la Cour de justice de l'Ontario:*
   (include name of Judge or Justice of Peace appealed from, if known /*inscrire le nom du juge ou du juge de paix dont la décision est portée en appel, s'il est connu*)

8. Date of decision:/*Date de la décision :*

9. The Appellant appeals against:/*L'appelant(e) interjette appel :*
   ☐ Conviction   ☐ Dismissal   ☐ Sentence
      de la déclaration de culpabilité   *du rejet de l'accusation*   *de la sentence*

10. If Appellant is in custody, place where held:
    Si l'appelant(e) est sous garde, lieu de détention :

11. (a) Description of offence[1]
        Description de l'infraction[1]

    (b) Certificate number *(if known)*:/*Numéro du procès-verbal (s'il est connu) :*

FOR INFORMATION ON ACCESS
TO ONTARIO COURTS
FOR PERSONS WITH DISABILITIES, CALL
1-800-387-4456
TORONTO AREA **416-326-0111**

POUR PLUS DE RENSEIGNEMENTS SUR L'ACCÈS
DES PERSONNES HANDICAPÉES
AUX TRIBUNAUX DE L'ONTARIO, COMPOSEZ LE
1-800-387-4456
RÉGION DE TORONTO **416-326-0111**

(Continued)

Figure 13.4   Notice of Appeal for Parts I and II Matters (*Continued*)

12. Statute[2]: _____
    Loi[2]

13. Date of offence: _____
    Date de l'infraction :

14. Plea at trial:
    Plaidoyer au procès :

    The plea entered was:
    Le plaidoyer inscrit :
    (check one / *cocher la case appropriée*)

    ☐ guilty   ☐ not guilty   ☐ not known
       coupable   *non coupable*   *non connu*

15. The Appellant wants the appeal court to:
    L'appelant(e) désire que le tribunal d'appel :
    (check one/*cocher la case appropriée*)

    ☐ Find the Defendant not guilty/*Déclare la partie défenderesse non coupable*

    ☐ Find the Defendant guilty/*Déclare la partie défenderesse coupable*

    ☐ Order a new trial/*Ordonne la tenue d'un nouveau procès*

    ☐ Change the sentence/*Modifie la sentence*

    ☐ Other:/*Autre:*
       (specify/*préciser*)

16. The grounds of appeal are:/*Les motifs d'appel sont les suivants :*

Complete No. 17 for *Provincial Offences Act*, Part II, parking Offences where the municipality is collecting its own parking fines.
Remplir le N°17 dans le cas des infractions de stationnement visées par la partie II de la Loi sur les infractions provinciales, lorsque la municipalité perçoit ses propres amendes de stationnement.

17. The fine has been paid in full at: _____ on _____
    L'amende a été payée intégralement à   (municipality/*municipalité*)   *le*   (date)

18. Date: _____

19. Signature of Appellant or Counsel or Agent: _____
    Signature de l'appelant(e) ou de son avocat(e) ou représentant(e):

I request a _____ language interpreter for the appeal.
Je demande les services   (leave blank if inapplicable/*à remplir, le cas échéant*)   *pour l'appel.*
d'un interprète de langue

NOTES:

(1) If Appellant's address for service is that of the Appellant's Counsel, state Counsel's full address and Appellant's own full address.

(2) Please notify the clerk of the court in writing immediately of any change of address. The court will communicate with you by mail at the address shown by you in this notice unless you notify the court of a change in your address.

(3) This notice of appeal must be filed with the local registrar of the Superior Court of Justice or Ontario Court of Justice.

Sections 111 and 112 of the *Provincial Offences Act* are as follows:

111. (1) A notice of appeal by a Defendant shall not be accepted for filing if the Defendant has not paid in full the fine imposed by the decision appealed from.

   (2) A judge may waive compliance with subsection (1) and order that the Appellant enter into a recognizance to appear on the appeal, and the recognizance shall be in such amount, with or without sureties, as the judge directs.

112. The filing of a notice of appeal does not stay the conviction unless a judge so orders.

REMARQUES :

1) *Si le domicile élu de l'appelant(e) est celui de son avocat(e), indiquer l'adresse au complet de l'avocat(e) de même que l'adresse au complet de l'appelant(e) lui-même(elle-même).*

2) *En cas de changement d'adresse, en aviser immédiatement le greffier du tribunal par écrit. Si le tribunal n'est pas avisé, il communiquera avec vous par courrier à l'adresse indiquée au présent avis.*

3) *Le présent avis d'appel doit être déposé auprès du greffier local de la Cour supérieure de justice ou de la Cour de justice de l'Ontario.*

Les articles 111 et 112 de la Loi sur les infractions provinciales se lisent comme suit:

111. 1) *l'avis d'appel d'un défendeur n'est pas accepté pour dépôt s'il n'a pas payé intégralement l'amende imposée par la décision portée en appel.*

   2) *Un juge d'appel peut dispenser l'appelant de se conformer au paragraphe (1) et lui ordonner de consentir un engagement à comparaître en appel. Le juge décide du montant de l'engagement, avec ou sans caution.*

112. *Le dépôt d'un avis d'appel ne suspend pas la déclaration de culpabilité à moins qu'un juge d'appel ne l'ordonne.*

[2]for example, *Highway Traffic Act*/*par example,* Code de la route

Figure 13.5 Application for Extension of Time to Appeal

APPLICATION FOR EXTENSION OF TIME TO APPEAL
DEMANDE DE PROROGATION DU DÉLAI D'APPEL

ONTARIO COURT OF JUSTICE
COUR DE JUSTICE DE L'ONTARIO
PROVINCE OF ONTARIO
PROVINCE DE L'ONTARIO

Section 85 of the *Provincial Offences Act*
O. Reg 723/94 (s.7), O. Reg 722/94 (s.8)
Aux termes de l'article 85 de la Loi sur les infractions provinciales,
Règl. de l'Ont. 723/94 (a.7), Règl. de l'Ont. 722/94 (a. 8)

Pursuant to Section 85(2) of the *Provincial Offences Act*, no more than one application for extension of time to appeal may be made in respect of a conviction.
Aux termes du paragraphe 85(2) de la Loi sur les infractions provinciales, pas plus d'une demande de prorogation du délai d'appel ne peut être présentée à la suite d'une déclaration de culpabilité.

1. I, ...
    Je soussigné(e)

    of ....
    de
    (occupation/*profession*)

    was convicted in the Ontario Court of Justice at ....
    ai été déclaré(e) coupable par le ou la juge siégeant à la Cour de justice de l'Ontario à

    on the .... day of .... , yr. .... of the offence of:
    le .... *jour de* .... *an* .... *pour avoir commis l'infraction suivante :*

    ....
    ....
    ....

    contrary to .... section ....
    contrairement à .... *article* ....

    and was sentenced to pay a fine of $ .... (including costs).
    et le tribunal m'a ordonné de payer une amende de $ *(y compris les frais).*

2. Reason for failure to appeal within allotted time:
    Motif du défaut d'interjeter un appel dans le délai imparti :

    ....
    ....
    ....
    ....
    ....
    ....
    ....
    ....

    I request a .... language interpreter for the appeal.
    Je demande les services (leave blank if inapplicable / *à remplir, le cas échéant*) *pour l'appel.*
    d'un(e) interprète de langue

    Dated at ....
    Fait à

    this .... day of .... , 20 ....   _____
    ce .... *jour de* ....   Signature of Applicant/*Signature du(de la) requérant(e)*

    Extension Granted ☐ (appeal to be filed within 30 days of approval date)
    Prorogation accordée (*l'appel doit être déposé dans les 30 jours qui suivent la date d'approbation*)

    Denied ☐
    Rejetée

    Dated on the .... day of .... , 20 ....   _____
    Fait le .... *jour de* ....   Judge/*Juge*

    FOR INFORMATION ON ACCESS TO
    ONTARIO COURTS
    FOR PERSONS WITH DISABILITIES, CALL
    1-800-387-4456
    TORONTO AREA **416-326-0111**

    POUR PLUS DE RENSEIGNEMENTS SUR
    L'ACCÈS DES PERSONNES HANDICAPÉES
    AUX TRIBUNAUX DE L'ONTARIO, COMPOSEZ LE
    1-800-387-4456
    RÉGION DE TORONTO **416-326-0111**

Source: https://www.niagararegion.ca/living/provincial-offences/pdf/Application-for-Extension-of-Time-to-Appeal-POA-0206.pdf

CASE IN POINT

Transcripts for Part I Appeal

R v Ovided, 2008 ONCJ 317, 91 OR (3d) 593

Facts

This case dealt with four unrelated defendants who were each convicted of a Part I offence or offences. Each defendant filed a notice of appeal, submitted requests for transcripts to support the appeal, and followed up with the court administration office to obtain the transcripts. The amount of time to receive the transcripts ranged from 15.5 months to 27 months. As a result, each defendant filed a notice of constitutional question and application seeking a stay of proceedings under section 7 of the Charter because of the lengthy delay in obtaining the transcripts. The prosecution's position was that since there is no mandatory transcript requirement for Part I matters, they cannot be faulted for a delay in preparing the transcripts.

Relevant Issue

Transcripts for Part I Appeal

Decision

The judge found that in order for the provincial offences appeal court to conduct a meaningful review of the proceedings giving rise to the appeal, a transcript of the trial needs to be produced. The lack of a mandatory transcript requirement does not mean that there is no need to prepare requested transcripts in a timely and efficient way. The judge concluded that the right to fundamental justice under section 7 of the Charter was violated as a result of the excessive delays in receiving the transcripts. Since the appellants had incurred additional costs as a result of the delays, they were each awarded $300 in costs. The appeals were allowed and a stay of proceedings was entered for each of the appellants.

Part III

For Part III matters, section 116(3) of the POA indicates that "the appellant shall give notice of appeal in such manner and within such period as is provided by the rules of court." In accordance with Regulation 723/94 of the Courts of Justice Act, the notice of appeal must be served on the opposing party within 30 days of the date of the decision. Then, within 5 days of service, the appeal must be filed with the court office (with proof that the opposing party has been served). As discussed for Part I and Part II matters, if more time is needed to prepare the Part III appeal, the defendant can apply for an extension under section 85 of the POA.

The required form for Part III appeals is Form 1, notice of appeal under Regulation 723/94 of the *Courts of Justice Act* (see Figure 13.6). The appellant must order a transcript of the original trail (most courts require that the transcript be ordered and paid for when the notice of appeal is filed). In many cases, a factum is not necessary (unless required by the presiding judge).

In accordance with section 110 of the POA, if a defendant is imprisoned for a Part III matter, the defendant will remain in custody pending the appeal unless a judge orders the defendant's release pursuant to the grounds set out in section 150(2).

Figure 13.6   Notice of Appeal for Part III Matters

NOTICE OF APPEAL UNDER SECTION 116 OF THE *PROVINCIAL OFFENCES ACT*
AVIS D'APPEL INTERJETÉ EN VERTU DE L'ARTICLE 116 DE LA LOI SUR LES INFRACTIONS PROVINCIALES

ONTARIO COURT OF JUSTICE *COUR DE JUSTICE DE L'ONTARIO* PROVINCE OF ONTARIO *PROVINCE DE L'ONTARIO*	(Part III) *(Partie III)*	**Form / Formule 1** *Courts of Justice Act* Loi sur les tribunaux judiciaires O.Reg. / Règl. de l'Ont. 723/94

1. **Superior/Ontario* Court of Justice/*Cour supérieure de justice/de justice de l'Ontario** at / à**

2. Appellant is/*La partie appelante est*

    ☐ Defendant
    le défendeur (la défenderesse)

    ☐ Attorney General
    le procureur général

    ☐ Prosecutor
    le poursuivant

3. Name of Appellant:
    Nom de l'appelant(e) :

    Address for service:
    Domicile élu :

4. Counsel for Appellant: Name:
    Avocat(e) de l'appelant(e) : Nom :

    Address for service:
    Domicile élu :

5. Name of respondent *(if known)*:
    Nom de l'intimé(e) (s'il est connu) :

    Address for service:
    Domicile élu :

6. Counsel for respondent *(if known)*:
    Nom de l'avocat(e) de l'intimé(e) (s'il est connu) :

    Address for service:
    Domicile élu :

7. Decision of Ontario Court of Justice/*Décision rendue par la Cour de justice de l'Ontario :*
    (include name of Judge or Justice of Peace appealed from, if known):/*inscrire le nom du juge ou du juge de paix dont la décision est portée en appel, s'il est connu) :*

8. Date of decision:/*Date de la décision:*

9. The Appellant appeals against:/*L'appelant(e) interjette appel :*
    ☐ conviction/*de la déclaration de culpabilité*
    ☐ dismissal/*du rejet de l'accusation*
    ☐ finding as to ability to conduct a defense/*de la conclusion quant à la capacité du défendeur (de la défenderesse) d'assurer sa défense*
    ☐ sentence/*de la sentence*
    ☐ order (s. 161 of the P.O.A.)/*de l'ordonnance (art. 161 de la L.I.P.)*
    ☐ any other order as to costs.

    by the Ontario Court of Justice/*de la Cour de justice de l'Ontario*

    at
    à/au
    (address of court/*adresse du tribunal*)

* Strike out inapplicable/
* *Rayer ce qui ne s'applique pas*

FOR INFORMATION ON ACCESS
TO ONTARIO COURTS
FOR PERSONS WITH DISABILITIES, CALL
1-800-387-4456
TORONTO AREA **416-326-0111**

POUR PLUS DE RENSEIGNEMENTS SUR L'ACCÈS
DES PERSONNES HANDICAPÉES
AUX TRIBUNAUX DE L'ONTARIO, COMPOSEZ LE
1-800-387-4456
RÉGION DE TORONTO **416-326-0111**

(Continued)

Figure 13.6 Notice of Appeal for Part III Matters (*Continued*)

10. If Defendant is in custody, place where held: ....
    Si l'appelant(e) est sous garde, lieu de détention : ....
    ....

11. (a) Description of offence[1]:/*Description de l'infraction[1] :* ....
    ....

    (b) Information number *(if known):* ....
    Numéro de la dénonciation (s'il est connu): ....

12. (1) Statute[2]:/Loi[2]: ....

    (2) Section[3] :/Article[3] : ....

13. Date of offence:/*Date de l'infraction:* ....

14. Plea at trial:/*Plaidoyer au procès:* ....

15. The grounds for appeal are:/*Moyens d'appel :*
    (specify the question of law or issue where the appeal is from conviction or acquittal or finding as to ability to conduct a defense or specify the ground for appeal against sentence/*préciser la question de droit ou la question en litige lorsqu'il est interjeté appel de la déclaration de culpabilité, de l'acquittement ou de la conclusion quant à la capacité de la partie défenderesse d'assurer sa défense, ou préciser les moyens d'appel contre la sentence)*

    ....

    ....

    ....

    ....

16. In support of this appeal, the Appellant relies upon the following:
    À l'appui du présent appel, l'appelant(e) se fonde sur les documents suivants :
    (set out documents such as transcript, etc. upon which the Appellant relies / *indiquer les documents, tels que les transcriptions, sur lesquels se fonde l'appelant(e))*

    ....

    ....

    ....

    ....

17. The relief sought is: ....
    Mesure de redressement demandée :

18. The Appellant intends:/*Intention de l'appelant(e) :*

    ☐ to be present in person or by counsel and to present the issues and the Appellant's arguments orally.
    comparaître en personne ou par l'entremise d'un(e) avocat(e) et débattre les questions en litige et présenter ses arguments oralement.

    ☐ not to be present in person or by counsel and to present the issues and the Appellant's arguments in writing.
    ne comparaître ni en personne ni par l'entremise d'un(e) avocat(e) et débattre les questions en litige et présenter ses arguments par écrit.

19. Does the Appellant intend to make a motion for an order that the appeal be heard by way of a new trial in the appeal court?
    L'appelant(e) a-t-il(elle) l'intention de présenter une motion en vue d'obtenir une ordonnance prévoyant la tenue de l'appel sous forme d'un nouveau procès devant le tribunal d'appel?

    ☐ Yes/*Oui*   ☐ No/*Non*

20. Date: ....

21. Signature of Appellant or Counsel: _____
    Signature de l'appelant(e) ou de son avocat(e) :

I request a .... language interpreter for the appeal.
Je demande les services _____(leave blank if inapplicable/*à remplir, le cas échéant)* *pour l'appel.*
d'un interprète de langue

NOTES:

(1) If Appellant's address for service is that of the Appellant's Counsel, state Counsel's full address and Appellant's own full address.

(2) Please notify the clerk of the court in writing immediately of any change of address. The court will communicate with you by mail at the address shown by you in this notice unless you notify the court of a change in your address.

(3) This court of appeal must be filed with the local registrar of the Superior Court of Justice or Ontario Court of Justice.

[1] for example, careless driving/*par exemple, conduite imprudente*

[2] for example, *Highway Traffic Act*/*par exemple,* Code de la route

[3] for example, Section 130/*par exemple, article 130*

REMARQUES :

1) Si le domicile élu de l'appelant(e) est celui de son avocat(e), indiquer l'adresse au complet de l'avocat(e) de même que l'adresse au complet de l'appelant lui-même (elle-même).

2) En cas de changement d'adresse, en aviser immédiatement le greffier du tribunal par écrit. Si le tribunal n'est pas avisé, il communiquera avec vous par courrier à l'adresse indiquée au présent avis.

3) Le présent avis d'appel doit être déposé auprès du greffier local de la Cour supérieure de justice ou de la Cour de justice de l'Ontario.

Grounds for Appeal

The notice of appeal must state the grounds for appeal. The POA sets out the types of appeals that can be brought, as well as the grounds for appeal.

For Part I and Part II matters, the defendant or the prosecution can appeal an acquittal, a conviction, or a sentence. Part III matters provide broader opportunities of appeal, including appeals of a conviction; a dismissal; a finding as to the ability to conduct a defence because of mental disorder; a sentence; or an order for costs.

The POA provides further guidance for Part III appeals. A conviction or a finding of ability to conduct a defence can be appealed on the grounds that the verdict is unreasonable or cannot be supported by the evidence. This may include the justice's failure to provide sufficient reasons or an error in findings concerning the credibility of witnesses. A conviction can also be appealed if there has been a miscarriage of justice or if there has been a wrong decision on a question of law. A wrong decision on a question of law can include interpretation of a case or statute, or admissibility of evidence.

An acquittal can be appealed by the prosecution if there are sufficient grounds to believe that the defendant was wrongly acquitted based on a question of law. The prosecution can appeal the sentence on the grounds that it is clearly unfit or unreasonable.

Procedure for Part I and Part II Appeals (Section 135 Appeals)

An acquittal, a conviction, or a sentence can be appealed for Part I and Part II matters. Although either the defence or the prosecution may decide to appeal the sentence (e.g., the prosecutor believes the sentence was too lenient; the defendant believes the sentence was too harsh), it would be the prosecutor who considers appealing an acquittal and the defence who decides to appeal a conviction.

Sections 135 to 139 of the POA set out the procedure for Part I and Part II appeals. With the exception of appeals by a young person, Part I and Part II appeals are heard by a provincial court judge in the Ontario Court of Justice. Appeals by a young person are heard in the Superior Court of Justice, but, in accordance with section 105 of the Act, the procedures and the powers of the court and any appeal from the judgment of the court are the same as if the appeal were heard in the Ontario Court of Justice by a provincial judge. However, paralegals cannot appear in the Superior Court of Justice.

While the court will give the parties an opportunity to be heard in order to determine the issues, the appeal is conducted by way of a review. In reviewing the original decision, section 136 of the POA indicates that the appeal judge can hear or rehear recorded evidence, require any party to provide a transcript or exhibit, receive evidence from any witness, and require the trial justice to provide a written report, or the appeal judge may make a decision based on agreed statements of fact or admissions. The following case examines the powers of an appeal judge on a Part I appeal.

CASE IN POINT

Powers of a Judge on a Part I Appeal

R v Michaud, 2015 ONCA 585

Facts

As a commercial truck driver, the defendant was required by law to equip his truck with a functional speed limiter set to a maximum speed of 105km/h. When his vehicle was inspected at a Ministry of Transportation inspection station the officer discovered that the speed limiter was set at 109.4km/h. The defendant was charged with two Part I offences under the *Highway Traffic Act.* At trial, the justice accepted the defendant's argument that the legislation under which he was charged violated the Charter and the defendant was acquitted.

The prosecution appealed to the Ontario Court of Justice. The defendant passed away before the appeal, but his wife was substituted as the party and the appeal proceeded. At the appeal, the judge admitted fresh expert evidence, found that there was no Charter violation, and set aside the trial decision. The defence appealed to the Ontario Court of Appeal on the grounds that the appeal court's Part I review powers do not permit an appeal judge to engage in extensive re-weighing of the evidence or to interfere with credibility findings. The defence argued that, in doing so, the appeal judge impermissibly conducted a re-trial.

Relevant Issue

Powers of a Judge on a Part I Appeal

Decision

The court ruled that once fresh evidence was admitted, the appeal judge was entitled, if not obliged, to consider it along with all of the other evidence. The justice was also required to consider whether the trial justice's views of the trial evidence were reasonable. The court indicated that the scope of a review by the Ontario Court of Justice on a Part I appeal is broad and that the legislature clearly intended Part I appeals to be conducted as robust reviews. The appeal was dismissed.

Procedure for Part III Appeals (Section 116 Appeals)

For Part III matters, the POA allows a conviction; a dismissal; a finding as to the ability to conduct a defence because of mental disorder; a sentence; or an order for costs to be appealed.

Sections 116 to 134 of the Act set out the procedure for Part III appeals. The court that will hear the appeal depends on whether the original decision was made by a justice of the peace or a judge. If the appeal stems from a decision of a justice of the peace, it will be heard in the Ontario Court of Justice by a provincial judge and can be handled by paralegals. If a provincial judge's decision is being appealed, it goes before the Superior Court of Justice, which is outside of a paralegal's scope of practice. Although some charging acts specify that a trial is to be conducted by a judge, most trials take place before justices of the peace and therefore most appeals will go to the Ontario Court of Justice, which is within a paralegal's scope of practice.

The court's powers for a Part III appeal are set out in section 117 of the POA. Specifically, the court has the ability to:

> (a) order the production of any writing, exhibit or other thing relevant to the appeal;
>
> (a.1) amend the information, unless it is of the opinion that the defendant has been misled or prejudiced in his or her defence or appeal;

(b) order any witness who would have been a compellable witness at the trial, whether or not he or she was called at the trial,

(i) to attend and be examined before the court, or

(ii) to be examined in the manner provided by the rules of court before a judge of the court, or before any officer of the court or justice of the peace or other person appointed by the court for the purpose;

(c) admit, as evidence, an examination that is taken under subclause (b)(ii);

(d) receive the evidence, if tendered, of any witness;

(e) order that any question arising on the appeal that,

(i) involves prolonged examination of writings or accounts, or scientific investigation, and

(ii) cannot in the opinion of the court conveniently be inquired into before the court,

be referred for inquiry and report, in the manner provided by the rules of court, to a special commissioner appointed by the court; and

(f) act upon the report of a commissioner who is appointed under clause (e) in so far as the court thinks fit to do so.

It is important to note that either the defence or the prosecution may make appeal arguments in writing instead of orally.

The court's options on an appeal depend on the type of appeal that has been brought. Section 120(1) of the POA sets out the court's powers when dealing with an appeal of a conviction and of a finding of the ability to conduct a defence. The court can allow the appeal or dismiss the appeal based on several grounds.

The court will allow the appeal if the findings are unreasonable or cannot be supported by the evidence, a wrong decision was made on a question of law, or a miscarriage of justice took place. If the appeal is allowed, the court can direct an acquittal or order a new trial. If the appeal is related to a finding of ability, the proper remedy is to order a new trial. An appeal of the conviction can be dismissed if the court believes that the appellant was properly convicted.

Where the appeal is against an acquittal, section 121 stipulates that the court may dismiss the appeal or set aside the acquittal. If the acquittal is set aside, the court can order a new trial or enter a finding of guilt and sentence the defendant.

The specifics of an appeal against a sentence are outlined in section 122. The court is obligated to consider the fitness of the sentence that is being appealed. It can then decide to dismiss the appeal or vary the sentence within the limits of the original charging act.

If the appeal is based on a defect with the information, the certificate, or the process, the judgment will be in the appellant's favour only if it can be shown that an objection was made at trial. An appeal can also be brought if there was a variance between the information, the certificate, or the process and the evidence at trial. In this case, the appellant can obtain a favourable judgment only if there was an objection at trial and a refusal to adjourn the trial, despite the variance.

Outcome of the Appeal

When the review is complete, the court has the authority to uphold, reverse, or vary the original decision, or to order a new trial. A new trial will be ordered only if it is necessary to satisfy the ends of justice. It will be held in the Ontario Court of Justice before a justice other than the trial justice, unless the parties consent otherwise.

If dissatisfied with the outcome of the appeal, a party can apply for **leave to appeal** to the Ontario Court of Appeal. Pursuant to section 139(1) of the POA for Part I or II matters:

> An appeal lies from the judgment of the Ontario Court of Justice in an appeal under section 135 to the Court of Appeal, with leave of a judge of the Court of Appeal, on special grounds, upon any question of law alone.

Or pursuant to section 131(1) for Part III matters:

> A defendant or the prosecutor or the Attorney General by way of intervention may appeal from the judgment of the court to the Court of Appeal, with leave of a judge of the Court of Appeal on special grounds, upon any question of law alone or as to sentence.

However, under sections 139(2) and 131(2), the grounds for leave to appeal can be difficult to satisfy. For Parts I, II, and III matters the leave to appeal to the Court of Appeal will not be granted unless the judge of the Court of the Appeal considers it essential in the public interest or for the due administration of justice that leave be granted. Part VII of the POA and Ontario Regulation 721/94 set out the rules that apply in the Court of Appeal. However, since paralegals are not permitted to appear on appeals before the Court of Appeal, the defendant would be required to self-represent or retain a new legal representative for the appeal.

leave to appeal
permission from the court to bring an appeal

KEY TERMS

appellant, 164
fresh evidence, 166
leave to appeal, 176
surety, 166

REVIEW QUESTIONS

Multiple Choice

The following scenario applies to questions 1-2:

Roy was convicted when his paralegal did not show up for trial. Roy fired the paralegal and retained a new paralegal to assist with a reopening for the matter.

1. How many days does Roy have to file the request for a reopening in this case?

    a. Within 15 days of the conviction.

    b. Within 15 days of learning of the conviction.

    c. Within 30 days of the conviction.

    d. Within 30 day of learning of the conviction.

2. Under whose name should the affidavit for reopening be filed?

    a. Roy's.

    b. The name of the paralegal who did not show up for trial.

    c. Roy's new paralegal.

    d. An affidavit is not used for a reopening.

3. Which of the following explanations would likely meet the requirements for a reopening?

    a. The defendant forgot to respond to the ticket within the 15-day time frame because she was very busy at work.

    b. The defendant missed her trial because she was rushed to the hospital for emergency surgery.

    c. The defendant mailed in a request for a trial, but it was returned to her for insufficient postage.

    d. The defendant missed her trial because she got lost on the way to the courthouse.

4. Which of the following statements is a correct statement about Part III matters?

    a. Part III matters can be reopened.

    b. Part III matters can be appealed.

    c. Part III matters can either be reopened or appealed.

    d. Part III matters cannot be reopened nor appealed.

5. For which procedural stream can an appeal be brought?

    a. Part I.

    b. Part II.

    c. Part III.

    d. All procedural streams.

6. How can Part III appeal arguments be made?

    a. Orally.

    b. In writing.

    c. Both orally and in writing.

    d. Neither orally nor in writing.

7. What options are available for a defendant who missed the deadline for filing an appeal?

    a. Can apply for an extension of time to file.

    b. Can swear an affidavit to prove the missed deadline was through no fault of the defendant.

    c. Can swear an affidavit to prove that the missed deadline was because a document relating to the matter was not delivered to the defendant.

    d. There are no further options.

The following scenario applies to questions 8–10:

Your client was convicted at trial before a justice of the peace for careless driving and fined $1,200. He has retained you to appeal the decision.

8. What is the appropriate court to hear this appeal?

    a. Ontario Court of Appeal.

    b. Superior Court of Justice.

    c. Ontario Court of Justice presided over by a provincial judge.

    d. Ontario Court of Justice presided over by a justice of the peace.

9. How much time do you have to file the appeal in this case?

    a. Within 15 days of the conviction.

    b. Within 15 days of learning of the conviction.

    c. Within 30 days of the conviction.

    d. Within 30 days of learning of the conviction.

10. Assume that the appeal is successful and a new trial is ordered. Unless otherwise agreed, the trial will be held:

    a. before the original justice who tried the defendant in first instance.

    b. before a Superior Court judge.

    c. before a Court of Appeal judge.

    d. before a justice, other than the original justice who tried the defendant in the first instance.

Short Answer

The following scenario applies to questions 1-5:

Gary was convicted by a justice of the peace on October 2 for "Fail to Yield to Pedestrian" contrary to section 144(7) of the *Highway Traffic Act*. At trial, he had tried unsuccessfully to quash his offence notice for a spelling error. He believes a wrong decision was made on a question of law and plans to appeal.

1. What is the deadline to file the appeal?

2. Which court would hear Gary's appeal?

3. Which type of justice would handle the appeal?

4. Can a paralegal represent Gary on the appeal? Explain.

5. If Gary's matter was further appealed to the Ontario Court of Appeal, could he retain the same paralegal? Explain.

6. After a defendant has been convicted and sentenced, which party is permitted to appeal the defendant's sentence?

7. Dawn was convicted of an environmental offence after a lengthy trial before a provincial court judge. She has retained a paralegal to represent her on the appeal. Which court would hear the appeal?

8. Is there an issue with Dawn's legal representation?

9. Explain why Part III matters cannot be reopened.

10. Marc contacted you for legal advice. He had been charged with using his cellphone while driving. He requested a trial by checking off the appropriate box on the back of his offence notice and mailed it to the address provided. Several months later, he was surprised to find out that he had been convicted of the offence. When he contacted the court office he was told that they never received his trial request. He was deemed not to wish to dispute the charge and convicted. Marc requested a reopening but it was denied. He has come to you two months later in order to appeal the reopening decision and see if there is anything else that he can do. What advice would you give to Marc?

11. You are retained by a taxi driver who is very concerned about having a conviction appear on his driving record because he does not want any demerit points. He has grounds to appeal his recent speeding conviction. What steps would you take to ensure that his driving record is not affected while waiting for the appeal?

Common Highway Traffic Act Offences

14

LEARNING OUTCOMES

After reading this chapter, you will understand

- the terminology used in the *Highway Traffic Act*;

- common offences under the *Highway Traffic Act*; and

- penalties associated with common offences under the *Highway Traffic Act*, including fines, demerit points, incarceration, and licence suspension.

Introduction

Most of the charges prosecuted in provincial offences court are laid under the *Highway Traffic Act* (HTA).[1] Because the HTA is provincial legislation, its provisions apply to drivers throughout Ontario. Each province has its own version of the HTA, which applies to drivers in those provinces. The offences and their wording vary from province to province. A slight change in the wording can alter how an offence is classified (*mens rea*, strict liability, or absolute liability) and can change the court's interpretation of an offence.

That slight change in wording or interpretation can also modify the defence(s) available for that charge. For example, in Ontario speeding is classified as an absolute liability offence, but in some of the other provinces it is a strict liability offence. Therefore, a driver in a province with a strict liability classification is able to justify his or her actions by demonstrating due diligence, but due diligence would be irrelevant in Ontario because of the absolute liability classification for speeding.

PRACTICE TIP

When conducting case research, be sure to check in which province the charges originated. You do not want to present an argument about an interpretation that is based on wording of a charge from a different province. If the case is from another province, it may be persuasive, but it would not be binding in Ontario.

The HTA is divided into the following parts:

Part I: Administration
Part II: Permits
Part III: Parking Permits
Part IV: Licences
Part V: Garage and Storage Licences
Part VI: Equipment
VII: Load and Dimension
VIII: Weight
IX: Rate of Speed
X: Rules of the Road
XI: Civil Proceedings
XII: Municipal By-laws
XIII: Suspension for Failure to Pay Judgments or Meet Support Obligations
XIV: Records and Reporting of Accidents and Convictions
XV: Procedure, Arrests and Penalties
XVI: Pilot Projects

---

1 RSO 1990, c H.8.

Of particular relevance to paralegals are Part IV, Part VI, Part IX, Part X, Part XIV, and Part XV (in bold above), with the majority of the offences that paralegals deal with in court itemized under Part VI, Part IX, and Part X.

There are more than 80 regulations made under the HTA. These regulations cover a wide range of driving-related matters. Some of the more commonly consulted regulations include display screens and hand-held devices;[2] races, contests, and stunts;[3] and red light camera system evidence;[4] however, it is advisable for paralegals to be familiar with all of the different regulations under the HTA because they are an important source of information.

Terminology

In order to understand the HTA, it is important to first examine some of the definitions found in section 1(1) of the Act.

Highway

> 1(1) ... "highway" includes a common and public highway, street, avenue, parkway, driveway, square, place, bridge, viaduct or trestle, any part of which is intended for or used by the general public for the passage of vehicles and includes the area between the lateral property lines thereof.

Although the common, everyday understanding of the word "highway" tends to be an expressway (e.g., a 400-series highway), the HTA broadens that definition to include all types of roads and some other areas commonly driven on. Case law helps to further define areas that are, and are not, classified as part of a highway.

The following is an example of an HTA section that specifies "highway":

> 130.   Every person is guilty of the offence of driving carelessly who drives a vehicle or street car on a highway without due care and attention or without reasonable consideration for other persons using the highway ... .

If the charging section of the HTA specifies that the prohibited behaviour must take place on a highway, as above, this offence only occurs when the behaviour takes place on areas that are included within the definition or interpretation of highway. For example, section 130 prohibits careless driving on a highway, but a charge could not be laid under this section if the motorist was driving carelessly in a parking lot, because a parking lot is not considered to be part of a highway. Other charges may be applicable in this example, but not a charge under section 130.

---

2   O Reg 366/09.

3   O Reg 455/07.

4   O Reg 277/99.

Roadway

> 1(1) ... "roadway" means the part of the highway that is improved, designed or ordinarily used for vehicular traffic, but does not include the shoulder, and, where a highway includes two or more separate roadways, the term "roadway" refers to any one roadway separately and not to all of the roadways collectively.

Notice that the definition of "roadway" does not include the shoulder of the highway; it only includes the part of the highway that is most commonly driven on. When "roadway" is used within a charging section, it means that the behaviour is not prohibited on the shoulder. If a section of the Act is intended to apply to motorists who drive on the shoulder, the charging section will specify "highway" instead of "roadway."

The following is an example of an HTA section that specifies "roadway":

> 147(1) Any vehicle travelling upon a roadway at less than the normal speed of traffic at that time and place shall, where practicable, be driven in the right-hand lane then available for traffic or as close as practicable to the right-hand curb or edge of the roadway.

This section prohibits a driver from travelling too slow in a "fast" lane of traffic (i.e., the left lane) and allows a slow-moving vehicle to travel in the right lane. By using the word "roadway," a motorist driving at below the normal speed of traffic on the shoulder would not be charged under section 147(1). Other charges may be applicable in this example, but not a charge under section 147(1).

Motor Vehicle

> 1(1) ... "motor vehicle" includes an automobile, a motorcycle, a motor-assisted bicycle unless otherwise indicated in this Act, and any other vehicle propelled or driven otherwise than by muscular power, but does not include a street car or other motor vehicle running only upon rails, a power-assisted bicycle, a motorized snow vehicle, a traction engine, a farm tractor, a self-propelled implement of husbandry or a road-building machine.

Based on the definition, a motor vehicle does not use muscular power. Therefore, charges in the HTA that apply to motor vehicles would not apply to any vehicle that does use muscular power (e.g., a bicycle).

The following is an example of an HTA section that specifies "motor vehicle":

> 165. No person shall,
>
> (a) open the door of a motor vehicle on a highway without first taking due precautions to ensure that his or her act will not interfere with the movement of or endanger any other person or vehicle; ... .

This section ensures the safety of approaching persons and vehicles. The term "motor vehicle" was likely used because vehicles propelled by muscular power do not typically have doors.

Case law helps to determine which vehicles are, and are not, classified as motor vehicles.

Vehicle

1(1) ... "vehicle" includes a motor vehicle, trailer, traction engine, farm tractor, road-building machine, bicycle and any vehicle drawn, propelled or driven by any kind of power, including muscular power, but does not include a motorized snow vehicle or a street car.

"Vehicle" encompasses more than "motor vehicle." It includes all vehicles that use any power, including motor and muscular power. Therefore, any sections in the Act that refer to "vehicle" are intended to apply to such things as bicycles and wheelchairs, as well as to motor vehicles.

If a section of the HTA is intended to apply to one of the excluded vehicles, the definition will be amended within the Act (e.g., section 144(1) specifies that "vehicle" will include a street car for that section, even though street car was excluded in section 1(1)).

The following is an example of an HTA section that specifies "vehicle":

163(1) When the driver of a vehicle is approaching a railway crossing at a time when a clearly visible electrical or mechanical signal device or a flagman is giving warning of the approach of a railway train, he or she shall stop the vehicle not less than 5 metres from the nearest rail of the railway and shall not proceed until he or she can do so safely.

This section ensures that all types of vehicles stop at a railway crossing. It is not limited to motor vehicles.

Driver

1(1) ... "driver" means a person who drives a vehicle on a highway.

While the definition is quite vague, case law has assisted with interpreting the term "driver." A commonly accepted definition would be someone exercising control over a vehicle and substantially controlling the movement and direction of a vehicle.

The following is an example of an HTA section that specifies "driver":

144(5) A driver who is directed by a traffic control signal erected at an intersection to stop his or her vehicle shall stop ... .

This section places the responsibility to ensure that a vehicle properly comes to a stop on the person in control of the vehicle (i.e., the driver). Therefore, the driver can be charged under section 144(5). Other sections in the HTA may specifically apply to passengers, occupants, or owners of vehicles.

Owner

The term "owner" is not defined in section 1(1) of the HTA, but the term is used in various sections to refer to the person who has registered ownership of the vehicle.

There are some offences where the owner can be charged instead of the driver. As an example, if a school bus driver makes note of a motor vehicle's plate number, the owner of the motor vehicle can be charged under section 175(19) if the driver failed to stop for a school bus.

Penalties

Fines

The set fines that have been established for Part I offences are intended to be used as the amount payable for out-of-court settlement (i.e., paying the ticket). Once a defendant proceeds to trial, the set fine is only persuasive and a different fine or fine range will apply in the event of a conviction. The set fines for HTA offences are listed in *Provincial Offences Act* RRO 1990, Reg 950, which is Schedule 43 for the HTA (see Appendix C, Set Fines from the *Provincial Offences Act* for the *Highway Traffic Act*).

The justice has discretion to order a fine up to the $1,000 maximum for Part I offences specified in the POA, unless otherwise stated in the HTA. Set fines do not apply to Part III offences. Instead, the justice has the discretion to order a fine of up to the $5,000 maximum for Part III offences set by the POA, unless otherwise stated in the HTA.

However, many—but not all—of the offences under the HTA have a specified fine range or a specified maximum fine that can be ordered upon conviction. If not specified in the charging section 214 of the HTA will apply:

> Every person who contravenes this act is guilty of an offence and on conviction, where a penalty for the contravention is not otherwise provided for herein, is liable to a fine of not less than $60 and not more than $500.

For maximum fines, the default provisions of the HTA override the statutory default maximums set out in the POA for both Part I and Part III offences. Therefore, unless otherwise specified in the HTA, the maximum fine for an HTA offence is $500. With regard to minimum fines, section 214 must be considered in conjunction with section 59(2) of the POA, which indicates that a court may impose a fine lower than the minimum fine where the court is of the opinion that exceptional circumstances exist. As such, in limited circumstances, a defendant could be ordered to pay a fine that is lower than the $60 minimum specified in the HTA.

Section 214.1 of the HTA deals with community safety zones and allows for increased fines for specified offences when an offence takes place in a community safety zone.

Demerit Points

An additional type of penalty, unique to highway traffic offences, is demerit points. Demerit points are administered by the Ministry of Transportation and not by the courts. Therefore, the prosecutor and the justice cannot take away or lower any demerit points that correspond with an offence.

It is a common misconception that drivers lose demerit points. A defendant who has been convicted of an HTA offence that carries demerit points will have the points added to his or her **driving record**. The points will stay on the record with the

driving record
a record of convictions against a driver maintained by the Ministry of Transportation

Ministry of Transportation for two years from the date of the offence. Accumulation of points will typically increase the driver's insurance rates and may lead to further penalties and involvement by the Ministry of Transportation. The following indicates the series of events that occur as demerit points are accumulated:

- 6 points: driver is advised of record
- 9 points: driver is required to attend an interview with the ministry
- 15 points: driver's licence will be suspended for 30 days

After a suspension, the number of demerit points will be reduced to 7. If the driver reaches 15 points again, his or her licence will be suspended for six months.

PRACTICE TIP

Many of your clients will be concerned about the demerit points associated with an offence—especially if they rely upon a driver's licence for their job and a "clean driving record" may be a condition of employment. It is important to try to negotiate with the prosecutor in order to get a reduced (included) offence that would result in fewer demerit points or no points for your client.

The demerit points that correspond with HTA offences are set out in Ontario Regulation 339/94 (see Appendix D, *Highway Traffic Act* Demerit Point System).

Additional Penalties

Some HTA offences specify that the defendant's licence may be suspended for a period of time. This typically applies to the more serious Part III HTA offences. For example, section 130 (careless driving) indicates that a defendant's licence may be suspended for a period of not more than two years, and section 172(2) (stunt driving) specifies a suspension for a period of not more than two years for the first conviction and not more than ten years for a subsequent conviction. In rare situations, a justice may order a lifelong suspension. For example, pursuant to section 216(4) a defendant who continued to avoid a police officer when the police officer gave pursuit (e.g., a police chase) may have his or her licence suspended for the remainder of the person's life.

Imprisonment is a possible penalty for some of the more serious Part III offences. For example, pursuant to section 172(17), obstructing or interfering with a police officer in the performance of his or her duties under section 172 can lead to a jail term of not more than six months.

Common Offences

Although it is beyond the scope of this text to discuss all of the charges listed in the HTA, the pages that follow are intended to provide an overview of some of the more common offences that paralegals are likely to defend against in provincial offences court.

Speeding

Although the term "speeding" is not defined in the HTA, a commonly accepted definition is "driving a motor vehicle at a rate of speed in excess of that permitted on the specified highway." The HTA sets out the rules pertaining to the offence of speeding:

128(1) No person shall drive a motor vehicle at a rate of speed greater than,

(a) 50 kilometres per hour on a highway within a local municipality or within a built-up area;

(b) despite clause (a), 80 kilometres per hour on a highway, not within a built-up area, that is within a local municipality that had the status of a township on December 31, 2002 and, but for the enactment of the *Municipal Act, 2001*, would have had the status of a township on January 1, 2003, if the municipality is prescribed by regulation;

(c) 80 kilometres per hour on a highway designated by the Lieutenant Governor in Council as a controlled-access highway under the *Public Transportation and Highway Improvement Act*, whether or not the highway is within a local municipality or built-up area;

(d) the rate of speed prescribed for motor vehicles on a highway in accordance with subsection (2), (5), (6), (6.1) or (7);

(e) the maximum rate of speed set under subsection (10) and posted in a construction zone designated under subsection (8) or (8.1); or

(f) the maximum rate of speed posted on a highway or portion of a highway pursuant to section 128.0.1.

Notice that in each of these paragraphs, the rate of speed applies to motor vehicles on highways (one exception: (e) applies to a construction zone). Therefore, someone driving a non-motorized vehicle, such as a bicycle, could not be charged with speeding under this section. Further, a police officer would not charge someone with speeding under section 128 if he or she was driving in an area that is considered a non-highway, such as a parking lot—although other charges may apply for speeding in a parking lot.

In most cases, a speed limit sign is posted to advise drivers on how fast they are permitted to drive. However, paragraphs (a) to (c) set the default rate of speed for a highway even if a sign is not visible—making it difficult for a defendant to argue that he or she did not know the speed limit or did not see a sign. Drivers are expected to know the rules of the road and the default rates of speed.

PRACTICE TIP

Take a close look at the offence notice. If the letter "R" is written in the Code box, it is unlikely that the prosecutor will reduce the defendant's alleged rate of speed. The "R" stands for "reduced," meaning that the officer already reduced the speed when the defendant was pulled over. Some officers will use this as a signal to the prosecutor to avoid a further reduction.

Commentary

There are four primary ways for the police to detect and measure the rate of speed:

1. *Laser*: The officer uses a device that sends infrared light pulses, which take a measurement based on the speed of light. Because multiple readings are taken in a second, the device is considered to be very accurate. The laser ("light amplification by stimulated emission radiation") device allows the officer to pinpoint one particular motor vehicle in a specific lane of traffic because the laser beam is very narrow. Typically, the laser device is mounted on a tripod because movement of the device can cause an inaccurate reading. The officer's evidence will include that he or she has been trained on the device and that the officer tested for correct readings by comparing readings for the laser gun to independent technology.

2. *Radar*: The officer uses a device that sends a radio beam and takes a measurement based on the speed of sound. While it is considered to be quite accurate, radar technology does not allow an officer to pinpoint a specific motor vehicle within a cluster of motor vehicles. Radar devices can be used as a hand-held device or mounted on the police cruiser's dashboard to take readings while the officer is driving. The officer must state in his or her testimony that the radar gun was tested and that he or she has been properly trained on how to operate it.

3. *Pacing*: The officer can follow directly behind a motor vehicle at the same speed and measure the motor vehicle's speed by the reading on the police cruiser's speedometer. Pacing is considered to be accurate as long as the officer keeps the distance between the motor vehicles constant and never loses sight of the defendant's motor vehicle. As well, the officer must give evidence that the officer's motor vehicle was reliably calibrated and tested to verify that the speedometer was in proper working order at the time of the offence.

4. *Aircraft*: There are signs along many Ontario highways that indicate speed can be detected by aircraft (e.g., a helicopter or fixed-wing plane). One officer will be in the aircraft and use a stop watch to measure how long it takes a motor vehicle to travel a predetermined fixed distance. If the officer in the aircraft determines that a motor vehicle is speeding, he or she will radio an officer on the highway to pull over the motor vehicle and issue a ticket.

Penalties

The set fines for speeding are listed in Schedule B of the *Provincial Offences Act* RRO 1990, Reg 950, which is Schedule 43 for the HTA (Appendix C in this text):

- 1 to 19 kilometres per hour over the posted speed limit = $2.50/km
- 20 to 29 kilometres per hour over the posted speed limit = $3.75/km
- 30 to 49 kilometres per hour over the posted speed limit = $6.00/km
- 50 kilometres per hour or more over the posted speed limit = no out-of-court settlement

It should be noted that when speeding takes place in a community safety zone or in a construction zone where a worker is present, the set fines are doubled, pursuant to Schedules D and E of Schedule 43 to the HTA.

The above amounts refer to the amount that appears on the offence notice and can be paid as an out-of-court settlement. Once a defendant takes the matter to court, the per-kilometre penalty for a speeding conviction increases, as set out in section 128(14):

> 128(14) Every person who contravenes this section or any by-law or regulation made under this section is guilty of an offence and on conviction is liable, where the rate of speed at which the motor vehicle was driven,
>
> (a) is less than 20 kilometres per hour over the speed limit, to a fine of $3 for each kilometre per hour that the motor vehicle was driven over the speed limit;
> (b) is 20 kilometres per hour or more but less than 30 kilometres per hour over the speed limit, to a fine of $4.50 for each kilometre per hour that the motor vehicle was driven over the speed limit;
> (c) is 30 kilometres per hour or more but less than 50 kilometres per hour over the speed limit, to a fine of $7 for each kilometre per hour that the motor vehicle was driven over the speed limit; and
> (d) is 50 kilometres per hour or more over the speed limit, to a fine of $9.75 for each kilometre per hour that the motor vehicle was driven over the speed limit.

It should be noted that when speeding takes place in a community safety zone, upon conviction the fines are doubled pursuant to section 214.1(6).

A higher per-kilometre penalty is charged for higher rates of speed. The actual offence is speeding; the rate of speed only determines the fine. Technically, driving even one kilometre over the posted rate of speed is considered to be an offence and a driver could be charged with speeding.

PRACTICE TIP

Caution your client about providing an estimate in court as to how fast he or she was driving. Defendants will sometimes take the stand and state that they were driving only five kilometres over the speed limit. This is an admission to the offence, because the offence itself is speeding; rate of speed only determines the fine. Your client should be careful not to give evidence that supports his or her own conviction.

Demerit points for speeding are based on the rate of speed, as set out in Ontario Regulation 339/94, as follows:

- 0 to 15 kilometres over the limit: 0 demerit points
- 16 to 29 kilometres over the limit: 3 demerit points
- 30 to 49 kilometres over the limit: 4 demerit points
- 50 and plus kilometres over the limit: 6 demerit points

For example, if a defendant had been driving 75km/h in a 50km/h zone, he or she would have been driving 25 kilometres over the posted speed limit, which would result in three demerit points. For speeding charges, the points automatically correspond with the number of kilometres over the limit. Neither the prosecutor nor the justice have the discretion to reduce or eliminate the points. However, negotiations with the prosecutor could lead to an amended speed that may correspond with fewer demerit points.

For speeding charges, it is not possible to receive just one or two demerit points. The points jump from zero to three which can make it difficult to negotiate a more desirable outcome for your client. A prosecutor may be willing to amend the charge and reduce the speed, but not always by an amount that would lower the demerit points to zero. However, there may be other offences within the HTA that correspond with the fact scenario and carry fewer demerit points. For example, a guilty plea to the offence of "disobey sign" under section 182(2) could be negotiated instead, because a driver who is speeding is also disobeying the sign that posts the speed limit. Therefore, when negotiating with the prosecutor, it is important to thoroughly review the HTA, looking for charges that fit your client's situation and carry fewer demerit points.

PRACTICE TIP

Caution your client that a decision to take a speeding charge to trial not only means a higher per-kilometre penalty, but also means that he or she could be faced with an "**amending up**" situation. This means that the trial would be based on the actual rate of speed that the defendant was driving instead of the reduced rate of speed specified by the officer when the charges were laid. The practice of amending up is permitted, as long as there is no prejudice or injustice to the defendant and the requirements of the POA are met.

amending up
the practice of having the defendant tried on the actual rate of speed instead of the reduced rate of speed specified by the officer when the charges were laid

CASE IN POINT

Amending Up for Speeding Offences

York (Regional Municipality) v Winlow, 2009 ONCA 643, 99 OR (3d) 337

Facts

The defendant was caught speeding on Highway 400 in York Region. The officer who stopped him indicated that the defendant was driving 30 kilometres per hour over the speed limit. However, the officer used discretion and charged him with travelling 15 kilometres per hour over the limit. At trial, the prosecutor sought an amendment to the certificate to specify that the defendant was driving 30 kilometres per hour over the posted speed limit. The justice refused to amend the charge. On appeal, the judge in the Ontario Court of Justice upheld the decision and refused to amend the certificate to reflect the original rate of speed. The prosecution appealed to the Ontario Court of Appeal.

Relevant Issue

Amending Up for Speeding Offences

Decision

The Court of Appeal ruled that the practice of amending up is permissible as long as there is no prejudice or injustice to the defendant and that the requirements of the *Provincial Offences Act* are met. The appeal was granted.

Racing, Contests, and Stunt Driving

Stunt driving is considered to be a serious Part III offence under the HTA. It encompasses a wide range of wrongful driving behaviours, including racing, and a number of behaviours that are classified as stunts.

Section 172(1) of the HTA states: "No person shall drive a motor vehicle on a highway in a race or contest, while performing a stunt or on a bet or wager."

The particulars of what constitutes racing and stunt driving are not within the HTA, but instead are set out in sections 2 and 3 of Ontario Regulation 455/07, as follows:

A race and contest, under section 2(1), includes any activity where one or more persons engage in the following driving behaviours:

1. Driving two or more motor vehicles at a rate of speed that is a marked departure from the lawful rate of speed and in a manner that indicates the drivers of the motor vehicles are engaged in a competition.
2. Driving a motor vehicle in a manner that indicates an intention to chase another motor vehicle.
3. Driving a motor vehicle without due care and attention, without reasonable consideration for other persons using the highway or in a manner that may endanger any person by,
    i. driving a motor vehicle at a rate of speed that is a marked departure from the lawful rate of speed,
    ii. outdistancing or attempting to outdistance one or more other motor vehicles while driving at a rate of speed that is a marked departure from the lawful rate of speed, or
    iii. repeatedly changing lanes in close proximity to other vehicles so as to advance through the ordinary flow of traffic while driving at a rate of speed that is a marked departure from the lawful rate of speed.

While most people tend to think of stunt driving as behaviour related to speeding or racing, it actually encompasses a wide range of different driving behaviours.

Stunts, under section 3, include any activity where one or more persons engage in the following driving behaviours:

1. Driving a motor vehicle in a manner that indicates an intention to lift some or all of its tires from the surface of the highway, including driving a motorcycle with only one wheel in contact with the ground, but not including the use of lift axles on commercial motor vehicles.
2. Driving a motor vehicle in a manner that indicates an intention to cause some or all of its tires to lose traction with the surface of the highway while turning.
3. Driving a motor vehicle in a manner that indicates an intention to spin it or cause it to circle, without maintaining control over it.
4. Driving two or more motor vehicles side by side or in proximity to each other, where one of the motor vehicles occupies a lane of traffic or other portion of the highway intended for use by oncoming traffic for a period of time that is longer than is reasonably required to pass another motor vehicle.

5. Driving a motor vehicle with a person in the trunk of the motor vehicle.
6. Driving a motor vehicle while the driver is not sitting in the driver's seat.
7. Driving a motor vehicle at a rate of speed that is 50 kilometres per hour or more over the speed limit.
8. Driving a motor vehicle without due care and attention, without reasonable consideration for other persons using the highway or in a manner that may endanger any person by,

  i. driving a motor vehicle in a manner that indicates an intention to prevent another vehicle from passing,

  ii. stopping or slowing down a motor vehicle in a manner that indicates the driver's sole intention in stopping or slowing down is to interfere with the movement of another vehicle by cutting off its passage on the highway or to cause another vehicle to stop or slow down in circumstances where the other vehicle would not ordinarily do so,

  iii. driving a motor vehicle in a manner that indicates an intention to drive, without justification, as close as possible to another vehicle, pedestrian or fixed object on or near the highway, or

  iv. making a left turn where,

  (A) the driver is stopped at an intersection controlled by a traffic control signal system in response to a circular red indication;

  (B) at least one vehicle facing the opposite direction is similarly stopped in response to a circular red indication; and

  (C) the driver executes the left turn immediately before or after the system shows only a circular green indication in both directions and in a manner that indicates an intention to complete or attempt to complete the left turn before the vehicle facing the opposite direction is able to proceed straight through the intersection in response to the circular green indication facing that vehicle.

Commentary

The sections of the HTA that deal with stunt driving came into effect in September 2007. Initially, many of the charges under section 172 of the HTA were laid for stunt driving by speeding. At the trial level, since it involved an excessive rate of speed, justices typically treated the offence as an absolute liability offence, like speeding. However, because a jail term is a possible penalty, an absolute liability classification is contrary to section 7 of the *Canadian Charter of Rights and Freedoms* [the Charter],[5] which guarantees life, liberty, and security of the person. The possibility of being absolutely liable and going to jail without being able to thoroughly defend oneself is contrary to the Charter. As a result, in 2010 the Ontario Court of Appeal classified stunt driving, under section 172 of the HTA, as a strict liability offence—which gives defendants an opportunity to raise a due diligence defence. See *R v Raham*, Case in Point in Chapter 7.

---

5 Part I of the *Constitution Act, 1982*, being Schedule B to the *Canada Act 1982* (UK), 1982, c 11.

Penalties

The possible penalties for racing, contests, and stunt driving are set out in section 172 of the HTA:

- an immediate seven-day driver's licence roadside suspension (defendant has to go to the Ministry of Transportation and pay a fee to get the licence back);
- a seven-day vehicle impound (defendant is responsible to pay the costs for towing and storage of the impounded vehicle);
- a minimum fine of $2,000 to a maximum of $10,000;
- a jail term for up to six months; or
- a driver's licence suspension for up to two years on a first conviction.

In addition, a conviction under section 172 results in six demerit points.

It should be noted that when stunt driving takes place in a community safety zone the minimum fine is increased. Upon conviction the defendant will be liable to a fine of not less than double the minimum set fine and not more than the maximum set fine.

PRACTICE TIP

If your client has been charged with stunt driving because they were exceeding the speed limit by 50km/h or more, discuss the various options available to your client, which may include trying to negotiate a deal with the prosecutor for a plea of guilty to the offence of speeding. Speeding is considered to be an included offence of stunt driving and carries only a fine and demerit points as the possible penalties.

Stop Signs

Section 136(1) of the HTA sets out the requirements for obeying stop signs:

136(1) Every driver or street car operator approaching a stop sign at an intersection,
(a) shall stop his or her vehicle or street car at a marked stop line or, if none, then immediately before entering the nearest crosswalk or, if none, then immediately before entering the intersection; and
(b) shall yield the right of way to traffic in the intersection or approaching the intersection on another highway so closely that to proceed would constitute an immediate hazard and, having so yielded the right of way, may proceed.

This section states that drivers must stop their vehicles at a stop sign and also indicates where, physically, they must stop. It also specifies the requirement of yielding the right-of-way, when appropriate. Therefore, a charge under section 136(1) is not necessarily laid because the defendant did not come to a stop; charges can be laid for other wrongful driving behaviour at a stop sign.

Commentary

There is nothing in the wording of this section to indicate how long drivers must stop at a stop sign. It is a common misconception that drivers are required to stop their vehicle for a specified amount of time. The requirement is for drivers to come to a full and complete stop, which is not a "rolling stop." Drivers must also be mindful of where to stop—a charge can be laid based on how far away they stop from the stop line or intersection. Since it is an absolute liability offence, it is not relevant to indicate that a driver intended to stop or attempted to stop.

Penalties

As set out in Schedule 43 to the HTA, the set fine for failing to stop, stopping at the wrong place, or failing to yield at a stop sign is $85. The schedule also includes the set fines if the offence takes place in a community safety zone. A driver who stops in the wrong place in such a zone will face a $120 set fine, while those who fail to stop or to yield in a community safety zone face a set fine of $150.

There is no minimum fine or fine range specified for this offence. Therefore, upon conviction, the default range specified in section 214 of the HTA will apply.

Three demerit points are associated with this charge. Some prosecutors may consider negotiating a lesser and included offence with no demerit points, but it is discretionary.

Traffic Lights

Section 144 of the HTA deals with traffic control signals, otherwise known as stop lights or traffic lights. Within this section are many different subsections setting out the various behaviours that are prohibited at traffic lights, including charges that involve motor vehicles, pedestrians, and cyclists.

Much like the stop sign offence, this section sets out not only the need to come to a stop, but also where on the road the driver is expected to stop the vehicle. According to section 144(5) of the HTA:

> 144(5) A driver who is directed by a traffic control signal erected at an intersection to stop his or her vehicle shall stop,
>   (a) at the sign or roadway marking indicating where the stop is to be made;
>   (b) if there is no sign or marking, immediately before entering the nearest crosswalk; or
>   (c) if there is no sign, marking or crosswalk, immediately before entering the intersection.

Not only must a driver stop at a traffic control signal when the light is red, but according to the HTA, a driver must also stop when the light is amber (yellow) if it is safe to do so. As set out in section 144(15):

> 144(15) Every driver approaching a traffic control signal showing a circular amber indication and facing the indication shall stop his or her vehicle if he or she can do so safely, otherwise he or she may proceed with caution.

If a driver is charged under section 144(15), the officer must have believed that he or she could have stopped safely or did not proceed with caution through the intersection. An accident could be caused by not proceeding with caution.

Section 144(18) deals with coming to a stop for a red traffic light. This section states:

> 144(18) Every driver approaching a traffic control signal showing a circular red indication and facing the indication shall stop his or her vehicle and shall not proceed until a green indication is shown.

Commentary

A variety of charges can be laid for a violation at a traffic light. While drivers understand the need to stop at a red light, many seem to believe that an amber light means to slow down or speed up—not realizing that it also means to stop as long as it is safe to do so.

Penalties

The set fines under section 144 vary across the different subsections. The common charge of failing to stop under section 144(18) has a set fine of $260. But if the offence takes place in a community safety zone, the set fine rises to $400.

While most of the subsections do not have a minimum fine or fine range specified, section 144(31.2) prescribes the fine range of $150-$500 on a conviction for disobeying an amber light under subsection (15), and section 144(31.2.1) sets out the fine range of $200-$1,000 on a conviction for disobeying a red light. The other subsections use the default range specified in section 214 of the HTA.

While some of the offences outlined in the subsections to section 144 do not have demerit points, other subsections have two or three demerit points. For example, a charge under section 144(18) carries three demerit points, but a charge under section 144(5) carries none.

> **PRACTICE TIP**
>
> If your client has been charged under section 144, carefully review all of the other subsections to determine whether a different subsection could apply. Recommending a subsection to the prosecutor that is worded in a slightly different manner could result in a lesser penalty for your client.

Red Light Cameras

The offence of failing to stop at a red light and being detected by a red light camera, instead of by a police officer, is set out in section 144(18.1), which states:

> 144(18.1) A person who issues a certificate of offence and offence notice under subsection 3(2) of the *Provincial Offences Act* for a contravention of subsection (18)

shall, despite that Act and the regulations under that Act, specify this subsection, instead of subsection (18), as the provision that was contravened, if,

    (a) the person who issues the certificate of offence and offence notice believes that the offence was committed on the basis of evidence obtained through the use of a red light camera system; and

    (b) the defendant is being charged as the owner of the vehicle.

If the red light camera photographs a driver who does not stop at an intersection, the owner of the vehicle will be served with an offence notice by mail, pursuant to section 144(18.1) of the HTA. While section 144(18.2) does allow for the driver to be charged, it is usually the owner who will be charged. This is because the owner of the vehicle can easily be identified through a Ministry of Transportation search, but it would be very difficult to identify who was driving the vehicle at the time of the offence.

The offence notice contains a series of photographs of the vehicle as it crossed into and proceeded through the intersection. Each photograph is marked with rows of codes, symbols, and abbreviations that provide information about the commission of the offence, including the time, date, the length of time that the indication was showing red/amber before the photo was taken, and the speed of the vehicle. The interpretation guide for this coding system is described in sections 3(1) and 3.1-3.3 of Ontario Regulation 277/99.

Commentary

In response to an increase in "red light running" and in an effort to increase road safety, red light camera intersections were introduced in Ontario in 2000. Not all municipalities use cameras at their intersections, but as listed in section 1.1 of Ontario Regulation 277/99, red light cameras are currently being used in: Halton, Hamilton, London, Ottawa, Peel, Toronto, Waterloo, and York regions.

Designated intersections have a posted sign to indicate that it is a red light camera intersection. An offence takes place if a vehicle enters the intersection after the traffic light has turned red. The camera will take a series of photos of any vehicle that enters the intersection on red. Entering the intersection on an amber light will not trigger the camera and will not result in a charge. Similarly, a driver already in the intersection (e.g., waiting to turn left) when the light changed to red will not trigger the red light camera.

Section 2(4) of Ontario Regulation 277/99 states that a red light camera system may be permanently or temporarily installed at an intersection. This allows cameras to be rotated throughout designated intersections, so not necessarily all of the intersections will have an active camera at all times. Since drivers can never really be certain whether there is an active camera at an intersection, it has a deterrent effect and drivers are reluctant to run a red light.

The procedures for red light camera offences are different from other HTA offences. Ontario Regulation 277/99 provides the unique procedures and time frames for service of the offence notice. For example, the offence notice must be sent by mail or courier within 23 days after the occurrence and it is deemed to be effected on the seventh day following the day on which it was mailed or couriered.

Section 205 of the HTA sets the unique rule for evidence at trial. For example, section 205.21(1) indicates that the certified statements in a certificate of offence are admissible in evidence as proof, and in accordance with section 205.20(1) and section 205.20(2), the officer is not required to give oral evidence at trial.

Penalty

Although the set fine of $260 is the same as when a red light charge is laid by a police officer, it would not be reasonable to penalize the owner with demerit points, because the owner has no direct control over or responsibility for how the driver operates the vehicle. Therefore, there are no demerit points for a red light camera offence.

There is no minimum fine or fine range specified for this offence. Therefore, upon conviction, the default range specified in section 214 of the HTA will apply.

Improper Turn

The offence of making an improper turn is addressed in section 141 of the HTA. Under subsections (2) and (3), a driver who wants to turn right at an intersection must approach the intersection in the right lane and turn into the right lane. If there are multiple marked turn lanes, the driver must stay in the corresponding lane while making the turn.

For left turns, subsection (5) states: "No driver or operator of a vehicle in an intersection shall turn left across the path of a vehicle approaching from the opposite direction unless he or she has afforded a reasonable opportunity to the driver or operator of the approaching vehicle to avoid a collision." Subsection (6) sets out the proper lanes from which to make a turn, so that the driver approaches the intersection immediately to the right of the centre line of the highway and turns left into the corresponding lane.

Commentary

Improper turns usually fall under the HTA, while illegal turns often come under a municipal by-law. For example, a municipality may prohibit left-hand turns during rush hour, making it an illegal turn and leading to a charge under a local by-law. But if a driver turned into the wrong lane, it would likely be an improper turn and bring a charge under the HTA.

Penalties

The set fines vary for the type of improper turn. In many cases, the set fine is $85, but if the offence takes place in a community safety zone, the set fine is either $120 or $150, depending on the circumstances.

There is no minimum fine or fine range specified for this offence. Therefore, upon conviction, the default range specified in section 214 of the HTA will apply. Most of the improper turn offences come with two demerit points. An exception is an improper turn that results in a collision, which carries three demerit points.

Following Too Closely

Provisions in the HTA that govern following too closely are found in section 158, entitled "Headway of Motor Vehicles."

General Provisions

Section 158(1) sets out the general provisions:

> 158(1) The driver of a motor vehicle or street car shall not follow another vehicle or street car more closely than is reasonable and prudent having due regard for the speed of the vehicle and the traffic on and the conditions of the highway.

COMMENTARY

Many drivers charged with this offence have been involved in a rear-end collision. The police officer who attends to the accident scene will examine the position of the vehicles, the damage to the vehicles, and tire marks on the road, and then talk to witnesses. From there, the officer may deduce that a motor vehicle was following another vehicle too closely, because the driver was unable to stop in time. In most cases, the officer has not actually witnessed the accident, and the other driver and civilian witnesses will be asked to testify for the prosecution in court.

The wording of this subsection also allows an officer to lay charges if a motor vehicle was tailgating another vehicle. However, it can be difficult for a prosecutor to prove the elements of the offence because section 158(1) does not specify what distance would be considered too close. Without a specified distance, the appropriate distance will vary from situation to situation.

Notice that this subsection refers to reasonableness and considers the conditions of the highway. There is substantial opportunity to defend this charge because it provides subjective standards and because it is classified as a strict liability offence, which means that the defence of due diligence is available.

Commercial Motor Vehicles

In accordance with section 158(2), a different standard applies to commercial motor vehicles:

> 158(2) The driver of a commercial motor vehicle when driving on a highway at a speed exceeding 60 kilometres per hour shall not follow within 60 metres of another motor vehicle, but this shall not be construed to prevent a commercial motor vehicle overtaking and passing another motor vehicle.

COMMENTARY

The wording of this subsection provides an objective standard for commercial motor vehicles by setting out a specific rate of speed and distance.

PRACTICE TIP

Be sure to listen to the officer's evidence as to how he or she determined that the distance between the vehicles was 60 metres or less. Depending on his or her explanation, you may be able to build a defence around the reliability of the evidence.

Penalties

The set fine for both commercial and non-commercial motor vehicles is $85, or $120 if the offence takes place in a community safety zone. There is no minimum fine or fine range specified for this offence. Therefore, upon conviction, the default range specified in section 214 of the HTA will apply. This offence also carries four demerit points.

Careless Driving

Section 130 of the HTA sets out careless driving as follows:

> 130. Every person is guilty of the offence of driving carelessly who drives a vehicle or street car on a highway without due care and attention or without reasonable consideration for other persons using the highway ... .

It is important to note that the offence of careless driving is for a "vehicle," not a "motor vehicle," so that a cyclist could be charged with careless driving. As well, note that the offence must take place on a highway.

Commentary

The broad wording of this section means that a wide range of behaviours could fall within the requirements of "without due care and attention" or "without reasonable consideration." Examples include shaving while driving, cutting off another driver, falling asleep at the wheel, and hitting a parked car.

Penalties

Careless driving is considered to be one of the more serious charges in the HTA. The officer has discretion to lay charges under Part I or Part III. The officer would likely opt for Part III charges if there is an accident or serious injury, if the officer wants to require a court appearance, or if the offence takes place in a community safety zone.

The set fine when a careless driving charge is laid under Part I is $400 plus six demerit points. Most drivers will be more concerned about the points than the fine because the number of points for this offence is significant, especially for insurance purposes. A defendant who does not resolve this charge out of court will face a fine in the range of $400 to $1,000.

Defendants charged under Part III do not have an opportunity for out-of-court settlement and will be summoned to attend court. Upon conviction, they will face a fine in the range of $400 to $2,000, at the justice's discretion. A conviction under Part III also brings six demerit points, plus the possibility of up to six months in jail and a driver's licence suspension of up to two years.

It should be noted that when careless driving takes place in a community safety zone, the minimum fine is increased. Upon conviction the defendant will be liable to a fine of not less than double the minimum set fine and not more than the maximum set fine.[6]

PRACTICE TIP

Because a careless driving conviction results in six demerit points and a significant increase in insurance rates, it is a good idea to try to negotiate with the prosecutor. You may be able to negotiate a guilty plea to an included offence that carries fewer points. Depending on the facts of the defendant's case, some of the relevant included offences for careless driving may include:

- follow too closely;
- improper lane change;
- turn not in safety;
- fail to yield; and
- fail to drive in marked lane.

Fail to Report

Section 199(1) sets out the duty to report an accident:

> 199(1) Every person in charge of a motor vehicle or street car who is directly or indirectly involved in an accident shall, if the accident results in personal injuries or in damage to property apparently exceeding an amount prescribed by regulation, report the accident forthwith to the nearest police officer and furnish him or her with the information concerning the accident as may be required by the officer under subsection (3).

This section places a special legal obligation on drivers involved in accidents. Not only must they report the accident to the police, but they must report it immediately and without delay.

Notice that there is no requirement that the accident take place on a highway. That means a driver could be charged under section 199(1) even if the accident occurred

---

6 In the fall of 2017, the Ontario government is expected to introduce proposed legislation that would add a new offence to the HTA. Specifically, it is anticipated that a charge of "careless driving causing bodily harm or death" will be added to the HTA with penalties of between $2,000 and $50,000, up to two years in jail, and a licence suspension for up to five years.

in a parking lot. The duty to report also applies to drivers who are indirectly involved in an accident, such as a driver who cut off another vehicle, causing an accident.

Commentary

The amount of damage to property that triggers this duty is set out in Regulation 596, which currently states that "the prescribed amount for damage to property is $1,000."

Therefore, a reasonable inspection must take place, and if the damage is more than $1,000, the accident must be reported. In many cases, drivers will report the accident to a collision reporting centre instead of calling an officer to the scene.

Penalties

Three demerit points accompany a charge under section 199(1), as well as a set fine of $85. There is no minimum fine or fine range specified for this offence. Therefore, upon conviction, the default range specified in section 214 of the HTA will apply.

Fail to Remain

Section 200(1) of the HTA deals with the duty to remain at the scene of an accident:

> 200(1) Where an accident occurs on a highway, every person in charge of a vehicle or street car that is directly or indirectly involved in the accident shall,
> (a) remain at or immediately return to the scene of the accident;
> (b) render all possible assistance; and
> (c) upon request, give in writing to anyone sustaining loss or injury or to any police officer or to any witness his or her name, address, driver's licence number and jurisdiction of issuance, motor vehicle liability insurance policy insurer and policy number, name and address of the registered owner of the vehicle and the vehicle permit number.

The duty to remain at the scene of an accident, under section 200(1), applies only if the accident occurs on a highway. It pertains to all vehicles at the scene, whether directly or indirectly involved. Because there is no threshold amount, the duty to remain begins as soon as there is an accident and is not connected to the seriousness of the accident. It should be noted that leaving the scene of an accident that did not occur on a highway could also lead to criminal charges and/or a civil lawsuit.

Commentary

Not only does the driver have a duty to remain, but he or she also has a duty to assist and to provide particulars. In defending this strict liability offence, a paralegal should consider why the defendant left the scene and the reasonableness of that decision.

Penalties

This is considered to be a very serious charge. The fine ranges from $400 to $2,000, but because there is no set fine available, the charges will be laid under Part III. A jail term of up to six months is also possible. The driver's licence may be suspended for up to two years, or seven demerit points will be added to the defendant's driving record.

Fail to Pull Over for a Police Officer

Section 216(1) establishes the need to pull over for a police officer when requested to do so:

> 216 (1) A police officer, in the lawful execution of his or her duties and respon-sibilities, may require the driver of a vehicle, other than a bicycle, to stop and the driver of a vehicle, when signalled or requested to stop by a police officer who is readily identifiable as such, shall immediately come to a safe stop.

This section places an obligation on drivers to immediately pull over when requested to do so by a police officer provided it is possible to come to a safe stop. Notice that it applies to all vehicles other than a bicycle and does not have to take place on a highway.

Further, it specifies that the police officer must be readily identifiable as a police officer, meaning that there would a possible defence for someone who didn't pull over for an unmarked cruiser or didn't respond to an officer who was not in uniform.

Commentary

As outlined below in the discussion on penalties, this strict liability offence becomes much more severe if it is determined that that the person wilfully avoided the police officer when the officer gave pursuit (under the heading of "escape by flight," other-wise referred to as a police chase). Pursuant to section 216(3) it becomes a *mens rea* offence. This offence is unique in the HTA because the charge is still laid as fail-ure to pull over for the police officer, but upon hearing the evidence the justice will determine if the charge should be bumped up to the more serious component of the offence.

Penalties

There are no set fines associated with the offence since it is considered to be a Part III offence.

Upon conviction, the defendant is liable to a fine in the range of $1,000 to $10,000, imprisonment for up to six months, or both a fine and imprisonment.

Further, if there is a conviction of this offence and the court is satisfied on the evidence that the person wilfully continued to avoid police when a police officer gave pursuit, section 216(3) applies and the penalties increase substantially. Specifically, the fine range is $5,000 to $25,000, there is a mandatory jail term of 14 days to 6 months, and a mandatory licence suspension for 5 years. If the person's conduct or the pursuit resulted in death or bodily harm to any person, the licence suspension will be for a minimum of 10 years to the maximum of a lifetime suspension.

Seven demerit points apply when there is a conviction for this offence.

Seat Belts

The rules regarding the use of seat belts are set out in section 106 of the HTA. Section 106(2), which is directed at drivers, states:

> 106(2) Every person who drives on a highway a motor vehicle in which a seat belt assembly is provided for the driver shall wear the complete seat belt assembly as required by subsection (5).

With regard to passengers, section 106(3) indicates:

> 106(3) Every person who is at least 16 years old and is a passenger in a motor vehicle on a highway shall,
>   (a) occupy a seating position for which a seat belt assembly has been provided; and
>   (b) wear the complete seat belt assembly as required by subsection (5).

Section 106(5) sets out the manner in which the seat belt is to be worn so that both the pelvic restraint and the torso restraint are securely fastened.

Commentary

Sections 106(6) and 106(7) of the HTA set out exceptions to the seat belt requirements. Specifically, a seat belt is not required when driving in reverse, presumably to allow the driver to turn his or her body for the best rear view. In addition, with proper documentation from a medical practitioner, a person may be exempt from wearing a seat belt for medical reasons (e.g., abdominal surgery) or because of size, build, or other physical characteristics (e.g., the person is too tall for the seat belt to be an effective restraint). There is a further exemption for someone whose work requires frequent entry into and exit from a motor vehicle, such as a garbage truck driver. Seat belt offences are strict liability offences, which means that the defendant has the opportunity to demonstrate due diligence. See *R v Kanda*, Case in Point in Chapter 4.

For more information about seat belts and child restraints, review Regulation 613 under the HTA.

Penalties

There is a set fine of $200 for all seat belt-related charges. Upon conviction the defendant is liable to a fine of not less than $200 and not more than $1,000. Two demerit points are applied against a driver who was not wearing a seat belt or who did not ensure that a passenger under the age of 16 was wearing a seat belt. Passengers can be charged for not wearing a seat belt, but demerit points will not be applied. Many defendants will try to negotiate a guilty plea to the related charge of inoperable seat belt under section 106(1), but it is the discretion of the prosecution and the justice to determine if the facts of the case would apply (e.g., if the seat belt was broken).

Display Screens and Hand-Held Devices

In Ontario, the ban on display screens and hand-held devices took effect on October 26, 2009, with an increase in penalties effective September 1, 2015. In Ontario, recent statistics show:

- one person is injured in a distracted-driving collision every half hour
- a driver using a phone is four times more likely to crash than a driver focusing on the road[7]

There are two primary charges: viewing a display screen while driving and using a hand-held device while driving. It is worth noting that the officer has the discretion to lay a careless driving charge if the driver endangers other people, or a criminal charge of dangerous driving if there has been bodily harm or death.

Display Screens

Section 78(1) of the HTA, which concerns display screens, states:

> 78(1) No person shall drive a motor vehicle on a highway if the display screen of a television, computer or other device in the motor vehicle is visible to the driver.

COMMENTARY

Sections 78(2) and 78(3) set out some of the exceptions to this provision (e.g., GPS devices; drivers of ambulance, fire, or police vehicles). Ontario Regulation 366/09 provides additional exceptions from the ban on display screens (e.g., couriers, taxis, and limousines).

Hand-Held Devices

Hand-held communication devices, such as cellphones, are also banned. Specifically, section 78.1(1) states:

> 78.1(1) No person shall drive a motor vehicle on a highway while holding or using a hand-held wireless communication device or other prescribed device that is capable of receiving or transmitting telephone communications, electronic data, mail or text messages.

Section 78.1(2) bans hand-held entertainment devices, such as gaming devices:

> 78.1(2) No person shall drive a motor vehicle on a highway while holding or using a hand-held electronic entertainment device or other prescribed device the primary use of which is unrelated to the safe operation of the motor vehicle.

The wording of both of these subsections indicates that hand-held devices are not permitted while driving a motor vehicle on a highway. In addition to not using a hand-held device, a motorist cannot even hold the device while driving.

---

7   Ministry of Transportation Ontario, *Distracted Driving*, online: <https://www.ontario.ca/page/distracted-driving>.

COMMENTARY

There are several exemptions to the ban on display screens and hand-held devices. Section 78.1(3) allows for a hands-free mode to be used, and section 78.1(5) permits a hand-held communication device to be used to contact ambulance, police, or fire department emergency services. Additional exemptions are set out in section 78.1(4) and in Ontario Regulation 366/09.

As well, section 78.1(6) indicates that hand-held device charges will not apply if the vehicle is off the roadway, such as on the shoulder, is not in motion, and is not impeding traffic. This allows drivers to safely pull to the side of the road and stop their vehicle in order to make a phone call or check messages.

As demonstrated by *R v Kazemi*, below, a defendant can be convicted under this section for briefly holding a cellphone while driving even if it was not being used.

CASE IN POINT

Holding Cellphone while Driving

R v Kazemi, 2013 ONCA 585

Facts

The defendant had been driving with her cellphone on the passenger seat, but when she braked for a red light it fell to the floor of her vehicle. While stopped at the red light she bent over to pick up her cellphone. At trial, the defendant was convicted. On appeal to the Ontario Court of Justice the judge accepted that she had only momentarily touched the phone and the defendant was acquitted. The prosecution appealed to the Ontario Court of Appeal.

Relevant Issue

Holding Cellphone while Driving

Decision

The Court of Appeal considered the legislature's intention and purpose when drafting the legislation and ruled that this simple act of "holding" was in violation of the law. Any type of handling for any length of time is prohibited, and it is not necessary to prove sustained physical holding. The appeal was granted and the conviction against the defendant was restored.

Penalties

In 2015, the set fine increased from $280 with no demerit points to a $400 set fine with three demerit points. Upon conviction, the defendant will be faced with a fine of not less than $300 and not more than $1,000. As well, the officer still has the option of laying charges under these specific sections or as a careless driving charge, which carries six demerit points.

The following case indicates that it is not necessary to for the prosecution to prove that the hand-held device was operable.[8]

---

8 In the fall of 2017, the Ontario government is expected to introduce proposed legislation that would add licence suspensions and increased fines for subsequent convictions of distracted driving.

CASE IN POINT

Proof That Cellphone Is Operational

R v Pizzurro, 2013 ONCA 584

Facts

The defendant was observed holding a cellphone while driving. At trial, he did not dispute that he was holding the phone, but indicated that the prosecution failed to produce evidence that his cellphone was operational. The defendant was convicted and he appealed to the Ontario Court of Justice. The judge agreed that an operational cellphone would be an essential element of the offence and reversed the trial decision. The prosecution then appealed to the Court of Appeal.

Relevant Issue

Proof That Cellphone Is Operational

Decision

In restoring the conviction, the Court of Appeal indicated that the legislature's intention was to ensure road safety and driver attentiveness to driving. The court found that cellphones are presumed to be capable of receiving or transmitting telephone communication, electronic data, mail or text messages and that this does not have to be proven by the prosecution. The appeal was granted.

PRACTICE TIP

It is important to be aware of the interrelationship of the various sections of the HTA. As an example, section 207(1) states:

Subject to subsection (2), the owner of a vehicle may be charged with and convicted of an offence under this Act or the regulations or any municipal by-law regulating traffic for which the driver of the vehicle is subject to be charged unless, at the time of the offence, the vehicle was in the possession of some person other than the owner without the owner's consent and on conviction the owner is liable to the penalty prescribed for the offence.

There may be situations where the prosecutor would be willing to accept a guilty plea from the defendant as the owner instead of as the driver. This is beneficial to the defendant because convictions where section 207(1) have been applied would not carry any demerit points.

KEY TERMS

REVIEW QUESTIONS

Multiple Choice

1. Which of the following speed measuring devices measures the round-trip time for a beam of light to reach a car and reflect back?

   a. Radar.

   b. Laser.

   c. Pacing.

   d. Aircraft.

2. What type of legislation is the *Highway Traffic Act*?

   a. Municipal legislation.

   b. Provincial legislation.

   c. Federal legislation.

   d. Hybrid legislation.

3. For what period of time does the *Highway Traffic Act* specify that a driver must stop at a stop sign?

   a. Three seconds.

   b. Five seconds.

   c. Long enough to spell the word "S-T-O-P."

   d. It does not specify a length of time.

4. Which of the following could potentially be suggested as an included offence to "fail to stop at a stop sign" contrary to section 136(1)(a) and would put your client in a better position for demerit points?

   a. Disobey sign, section 182(2).

   b. Careless driving, section 130.

   c. Red light—fail to stop, section 144(18).

   d. Traffic on through highway—fail to yield, section 136(2).

5. Which of the following devices is exempt from the ban on display screens?

   a. GPS.

   b. Cellphone that is not working properly.

   c. Portable video player.

   d. Portable gaming system.

6. How many points would a defendant lose for a conviction for failing to remain at the scene of an accident?

   a. 0.

   b. 3.

   c. 4.

   d. 7.

7. Rosie was charged with "improper right turn" contrary to section 141(2) of the HTA. If she is convicted at trial, what is the maximum fine that will apply?

   a. The set fine of $85.

   b. The POA maximum of $1,000.

   c. The HTA maximum of $500.

   d. There is no maximum.

8. What is the minimum fine that will apply to Rosie?

   a. The set fine of $85.

   b. The POA minimum.

   c. The HTA minimum of $60.

   d. There is no minimum.

Short Answer

1. Outline four methods that are used to detect a vehicle's rate of speed.

2. List three situations in which a motorist is more likely to be charged with careless driving under Part III than under Part I.

3. Your client was charged with speeding. He tells you that no speed limit was posted, so he drove through a developed area in his municipality at 60 km/h. What should your client have done?

4. List three situations in which the police will come to the scene of an accident, instead of sending the driver to a collision reporting centre.

5. In an effort to ensure he was not using his cellphone while driving, Bob passed his cellphone to his son who was in the back seat and asked him to make a phone call. Bob was charged under section 78.1(2) of the HTA. What should he have done to ensure he was not breaking the law?

Exercises

1. Your client has been charged with driving 80km/h in a posted 50km/h zone. After negotiating with the prosecutor, you were able to reduce the speeding charge to 65km/h in a 50km/h zone.

   a. How many demerit points are associated with this offence at the original rate of speed?

   b. What is the set fine for the original rate of speed?

   c. What is the victim fine surcharge for the original rate of speed? Hint: refer to Chapter 12 for victim fine surcharges.

   d. How many demerit points are associated with the reduced rate of speed?

   e. What is the set fine for the reduced rate of speed?

   f. What is the victim fine surcharge for the reduced rate of speed?

   g. If your client had not negotiated with the prosecutor and had instead been convicted at trial, what would the fine be (do not include court costs and victim fine surcharge)?

2. Your client has been charged with "failure to stop at a stop sign" contrary to section 136(1)(a).

   a. How many demerit points are associated with this offence?

   b. What is the set fine for this offence?

   c. What is the victim fine surcharge for this offence?

   d. If your client is convicted at trial, what would the fine range be?

3. Review Regulation 339/94 (see Appendix D). How many demerit points would a defendant receive if convicted of the following offences?

   a. Driving at 35km/h over the speed limit.

   b. Driving the wrong way on a divided highway.

   c. Using a cellphone while driving.

   d. Detection by a provincial offences officer for failure to stop at a red light.

   e. Detection by a red light camera for failure to stop at a red light.

Other Common Acts

15

LEARNING OUTCOMES

After reading this chapter, you will understand

- the statutes and common charges that are commonly prosecuted in Ontario;

- Charter applicability and notice requirements;

- the areas of responsibility for which municipalities may enact by-laws; and

- why some federal statutes may be prosecuted under the *Provincial Offences Act*.

Introduction

Many of the previous chapters focused on laying the groundwork for the various procedures and processes involved in the regulatory framework in Ontario. It is important to understand how the framework functions, but you also need to understand the provisions of the charging act under which a proceeding is commenced.

This chapter will discuss some of the more common statutes besides the *Highway Traffic Act* that are prosecuted in Ontario using the procedures set out in the POA.

> ## PRACTICE TIP
>
> When representing a client, it is essential that you review the charging act or by-law that created the offence as part of case preparation. This will allow you to determine the essential elements of the offence and will help you develop a defence for your client.

Compulsory Automobile Insurance Act

The *Compulsory Automobile Insurance Act* (CAIA) requires every owner or operator of a motor vehicle on an Ontario highway to have an automobile insurance contract and to abide by certain rules relating to the insurance.[1] Under the CAIA, the term "motor vehicle" has the same meaning as under the HTA and includes motorized snow vehicles, all-terrain vehicles, trailers, and accessories of a motor vehicle.

The CAIA is unique in that it provides a lengthy limitation period. Charges can be laid at any time within three years from the date that the offence was, or is alleged to have been, committed. This is much longer than the default statutory maximum of six months under the POA.

The CAIA creates several offences. Some offences, like those under other provincial statutes, are minor and relatively straightforward (e.g., failing to carry proof of insurance, section 3(1)). However, others are quite serious and can have a significant impact on your client if he or she is convicted (e.g., driving without insurance, section 2(1)).

Minor Offences

The chief justice has prescribed short-form wording for five minor offences that may be commenced under Part I of the POA. These minor offences under the CAIA are:

- failing to surrender suspended driver's licence when required by a police officer (section 2(6))
- refusing to surrender suspended driver's licence when required by a police officer (section 2(6))

---

1   RSO 1990, c. C.25.

- failing to carry or produce the insurance card for the motor vehicle being operated (section 3(1))

- failing to carry or produce evidence that the operator is covered under a contract of insurance (section 3(1))

- failing to disclose the particulars of an insurance contract when requested by an individual involved in the accident (section 4(1)).

With regard to section 4(1), the operator of a motor vehicle who is involved in an accident is required to disclose certain particulars about the automobile insurance for the motor vehicle. Specifically, section 4(2) defines which particulars or information should be disclosed at a collision scene as follows: the name and address of the insured; the make, model, and serial number of the insured vehicle; the effective date and expiry date of the insurance contract; the name of the insurer and insurer's agent (if any); and the policy number of the contract.

PRACTICE TIP

Many of the minor offences under the CAIA are often laid in conjunction with other driving-related charges. If your client took steps to update his or her insurance—or had valid insurance but was unable to produce proof at the time of interaction with the police officer (e.g., forgot wallet at home)—coming to court with all the necessary documentation may provide persuasive arguments for the prosecutor to accept a favourable plea settlement.

Serious Offences

Several serious offences are prosecuted under the CAIA. Given the nature of these offences and the penalties that are prescribed, they are commenced under Part III of the POA. The serious offences under the CAIA are:

- operating a motor vehicle with no insurance (section 2(1))

- vehicle owner permitting the operation of a motor vehicle without insurance (section 2(1))

- possessing/using/selling/producing an insurance card that is known or ought to be known to be false or invalid (section 13.1(1))

- making false statements with respect to any information provided for the purposes of the Act, including purporting to be insured when renewing validation permits with the Ministry of Transportation and knowing that to be false (section 13(11)).

The consequences of being convicted of one of the serious offences under the CAIA are significant and represent some of the most serious of the regulatory offences that involve the general public. The legislature has enacted heavy penalty provisions to serve as a deterrent to all drivers.

Penalties

The set fines for the Part I offences can be found in the Ontario Court of Justice, Schedule 1 of the consolidated Set Fines Schedules, under the *Compulsory Automobile Insurance Act*:

TABLE 15.1 Set Fines for Part I Offences

	SHORT-FORM WORDING	SECTION	SET FINE
1.	Fail to surrender suspended driver's licence	2(6)	$25.00
2.	Refuse to surrender suspended driver's licence	2(6)	$25.00
3.	Fail to have insurance card	3(1)	$50.00
4.	Fail to surrender insurance card	3(1)	$50.00
5.	Fail to disclose particulars of insurance	4(1)	N.S.F.*

* No set fine: A proceeding may still be commenced under Part I, but a summons is required.

These set fines apply for an out-of-court settlement. An offence dealt with at trial will have a specified maximum fine. A defendant who is convicted of failing or refusing to surrender his or her driver's licence (section 2(6)) is liable to a fine of not more than $200. A defendant who is convicted of failing to have or surrender his or her insurance card (section 3(1)) or failing to disclose particulars of insurance (section 4(1)) is liable for a maximum fine of $400.

Section 2(3) of the CAIA provides the statutory framework for the penalty provisions for the Part III offences under sections 2(1) and 13(11) of the Act. An owner or lessee of a motor vehicle who operates or permits the vehicle to be operated without insurance or shows false insurance documents to a police officer is guilty of an offence and is liable on a first conviction to a minimum fine of $5,000 and up to $25,000 and on a subsequent conviction to a minimum fine $10,000 and up to $50,000. In addition, his or her driver's licence may be suspended for up to one year. The penalties for offences under section 13.1 (false or invalid insurance card) are even more severe with a fine range of $10,000 to $50,000 for a first conviction and a fine range of $20,000 to $100,000 on a subsequent conviction.

Outside of the fines specified in the CAIA, driving convictions will also affect your client's insurance rating and how insurance companies will bill your client. To receive preferred or discounted rates, drivers must have a clean record; that is, usually no more than two minor convictions within a three-year period. Additional convictions can have serious implications for your client's ability to obtain insurance. Insurance rates can rise as much as 250 percent for serious convictions or multiple offences.

PRACTICE TIP

As a value-added service, paralegals should become familiar with the Facility Association rules and guidelines so that they can explain this option to clients who might not have other insurance options. The Facility Association is an unincorporated non-profit organization of all automobile insurers that was established to ensure that automobile insurance is available to all owners and licensed drivers of motor vehicles. The association serves owners or drivers who are otherwise unable to obtain automobile insurance from regular insurance companies because of prior accidents, a poor driving record, or numerous insurance policy cancellations.[2] However, insurance rates obtained through the Facility Association are substantially higher than those obtained through regular insurers.

Liquor Licence Act

The *Liquor Licence Act* (LLA) is a robust and sophisticated piece of legislation that is primarily responsible for establishing licensing and the safe and responsible use of alcohol in Ontario.[3]

The LLA regulates the manner in which alcohol is sold, purchased, brewed, and consumed in Ontario. Licensing and brewing are highly regulated and compliance is largely achieved through orders and threats of revocation of permits. As such, most administrative or non-compliance matters are dealt with through administrative monetary fines.

Regulation 719 under the LLA describes the terms and conditions for licensees who sell liquor. Sections 25 and 29 cover the service of alcohol outside of prescribed hours and the licence holder's failure to clear away within a specified time all evidence that alcohol has been served and consumed on a premises. Sections 41 and 42 deal with serving minors and the failure to check ID. Section 43 deals with over crowding in premises that are licensed to serve alcohol, and sections 45, 45.1, 45.2, and 46 prescribe that drunkenness, unlawful gambling, violence, and disorderly conduct are not permitted on the premises or in areas adjacent to the premises under the exclusive control of the licence holder.

The Alcohol and Gaming Commission of Ontario (AGCO) is responsible for administering the *Liquor Licence Act*. Although the commission will often perform inspections to ensure compliance, it will also form partnerships with local and regional police services to ensure effective enforcement of the responsible-use provisions of the LLA.

---

2 The Facility Association, online: <www.facilityassociation.com>.

3 RSO 1990, c L.19.

Offences

The LLA creates a number of offences with regard to both the consumer and the establishment/server.

Some of the offences that may be applicable to a consumer include:

- Person under 19 having, consuming or attempting to purchase liquor (s 30(8));
- Presenting as evidence of age documentation not lawfully issued to person (s 30(12));
- Consuming liquor in other than licensed premises, residence or private place (s 31(2));
- Being intoxicated in a public place (s 31(4));
- Driving motor vehicle with open container of liquor (s 32(1)).

Offences that are applicable to a licensed establishment or server include:

- Selling or supplying liquor to intoxicated person (s 29);
- Knowingly selling or supplying liquor to person who appears to be under the age of 19 (s 30(1));
- Licensee failing to ensure that person who is unlawfully on premises does not remain on premises (s 34(1)).

Penalties

Most of the consumer-focused offences listed in sections 30 to 33 of the LLA have set fines pursuant to Schedule 61 of the consolidated Set Fines Schedules ranging from $50 to $175.

Section 61 of the LLA establishes the penalties upon conviction for the range of offences under the LLA. Of particular relevance is section 61(3), which indicates that upon conviction (other than for a conviction on one of the subsections that relate to providing liquor to someone under 19):

(a) a corporation is liable to a fine of not more than $250,000; and

(b) an individual is liable to a fine of not more than $100,000 or to imprisonment for a term of not more than one year or both.

Specific penalties are provided for convictions on contraventions relating to providing liquor to a person under 19 years of age. Specifically, if the offence involves a contravention of section 30(1) or (2),

- a corporation is liable to a fine in the range of $1,000 to $500,000 (with a licence suspension of the licensee for a minimum of 7 days; and
- an individual is liable to a fine in the range of $200 to $200,000 or to imprisonment for a term of not more than one year or both.

It should also be noted that an individual who is convicted for consuming liquor in non-licensed premises (section 31(2)) or being intoxicated in public (section 31(4)) is not faced with the possibility of imprisonment.

Environmental Protection Act

A particularly important area of provincial regulation today is environmental protection. The *Environmental Protection Act* (EPA) is an example of provincial legislation that creates obligations to protect the environment and establishes offences when breached. The seriousness of environmental matters can be recognized by the fact that section 185 of the EPA allows the Crown to require that a provincial judge, instead of a justice of the peace, preside over a proceeding in respect of an offence under the EPA.[4]

Offences

The EPA regulates the actions of those in charge of pollutants, creating offences in such areas as spillage and littering. For example, a person in charge of a pollutant must develop a plan to reduce the risk of spillage and respond effectively if spillage occurs. The EPA also addresses less serious Part I environmental offences relating to emission control equipment and waste disposal/management.

Penalties

The general penalty provisions indicate that for a first conviction an individual is liable to a fine up to $50,000 for each day on which the offence occurs or continues (and on a subsequent conviction a daily fine up to $100,000 and the possibility of jail for up to one year). For a corporation, the maximum daily fine is $250,000 for a first conviction and $500,000 for each day, or part of a day, in which an offence occurs or continues.

However, not all EPA offences are subject to severe penalty provisions of the EPA. For example, pursuant to section 89(1), an individual convicted of littering is liable to a fine of up to $1,000 for a first offence and up to $2,000 for a subsequent offence. A corporation is liable to a maximum fine of $2,000 on a first conviction and $5,000 on each subsequent conviction.

Other penalties may apply under the EPA, including amending, reviewing, suspending, and revoking an environmental compliance approval or renewable energy approval; issuing an order of conformance; or issuing a control order or stop order.

---

4 RSO 1990, c E.19.

Additional Environmental Statutes

Additional statutes that are aimed at environmental protection include the *Clean Water Act, 2006*[5] and the *Pesticides Act.*[6]

The *Clean Water Act* stipulates a number of obligations pertaining to safe drinking water. Under this act, if a person with source protection authority becomes aware of a drinking-water hazard, he or she must alert the Ministry of the Environment. It is also an offence to continue to engage in an activity that endangers a water supply.

The *Pesticides Act* imposes penalties on those who release pesticides into the environment outside of an ordinary course of events, and injury to the environment, animals, or persons is likely to occur.

PRACTICE TIP

If the prosecution has a strong case, you may need to work with subject-matter experts to determine the best strategy for advancing the defence and mitigating the evidence of the prosecution. Experts on soil analysis, air analysis, environmental impacts, and best practices may form a key part of a due-diligence defence.

Occupational Health and Safety Act

The *Occupational Health and Safety Act* (OHSA) sets out duties for all workplace parties and establishes rights for workers.[7] Further, the OHSA establishes procedures for dealing with workplace hazards and provides for enforcement where compliance has not been achieved voluntarily. The importance of occupational health and safety matters can be recognized by the fact that section 68(2) of the OHSA allows for the attorney general or agent for the attorney general to require that a provincial judge preside over the proceeding, instead of a justice of the peace.

Duties Under the OHSA

The OHSA establishes a positive duty on employers to:

- provide a safe work environment,
- educate and train workers,
- develop and implement an occupational health and safety policy,
- create a violence and harassment policy,
- appoint competent supervision,

---

5   SO 2006, c 22.

6   RSO 1990, c P.11.

7   RSO 1990, c O.1.

- ensure that workers and supervisors comply with the Act,
- immediately report accidents causing critical injury or death.

The duties that workers must comply with are described in section 28 of the OHSA, including:

- comply with OHSA and regulations,
- use/wear the equipment, protective devices, or clothing specified by the employer,
- report to the employer or supervisor any missing or defective equipment or protective device that may be dangerous,
- report to the employer the existence of any workplace hazard.

The OHSA also deals with the protocol for dealing with a workplace accident. A thorough investigation should begin as soon as medical help has been given. In the event of a critical or fatal injury, a written report must be made to the Minister of Labour within 48 hours. Pursuant to section 2, all other non-critical injuries must be reported within four days.

The Ministry may prosecute any person for violating the Act or the regulations, or for failing to comply with an order issued by an inspector or director of the Ministry of Labour (section 66(1)). In deciding whether or not to prosecute, the ministry will take into account factors that include, but are not limited to, the seriousness of the offence and whether there have been repeated contraventions or ignored orders. Offences under the OHSA are strict liability offences. This means that the Ministry of Labour does not have to prove an intention to violate the legislation and the employer will have an opportunity to demonstrate due diligence. For example, in the case of a workplace accident, the Ministry of Labour must prove beyond a reasonable doubt that an act or omission by the employer caused the danger to exist. Once the Ministry of Labour has proven their case, the onus then switches to the employer to show on a balance of probabilities that every reasonable precaution was taken to prevent the accident.

Penalties

Section 66 of the OHSA provides that any person who contravenes or fails to comply with a provision of the OHSA or the regulations, an order or requirement of an inspector or a director, or an order of the minister is guilty of an offence. Failure to comply with provisions in the OHSA can result in maximum fines of $25,000 or up to 12 months in jail for persons, and a maximum fine of $500,000 for corporations.

PRACTICE TIP

In preparing to represent a client charged under the OHSA, you should review the workplace policies, procedures, and training documents. Review them again with the client and ensure that you have a functional understanding of the workplace operations.

Trespass to Property Act

The *Trespass to Property Act* (TPA) is one of the more common acts enforced by peace officers, security guards, and private citizens.[8] It gives ordinary citizens the authority to remove unwanted individuals from their property and to post signs restricting access. There are two important definitions found in section 1 of the TPA:

1. "Occupier," which includes a person who is in physical possession of a premises or a person (this can include a security guard or ticket collector) who has responsibility for and control over the condition of premises or the activities there carried on, or control over persons allowed to enter the premises, even if there is more than one occupier of the same premises.

   This includes anyone who is responsible for a property at any given time. It can include the owner, a security guard, or anyone else who has some written authority to act on behalf of the occupier. Anyone having control over entering a premises can act as an occupier.

2. "Premises" refers to lands and/or structures, and includes water; ships and vessels; trailers and portable structures designed or used for residence, business, or shelter; and trains, railway cars, vehicles, and aircraft, except while they are in operation.

   It is important to know what constitutes a premises, because many of the offence-related sections deal with access or non-access to premises, failing to leave a premises when directed, or engaging in prohibited activities on these premises. Mobile items can also be considered premises; for example, if someone rents a trailer and a private campsite, that person would be the occupier of a premises.

Offences

Most offences under the TPA are dealt with in section 2(1). There are three important offence categories:

1. Entering a premises when it is prohibited.
2. Carrying out a prohibited activity.
3. Failing to leave when directed.

However, before any entry can be deemed unlawful, there must be some form of notice prohibiting the entry or action. The different forms of notice can be found in section 5(1) of the TPA. Notice can be provided orally, in writing, or through signage. For example, if hunters are found on a farmer's property, the farmer can ask them to leave. If they do not leave, they can be charged with failing to leave the premises when directed because they have been given oral notice. As a further example,

---

8 RSO 1990, c T.21.

a sign that reads "No Trespassing" or that contains one large red dot are familiar types of notices. The large red dot marking system is frequently used by farmers or property owners in rural areas.

Notice becomes more complicated where stores or other commercial outlets are involved. Stores often post a sign on the door that reads "No Shoplifting" or "Shoplifters will be prosecuted." If someone steals an item and is caught by store security, there is some jurisprudence, as well as commonly held interpretations, that store security is acting under the authority of both the *Criminal Code*[9] and the *Trespass to Property Act*.[10]

Under section 9, a police officer or occupier of the premises has the authority to arrest anyone whom he or she believes, on reasonable and probable grounds, is committing an offence under section 2. It is important to remember that an occupier who arrests a suspect must immediately turn him or her over to a police officer.

PRACTICE TIP

In reviewing any case that involves an arrest for an offence under the TPA, turn your mind to whether your client's rights under the Charter were preserved throughout the arrest. If your client's rights were violated (no right to counsel, illegal search, or unlawful arrest), successfully bringing a motion before the court alleging the Charter breach may result in a stay of the charges.

Penalties

The chief justice has prescribed the set fines for offences under the Ontario Court of Justice, Schedule 85 of the consolidated Set Fines schedules, under the *Trespass to Property Act*:

TABLE 15.2   Set Fines under Section 85

	CHARGE	SECTION	SET FINE
1.	Enter premises when entry prohibited	2(1)(a)(i)	$50.00
2.	Engage in prohibited activity on premises	2(1)(a)(ii)	$50.00
3.	Fail to leave premises when directed	2(1)(b)	$50.00

Since there is a set fine of $50, charges are often laid under Part I. If there is not an out-of-court settlement, the maximum fine upon conviction is $2,000.

---

9   RSC, 1985, c C-46.

10   RSO 1990, c T.21.

PRACTICE TIP

Your client may be able to use the defence of "colour of right." This defence has been defined in various court decisions to mean "an honest belief in a set of facts that, if they existed, would provide a legal justification or excuse for the act committed." Conducting a proper client interview and establishing the facts are crucial to successfully advancing this defence. The defence operates to excuse behaviour where ownership (or an ownership-like interest), or honest belief of the same, constitutes a valid legal justification or excuse. For example, the property had been recently sold but your client mistakenly believed it was still owned by a relative.

Blind Persons' Rights Act

The intent of the *Blind Persons' Rights Act* (BPRA) is to ensure that people who are visually impaired and who use guide dogs receive the same access to accommodation, services, and facilities as sighted people.[11] The BPRA also guarantees the user of a guide dog the right to equal housing opportunities with no special terms or conditions.

Offences

Many landlords impose a "no pets" clause, and establishments (such as hotels and restaurants) often do not allow patrons to bring their pet dogs inside. For blind persons, however, their dogs are not merely pets, but are service dogs.

This is why section 2(1) of the Act clearly stipulates access:

> 2(1) No person, directly or indirectly, alone or with another, by himself, herself or itself or by the interposition of another, shall,
>> (a) deny to any person the accommodation, services or facilities available in any place to which the public is customarily admitted; or
>> (b) discriminate against any person with respect to the accommodation, services or facilities available in any place to which the public is customarily admitted, or the charges for the use thereof,
> for the reason that he or she is a blind person accompanied by a guide dog.

The first part of this section states that no one, regardless of the circumstances, may deny access or discriminate against a blind person in relation to accommodation, services, or facilities. For example, an employee who claims that he or she was merely following directions from an employer in denying access would not be able

---

11 RSO 1990, c B.7.

to use that as a defence under this section, and everyone (whether employer or employee) is equally liable.

Paragraphs (a) and (b) clarify the law by stating that a person with a guide dog cannot be denied access or be discriminated against when entering a place normally used by the public.

Section 3 limits the use of a white cane in public such that it can be used only by a blind person, and sections 4(1) and 4(2) allow for an identification card to be issued as proof that the blind person and the guide dog identified herein are qualified for the purposes of the BPRA.

Penalties

There are no set fines established under this Act.

Anyone who is convicted of contravening section 2 by denying accommodation, services, or facilities to a blind person accompanied by a guide dog faces a maximum fine of $5,000. With a fine of up to $5,000, officers would proceed by way of a Part III summons and information.

Section 6(2) states that any person who falsely identifies themselves as a blind person or who uses a white cane to benefit from the *Blind Persons' Rights Act* is guilty of an offence and if convicted is liable to a fine not exceeding $500. It must be proven that the person wanted to appear to be blind and was trying to establish some benefit. It would not be an offence for a person to pretend that he or she was blind and to use a white cane unless a benefit was received (e.g., attempting to obtain a discount in transit fares).

Dog Owners' Liability Act

The *Dog Owners' Liability Act* (DOLA) contains provisions for court proceedings against dog owners who do not exercise reasonable precautions to prevent their dog from biting, attacking, or behaving in a manner that poses a menace to the safety of persons or domestic animals.[12]

Section 1(1) of the Act defines a dog owner as "a person who possesses or harbours the dog and, where the owner is a minor, the person responsible for the custody of the minor." Under this definition, the DOLA could apply to someone who is only looking after a dog.

Dog owners have a positive duty to control a dog's behaviour and will be strictly liable for any injury or damage caused by their dog. With regard to dog bites, dog owners have a legal responsibility to any person or animal who comes into contact with their dog.

The pit bull ban is set out in sections 6 to 11 of the DOLA, and Ontario Regulation 157/05 sets out the rules and requirements for the control of dogs that are classified as pit bulls.

---

12   RSO 1990, c D.16.

Offences

There are two "streams" of offences set out in the DOLA. The first is for an order if there has been an incident where a dog was in involved in a biting, attacking, or menacing incident. The other is for the prosecution of offences for general DOLA-related contraventions and pit bull matters.

Under section 4(1), a proceeding may be commenced in the Ontario Court of Justice for an order against an owner to destroy or control a dog if it is alleged that:

> 4(1) ...
>> (a) the dog has bitten or attacked a person or domestic animal;
>> (b) the dog has behaved in a manner that poses a menace to the safety of persons or domestic animals; or
>> (c) the owner did not exercise reasonable precautions to prevent the dog from,
>>> (i) biting or attacking a person or domestic animal, or
>>> (ii) behaving in a manner that poses a menace to the safety of persons or domestic animals.

Section 4(1.2) of the DOLA indicates that Part IX of the *Provincial Offences Act* applies to proceedings against an owner of a dog. Part IX of the POA contains only one section, section 161. This section allows a statement under oath to be used in place of an information and sets out the process to be followed. Specifically, in accordance with section 161,

> 161. Where, by any other Act, a proceeding is authorized to be taken before the Ontario Court of Justice or a justice for an order, including an order for the payment of money, and no other procedure is provided, this Act applies with necessary modifications to the proceeding in the same manner as to a proceeding commenced under Part III, and for the purpose,
>> (a) in place of an information, the applicant shall complete a statement in the prescribed form under oath attesting, on reasonable and probable grounds, to the existence of facts that would justify the order sought; and
>> (b) in place of a plea, the defendant shall be asked whether or not the defendant wishes to dispute the making of the order.

If there is an allegation that the dog has bitten, attacked, or behaved as a menace, the complainant will file a sworn statement that could justify the order being sought. The form that should be used to make a statement under section 161 of the POA is Form 142 of the "POA Rules," and the matter will be brought before a justice in the Ontario Court of Justice.

Instead of being asked to enter a plea, the defendant will be asked whether he or she intends to dispute the making of the order, under section 161(b) of the POA. Pursuant to section 4(1.3) of the DOLA, when hearing an application for such an order, the court will use the civil standard of proof on a balance of probabilities in making findings of fact. This distinguishes such proceedings from typical criminal or regulatory prosecutions, where the higher standard of beyond a reasonable doubt is used.

This civil standard applies to a court order proceeding even if it is commenced in conjunction with a prosecution, although the prosecution of another DOLA offence will be decided using the higher standard.

Penalties

If the court finds that a dog has bitten, attacked, or that the dog's behaviour was a menace to the safety of persons or domestic animals, then that court will issue an order. Pursuant to section 4(3), the order may either state that:

- the dog be destroyed, or
- the owner of the dog take specific measures for more effective control of the animal (e.g., confining the dog to owner's property, leash order, muzzle order, warning signs).

If a dog in question is a pit bull, the order will be for the dog to be destroyed. In such a case, an owner would have the onus to prove that the dog is not a pit bull and therefore should not be destroyed.

In addition to any special measures that are ordered, the owner is also required to have the dog spayed or neutered within 30 days of the order. The justice may also prohibit the owner from owning another dog for a specific period of time.

Penalties can be reduced because of contributory negligence. This occurs when the injured person contributed to the situation (e.g., provoked the dog in some way).

Since the chief justice has not prescribed short-form wordings or set fines for DOLA offences, any DOLA charges are laid under Part III of the POA. Alternatively, if the municipality has established animal control offences within a municipal by-law, the proceedings can be commenced under Part I or under the municipality's administrative penalty system, if applicable.

Section 18 provides the penalties for violating the DOLA. Any individual who contravenes any provision of the Act or its regulations or who contravenes an order made under the Act or the regulations is liable upon conviction to a fine of not more than $10,000 or to imprisonment for a term of not more than six months, or both. The maximum fine for a corporation is $60,000. Section 18(3) authorizes additional penalties as determined by the court making the conviction—specifically, in addition to any other penalty, a court may order the person convicted to make compensation or restitution in relation to the offence.

PRACTICE TIP

It is important to remember that in a DOLA case your client may be under significant emotional stress. Most dog owners are very attached to their pets and the process is challenging for them. Take extra time to prepare your client for the proceeding and ensure that they are able to control their emotional reactions.

Municipal By-Laws

Municipal by-laws are an area of specialty within provincial law. Every paralegal practising regulatory law in Ontario should have an understanding of the *Municipal Act, 2001*, and its spheres of jurisdiction and enforcement sections.[13] Sections 9, 10, and 11 of the Act, as well as Part IV, should form part of your required knowledge base.

Section 9 of the Act provides a municipality the powers of a natural person for the purpose of exercising its authority under this or any other Act.

Sections 10 and 11 are substantially similar but distinguish between a single-tier municipality and an upper-tier/lower-tier municipality. An example of a single-tier municipality would be the City of Barrie in Ontario. An example of a lower-tier/upper-tier municipality is that of the Town of Aurora (lowertier) being within the Regional Municipality of York (upper-tier).

Regardless of whether a municipality is single, lower, or upper tier, the Act provides a broad, general power for municipalities to license businesses and to license, regulate, and govern persons carrying on or engaged in businesses.

Paralegals must have an operational understanding of the legislative requirements and the enabling statutory provisions. Sections 10(2) and 11(3) and Part IV of the Act give municipalities a substantial arsenal to enact by-laws in the public interest, addressing a wide variety of activities and issues:

- governance structure of the municipality and its local boards;
- accountability and transparency of the municipality and its operations and of its local boards and their operations;
- financial management of the municipality and its local boards;
- public assets of the municipality acquired for the purpose of exercising its authority under this or any other Act;
- economic, social, and environmental well-being of the municipality;
- health, safety, and well-being of persons;
- services and things that the municipality is authorized to provide under section 10(1);
- protection of persons and property, including consumer protection;
- animals;
- structures, including fences and signs; and
- business licensing.

Part IV of the Act includes the licensing of adult entertainment establishments, tow trucks, taxicabs, trailers, and motor vehicle racing.

Municipalities are increasingly involved in regulating everyday elements of our lives and have broad legislative authority under the Act. A paralegal needs to understand the links between municipal authority and provincial authority. Municipalities may be responsible for enforcing various provincial statutes, such as the *Building*

---

13 SO 2001, c 25.

Code,[14] the *Planning Act*,[15] and various public welfare statutes that are regulatory in nature.

Offences

Paralegals may be called on to represent clients in cases involving charges for:

- *Building Code* violations,
- licensing appeal tribunals and hearings,
- animal control offences,
- massage parlour offences,
- property standards concerns,
- noise by-law infractions,
- and health code violations.

Penalties

Penalties are established by the municipality for each offence within the specific by-law.

PRACTICE TIP

Municipal by-law and regulatory schemes can be very complex and may involve various procedural streams. Proceedings may take place in provincial offences court, the Superior Court of Justice, or administrative tribunals. If you are pursuing a municipal law practice, ensure that you improve your skills with specific training in the areas of municipal law and administrative law. Visit the Association of Municipal Managers, Clerks, and Treasurers of Ontario (AMCTO) website[16] for training courses or consult the Law Society of Ontario's website[17] for professional development opportunities in these areas.

Federal Acts

Designated federal statutes may be prosecuted under the POA through a modified procedure authorized by the *Contraventions Act*.[18]

The *Contraventions Act* provides a procedure to prosecute a failure to comply with federal provisions of a regulatory nature. The Act allows the federal government to

---

14 SO 1992, c 23.

15 RSO 1990, c P.13.

16 Association of Municipal Managers, Clerks, and Treasurers of Ontario, online: <http://www.amcto.com>.

17 Law Society of Ontario, *Continuing Professional Development*, online: <https://ecom.lsuc.on.ca/cpd>.

18 SC 1992, c 47.

make regulations designating federal statutory offences as "contraventions" and to distinguish them from criminal offences. It reflects the distinction between these minor offences and criminal offences, and alters the legal consequences of being convicted of a contravention.

The Act also allows Ottawa to establish the fine associated with a federal contravention. That amount is systematically lower than the maximum fine an offender could face should the offence be prosecuted by way of summary conviction.

The following example illustrates this principle. According to the Historic Canals Regulations,[19] adopted under the *Department of Transport Act*,[20] "no person shall take off, land or moor an aircraft ... on the navigation channel of a historic canal." The federal government has designated this offence as a contravention. Therefore, an enforcement authority may elect to issue a ticket to someone accused of violating this provision. Should the person be found guilty, he or she will be required to pay a fine of $200.

It is impossible to list all federal statutory offences that have been designated as contraventions. To date, there are close to 3,000 such offences, involving more than 20 federal statutes and more than 45 sets of regulations.

Only those offences that have been designated as contraventions by the governor in council may be prosecuted under the *Contraventions Act*. To be designated as a contravention, an offence must be consistent with the underlying philosophy of the Act, which centres on the prosecution of less serious federal offences. The short-form wording of these designated offences and the applicable fines are found in the *Contraventions Regulations* (SOR/96-313).

In all provinces and territories, except Ontario and Quebec, the attorney general of Canada is responsible for prosecutions under the Act, either through the department's regional offices or Crown agents. Ontario and Quebec have chosen to prosecute contraventions under the Act on their own, in part to ensure the integrity of their respective offence schemes.

Although the *Contraventions Act* is comprised of more than 80 sections, only certain provisions create an adequate legal framework that permits the designated offences to be prosecuted under a modified procedure under the POA. Essentially, once a contravention proceeding has begun under the POA, the procedures and processes are identical to those of a regular POA proceeding. These provisions are listed in section 65.1(2) of the *Contraventions Act* and are the only provisions that apply in this context.

Charter Issues

It is clear that the *Canadian Charter of Rights and Freedoms* applies to regulatory offences in general. While provincial offences may not be held to the same stringent standard as criminal matters, the provisions of the Charter still apply and should always be reviewed in the context of any proceeding.

---

19   SOR/93-220.

20   RSC 1985, c T-18.

Legal arguments have been made that the Charter applies less to matters commenced under Part I or Part II of the POA than to those under Part III, as the only penalty is economic and the Charter provides no right to economic security. Even so, your client is still entitled to the common-law protection of procedural fairness, and has an inherent right to know the charges and be provided with disclosure.

As a licensed paralegal, it is very important that you be aware of the notice requirements under the *Courts of Justice Act* for bringing an application for a violation of the Charter, which is called a notice of constitutional question:

109(1) Notice of a constitutional question shall be served on the Attorney General of Canada and the Attorney General of Ontario in the following circumstances:

1. The constitutional validity or constitutional applicability of an Act of the Parliament of Canada or the Legislature, of a regulation or by-law made under such an Act or of a rule of common law is in question.

2. A remedy is claimed under subsection 24(1) of the *Canadian Charter of Rights and Freedoms* in relation to an act or omission of the Government of Canada or the Government of Ontario.

109(2) If a party fails to give notice in accordance with this section, the Act, regulation, by-law or rule of common law shall not be adjudged to be invalid or inapplicable, or the remedy shall not be granted, as the case may be.

A form has been approved for filing a notice of constitutional question (see Figure 8.3), but it would be wise to prepare a factum detailing your legal arguments and the facts and the law upon which you are relying in advancing the constitutional issue.

PRACTICE TIP

Take time to build relationships with other practising paralegals. Rely on the mentoring of more experienced practitioners and seek out opportunities to share information and sample templates on how to best structure a proper factum for a notice of constitutional question.

REVIEW QUESTIONS

Multiple Choice

1. Which of the following *Compulsory Automobile Insurance Act* offences could be commenced under Part III?

   a. Failing to surrender suspended driver's licence.

   b. Failing to produce insurance card.

   c. Permitting operation of a motor vehicle without insurance.

   d. Failing to disclose particulars of insurance when involved in an accident.

2. Which of the following statutes contains a section that provides the authority for a provincial court judge to deal with the matter instead of a justice of the peace?

   a. *Liquor Licence Act*.

   b. *Environmental Protection Act*.

   c. *Trespass to Property Act*.

   d. *Dog Owners' Liability Act*.

3. Which of the following statutes has no set fines?

   a. *Compulsory Automobile Insurance Act*.

   b. *Liquor Licence Act*.

   c. *Trespass to Property Act*.

   d. *Dog Owners' Liability Act*.

4. Which of the following is NOT a category of offences under the *Trespass to Property Act*?

   a. Entering a premises when it is prohibited.

   b. Failing to read trespassing notice.

   c. Carrying out a prohibited activity.

   d. Failing to leave when directed.

5. What is the maximum fine upon conviction under the *Trespass to Property Act*?

   a. $200.

   b. $500.

   c. $2,000.

   d. $5,000.

6. Which of the following penalties prescribes a daily fine for each day on which the offence occurs or continues to occur?

   a. *Liquor Licence Act*.

   b. *Environmental Protection Act*.

   c. *Occupational Health and Safety Act*.

   d. *Trespass to Property Act*.

7. Oscar is an eight-month-old puppy who nipped at a jogger who ran up behind him and frightened him. The jogger has contacted an animal control officer and wants the owner to take responsibility for the dog's bite. Which of the following is NOT a way that charges could proceed?

   a. As a Part I offence under the *Dog Owners' Liability Act*.

   b. As a Part III offence under the *Dog Owners' Liability Act*.

   c. As a Part I offence under a municipal animal control by-law.

   d. As an administrative penalty under a municipal by-law.

Short Answer

1. What was a primary reason for the federal government enacting the *Contraventions Act*?

2. How can a property owner or agent give notice that entry is prohibited under the *Trespass to Property Act*?

3. Describe the procedure and standard of proof for orders under the *Dog Owners' Liability Act*.

4. Would it be an offence under the *Blind Persons' Rights Act* for Renata to tell her friend Richard that she can't give him and his guide dog a ride in her car because she is allergic to dogs? Explain.

Scenario 1

Yvonne was driving a friend's vehicle when she was pulled over and charged with "fail to produce an insurance card" contrary to section 3(1) of the *Compulsory Automobile*

Insurance Act. Yvonne later found out that her friend had forgotten to renew the insurance policy and that she had actually been driving without insurance. When she went to the court administration office to pay the fine, she was told that the officer never filed the certificate of offence. However, almost nine months after she was pulled over, an officer came to the door and served her with a Part III summons to appear in court for the driving with no insurance. She has come to you for advice.

1. Is the officer allowed to charge her so long after the offence date? Explain.

2. Does Yvonne have a valid defence that she did not know she was driving without insurance?

Scenario 2

Graham works for a trendy downtown restaurant. On weekends, it is filled to capacity and lined up around the block. One Saturday evening, Graham's boss noticed that one of the customers in line had a guide dog and told Graham to make him "go away" since the dog would take up too much floor space and posed a tripping risk for the restaurant's wait staff. Graham tried to offer the customer and his friends a free meal if they would be willing to come back another night, but they asked why they were getting the special offer. Graham explained that the owner didn't want the dog in the restaurant and told him he would have to tie the dog up outside instead.

1. Was Graham's conduct appropriate in this case? Explain.

2. Who could be charged in this case? Explain.

3. What are the possible penalties in this case?

Administrative Monetary Penalties

16

LEARNING OUTCOMES

After reading this chapter, you will understand

■ how an administrative penalty system is currently being used in Ontario;

■ the difference when dealing with parking infractions in the POA system compared with an AMPs system; and

■ the benefits of using an administrative penalty system.

Introduction

Within their 2011 report titled *Modernizing the Provincial Offences Act: A New Framework and Other Reforms*,[1] the Law Commission of Ontario (LCO) made several recommendations related to the expanded use of administrative penalty systems throughout Ontario to deal with minor regulatory offences, notably parking infractions. Included was a recommendation to amend the *Provincial Offences Act* in order to remove the prosecution of Part II parking infractions from the Ontario Court of Justice. Instead, the LCO recommended that each municipality adopt and implement a by-law for administrative penalties in order to enforce by-laws relating to parking infractions.

Several years have passed since the LCO recommendations were made, but Part II offences still remain in the POA, and many municipalities continue to prosecute parking infractions in the Ontario Court of Justice. At the time of the initial LCO report, the only two municipalities that were using an administrative penalty system for parking infractions were Vaughan and Oshawa. Since the LCO report, several large municipalities in Ontario have opted to utilize administrative penalties for parking and other matters, including Mississauga, Windsor, Hamilton, and Toronto. When an administrative penalty system is put into place for a particular by-law, it replaces the POA provisions that would otherwise have been applicable to that by-law.

Overview of AMPs

Administrative monetary penalties (AMPs)[2] can be used as a system for enforcing compliance with by-laws and regulatory statutes. This approach has been adopted by numerous municipalities, provinces, and the federal government as an alternative way to enforce and adjudicate minor infractions. Administrative penalties have been used for parking infractions in cities throughout the United States (e.g., New York and Chicago) for several decades, as well as in other countries (e.g., Australia).[3] An AMP system takes disputes out of the courtroom as a judicial process and moves them to a municipal office or hearing room as more of an administrative review process.

Administrative penalty systems are not new in Ontario. They have been used for the enforcement of some Ontario statutes for many years. Administrative penalties are established for some of the offences in the *Compulsory Automobile Insurance Act*,[4]

---

1 Law Commission of Ontario, *Modernization of the Provincial Offences Act* (Toronto: Osgoode Hall Law School, York University, August 2011), online: <http://www.lco-cdo.org/en/our-current-projects/provincial-offences-act/poa-final-report-august-2011>.

2 Also known as the administrative penalty system (APS).

3 Law Commission of Ontario, *V. Administrative Monetary Penalties as an Alternative to the Court Process* (Toronto: Osgoode Hall Law School, York University, August 2011), online: <http://www.lco-cdo.org/en/our-current-projects/provincial-offences-act/poa-interim-report-march-2011/v-administrative-monetary-penalties-as-an-alternative-to-the-court-process>.

4 RSO 1990, c C.25.

the *Accessibility for Ontarians with Disabilities Act, 2005*,[5] the *Environmental Protection Act*,[6] and dozens of other Ontario statutes.

Bill 130, the *Municipal Statute Law Amendment Act, 2006*,[7] was amended the *Municipal Act, 2001* on January 1, 2007,[8] to allow municipalities to develop an administrative penalty system for the enforcement of parking matters. Specifically, section 102.1 of the *Municipal Act* establishes the authority for a municipality to require a person to pay an administrative penalty if that person has failed to comply with a parking by-law.

Licensing matters can also be dealt with through administrative penalties because sections 9 and 10 of the *Municipal Act* establish the broad authority of municipalities to establish systems of administrative penalties for the enforcement of any by-law passed under the *Municipal Act*.

Ontario Regulation 333/07 ("AMP Regulation") was created to establish guidelines and procedures for municipal administrative penalty systems (see Appendix E). Section 3(2) of the AMP Regulation sets out the purpose of a system of administrative penalties as follows:

> The purpose of the system of administrative penalties established by the municipality shall be to assist the municipality in regulating the flow of traffic and use of land, including highways, by promoting compliance with its by-laws respecting the parking, standing or stopping of motor vehicles.

Note the dual purpose—not only is there an enforcement aspect of the AMP system, but administrative penalties are also focused on improving compliance. The AMP Regulation does not set out a monetary limit for the administrative penalties, but instead indicates that the penalty amount must not be punitive in nature and that it must not exceed the amount reasonably required to promote compliance with the by-law. This gives municipalities an opportunity to set their own penalties and to vary the penalties from any set fines that had been previously been established. Further, the AMP Regulation requires a municipality to develop standards that include policies and procedures relating to political interference, conflict of interest, and financial management and reporting, as well as to develop a process for filing and processing complaints made by the public.

Parking Infractions Under the POA

Traditional POA enforcement of parking violations involves service of a Part II parking infraction notice by affixing it to the vehicle or serving it on the owner/operator of the vehicle at the time and the place of the infraction. If a trial date is requested for the matter, the trial will be held in the Ontario Court of Justice (or, in rare cases, the Superior Court), adjudicated by a justice of the peace or a judge (most often, a justice of the peace). Since this process can take several months, the courts tend to become backlogged in some of the larger municipalities.

---

5 SO 2005, c 11.

6 RSO 1990, c E.19.

7 SO 2006, C.32.

8 SO 2001, c 25.

Under the POA system, a defendant who is not satisfied with the trial level decision and who has grounds for appeal can still go through several levels of appeal. Appeals may be brought to the Ontario Court of Justice and, with leave to appeal, Ontario Court of Appeal, and the Supreme Court of Canada.

Penalties for parking convictions result in a fine for the owner of the vehicle, but do not carry any demerit points and include no possibility of imprisonment. However, it is worth noting that unpaid parking tickets can lead to plate denial by the Ministry of Transportation.

Concerns with the POA System

The use of the provincial offences system to deal with parking infractions has been criticized for being overly expensive. Part II parking trials are conducted in the same courtrooms as Part I and Part III trials and, much like the trials for the more serious provincial offences, require the presence of a justice, clerk, prosecutor, and the provincial offences officer who laid the charge. In addition, any defendant who requests an interpreter will be provided with one (paid for by the court). With the expenses of the courtroom and the number of people who are required to be in attendance, the POA system is a costly method of dealing with infractions that generally carry a fine of less than $100 (and often fall in the $20-$50 range).

Time delays are another concern with the POA system. It is not uncommon for a matter to take several months to proceed to trial. Judicial resources are strained and courtrooms are in demand, particularly in the Greater Toronto Area. Part II matters are not allocated a significant proportion of available court time. With these lengthy delays, defendants and their representatives have been successful in bringing 11B Charter motions for unreasonable delay. Having such charges stayed for unreasonable delay results in a loss of revenue for the municipality and is a waste of courtroom resources. This is also a time-consuming process for defendants as they prepare for and wait for the trial date.

The POA system isn't considered to be a user-friendly system. It has a very formal and complex process for dealing with a minor violation. It can be overwhelming for the average person to navigate through and is an intimidating atmosphere for someone who hasn't had prior exposure to the legal system.

At the time that the POA was drafted, some of the enforcement difficulties that arise today had not been anticipated. For example, since the POA requires the parking infraction notice to be served at the time and place of the infraction, it does not allow for service after the infraction has taken place or for other methods of service. Some drivers, aware of this limitation, decide to drive away when they see a parking enforcement officer taking down the details to prepare a parking infraction notice. This leaves no opportunity for the officer to serve the notice. Some municipalities have advocated for changes to the service provisions of the POA, but to date, no such changes have been made.

Parking Infractions Under AMPs

While some aspects of the AMP process will seem similar to the POA process, an AMP system is designed to be more streamlined and efficient. Each municipality can draft its own administrative penalty by-law and determine the processes that meet the needs of the municipality. Therefore, by-laws and procedures will vary from municipality to municipality.

PRACTICE TIP

The AMP Regulation requires a municipality to ensure the administrative penalty by-law is made available to the public. Since there can be variances in by-laws between municipalities, it is essential to review the relevant by-law each time you represent a client in a different municipality. Municipal by-laws are generally posted online or are available from the municipality.

Parking infractions involve the service of a document called a **penalty notice** (for a sample of the penalty notice used by the City of Markham, see Figure 16.1). Each municipality is able to establish the relevant service requirements for their notices. A common theme among administrative penalty by-laws established by many of the municipalities relates to expanded rules for service. For example, in the City of Brampton, a penalty notice can be served by: affixing it to the vehicle, delivering it

penalty notice
the document served on the registered owner of a vehicle under the administrative penalty system

Figure 16.1 Sample Penalty Notice

PARKING PENALTY NOTICE

City of Markham
Province of Ontario

Markham

City of Markham
Administrative
Penalty By Law

______________________________ certifies that the owner (or operator) of the vehicle upon which was displayed the numbered plate described below committed the Parking Contravention indicated below.

200000001

DATE: TIME OF INFRACTION:

FROM: TO:

MAKE:

PLATE:

PROV: VAL TAG:

LOCATION:

METER:
AREA MUN. CITY OF MARKHAM FORMER MUN.:

to the person with care and control of the vehicle, delivering it to the owner, sending it by registered mail or regular letter mail, or sending it by fax or email (see sections 8(1) and 33(1) of City of Brampton By-law 333-2013). This expands the ability for service of the notice at a later date, even if the driver has driven away.

The monetary penalty is due when the enforcement officer discovers a contravention of a by-law and serves the penalty notice; however, the registered owner of the vehicle has the right to request a review of the penalty. Upon request, it is initially reviewed by a **screening officer**, who has the ability to affirm, reduce, or cancel the penalty. If the registered owner is not satisfied with the result of the screening, he or she can request a review of the penalty by a **hearing officer**, who is able to affirm, reduce, or cancel the decision of the screening officer. The hearing officer's decision is final with no further rights to appeal. The procedural requirements and responsibilities of both the screening officer and the hearing officer are set out in section 8(1) of the AMP Regulation. While screening officers are usually employees of the municipality, hearing officers are typically independent, impartial third parties who are contracted by the municipality to provide adjudication services on an as-needed basis.

Similar to the POA process, there are no demerit points and no possibility of imprisonment under an AMP by-law, just the penalty and any associated fees. If the penalty and fees remain unpaid, a notice of default will be sent to the Ontario registrar of Motor Vehicles, which will then deny the renewal of existing vehicle licence permits or the issuance of new permits.[9]

The AMP approach is a paradigm shift in utilizing penalties instead of fines. The monetary penalty is not considered to be a fine and is not intended as a punishment. Instead the penalty under an AMP system is intended to encourage compliance. The process is considered to be more of a civil process than a quasi-criminal process. Administrative monetary penalties are imposed without a courtroom trial and do not require an admission or a finding of guilt. Requirements are put in place to ensure that the AMP process is fair and in accordance with the principles of natural justice.

Municipalities can also use a combined process where they continue to use the POA process for some parking infractions but use an AMP system for other parking infractions. As an example, the City of Mississauga has transferred most of the parking infractions to an AMP system, but has opted to continue to use the POA system for tickets issued at Toronto Pearson International Airport.

Other Matters Under AMPs

It is possible for municipalities to use an AMP system for more than parking infractions. Some municipalities have moved a portion of their licensing matters into an AMPs system. For example, the City of Mississauga uses AMPs to deal with animal licenses and mobile licensing (i.e., taxi or limousine licensees) and the City of Oshawa uses the administrative penalty process to deal with business licenses and residential rental housing licenses. It is anticipated that, in the future, many of the municipalities that are currently using an AMPs system will expand their use of it for additional matters.

screening officer
a municipal employee who provides an initial review of an administrative penalty

hearing officer
an administrative law judge who provides a final review of a screening officer's decision

---

9 For licensing matters, outstanding payments may result in the revocation or denial of a licence.

Benefits of AMPs

The movement to an AMP system is anticipated to have a number of benefits for both the municipality and the **contravener.**

contravener
a person who has violated an administrative penalty by-law

More Efficient

Under an AMP system, matters are dealt with more quickly than under the POA system. Many municipalities cite a 10-month-plus wait to hear parking tickets in court, while an AMP system will typically have a matter heard within a couple of months.

More Convenient

Most municipalities have flexibility with their screening times and some municipalities have opted to offer walk-in screenings. The hearings also tend to be more convenient as some of the municipalities offer a fixed time for each hearing (e.g., Oshawa, Vaughan). This is in contrast to the POA system, where dozens of matters are scheduled within a court tier and require defendants to wait until their matter is called.

Cost Savings

While the processes and requirements vary between municipalities, it seems that there are significant cost savings in terms of staffing and required attendance at screenings and hearings. Screenings are conducted between the contravener/representative and the screening officer, with no other parties required to attend. With regard to hearings, some municipalities (e.g., Mississauga) conduct hearings with reliance on the officer's notes and photographs instead of requiring attendance by the officer. In other municipalities (e.g., Vaughan) hearings are scheduled during the officer's regular work shift so that it is not necessary to pay overtime. Further cost savings occur since hearing officers are not employees of the municipality and are only scheduled and paid on an as-needed basis.

Reduction in the Number of Hearings

The use of an AMP system may lead to fewer hearings being requested. According to the Law Commission of Ontario's *Interim Report*, the City of Vaughan indicated that the percentage of matters going to a hearing officer is roughly 1.5 percent of tickets issued, which is lower than the roughly 3.5 percent of tickets that are challenged in court.[10]

Opportunity for Education

With fewer matters before the hearing officer and/or fixed time slots, there is more time for one-on-one dialogue with the contraveners, which provides an opportunity

---

10 *Supra* note 3.

to educate residents about the by-laws. This contributes to improving compliance. For example, a person who disputes a penalty notice for parking in a fire route because he or she was parked only briefly will learn that there is no grace period for fire routes and that the length of time he or she was stopped is irrelevant.

Fewer Loopholes in the System

In the POA system, matters are sometimes dismissed due to delay or because of the non-attendance of the enforcement officer. With fewer delays and more officers attending as part of their regular workday or not being required to attend for some matters, there are fewer loopholes or opportunities to beat the system. This translates into cost savings for taxpayers.

Court Used for More Serious Matters

Parking infractions take up valuable court time and resources. With the implementation of an AMP system, court time is freed up to deal with Part I and Part III matters. Reducing congestion in the courts will bring the more serious POA matters to court with fewer delays.

Increased Accessibility

An AMP system provides a more local and accessible dispute resolution system. Hearings and screenings are held at local municipal offices instead of the nearest provincial offences courts. For example, contraveners can go to the City of Markham offices for an AMP parking matter instead of being required to drive to Richmond Hill or Newmarket to deal with a POA parking matter.

User-Friendly

The AMP system is considered to be a more user-friendly approach to dealing with minor infractions without the formality and intimidation of a courtroom. While lawyers and paralegals are still able to act as legal representatives, there may be less of a need for representation in this context because it is a more personalized process that simplifies the procedure without sacrificing justice.

KEY TERMS

contravener, 237
hearing officer, 236
penalty notice, 235
screening officer, 236

REVIEW QUESTIONS

Multiple Choice

1. Which of the following statements is FALSE in relation to the penalties under an AMP system?

   a. The penalty must not be punitive in nature.

   b. The penalty cannot exceed the amount reasonably required to promote compliance.

   c. Municipalities can set their own penalty amounts.

   d. The penalties must be consistent with previously established set fines.

2. Which of the following statements describes the role of a hearing officer?

   a. Provides an initial review of the penalty in an AMP system.

   b. Provides a review of the enforcement officer's penalty in an AMP system.

   c. Provides a review of the screening officer's decision in an AMP system.

   d. Provides a review of the justice's decision in a POA system.

Short Answer

1. List four benefits of an AMP system.

2. Explain some of the concerns with the POA system for parking infractions.

Scenario

The following scenario applies to questions 1-3:

Clive had to pick up a few items at his local grocery store. It was pouring rain, so he decided to leave his car right in front of the store so he could quickly run in and out. There were a lot of other cars parked there too, so he assumed it would be okay. However, when he returned he noticed a penalty notice on his windshield for parking in a designated fire route. He wants to challenge the notice because there were other cars parked there and because he was only briefly parked.

1. Was this proper service of the penalty notice?

2. Do you think he will be successful? Explain.

3. Kasha was also parked in front of the grocery store. However, when she returned from making her purchase the traffic enforcement officer was still in the process of writing her penalty notice. She decided to quickly get into her car and drive away. Can she still be served?

Legislation

Access to Justice Act, 2006, SO 2006, c 21 (Bill 14)

Accessibility for Ontarians with Disabilities Act, 2005, SO 2005, c 11

Blind Persons' Rights Act, RSO 1990, c B.7

Building Code Act, 1992, SO 1992, c 23

Canadian Charter of Rights and Freedoms, Part I of the Constitution Act, 1982, being Schedule B to the Canada Act 1982 (UK), 1982, c 11

Canadian Environmental Protection Act, SC 1999, c 33

Canadian Shipping Act, 2001, SC 2001, c 26

City of Toronto Act, 2006, SO 2006, c 11, Sch A

Clean Water Act, 2006, SO 2006, c 22

Commissioners for Taking Affidavits Act, RSO 1990, c C.17

Compulsory Automobile Insurance Act, RSO 1990, c C.25

Constitution Act, 1982, RSC 1985, App II, No 44, Part I

Contraventions Act, SC 1992, c 47

Courts of Justice Act, RSO 1990, c C.43

Criminal Code, RSC 1985, c C-46

Compulsory Automobile Insurance Act, RSO 1990, c C.25

Department of Transport Act, RSC 1985, c T-18

Dog Owners' Liability Act, RSO 1990, c D.16

Environmental Protection Act, RSO 1990, c E.19

Evidence Act, RSO 1990 c E.23

Fisheries Act, RSC 1985, c F-14

Gaming Control Act, 1992, SO 1992, c 24

Highway Traffic Act, RSO 1990, c H.8

Historic Canals Regulations, SOR/93-220

Income Tax Act, RSC 1985, c 1 (5th Supp)

Law Society Act, RSO 1990, c L.8

Limitations Act, SO 2002, c 24, Sch B

Liquor Licence Act, RSO 1990, c L.19

Municipal Act, 2001, SO 2001, c 25

Municipal Statute Law Amendment Act, 2006, SO 2006, C.32 (Bill 130)

Occupational Health and Safety Act, RSO 1990, c O.1

Pesticides Act, RSO 1990, c P.11

Planning Act, RSO 1990, c P.13

Police Services Act, RSO 1990, c P.15, section 53(2)

Provincial Offences Act, RSO 1990, c P.33

Smoke-Free Ontario Act, SO 1994, c 10

Trespass to Property Act, RSO 1990, c T.21

Provincial Offences Act

RSO 1990, c P.33

INTERPRETATION

Interpretation

1(1) In this Act,

"certificate" means a certificate of offence issued under Part I or a certificate of parking infraction issued under Part II;

"court" means the Ontario Court of Justice;

"electronic" and "electronically" have the meanings set out in the Electronic Commerce Act, 2000;

"judge" means a provincial judge;

"justice" means a provincial judge or a justice of the peace;

"offence" means an offence under an Act of the Legislature or under a regulation or by-law made under the authority of an Act of the Legislature;

"police officer" means a chief of police or other police officer but does not include a special constable or by-law enforcement officer;

"prescribed" means prescribed by the rules of court;

"prosecutor" means the Attorney General or, where the Attorney General does not intervene, means the person who issues a certificate or lays an information and includes an agent acting on behalf of either of them;

"provincial offences officer" means,
   (a) a police officer,
   (b) a constable appointed pursuant to any Act,
   (c) a municipal law enforcement officer referred to in subsection 101(4) of the *Municipal Act, 2001* or in subsection 79(1) of the *City of Toronto Act, 2006*, while in the discharge of his or her duties,
   (d) a by-law enforcement officer of any municipality or of any local board of any municipality, while in the discharge of his or her duties,
   (e) an officer, employee or agent of any municipality or of any local board of any municipality whose responsibilities include the enforcement of a by-law, an Act or a regulation under an Act, while in the discharge of his or her duties, or
   (f) a person designated under subsection (3);

"representative" means, in respect of a proceeding to which this Act applies, a person authorized under the *Law Society Act* to represent a person in that proceeding;

"set fine" means the amount of fine set by the Chief Justice of the Ontario Court of Justice for an offence for the purpose of proceedings commenced under Part I or II.

(2) Repealed.

Designation of provincial offences officers

(3) A minister of the Crown may designate in writing any person or class of persons as a provincial offences officer for the purposes of all or any class of offences.

General
Purpose of Act

2(1) The purpose of this Act is to replace the summary conviction procedure for the prosecution of provincial offences, including the provisions adopted by reference to the *Criminal Code* (Canada), with a procedure that reflects the distinction between provincial offences and criminal offences.

Interpretation

(2) Where, as an aid to the interpretation of provisions of this Act, recourse is had to the judicial interpretation of and practices under corresponding provisions of the *Criminal Code* (Canada), any variation in wording without change in substance shall not, in itself, be construed to intend a change of meaning.

PART I   COMMENCEMENT OF PROCEEDINGS BY CERTIFICATE OF OFFENCE

Certificate of offence and offence notice

3(1) In addition to the procedure set out in Part III for commencing a proceeding by laying an information, a proceeding in respect of an offence may be commenced by filing a certificate of offence alleging the offence in the office of the court.

Issuance and service

(2) A provincial offences officer who believes that one or more persons have committed an offence may issue, by completing and signing in the form prescribed under section 13,

(a) a certificate of offence certifying that an offence has been committed; and

(b) either an offence notice indicating the set fine for the offence or a summons.

Service

(3) The offence notice or summons shall be served personally upon the person charged within thirty days after the alleged offence occurred.

(4) Repealed.

Certificate of service

(5) Where service is made by the provincial offences officer who issued the certificate of offence, the officer shall certify on the certificate of offence that he or she personally served the offence notice or summons on the person charged and the date of service.

Affidavit of service

(6) Where service is made by a person other than the provincial offences officer who issued the certificate of offence, he or she shall complete an affidavit of service in the prescribed form.

Certificate as evidence

(7) A certificate of service of an offence notice or summons purporting to be signed by the provincial offences officer issuing it or an affidavit of service under subsection (6) shall be received in evidence and is proof of personal service in the absence of evidence to the contrary.

Officer not to act as agent

(8) The provincial offences officer who serves an offence notice or summons under this section shall not receive payment of any money in respect of a fine, or receive the offence notice for delivery to the court.

Filing of certificate of offence

4. A certificate of offence shall be filed in the office of the court as soon as is practicable, but no later than seven days after service of the offence notice or summons.

Having a trial

5(1) A defendant who is served with an offence notice may give notice of intention to appear in court for the purpose of entering a plea and having a trial of the matter.

Notice of intention to appear in offence notice

(2) If the offence notice includes a part with a notice of intention to appear, the defendant must give notice of intention to appear by,

(a) completing the notice of intention to appear part of the offence notice; and

(b) delivering the offence notice to the court office specified in it in the manner provided in the offence notice.

Notice of intention to appear to be filed in person

(3) If the offence notice requires the notice of intention to appear to be filed in person, the defendant must give the notice of intention to appear by,

(a) attending in person or by representative at the court office specified in the offence notice at the time or times specified in the offence notice; and

(b) filing a notice of intention to appear in the form prescribed under section 13 with the clerk of the court.

Specified court office

(4) A notice of intention to appear under subsection (3) is not valid if the defendant files the notice of intention to appear at a court office other than the one specified on the offence notice.

Notice of trial

(5) Where a notice of intention to appear is received under subsection (2) or (3), the clerk of the court shall, as soon as is practicable, give notice to the defendant and the prosecutor of the time and place of the trial.

Rescheduling time of trial

(6) The clerk of the court may, for administrative reasons, reschedule the time of the trial by giving a revised notice to the defendant and the prosecutor within 21 days of giving the notice referred to in subsection (5).

Availability of meeting procedure

5.1(1) This section applies where the offence notice requires the notice of intention to appear to be filed in person in the form prescribed under section 13.

Option for meeting with the prosecutor

(2) Instead of filing a notice of intention to appear under subsection 5(3), a defendant may request a meeting with the prosecutor to discuss the resolution of the offence by,

(a) indicating that request on the offence notice; and

(b) delivering the offence notice to the court office specified on it within 15 days after the defendant was served with the offence notice.

Notice of meeting time

(3) Where a defendant requests a meeting with the prosecutor under subsection (2), the clerk of the court shall, as soon as is practicable, give notice to the defendant and the prosecutor of the time and place of their meeting.

Rescheduling the meeting time

(4) If the time for the meeting scheduled in the notice under subsection (3) is not suitable for the defendant, the defendant may, at least two days before the scheduled time of the meeting, deliver to the clerk of the court one written request to reschedule the time for the meeting and the clerk shall arrange a new meeting time to take place within 30 days of the time scheduled in the notice under subsection (3).

Notice of rescheduled meeting time

(5) Where a meeting time is rescheduled under subsection (4), the clerk of the court shall, as soon as is practicable, give notice to the defendant and the prosecutor of the rescheduled time and the place of their meeting.

Meeting by electronic method

(6) The defendant and the prosecutor may, if unable to attend in person because of remoteness, attend their meeting by electronic method in accordance with section 83.1.

Agreement on plea of guilty and submissions

(7) At their meeting, the defendant and the prosecutor may agree that,

(a) the defendant will enter a guilty plea to the offence or a substituted offence; and

(b) the defendant and the prosecutor will make submissions as to penalty, including an extension of time for payment.

Appearance before justice

(8) If an agreement is reached under subsection (7), the defendant shall, as directed by the prosecutor,

(a) appear with the prosecutor before a justice sitting in court and orally enter the plea and make submissions; or

(b) appear without the prosecutor before a justice sitting in court within 10 days, enter the plea orally and make the submissions in the form determined by the regulations.

Conviction

(9) Upon receiving the plea and submissions under subsection (8), the justice may,

(a) require the prosecutor to appear and speak to the submissions, if the submissions were submitted under clause (8)(b); and

(b) enter a conviction and impose the set fine or such other fine as is permitted by law in respect of the offence for which the plea was entered.

If no justice available

(10) If no justice is available after the meeting to conduct the proceeding under clause (8)(a), the clerk of the court shall, as soon as practicable, give notice to the defendant and the prosecutor of the time and place for their joint appearance before a justice.

Notice of trial

(11) The clerk of the court shall, as soon as is practicable, give notice to the defendant and the prosecutor of the time and place of the trial if,

(a) an agreement is not reached under subsection (7); or

(b) the justice does not accept the guilty plea and refers the matter to trial.

Rescheduling time of trial

(12) The clerk of the court may, for administrative reasons, reschedule the time of the trial by giving a revised notice to the defendant and the prosecutor within 21 days of giving the notice referred to in subsection (11).

5.1.1 Repealed.

5.2 Repealed.

6. Repealed.

Plea of guilty with submissions

7(1) A defendant who does not have the option of meeting with the prosecutor under section 5.1 and does not wish to dispute the charge in the offence notice, but wishes to make submissions as to penalty, including an extension of time for payment, may attend at the time and place specified in the notice and may appear before a justice sitting in court for the purpose of pleading guilty to the offence and making submissions as to penalty, and the justice may enter a conviction and impose the set fine or such lesser fine as is permitted by law.

Submissions under oath

(2) The justice may require submissions under subsection (1) to be made under oath, orally or by affidavit.

Payment out of court

8(1) A defendant who does not wish to dispute the charge in the offence notice may, in the manner indicated on the offence notice, pay the set fine and all applicable costs and surcharges fixed by the regulations.

Effect of payment

(2) Acceptance by the court office of payment under subsection (1) constitutes,

(a) a plea of guilty by the defendant;

(b) conviction of the defendant for the offence; and

(c) imposition of a fine in the amount of the set fine for the offence.

Deemed not to dispute charge

9(1) A defendant is deemed to not wish to dispute the charge where,

(a) at least 15 days have elapsed after the defendant was served with the offence notice and the defendant did not give notice of intention to appear under section 5, did not request a meeting with the prosecutor in accordance with section 5.1 and did not plead guilty under section 7 or 8;

(b) the defendant requested a meeting with the prosecutor in accordance with section 5.1 but did not attend the scheduled meeting with the prosecutor; or

(c) the defendant reached an agreement with the prosecutor under subsection 5.1(7) but did not appear at a sentencing hearing with a justice under subsection 5.1(8).

Action by justice

(2) Where a defendant is deemed to not wish to dispute the charge, a justice shall examine the certificate of offence and shall,

(a) where the certificate of offence is complete and regular on its face, enter a conviction in the defendant's absence and without a hearing and impose the set fine for the offence; or

(b) where the certificate of offence is not complete and regular on its face, quash the proceeding.

Conviction without proof of by-law

(3) Where the offence is in respect of an offence under a by-law of a municipality, the justice shall enter a conviction under clause (2)(a) without proof of the by-law that creates the offence if the certificate of offence is complete and regular on its face.

Failure to appear at trial

9.1(1) A defendant is deemed to not wish to dispute the charge where the defendant has been issued a notice of the time and place of trial and fails to appear at the time and place appointed for the trial.

Examination by justice

(2) If subsection (1) applies, section 54 does not apply, and a justice shall examine the certificate of offence and shall without a hearing enter a conviction in the defendant's absence and impose the set fine for the offence if the certificate is complete and regular on its face.

Quashing proceeding

(3) The justice shall quash the proceeding if he or she is not able to enter a conviction.

Signature on notice

10. A signature on an offence notice or notice of intention to appear purporting to be that of the defendant is proof, in the absence of evidence to the contrary, that it is the signature of the defendant.

Reopening

Application to strike out conviction

11(1) A defendant who was convicted without a hearing may, within 15 days of becoming aware of the conviction, apply to a justice to strike out the conviction.

Striking out the conviction

(2) Upon application under subsection (1), a justice shall strike out a conviction if satisfied by affidavit of the defendant that, through no fault of the defendant, the defendant was unable to appear for a hearing or for a meeting under section 5.1 or the defendant did not receive delivery of a notice or document relating to the offence.

If conviction struck out

(3) If the justice strikes out the conviction, the justice shall,

(a) proceed under section 7, if the offence notice does not require the notice of intention to appear to be filed in person and the defendant wishes to proceed under that section;

(b) direct the clerk of the court to give notice to the defendant and the prosecutor of the time and place of their meeting under subsection 5.1(3), if the offence notice requires the notice of intention to appear to be filed in person and the defendant wishes to proceed under that section; or

(c) direct the clerk of the court to give notice to the defendant and the prosecutor of the time and place of the trial.

Rescheduling time of trial

(4) The clerk of the court may, for administrative reasons, reschedule the time of the trial by giving a revised notice to the defendant and the prosecutor within 21 days of giving the notice referred to in clause (3)(c).

Certificate

(5) A justice who strikes out a conviction under subsection (2) shall give the defendant a certificate of the fact in the prescribed form.

Error by municipality

11.1(1) A municipality or other body may apply to a justice requesting that a conviction be struck out if the defendant was convicted because of an error made by the municipality or other body.

Striking out conviction

(2) On an application by a municipality or other body, if a justice is satisfied that an error was made, the justice shall strike out the conviction.

Notice to defendant

(3) If the justice strikes out the conviction, the municipality or other body shall notify the defendant of that fact.

Consequences of conviction

Penalty

12(1)   Where the penalty prescribed for an offence includes a fine of more than $1,000 or imprisonment and a proceeding is commenced under this Part, the provision for fine or imprisonment does not apply and in lieu thereof the offence is punishable by a fine of not more than the maximum fine prescribed for the offence or $1,000, whichever is the lesser.

Transitional

(1.1)   Subsection (1) applies only to an offence committed on or after the day subsection 1(18) of Schedule 4 to the *Good Government Act, 2009* comes into force.

Other consequences of conviction

(2)   Where a person is convicted of an offence in a proceeding initiated by an offence notice,

(a)   a provision in or under any other Act that provides for an action or result following upon a conviction of an offence does not apply to the conviction, except,

(i)   for the purpose of carrying out the sentence imposed,

(ii)   for the purpose of recording and proving the conviction,

(iii)   for the purposes of giving effect to any action or result provided for under the *Highway Traffic Act*, and

(iv)   Repealed.

(v)   for the purposes of section 16 of the *Smoke-Free Ontario Act*; and

(b)   any thing seized in connection with the offence after the service of the offence notice is not liable to forfeiture.

Regulations

13(1)   The Lieutenant Governor in Council may make regulations,

(a)   Repealed.

(b)   authorizing the use in a form prescribed under clause (1.1)(a) of any word or expression to designate an offence.

(c)   Repealed.

(d)   Repealed.

Same, Attorney General

(1.1)   The Attorney General may make regulations,

(a)   prescribing the form of certificates of offence, offence notices and summonses and such other forms as are considered necessary under this Part;

(b)   respecting any matter that is considered necessary to provide for the use of the forms under this Part.

Sufficiency of abbreviated wording

(2)   The use on a form prescribed under clause (1.1)(a) of any word or expression authorized by the regulations to designate an offence is sufficient for all purposes to describe the offence designated by such word or expression.

Idem

(3)   Where the regulations do not authorize the use of a word or expression to describe an offence in a form prescribed under clause (1.1)(a), the offence may be described in accordance with section 25.

PART II   COMMENCEMENT OF PROCEEDINGS FOR PARKING INFRACTIONS

"Parking infraction," Part II

14.   In this Part,

"parking infraction" means any unlawful parking, standing or stopping of a vehicle that constitutes an offence.

Proceeding, parking infraction

14.1   In addition to the procedure set out in Part III for commencing a proceeding by laying an information, a proceeding in respect of a parking infraction may be commenced in accordance with this Part.

Certificate and notice of parking infraction

15(1)   A provincial offences officer who believes from his or her personal knowledge that one or more persons have committed a parking infraction may issue,

(a)   a certificate of parking infraction certifying that a parking infraction has been committed; and

(b)   a parking infraction notice indicating the set fine for the infraction.

Idem

(2)   The provincial offences officer shall complete and sign the certificate and notice in the form prescribed under section 20.

Municipal by-laws

(3)   If the alleged infraction is under a by-law of a municipality, it is not necessary to include a reference to the number of the by-law on the certificate or notice.

Service on owner

(4)   The issuing provincial offences officer may serve the parking infraction notice on the owner of the vehicle identified in the notice,

(a)   by affixing it to the vehicle in a conspicuous place at the time of the alleged infraction; or

(b)   by delivering it personally to the person having care and control of the vehicle at the time of the alleged infraction.

Service on operator

(5)   The issuing provincial offences officer may serve the parking infraction notice on the operator of a vehicle by delivering it to the operator personally at the time of the alleged infraction.

Certificate of service

(6) The issuing provincial offences officer shall certify on the certificate of parking infraction that he or she served the parking infraction notice on the person charged and the date and method of service.

Certificate as evidence

(7) If it appears that the provincial offences officer who issued a certificate of parking infraction has certified service of the parking infraction notice and signed the certificate, the certificate shall be received in evidence and is proof of service unless there is evidence to the contrary.

Payment out of court

16. A defendant who does not wish to dispute the charge may deliver the notice and amount of the set fine to the place shown on the notice.

Intention to appear

17(1) A defendant who is served with a parking infraction notice may give notice of intention to appear in court for the purpose of entering a plea and having a trial of the matter by so indicating on the parking infraction notice and delivering the notice to the place specified in it.

Proceeding commenced

(2) If a defendant gives notice of an intention to appear, a proceeding may be commenced in respect of the charge if it is done within seventy-five days after the day on which the alleged infraction occurred.

Idem

(3) The proceeding shall be commenced by filing in the office of the court,

    (a) the certificate of parking infraction; and

    (b) if the parking infraction is alleged against the defendant as owner of a vehicle, evidence of the ownership of the vehicle.

Notice of trial

(4) As soon as practicable after the proceeding is commenced, the clerk of the court or a person designated by the regulations shall give notice to the defendant and prosecutor of the time and place of the trial.

Rescheduling time of trial

(4.1) The clerk of the court may, for administrative reasons, reschedule the time of the trial by giving a revised notice to the defendant and the prosecutor within 21 days of giving the notice referred to in subsection (4).

Certificate not invalid without by-law number

(5) A certificate of parking infraction issued for an infraction under a by-law of a municipality is not insufficient or irregular by reason only that it does not identify the by-law that creates the offence if the notice of trial given to the defendant identifies the by-law.

Application

17.1(1) This section applies where the parking infraction notice requires the notice of intention to appear to be filed in person at a place specified in the parking infraction notice.

Subss. 17(1), (3) and (4) inapplicable

(2) Subsections 17(1), (3) and (4) do not apply in a municipality in which this section applies.

Filing

(3) A defendant who is served with a parking infraction notice may give notice of intention to appear in court for the purpose of entering a plea and having a trial of the matter by attending in person or by representative at the place specified in the parking infraction notice at the time or times specified in the parking infraction notice and filing a notice of intention to appear with a person designated by the regulations.

Notice

(4) The notice of intention to appear shall be in the form prescribed under section 20.

Proceeding commenced

(5) The proceeding shall be commenced by filing the certificate of parking infraction in the office of the clerk of the court or the person designated by the regulations.

Notice of trial

(6) As soon as practicable after the proceeding is commenced, the clerk of the court or the person designated by the regulations shall give notice to the defendant and the prosecutor of the time and place of the trial.

Rescheduling time of trial

(6.1) The clerk of the court may, for administrative reasons, reschedule the time of the trial by giving a revised notice to the defendant and the prosecutor within 21 days of giving the notice referred to in subsection (6).

Evidence required at trial

(7) The court shall not convict the defendant unless the following are presented at the trial:

1. If the parking infraction is alleged against the defendant as owner of a vehicle, evidence of the ownership of the vehicle.

2. A copy of the notice of trial, with the certificate of the person who issued the notice under subsection (6), stating that the notice was given to the defendant and to the prosecutor and stating the date on which this was done.

3. The certificate of parking infraction.

Failure to respond

18(1) The person designated by the regulations may give the defendant a notice of impending conviction if,

(a) at least fifteen days and no more than thirty-five days have elapsed since the alleged infraction occurred;

(b) the defendant has not paid the fine; and

(c) a notice of intention to appear has not been received.

Form of notice

(2) The notice shall be in the form prescribed under section 20.

Contents of notice

(3) The notice shall,

(a) indicate the set fine for the infraction; and

(b) indicate that a conviction will be registered against the defendant unless the defendant pays the set fine or gives notice of an intention to appear in court for the purpose of entering a plea and having a trial of the matter.

Intention to appear

18.1(1) A defendant who receives a notice of impending conviction may give notice of intention to appear in court for the purpose of entering a plea and having a trial of the matter by so indicating on the notice of impending conviction and delivering the notice to the place specified in it.

Proceeding commenced

(2) If a defendant gives notice of an intention to appear after a notice of impending conviction has been given, a proceeding may be commenced in respect of the charge if it is done within seventy-five days after the day on which the alleged infraction occurred.

Idem

(3) The proceeding shall be commenced by filing in the office of the court,

(a) the certificate of parking infraction; and

(b) if the parking infraction is alleged against the defendant as owner of a vehicle, evidence of the ownership of the vehicle.

Notice of trial

(4) As soon as practicable after the proceeding is commenced, the clerk of the court or a person designated by the regulations shall give notice to the defendant and prosecutor of the time and place of the trial.

Rescheduling time of trial

(5) The clerk of the court may, for administrative reasons, reschedule the time of the trial by giving a revised notice to the defendant and the prosecutor within 21 days of giving the notice referred to in subsection (4).

Application

18.1.1(1) This section applies where the notice of impending conviction requires the notice of intention to appear to be filed in person at a place specified in the notice of impending conviction.

Subss. 18.1(1), (3) and (4) inapplicable

(2) Subsections 18.1(1), (3) and (4) do not apply in a municipality in which this section applies.

Subss. 17.1(5), (6) and (7) applicable

(2.1) Subsections 17.1(5), (6) and (7) apply to a proceeding begun under this section.

Filing notice of intention to appear

(3) A defendant who receives a notice of impending conviction may give notice of intention to appear in court for the purpose of entering a plea and having a trial of the matter by attending in person or by representative at the place specified in the notice of impending conviction at the time or times specified in the notice of impending conviction and filing a notice of intention to appear with a person designated by the regulations.

Form of notice

(4) The notice of intention to appear shall be in the form prescribed under section 20.

18.1.2 Repealed.

No response to impending conviction notice

18.2(1) A defendant who has been given a notice of impending conviction shall be deemed not to dispute the charge if fifteen days have elapsed since the defendant was given the notice, the fine has not been paid and a notice of intention to appear has not been received.

Request for conviction

(1.1) If subsection (1) applies, the person designated by the regulations may prepare and sign a certificate requesting a conviction in the form prescribed under section 20.

Idem

(2) The certificate requesting a conviction shall state,

(a) that the certificate of parking infraction is complete and regular on its face;

(b) if the defendant is liable as owner, that the person is satisfied that the defendant is the owner;

(c) that there is valid legal authority for charging the defendant with the parking infraction;

(d) that the defendant was given a notice of impending conviction at least fifteen days before the certificate requesting a conviction is filed;

(e) that the alleged infraction occurred less than seventy-five days before the certificate requesting a conviction is filed; and

(f) the prescribed information.

Idem

(3) If the certificate of parking infraction was issued for an infraction under a by-law of a municipality, the certificate requesting a conviction shall also state,

(a) that payment of the set fine has not been made; and

(b) that the defendant has not given notice of intention to appear in court for the purpose of entering a plea and having a trial of the matter.

Idem

(4) A certificate requesting a conviction purporting to be signed by the person authorized to prepare it shall be received in evidence and is proof, in the absence of evidence to the contrary, of the facts contained in it.

Proceeding commenced

(5) A proceeding may be commenced in respect of the charge by filing the certificate requesting a conviction in the office of the court, but only if the certificate is filed within seventy-five days after the alleged infraction occurred.

Recording of conviction

(6) Upon receiving a certificate requesting a conviction, the clerk of the court shall record a conviction and the defendant is then liable to pay the set fine for the offence.

Application where ticket defective

18.3(1) A defendant who is convicted of a parking infraction under section 18.2 may, within fifteen days after becoming aware of the conviction, apply to a justice requesting that the conviction be struck out for the reason that the parking infraction notice is defective on its face.

Idem

(2) On an application by the defendant, if a justice is satisfied that the parking infraction notice is defective on its face, the justice shall strike out the conviction and shall order that the municipality or other body that issued the certificate requesting a conviction pay $25 in costs to the defendant.

Failure to appear at trial

18.4(1) A defendant is deemed to not wish to dispute the charge where the defendant has been issued a notice of the time and place of trial and fails to appear at the time and place appointed for the trial.

Examination by justice

(2) If subsection (1) applies, section 54 does not apply, and a justice shall examine the certificate of parking infraction and shall without a hearing enter a conviction in the defendant's absence and impose the set fine for the offence if the certificate is complete and regular on its face.

Owner liability

(3) Despite subsection (2), if the defendant is alleged to have committed the parking infraction as owner of the vehicle involved in the infraction, the justice shall not enter a conviction and impose the set fine unless he or she is satisfied that the defendant is the owner of the vehicle.

Entering conviction

(4) The justice shall enter a conviction with respect to a parking infraction under a by-law of a municipality without proof of the by-law that creates the offence if the justice is satisfied that the other criteria for entering a conviction have been met.

Quashing proceeding

(5) The justice shall quash the proceeding if he or she is not able to enter a conviction.

Error by municipality

18.5(1) A municipality or other body may apply to a justice requesting that a conviction respecting a parking infraction be struck out if the defendant was convicted because of an error made by the municipality or other body.

Idem

(2) On an application by a municipality or other body, if a justice is satisfied that an error was made, the justice shall strike out the conviction.

Idem

(3) If the justice strikes out the conviction, the municipality or other body shall notify the defendant of that fact.

Authority to collect parking fines

18.6(1) A municipality may collect the fines levied for convictions respecting parking infractions under its by-laws if the municipality,

(a) enters into an agreement with the Attorney General to authorize it; or

(b) enters into a transfer agreement under Part X.

Agreement

(1.1) The Attorney General and a municipality may enter into an agreement for the purpose of clause (1)(a).

Notice to municipality

(2) If a conviction is entered respecting a parking infraction under a by-law of a municipality to which subsection (1) applies, the clerk of the court shall give notice of the conviction to the clerk of the municipality.

Notice of fine

(3) If the clerk of a municipality receives notice of a conviction, the clerk of the municipality or the person designated by the clerk shall give notice to the person against whom the conviction is entered, in the form prescribed under section 20, setting out the date and place of the infraction, the date of the conviction and the amount of the fine.

If default

(4) If the fine is in default, the clerk of the municipality may send notice to the person designated by the regulations certifying that it is in default.

Idem

(5) If a conviction is entered respecting a parking infraction and the parking infraction is not under a by-law of a municipality to which subsection (1) applies, the clerk of the court shall give notice to the person against whom the conviction is entered of the date and place of the infraction, the date of the conviction and the amount of the fine.

Reopening

Application to strike out conviction

19(1) A defendant who was convicted of a parking infraction without a hearing may, within 15 days of becoming aware of the conviction, apply to a justice to strike out the conviction.

Striking out the conviction

(2) Upon application under subsection (1), a justice shall strike out a conviction if satisfied by affidavit of the defendant or otherwise that, through no fault of the defendant, the defendant was unable to appear for a hearing or the defendant never received any notice or document relating to the parking infraction.

If conviction struck out

(3) If the justice strikes out the conviction, the justice shall,

(a) if the defendant enters a plea of guilty, accept the plea and impose the set fine; or

(b) direct the clerk of the court to give notice to the defendant and the prosecutor of the time and place of the trial.

Rescheduling time of trial

(4) The clerk of the court may, for administrative reasons, reschedule the time of the trial by giving a revised notice to the defendant and the prosecutor within 21 days of giving the notice referred to in clause (3)(b).

Regulations

20(1) The Lieutenant Governor in Council may make regulations,

(a) Repealed.

(b) authorizing the use in a form under this Part of any word or expression to designate a parking infraction;

(c), (d) Repealed.

(e) designating the persons or classes of persons who are required to prepare a notice of impending conviction or a certificate requesting a conviction for municipalities and for other bodies on whose behalf parking infraction notices are issued;

(e.1) designating a person or class of persons for the purposes of subsection 17(4), 17.1(3), 17.1(5), 17.1(6), 18.1(4) or 18.1.1(3);

(f) Repealed.

(g) authorizing Ontario to pay allowances to municipalities and other bodies that issue notices of impending conviction and that collect fines under this Part, providing for the payment of those allowances from the court costs received in connection with the fines levied under this Part and fixing the amount of the allowances;

(h) Repealed.

(i) designating the person to whom a notice certifying that a fine is in default under subsection 18.6(4) is to be sent;

(j) designating municipalities for the purposes of sections 17.1 and 18.1.1.

Same, Attorney General

(1.1) The Attorney General may make regulations,

(a) prescribing the forms that are considered necessary under this Part;

(b) respecting any matter that is considered necessary to provide for the use of the forms under this Part;

(c) prescribing information that is required to be included in a parking infraction notice, a notice of impending conviction or a certificate requesting a conviction;

(d) prescribing the information to be included in a notice certifying that a fine is in default under subsection 18.6(4).

Sufficiency of abbreviations

(2) The use on a form prescribed under clause (1.1)(a) of any word or expression authorized by the regulations to designate a parking infraction is sufficient for all purposes to describe the infraction designated by such word or expression.

Idem

(3) Where the regulations do not authorize the use of a word or expression to describe a parking infraction in a form prescribed under clause (1.1)(a), the offence may be described in accordance with section 25.

Note: Part II of this Act, as it read immediately before September 1, 1993 continues to apply to proceedings that were commenced before September 1, 1993. See: 1992, c. 20, s. 3.

PART III   COMMENCEMENT OF PROCEEDING BY INFORMATION

Commencement of proceeding by information

21(1) In addition to the procedure set out in Parts I and II for commencing a proceeding by the filing of a certificate, a proceeding in respect of an offence may be commenced by laying an information.

Exception

(2) Where a summons or offence notice has been served under Part I, no proceeding shall be commenced under subsection (1) in respect of the same offence except with the consent of the Attorney General or his or her agent.

Summons before information laid

22. Where a provincial offences officer believes, on reasonable and probable grounds, that an offence has been committed by a person whom the officer finds at or near the place where the offence was committed, he or she may, before an information is laid, serve the person with a summons in the prescribed form.

Information

23(1) Any person who, on reasonable and probable grounds, believes that one or more persons have committed an offence, may lay an information in the prescribed form and under oath before a justice alleging the offence and the justice shall receive the information.

Multiple defendants

(1.1) For greater certainty, an information laid under subsection (1) may include one or more persons.

Where information may be laid

(2) An information may be laid anywhere in Ontario.

Procedure on laying of information

24(1) A justice who receives an information laid under section 23 shall consider the information and, where he or she considers it desirable to do so, hear and consider in the absence of the defendant the allegations of the informant and the evidence of witnesses and,

(a) where he or she considers that a case for so doing is made out,

(i) confirm the summons served under section 22, if any,

(ii) issue a summons in the prescribed form, or

(iii) where the arrest is authorized by statute and where the allegations of the informant or the evidence satisfy the justice on reasonable and probable grounds that it is necessary in the public interest to do so, issue a warrant for the arrest of the defendant; or

(b) where he or she considers that a case for issuing process is not made out,

(i) so endorse the information, and

(ii) where a summons was served under section 22, cancel it and cause the defendant to be so notified.

Summons or warrants in blank

(2) A justice shall not sign a summons or warrant in blank.

Counts

25(1) Each offence charged in an information shall be set out in a separate count.

Allegation of offence

(2) Each count in an information shall in general apply to a single transaction and shall contain and is sufficient if it contains in substance a statement that the defendant committed an offence therein specified.

Reference to statutory provision

(3) Where in a count an offence is identified but the count fails to set out one or more of the essential elements of the offence, a reference to the provision creating or defining the offence shall be deemed to incorporate all the essential elements of the offence.

Idem

(4) The statement referred to in subsection (2) may be,

(a) in popular language without technical averments or allegations of matters that are not essential to be proved;

(b) in the words of the enactment that describes the offence; or

(c) in words that are sufficient to give to the defendant notice of the offence with which the defendant is charged.

More than one count

(5) Any number of counts for any number of offences may be joined in the same information.

Particulars of count

(6) A count shall contain sufficient detail of the circumstances of the alleged offence to give to the defendant reasonable information with respect to the act or omission to be proved against the defendant and to identify the transaction referred to.

Sufficiency

(7) No count in an information is insufficient by reason of the absence of details where, in the opinion of the court, the count otherwise fulfils the requirements of this section and, without restricting the generality of the foregoing, no count in an information is insufficient by reason only that,

(a) it does not name the person affected by the offence or intended or attempted to be affected;

(b) it does not name the person who owns or has a special property or interest in property mentioned in the count;

(c) it charges an intent in relation to another person without naming or describing the other person;

(d) it does not set out any writing that is the subject of the charge;

(e) it does not set out the words used where words that are alleged to have been used are the subject of the charge;

(f) it does not specify the means by which the alleged offence was committed;

(g) it does not name or describe with precision any person, place, thing or time; or

(h) it does not, where the consent of a person, official or authority is required before proceedings may be instituted for an offence, state that the consent has been obtained.

Idem

(8) A count is not objectionable for the reason only that,

(a) it charges in the alternative several different matters, acts or omissions that are stated in the alternative in an enactment that describes as an offence the matters, acts or omissions charged in the count; or

(b) it is double or multifarious.

Need to negative exception, etc.

(9) No exception, exemption, proviso, excuse or qualification prescribed by law is required to be set out or negatived, as the case may be, in an information.

Summons

26(1) A summons issued under section 22 or 24 shall,

(a) be directed to the defendant;

(b) set out briefly the offence in respect of which the defendant is charged; and

(c) require the defendant to attend court at a time and place stated therein and to attend thereafter as required by the court in order to be dealt with according to law.

Service

(2) A summons shall be served by a provincial offences officer by delivering it personally to the person to whom it is directed or if that person cannot conveniently be found, by leaving it for the person at the person's last known or usual place of abode with an inmate thereof who appears to be at least sixteen years of age.

Service outside Ontario

(3) Despite subsection (2), where the person to whom a summons is directed does not reside in Ontario, the summons shall be deemed to have been duly served seven days after it has been sent by registered mail to the person's last known or usual place of abode.

Service on corporation

(4) Service of a summons on a corporation may be effected,

(a) in the case of a municipal corporation by,

(i) delivering the summons personally to the mayor, warden, reeve or other chief officer of the corporation or to the clerk of the corporation, or

(ii) mailing the summons by registered mail to the municipal corporation at an address held out by it to be its address;

(b) in the case of any corporation, other than a municipal corporation, incorporated or continued by or under an Act by,

(i) delivering the summons personally to the manager, secretary or other executive officer of the corporation or person apparently in charge of a branch office of the corporation, or

(ii) mailing the summons by registered mail to the corporation at an address held out by it to be its address;

(c) in the case of corporation not incorporated or continued by or under an Act by,

(i) a method provided under clause (b),

(ii) delivering the summons personally to the corporation's resident agent or agent for service or to any other representative of the corporation in Ontario, or

(iii) mailing the summons by registered mail to a person referred to in subclause (ii) or to an address outside Ontario, including outside Canada, held out by the corporation to be its address.

Date of mailed service

(4.1) A summons served by registered mail under subsection (4) is deemed to have been duly served seven days after the day of mailing.

Substitutional service

(5) A justice, upon motion and upon being satisfied that service cannot be made effectively on a corporation in accordance with subsection (4), may by order authorize another method of service that has a reasonable likelihood of coming to the attention of the corporation.

Proof of service

(6) Service of a summons may be proved by statement under oath or affirmation, written or oral, of the person who made the service.

Contents of warrant

27(1) A warrant issued under section 24 shall,

(a) name or describe the defendant;

(b) set out briefly the offence in respect of which the defendant is charged; and

(c) order that the defendant be forthwith arrested and brought before a justice to be dealt with according to law.

Idem

(2) A warrant issued under section 24 remains in force until it is executed and need not be made returnable at any particular time.

PART IV   TRIAL AND SENTENCING

TRIAL

Application of Part

28. This Part applies to a proceeding commenced under this Act.

Territorial jurisdiction

29(1) Subject to subsection (2), a proceeding in respect of an offence shall be heard and determined by the Ontario Court of Justice sitting in the county or district in which the offence occurred or in the area specified in the transfer agreement made under Part X.

Idem

(2) A proceeding in respect of an offence may be heard and determined in a county or district that adjoins that in which the offence occurred if,

(a) the court holds sittings in a place reasonably proximate to the place where the offence occurred; and

(b) the place of sitting referred to in clause (a) is named in the summons or offence notice.

Transfer to proper county

(3) Where a proceeding is taken in a county or district other than one referred to in subsection (1) or (2), the court shall order that the proceeding be transferred to the proper county or district and may where the defendant appears award costs under section 60.

Change of venue

(4) Where, on the motion of a defendant or prosecutor made to the court at the location named in the information or certificate, it appears to the court that,

(a) it would be appropriate in the interests of justice to do so; or

(b) both the defendant and prosecutor consent thereto, the court may order that the proceeding be heard and determined at another location in Ontario.

Conditions

(5) The court may, in an order made on a motion by the prosecutor under subsection (3) or (4), prescribe conditions that it thinks proper with respect to the payment of additional expenses caused to the defendant as a result of the change of venue.

Time of order for change of venue

(6) An order under subsection (3) or (4) may be made even if a motion preliminary to trial has been disposed of or the plea has been taken and it may be made at any time before evidence has been heard.

Preliminary motions

(7) The court at a location to which a proceeding is transferred under this section may receive and determine any motion preliminary to trial although the same matter was determined by the court at the location from which the proceeding was transferred.

Delivery of papers

(8) Where an order is made under subsection (3) or (4), the clerk of the court at the location where the trial was to be held before the order was made shall deliver any material in his or her possession in connection with the proceeding forthwith to the clerk of the court at the location where the trial is ordered to be held.

Justice presiding at trial

30(1) The justice presiding when evidence is first taken at the trial shall preside over the whole of the trial.

When presiding justice unable to act before adjudication

(2) Where evidence has been taken at a trial and, before making his or her adjudication, the presiding justice dies or in his or her opinion or the opinion of the Chief Justice of the Ontario Court of Justice is for any reason unable to continue, another justice shall conduct the hearing again as a new trial.

When presiding justice unable to act after adjudication

(3) Where evidence has been taken at a trial and, after making his or her adjudication but before making his or her order or imposing sentence, the presiding justice dies or in his or her opinion or the opinion of the Chief Justice of the Ontario Court of Justice is for any reason unable to continue, another justice may make the order or impose the sentence that is authorized by law.

Consent to change presiding justice

(4) A justice presiding at a trial may, at any stage of the trial and upon the consent of the prosecutor and defendant, order that the trial be conducted by another justice and, upon the order being given, subsection (2) applies as if the justice were unable to act.

Retention of jurisdiction

31. The court retains jurisdiction over the information or certificate even if the court fails to exercise its jurisdiction at any particular time or the provisions of this Act respecting adjournments are not complied with.

Stay of proceeding

32(1) In addition to his or her right to withdraw a charge, the Attorney General or his or her agent may stay a proceeding at any time before judgment by direction in court to the clerk of the court and thereupon any recognizance relating to the proceeding is vacated.

Recommencement

(2) A proceeding stayed under subsection (1) may be recommenced by direction of the Attorney General, the Deputy Attorney General or a Crown Attorney to the clerk of the court but a proceeding that is stayed shall not be recommenced,

(a) later than one year after the stay; or

(b) after the expiration of any limitation period applicable, which shall run as if the proceeding had not been commenced until the recommencement,

whichever is the earlier.

Dividing counts

33(1) A defendant may at any stage of the proceeding make a motion to the court to amend or to divide a count that,

(a) charges in the alternative different matters, acts or omissions that are stated in the alternative in the enactment that creates or describes the offence; or

(b) is double or multifarious,

on the ground that, as framed, it prejudices the defendant in the defendant's defence.

Idem

(2) Upon a motion under subsection (1), where the court is satisfied that the ends of justice so require, it may order that a count be amended or divided into two or more counts, and thereupon a formal commencement may be inserted before each of the counts into which it is divided.

Amendment of information or certificate

34(1) The court may, at any stage of the proceeding, amend the information or certificate as may be necessary if it appears that the information or certificate,

(a) fails to state or states defectively anything that is requisite to charge the offence;

(b) does not negative an exception that should be negatived; or

(c) is in any way defective in substance or in form.

Idem

(2) The court may, during the trial, amend the information or certificate as may be necessary if the matters to be alleged in the proposed amendment are disclosed by the evidence taken at the trial.

Variances between charge and evidence

(3) A variance between the information or certificate and the evidence taken on the trial is not material with respect to,

(a) the time when the offence is alleged to have been committed, if it is proved that the information was laid or certificate issued within the prescribed period of limitation; or

(b) the place where the subject-matter of the proceeding is alleged to have arisen, except in an issue as to the jurisdiction of the court.

Considerations on amendment

(4) The court shall, in considering whether or not an amendment should be made, consider,

(a) the evidence taken on the trial, if any;

(b) the circumstances of the case;

(c) whether the defendant has been misled or prejudiced in the defendant's defence by a variance, error or omission; and

(d) whether, having regard to the merits of the case, the proposed amendment can be made without injustice being done.

Amendment, question of law

(5) The question whether an order to amend an information or certificate should be granted or refused is a question of law.

Endorsement of order to amend

(6) An order to amend an information or certificate shall be endorsed on the information or certificate as part of the record and the trial shall proceed as if the information or certificate had been originally laid as amended.

Particulars

35. The court may, before or during trial, if it is satisfied that it is necessary for a fair trial, order that a particular, further describing any matter relevant to the proceeding, be furnished to the defendant.

Motion to quash information or certificate

36(1) An objection to an information or certificate for a defect apparent on its face shall be taken by motion to quash the information or certificate before the defendant has pleaded, and thereafter only by leave of the court.

Grounds for quashing

(2) The court shall not quash an information or certificate unless an amendment or particulars under section 33, 34 or 35 would fail to satisfy the ends of justice.

Costs on amendment or particulars

37. Where the information or certificate is amended or particulars are ordered and an adjournment is necessary as a result thereof, the court may make an order under section 60 for costs resulting from the adjournment.

Joinder of counts or defendants

38(1) The court may, before trial, where it is satisfied that the ends of justice so require, direct that separate counts, informations or certificates be tried together or that persons who are charged separately be tried together.

Separate trials

(2) The court may, before or during the trial, where it is satisfied that the ends of justice so require, direct that separate counts, informations or certificates be tried separately or that persons who are charged jointly or being tried together be tried separately.

Issuance of summons

39(1) Where a justice is satisfied that a person is able to give material evidence in a proceeding under this Act, the justice may issue a summons requiring the person to attend to give evidence and bring with him or her any writings or things referred to in the summons.

Service

(2) A summons shall be served and the service shall be proved in the same manner as a summons under section 26.

Exception

(2.1) Despite subsection (2), a summons served under this section may be served by a person other than a provincial offences officer.

Attendance

(3) A person who is served with a summons shall attend at the time and place stated in the summons to give evidence and, if required by the summons, shall bring with him or her any

writing or other thing that the person has in his or her posses-sion or under his or her control relating to the subject-matter of the proceeding.

Remaining in attendance

(4) A person who is served with a summons shall remain in attendance during the hearing and the hearing as resumed after adjournment from time to time unless the person is excused from attendance by the presiding justice.

Arrest of witness

40(1) Where a judge is satisfied upon evidence under oath or affirmation, that a person is able to give material evidence that is necessary in a proceeding under this Act and,

(a) will not attend if a summons is served; or

(b) attempts to serve a summons have been made and have failed because the person is evading service,

the judge may issue a warrant in the prescribed form for the arrest of the person.

Idem

(2) Where a person who has been served with a summons to attend to give evidence in a proceeding does not attend or remain in attendance, the court may, if it is established,

(a) that the summons has been served; and

(b) that the person is able to give material evidence that is necessary,

issue or cause to be issued a warrant in the prescribed form for the arrest of the person.

Bringing before justice

(3) The police officer who arrests a person under a warrant issued under subsection (1) or (2) shall immediately take the person before a justice.

Release on recognizance

(4) Unless the justice is satisfied that it is necessary to de-tain a person in custody to ensure his or her attendance to give evidence, the justice shall order the person released upon con-dition that the person enter into a recognizance in such amount and with such sureties, if any, as are reasonably necessary to ensure his or her attendance.

Bringing before judge

(5) Where a person is not released under subsection (4), the justice of the peace shall cause the person to be brought before a judge within two days of the justice's decision.

Detention

(6) Where the judge is satisfied that it is necessary to detain the person in custody to ensure his or her attendance to give evidence, the judge may order that the person be detained in custody to testify at the trial or to have his or her evidence taken by a commissioner under an order made under subsection (11).

Release on recognizance

(7) Where the judge does not make an order under subsec-tion (6), he or she shall order that the person be released upon condition that the person enter into a recognizance in such amount and with such sureties, if any, as are reasonably neces-sary to ensure his or her attendance.

Maximum imprisonment

(8) A person who is ordered to be detained in custody under subsection (6) or is not released in fact under subsection (7) shall not be detained in custody for a period longer than ten days.

Release when no longer required

(9) A judge, or the justice presiding at a trial, may at any time order the release of a person in custody under this section where he or she is satisfied that the detention is no longer justi-fied.

Arrest on breach of recognizance

(10) Where a person who is bound by a recognizance to at-tend to give evidence in any proceeding does not attend or re-main in attendance, the court may issue a warrant in the prescribed form for the arrest of that person and,

(a) where the person is brought directly before the court, subsections (6) and (7) apply; and

(b) where the person is not brought directly before the court, subsections (3) to (7) apply.

Commission evidence of witness in custody

(11) A judge or the justice presiding at the trial may order that the evidence of a person held in custody under this section be taken by a commissioner under section 43, which applies thereto in the same manner as to a witness who is unable to attend by reason of illness.

Order for person in a prison to attend

41(1) Where a person whose attendance is required in court to stand trial or to give evidence is confined in a prison, and a judge is satisfied, upon evidence under oath or affirma-tion orally or by affidavit, that the person's attendance is neces-sary to satisfy the ends of justice, the judge may issue an order in the prescribed form that the person be brought before the court, from day to day, as may be necessary.

Idem

(2) An order under subsection (1) shall be addressed to the person who has custody of the prisoner and on receipt thereof that person shall,

(a) deliver the prisoner to the police officer or other person who is named in the order to receive the prisoner; or

(b) bring the prisoner before the court upon payment of the person's reasonable charges in respect thereof.

Idem

(3) An order made under subsection (1) shall direct the manner in which the person shall be kept in custody and returned to the prison from which he or she is brought.

Penalty for failure to attend

42(1) Every person who, being required by law to attend or remain in attendance at a hearing, fails without lawful excuse to attend or remain in attendance accordingly is guilty of an offence and on conviction is liable to a fine of not more than $2,000, or to imprisonment for a term of not more than thirty days, or to both.

Proof of failure to attend

(2) In a proceeding under subsection (1), a certificate of the clerk of the court or a justice stating that the defendant failed to attend is admissible in evidence as proof, in the absence of evidence to the contrary, of the fact without proof of the signature or office of the person appearing to have signed the certificate.

Order for evidence by commission

43(1) Upon the motion of the defendant or prosecutor, a judge or, during trial, the court may by order appoint a commissioner to take the evidence of a witness who is out of Ontario or is not likely to be able to attend the trial by reason of illness or physical disability or for some other good and sufficient cause.

Admission of commission evidence

(2) Evidence taken by a commissioner appointed under subsection (1) may be read in evidence in the proceeding if,

(a) it is proved by oral evidence or by affidavit that the witness is unable to attend for a reason set out in subsection (1);

(b) the transcript of the evidence is signed by the commissioner by or before whom it purports to have been taken; and

(c) it is proved to the satisfaction of the court that reasonable notice of the time and place for taking the evidence was given to the other party, and the party had full opportunity to cross-examine the witness.

Attendance of accused

(3) An order under subsection (1) may make provision to enable the defendant to be present or represented by representative when the evidence is taken, but failure of the defendant to be present or to be represented by representative in accordance with the order does not prevent the reading of the evidence in the proceeding if the evidence has otherwise been taken in accordance with the order and with this section.

Application of rules in civil cases

(4) Except as otherwise provided by this section or by the rules of court, the practice and procedure in connection with the appointment of commissioners under this section, the taking of evidence by commissioners, the certifying and return thereof, and the use of the evidence in the proceeding shall, as far as possible, be the same as those that govern like matters in civil proceedings in the Superior Court of Justice.

Trial of issue as to capacity to conduct defence

44(1) Where at any time before a defendant is sentenced a court has reason to believe, based on,

(a) the evidence of a legally qualified medical practitioner or, with the consent of the parties, a written report of a legally qualified medical practitioner; or

(b) the conduct of the defendant in the courtroom,

that the defendant suffers from mental disorder, the court may,

(c) where the justice presiding is a judge, by order suspend the proceeding and direct the trial of the issue as to whether the defendant is, because of mental disorder, unable to conduct his or her defence; or

(d) where the justice presiding is a justice of the peace, refer the matter to a judge who may make an order referred to in clause (c).

Examination

(2) For the purposes of subsection (1), the court may order the defendant to attend to be examined under subsection (5).

Finding

(3) The trial of the issue shall be presided over by a judge and,

(a) where the judge finds that the defendant is, because of mental disorder, unable to conduct his or her defence, the judge shall order that the proceeding remain suspended;

(b) where the judge finds that the defendant is able to conduct his or her defence, the judge shall order that the suspended proceeding be continued.

Application for rehearing as to capacity

(4) At any time within one year after an order is made under subsection (3), either party may, upon seven days notice to the other, make a motion to a judge to rehear the trial of the issue and where upon the rehearing the judge finds that the defendant is able to conduct his or her defence, the judge may order that the suspended proceeding be continued.

Order for examination

(5) For the purposes of subsection (1) or a hearing or rehearing under subsection (3) or (4), the court or judge may order the defendant to attend at such place or before such person and at or within such time as are specified in the order and submit to an examination for the purpose of determining whether the defendant is, because of mental disorder, unable to conduct his or her defence.

Idem

(6) Where the defendant fails or refuses to comply with an order under subsection (5) without reasonable excuse or where

the person conducting the examination satisfies a judge that it is necessary to do so, the judge may by warrant direct that the defendant be taken into such custody as is necessary for the purpose of the examination and in any event for not longer than seven days and, where it is necessary to detain the defendant in a place, the place shall be, where practicable, a psychiatric facility.

Limitation on suspension of proceeding

(7) Where an order is made under subsection (3) and one year has elapsed and no further order is made under subsection (4), no further proceeding shall be taken in respect of the charge or any other charge arising out of the same circumstance.

Taking of plea

45(1) After being informed of the substance of the information or certificate, the defendant shall be asked whether the defendant pleads guilty or not guilty of the offence charged in it.

Conviction on plea of guilty

(2) Where the defendant pleads guilty, the court may accept the plea and convict the defendant.

Conditions of accepting plea

(3) A court may accept a plea of guilty only if it is satisfied that the defendant,

(a) is making the plea voluntarily;

(b) understands that the plea is an admission of the essential elements of the offence;

(c) understands the nature and consequences of the plea; and

(d) understands that the court is not bound by any agreement made between the defendant and the prosecutor.

Validity of plea not affected

(4) The failure of a court to fully inquire into whether the conditions set out in subsection (3) are met does not affect the validity of the plea.

Refusal to plead

(5) Where the defendant refuses to plead or does not answer directly, the court shall enter a plea of not guilty.

Plea of guilty to another offence

(6) Where the defendant pleads guilty of an offence other than the offence charged, and whether or not it is an included offence and whether or not the defendant has pleaded not guilty to the offence charged, the court may, with the consent of the prosecutor, accept such plea of guilty and accordingly amend the certificate of offence, the certificate of parking infraction or the information, as the case may be, or substitute the offence to which the defendant pleads guilty.

Judicial pre-trial conferences

45.1(1) On application by the prosecutor or the defendant or on his or her own motion, a justice may order that a pretrial conference be held between the prosecutor and the defendant or a representative of the defendant.

Matters for consideration

(2) The court, or a justice of the court, shall preside over the pre-trial conference, the purpose of which is to,

(a) consider the matters that, to promote a fair and expeditious trial, would be better decided before the start of the proceedings and other similar matters; and

(b) make arrangements for decisions on those matters.

Trial on plea of not guilty

46(1) If the defendant pleads not guilty, the court shall hold the trial.

Right to defend

(2) The defendant is entitled to make full answer and defence.

Right to examine witnesses

(3) The prosecutor or defendant, as the case may be, may examine and cross-examine witnesses.

Agreed facts

(4) The court may receive and act upon any facts agreed upon by the defendant and prosecutor without proof or evidence.

Defendant not compellable

(5) Despite section 8 of the *Evidence Act*, the defendant is not a compellable witness for the prosecution.

Evidence and burden of proof

Evidence taken on another charge

47(1) The court may receive and consider evidence taken before the same justice on a different charge against the same defendant, with the consent of the parties.

Certificate as evidence

(2) Where a certificate as to the content of an official record is, by any Act, made admissible in evidence as proof, in the absence of evidence to the contrary, the court may, for the purpose of deciding whether the defendant is the person referred to in the certificate, receive and base its decision upon information it considers credible or trustworthy in the circumstances of each case.

Burden of proving exception, etc.

(3) The burden of proving that an authorization, exception, exemption or qualification prescribed by law operates in favour of the defendant is on the defendant, and the prosecutor is not required, except by way of rebuttal, to prove that the authorization, exception, exemption or qualification does not operate in favour of the defendant, whether or not it is set out in the information.

Exhibits

48(1) The court may order that an exhibit be kept in such custody and place as, in the opinion of the court, is appropriate for its preservation.

Release of exhibits

(2) Where any thing is filed as an exhibit in a proceeding, the clerk may release the exhibit upon the consent of the parties at any time after the trial or, in the absence of consent, may return the exhibit to the party tendering it after the disposition of any appeal in the proceeding or, where an appeal is not taken, after the expiration of the time for appeal.

Certified evidence

Application

48.1(1) This section applies to a hearing, including a hearing in the absence of a defendant under section 54, where,

(a) the proceeding for the offence was commenced by certificate under Part I or II; and

(b) the offence is specified by the regulations.

Admissibility of certified evidence

(2) The following are admissible in evidence as proof of the facts certified in it, in the absence of evidence to the contrary:

1. A certified statement in a certificate of offence.

2. A certified statement in a certificate of parking infraction.

3. Other types of certified evidence specified by the regulations.

Other provisions on admissibility

(3) For greater certainty, subsection (2) does not affect or interfere with the operation of a provision of this Act or any other Act that permits or specifies that a document or type of document be admitted into evidence as proof of the facts certified in it.

Onus

(4) For greater certainty, this section does not remove the onus on the prosecution to prove its case beyond a reasonable doubt.

No oral evidence

(5) A provincial offences officer who provides certified evidence referred to in subsection (2) in respect of a proceeding shall not be required to attend to give evidence at trial, except as provided under subsection 49(4).

Regulations

(6) The Lieutenant Governor in Council may make regulations,

(a) specifying offences for the purposes of clause (1)(b);

(b) respecting other types of certified evidence for the purposes of paragraph 3 of subsection (2);

(c) respecting restrictions or conditions on the admissibility of evidence under subsection (2).

Adjournments

49(1) The court may, from time to time, adjourn a trial or hearing but, where the defendant is in custody, an adjournment shall not be for a period longer than eight days without the consent of the defendant.

Early resumption

(2) A trial or hearing that is adjourned for a period may be resumed before the expiration of the period with the consent of the defendant and the prosecutor.

Adjournment

(3) Despite subsection (1) and subject to subsection (4), if the trial is being held in respect of a proceeding commenced under Part I or II, the court shall not adjourn the trial for the purpose of having the provincial offences officer who completed the certificate attend to give evidence unless the court is satisfied that the interests of justice require it.

Adjournment where certified evidence

(4) If certified evidence referred to in subsection 48.1(2) is being admitted as evidence in a trial referred to in subsection (1), the court shall not adjourn the trial for the purpose of having any of the following persons attend to give evidence unless the court is satisfied that the oral evidence of the person is necessary in order to ensure a fair trial:

1. The provincial offences officer who completed the certificate of offence or the certificate of parking infraction, as the case may be.

2. Any provincial offences officer who provided certified evidence in respect of the proceeding.

Power of clerk to adjourn

(5) The clerk of the court may, on behalf of the court, adjourn,

(a) the first trial date for a proceeding commenced under Part I or Part II to a date agreed to by the defendant and the prosecutor in a written agreement filed with the court; and

(b) any proceeding under this Act or any step in a proceeding under this Act, where no justice is able to attend in person, to a date chosen in accordance with the instructions of a justice.

Appearance by defendant

50(1) A defendant may appear and act personally or by representative.

Appearance by corporation

(2) A defendant that is a corporation shall appear and act by representative.

Exclusion of representatives

(3) The court may bar any person, other than a person who is licensed under the *Law Society Act*, from appearing as a

representative if the court finds that the person is not competent properly to represent or advise the person for whom he or she appears, or does not understand and comply with the duties and responsibilities of a representative.

Compelling attendance of defendant

51. Although a defendant appears by representative, the court may order the defendant to attend personally, and, where it appears to be necessary to do so, may issue a summons in the prescribed form.

Restrictions on hearing and publication

Excluding defendant from hearing

52(1) The court may cause the defendant to be removed and to be kept out of court,

   (a) when the defendant misconducts himself or herself by interrupting the proceeding so that to continue in the presence of the defendant would not be feasible; or

   (b) where, during the trial of an issue as to whether the defendant is, because of mental disorder, unable to conduct his or her defence, the court is satisfied that failure to do so might have an adverse effect on the mental health of the defendant.

Excluding public from hearing

(2) The court may exclude the public or any member of the public from a hearing where, in the opinion of the court, it is necessary to do so,

   (a) for the maintenance of order in the courtroom;

   (b) to protect the reputation of a minor; or

   (c) to remove an influence that might affect the testimony of a witness.

Prohibition of publication of evidence

(3) Where the court considers it necessary to do so to protect the reputation of a minor, the court may make an order prohibiting the publication or broadcast of the identity of the minor or of the evidence or any part of the evidence taken at the hearing.

Failure of prosecutor to appear

53(1) Where the defendant appears for a hearing and the prosecutor, having had due notice, does not appear, the court may dismiss the charge or may adjourn the hearing to another time upon such terms as it considers proper.

Idem

(2) Where the prosecutor does not appear at the time and place appointed for the resumption of an adjourned hearing under subsection (1), the court may dismiss the charge.

Costs

(3) Where a hearing is adjourned under subsection (1) or a charge is dismissed under subsection (2), the court may make an order under section 60 for the payment of costs.

Written order of dismissal

(4) Where a charge is dismissed under subsection (1) or (2), the court may, if requested by the defendant, draw up an order of dismissal stating the grounds therefor and shall give the defendant a certified copy of the order of dismissal which is, without further proof, a bar to any subsequent proceeding against the defendant in respect of the same cause.

Conviction in the absence of the defendant

54(1) Where a defendant does not appear at the time and place appointed for a hearing and it is proved by the prosecutor, having been given a reasonable opportunity to do so, that a summons was served, a notice of trial was given under Part I or II, an undertaking to appear was given or a recognizance to appear was entered into, as the case may be, or where the defendant does not appear upon the resumption of a hearing that has been adjourned, the court may,

   (a) proceed to hear and determine the proceeding in the absence of the defendant; or

   (b) adjourn the hearing and, if it thinks fit, issue a summons to appear or issue a warrant in the prescribed form for the arrest of the defendant.

Proceeding arising from failure to appear

(2) Where the court proceeds under clause (1)(a) or adjourns the hearing under clause (1)(b) without issuing a summons or warrant, no proceeding arising out of the failure of the defendant to appear at the time and place appointed for the hearing or for the resumption of the hearing shall be instituted, or if instituted shall be proceeded with, except with the consent of the Attorney General or his or her agent.

Included offences

55. Where the offence as charged includes another offence, the defendant may be convicted of an offence so included that is proved, although the whole offence charged is not proved.

SENTENCING

Pre-sentence report

56(1) Where a defendant is convicted of an offence in a proceeding commenced by information, the court may direct a probation officer to prepare and file with the court a report in writing relating to the defendant for the purpose of assisting the court in imposing sentence.

Service

(2) Where a report is filed with the court under subsection (1), the clerk of the court shall cause a copy of the report to be provided to the defendant or the defendant's representative and to the prosecutor.

Other information relevant to sentence

Submissions as to sentence

57(1) Where a defendant who appears is convicted of an offence, the court shall give the prosecutor and the defendant's representative an opportunity to make submissions as to sentence and, where the defendant has no representative, the court shall ask the defendant if he or she has anything to say before sentence is passed.

Omission to comply

(2) The omission to comply with subsection (1) does not affect the validity of the proceeding.

Inquiries by court

(3) Where a defendant is convicted of an offence, the court may make such inquiries, on oath or otherwise, of and concerning the defendant as it considers desirable, including the defendant's economic circumstances, but the defendant shall not be compelled to answer.

Proof of previous conviction

(4) A certificate setting out with reasonable particularity the finding of guilt or acquittal or conviction and sentence in Canada of a person signed by,

(a) the person who made the adjudication; or

(b) the clerk of the court where the adjudication was made,

is, upon the court being satisfied that the defendant is the person referred to in the certificate, admissible in evidence and is proof, in the absence of evidence to the contrary, of the facts stated therein without proof of the signature or the official character of the person appearing to have signed the certificate.

Time spent in custody considered

58. In determining the sentence to be imposed on a person convicted of an offence, the justice may take into account any time spent in custody by the person as a result of the offence.

Provision for minimum penalty

59(1) No penalty prescribed for an offence is a minimum penalty unless it is specifically declared to be a minimum.

Relief against minimum fine

(2) Although the provision that creates the penalty for an offence prescribes a minimum fine, where in the opinion of the court exceptional circumstances exist so that to impose the minimum fine would be unduly oppressive or otherwise not in the interests of justice, the court may impose a fine that is less than the minimum or suspend the sentence.

Idem, re imprisonment

(3) Where a minimum penalty is prescribed for an offence and the minimum penalty includes imprisonment, the court may, despite the prescribed penalty, impose a fine of not more than $5,000 in lieu of imprisonment.

Costs

Fixed costs on conviction

60(1) Upon conviction, the defendant is liable to pay to the court an amount by way of costs that is fixed by the regulations.

Costs respecting witnesses

(2) The court may, in its discretion, order costs towards fees and expenses reasonably incurred by or on behalf of witnesses in amounts not exceeding the maximum fixed by the regulations, to be paid,

(a) to the court or prosecutor by the defendant; or

(b) to the defendant by the person who laid the information or issued the certificate, as the case may be,

but where the proceeding is commenced by means of a certificate, the total of such costs shall not exceed $100.

Costs collectable as a fine

(3) Costs payable under this section shall be deemed to be a fine for the purpose of enforcing payment.

Surcharge

60.1(1) If a person is convicted of an offence in a proceeding commenced under Part I or III and a fine is imposed in respect of that offence, a surcharge is payable by that person in the amount determined by regulations made under this Act.

Collection

(2) The surcharge shall be deemed to be a fine for the purpose of enforcing payment.

Priorities

(3) Any payments made by a defendant shall be credited towards payment of the fine until it is fully paid and then towards payment of the surcharge.

Part X agreements

(3.1) When an agreement made under Part X applies to a fine, payments made by the defendant shall first be credited towards payment of the surcharge, not as described in subsection (3).

Special purpose account

(4) Surcharges paid into the Consolidated Revenue Fund shall be credited to the victims' justice fund account and shall be deemed to be money received by the Crown for a special purpose.

Same

(4.1) Subsection (4) also applies to payments received under clause 165(5)(a).

(5), (6) Repealed.

Regulations

(7) The Lieutenant Governor in Council may make regulations,

(a) prescribing the amount of the surcharges or the method by which they are to be calculated;

(b) Repealed.

(c) exempting any offence or class of offence from the application of subsection (1).

(8) Repealed.

General penalty

61. Except where otherwise expressly provided by law, every person who is convicted of an offence is liable to a fine of not more than $5,000.

Minute of conviction

62. Where a court convicts a defendant or dismisses a charge, a minute of the dismissal or conviction and sentence shall be made by the court, and, upon request by the defendant or the prosecutor or by the Attorney General or his or her agent, the court shall cause a copy thereof certified by the clerk of the court to be delivered to the person making the request.

Time when imprisonment starts

63(1) The term of imprisonment imposed by sentence shall, unless otherwise directed in the sentence, commence on the day on which the convicted person is taken into custody thereunder, but no time during which the convicted person is imprisoned or out on bail before sentence shall be reckoned as part of the term of imprisonment to which he or she is sentenced.

Idem

(2) Where the court imposes imprisonment, the court may order custody to commence on a day not later than thirty days after the day of sentencing.

Sentences consecutive

64. Where a person is subject to more than one term of imprisonment at the same time, the terms shall be served consecutively except in so far as the court has ordered a term to be served concurrently with any other term of imprisonment.

Warrant of committal

65(1) A warrant of committal is sufficient authority,

    (a) for the conveyance of the prisoner in custody for the purpose of committal under the warrant; and

    (b) for the reception and detention of the prisoner by keepers of prisons in accordance with the terms of the warrant.

Conveyance of prisoner

(2) A person to whom a warrant of committal is directed shall convey the prisoner to the correctional institution named in the warrant.

Prisoner subject to rules of institution

(3) A sentence of imprisonment shall be served in accordance with the enactments and rules that govern the institution to which the prisoner is sentenced.

When fine due

66(1) A fine becomes due and payable fifteen days after its imposition.

Extension of time for payment of a fine

(2) Where the court imposes a fine, the court shall ask the defendant if the defendant wishes an extension of the time for payment of the fine.

Inquiries

(3) Where the defendant requests an extension of the time for payment of the fine, the court may make such inquiries, on oath or affirmation or otherwise, of and concerning the defendant as the court considers desirable, but the defendant shall not be compelled to answer.

Granting of extension

(4) Unless the court finds that the request for extension of time is not made in good faith or that the extension would likely be used to evade payment, the court shall extend the time for payment by ordering periodic payments or otherwise.

Notice where convicted in the absence of the defendant

(5) Where a fine is imposed in the absence of the defendant, the clerk of the court shall give the defendant notice of the fine and its due date and of the defendant's right to make a motion for an extension of the time for payment under subsection (6).

Further motion for extension

(6) The defendant may, at any time by motion in the prescribed form filed in the office of the court, request an extension or further extension of time for payment of a fine and the motion shall be determined by a justice and the justice has the same powers in respect of the motion as the court has under subsections (3) and (4).

Defendant's address

66.1 If a court imposes a fine, grants an extension of time for payment of a fine or deals with a fine under section 69, and the defendant is before the court, the court shall require the defendant to provide the defendant's current address to the clerk of the court.

Fee for refused cheque collectable as a fine

66.2 When a person purports to pay a fine by a cheque that the drawee of the cheque refuses to cash and thereby becomes liable to pay a fee in the amount prescribed for the purpose of section 8.1 of the *Financial Administration Act*, the fee shall be deemed to be a fine for the purpose of enforcing payment.

Regulation for work credits for fines

67. The Lieutenant Governor in Council may make regulations establishing a program to permit the payment of fines by means of credits for work performed, and, for the purpose and without restricting the generality of the foregoing may,

    (a) prescribe classes of work and the conditions under which they are to be performed;

    (b) prescribe a system of credits;

(c) provide for any matter necessary for the effective administration of the program,

and any regulation may limit its application to any part or parts of Ontario.

Civil enforcement of fines

68(1) When the payment of a fine is in default, the clerk of the court may complete a certificate in the prescribed form as to the imposition of the fine and the amount remaining unpaid and file the certificate in a court of competent jurisdiction and upon filing, the certificate shall be deemed to be an order or judgment of that court for the purposes of enforcement.

(2) Repealed.

Certificate of discharge

(3) Where a certificate has been filed under subsection (1) and the fine is fully paid, the clerk shall file a certificate of payment upon which the certificate of default is discharged and, where a writ of execution has been filed with the sheriff, the clerk shall file a certificate of payment with the sheriff, upon which the writ is cancelled.

Costs of enforcement

(4) Costs incurred in enforcing the deemed court order or judgment shall be added to the order or judgment and form part of it.

More than one fine

(5) The clerk may complete and file one certificate under this section in respect of two or more fines imposed on the same person.

Default

69(1) The payment of a fine is in default if any part of it is due and unpaid for fifteen days or more.

Order on default

(2) A justice of the peace who is satisfied that payment of a fine is in default,

(a) shall order that any permit, licence, registration or privilege in respect of which a suspension is authorized under any Act because of non-payment of the fine be suspended until the fine is paid;

(b) shall order that any permit, licence, registration or privilege in respect of which any Act authorizes a refusal to renew, validate or issue the permit, licence, registration or privilege because of non-payment of the fine not be renewed, validated or issued until the fine is paid; and

(c) may direct the clerk of the court to proceed with civil enforcement under section 68.

Highway Traffic Act permits

(3) If section 7 of the *Highway Traffic Act* authorizes an order or direction under this section that any permit under that Act not be validated or issued because payment of a fine is in default, a person designated by the regulations who is satisfied that payment of a fine is in default shall direct that until the fine is paid,

(a) validation of any permit held by the person who has defaulted be refused; and

(b) issuance of any permit to the person who has defaulted be refused.

Highway Traffic Act restriction

(4) Orders or directions made under this section pursuant to section 7 of the *Highway Traffic Act* are subject to subsection 7(12) of that Act and any regulations made under section 7 of that Act.

Highway Traffic Act licences

(5) If section 46 of the *Highway Traffic Act* authorizes an order or direction under this section that any licence under that Act be suspended or not be issued because payment of a fine is in default, a person designated by the regulations who is satisfied that payment of a fine is in default shall direct that until the fine is paid,

(a) if the person who has defaulted holds a licence, the licence be suspended; or

(b) if the person who has defaulted does not hold a licence, no licence be issued to him or her.

Obtaining convicted person's attendance

(6) A justice may issue a warrant requiring that a person who has defaulted be arrested and brought before a justice as soon as possible if other reasonable methods of collecting the fine have been tried and have failed, or would not appear to be likely to result in payment within a reasonable period of time.

Alternative summons procedure

(7) The clerk of the court that imposed the fine that is in default may issue a summons requiring the person who has defaulted to appear before a justice if the conditions described in subsection (6) exist.

Service of summons

(8) The summons referred to in subsection (7) may be served by regular prepaid mail.

Hearing

(9) If a person who has defaulted in paying a fine is brought before a justice as a result of a warrant issued under subsection (6) or such a person appears before a justice as a result of a summons issued under subsection (7), the justice shall hold a hearing to determine whether the person is unable to pay the fine within a reasonable period of time.

Onus

(10) In a hearing under subsection (9), the onus of proving that the person is unable to pay the fine within a reasonable period of time is on the person who has defaulted.

Adjournment

(11) The justice may adjourn the hearing from time to time at the request of the person who has defaulted.

Warning

(12) When an adjournment is granted, the justice shall warn the person who has defaulted that if the person fails to appear for the resumption of the hearing, the hearing may proceed in the person's absence.

Failure to warn

(13) If a hearing was adjourned and the person who has defaulted does not appear when it is resumed, the hearing may proceed in the person's absence even if the warning required by subsection (12) was not given.

Warrant of committal

(14) If the justice is not satisfied that the person who has defaulted is unable to pay the fine within a reasonable period of time and that incarceration of the person would not be contrary to the public interest, the justice may issue a warrant for the person's committal or may order that such other steps be taken to enforce the fine as appear to him or her to be appropriate.

> **Note: On a day to be named by proclamation of the Lieutenant Governor, section 69 is amended by adding the following subsection:**
>
> **Inability to pay**
>
> (14.1) Despite subsection 165(3), a defendant may, in accordance with the regulations, apply to a justice to reduce or expunge a defaulted fine under subsection (15) where the defendant meets the criteria for inability to pay defined in the regulations.
>
> **See: 2009, c. 33, Sched. 4, ss. 1(45), 5(4).**

Inability to pay fine

(15) If the justice is satisfied that the person who has defaulted is unable to pay the fine within a reasonable period of time, the justice may,

    (a) grant an extension of the time allowed for payment of the fine;

    (b) require the person to pay the fine according to a schedule of payments established by the justice;

    (c) in exceptional circumstances, reduce the amount of the fine or order that the fine does not have to be paid.

Term of imprisonment

(16) Subject to subsection (17), the term of imprisonment under a warrant issued under subsection (14) shall be for three days, plus,

    (a) if the amount that has not been paid is not greater than $50, one day; or

    (b) if the amount that has not been paid is greater than $50, a number of days equal to the sum of one plus the number obtained when the unpaid amount is divided by $50, rounded down to the nearest whole number.

Limit

(17) The term of imprisonment shall not exceed the greater of,

    (a) ninety days; and

    (b) half of the maximum number of days of imprisonment that may be imposed on conviction of the offence that the person who has defaulted was convicted of.

Effect of payments

(18) Subject to subsection (19), a payment in respect of the fine in default that is made after a warrant is issued under subsection (14) shall result in a reduction of the term of imprisonment by the number of days that is in the same proportion to the term as the payment is to the amount in default.

Restriction

(19) A payment that is less than the amount outstanding on the fine shall not result in a reduction of the term of imprisonment unless it is an amount that would reduce the term by a number of days that is a whole number.

Exceptions

(20) Subsections (6) to (19) do not apply if,

    (a) the person who has defaulted is less than eighteen years old; or

    (b) the fine was imposed on conviction of an offence under subsection 31(2) or (4) of the *Liquor Licence Act*.

Exceptional circumstances

(21) In exceptional circumstances where, in the opinion of the court that imposed the fine, to proceed under subsections (6) to (14) would defeat the ends of justice, the court may order that no warrant be issued under subsection (6) and that no summons be issued under subsection (7).

Regulations

(22) The Lieutenant Governor in Council may make regulations,

    (a) designating a person or class of persons for purposes of subsections (3) and (5);

> **Note: On a day to be named by proclamation of the Lieutenant Governor, subsection (22) is amended by adding the following clause:**
>
> (a.1) prescribing the form and procedure for an application under subsection (14.1);
>
> **See: 2009, c. 33, Sched. 4, ss. 1(46), 5(4).**

(b) prescribing criteria to be considered by a justice in determining whether a person is unable to pay a fine within a reasonable period of time.

Disclosure to consumer reporting agency

69.1(1) When a fine has been in default for at least 90 days, the Ministry of the Attorney General may disclose to a consumer reporting agency the name of the defaulter, the amount of the fine and the date the fine went into default.

Same

(2) When a fine disclosed to a consumer reporting agency has been paid in full, the Ministry of the Attorney General shall inform the agency of this fact as soon as possible after payment.

Fee where fine in default

70(1) Where the payment of a fine is in default and the time for payment is not extended or further extended under subsection 66(6), the defendant shall pay the administrative fee prescribed by the regulations.

Fee collectable as a fine

(2) For the purpose of making and enforcing payment, a fee payable under this section shall be deemed to be part of the fine that is in default.

Collection agency costs payable

70.1(1) A defendant shall pay the costs that a municipality incurs by using a registered collection agency in good standing under the *Collection and Debt Settlement Services Act* to collect a fine that is in default, but the costs shall not exceed an amount approved by the municipality.

Costs collectable as a fine

(2) For the purpose of making and enforcing payment, costs payable under this section shall be deemed to be part of the fine that is in default.

Suspension of fine on conditions

71. Where an Act provides that a fine may be suspended subject to the performance of a condition,
   (a) the period of suspension shall be fixed by the court and shall be for not more than one year;
   (b) the court shall provide in its order of suspension the method of proving the performance of the condition;
   (c) the suspension is in addition to and not in lieu of any other power of the court in respect of the fine; and
   (d) the fine is not in default until fifteen days have elapsed after notice that the period of suspension has expired is given to the defendant.

Probation order

72(1) Where a defendant is convicted of an offence in a proceeding commenced by information, the court may, having regard to the age, character and background of the defendant, the nature of the offence and the circumstances surrounding its commission,

   (a) suspend the passing of sentence and direct that the defendant comply with the conditions prescribed in a probation order;
   (b) in addition to fining the defendant or sentencing the defendant to imprisonment, whether in default of payment of a fine or otherwise, direct that the defendant comply with the conditions prescribed in a probation order; or
   (c) where it imposes a sentence of imprisonment on the defendant, whether in default of payment of a fine or otherwise, that does not exceed ninety days, order that the sentence be served intermittently at such times as are specified in the order and direct that the defendant, at all times when he or she is not in confinement pursuant to such order, comply with the conditions prescribed in a probation order.

Statutory conditions of order

(2) A probation order shall be deemed to contain the conditions that,
   (a) the defendant not commit the same or any related or similar offence, or any offence under a statute of Canada or Ontario or any other province of Canada that is punishable by imprisonment;
   (b) the defendant appear before the court as and when required; and
   (c) the defendant notify the court of any change in the defendant's address.

Conditions imposed by court

(3) In addition to the conditions set out in subsection (2), the court may prescribe as a condition in a probation order,
   (a) that the defendant satisfy any compensation or restitution that is required or authorized by an Act;
   (b) with the consent of the defendant and where the conviction is of an offence that is punishable by imprisonment, that the defendant perform a community service as set out in the order;
   (c) where the conviction is of an offence punishable by imprisonment, such other conditions relating to the circumstances of the offence and of the defendant that contributed to the commission of the offence as the court considers appropriate to prevent similar unlawful conduct or to contribute to the rehabilitation of the defendant; or
   (d) where considered necessary for the purpose of implementing the conditions of the probation order, that the defendant report to a responsible person designated by the court and, in addition, where the circumstances warrant it, that the defendant be under the supervision of the person to whom he or she is required to report.

Form of order

(4) A probation order shall be in the prescribed form and the court shall specify therein the period for which it is to remain in force, which shall not be for more than two years from the date when the order takes effect.

Notice of order

(5) Where the court makes a probation order, it shall cause a copy of the order and a copy of section 75 to be given to the defendant.

Regulations for community service orders

(6) The Lieutenant Governor in Council may make regulations governing restitution, compensation and community service orders, including their terms and conditions.

Exception

(7) The court shall not make a probation order when an individual has been convicted of an absolute liability offence, unless the order is made in addition to a sentence of imprisonment imposed under section 69 in default of payment of a fine.

When order comes into force

73(1) A probation order comes into force,

(a) on the date on which the order is made; or

(b) where the defendant is sentenced to imprisonment other than a sentence to be served intermittently, upon the expiration of that sentence.

Continuation in force

(2) Subject to section 75, where a defendant who is bound by a probation order is convicted of an offence or is imprisoned in default of payment of a fine, the order continues in force except in so far as the sentence or imprisonment renders it impossible for the defendant to comply for the time being with the order.

Variation of probation order

74. The court may, at any time upon the application of the defendant or prosecutor with notice to the other, after a hearing or, with the consent of the parties, without a hearing,

(a) make any changes in or additions to the conditions prescribed in the order that in the opinion of the court are rendered desirable by a change in circumstances;

(b) relieve the defendant, either absolutely or upon such terms or for such period as the court considers desirable, of compliance with any condition described in any of the clauses in subsection 72(3) that is prescribed in the order; or

(c) terminate the order or decrease the period for which the probation order is to remain in force, and the court shall thereupon endorse the probation order accordingly and, if it changes or adds to the conditions prescribed in the order, inform the defendant of its action and give the defendant a copy of the order so endorsed.

Breach of probation order

75. Where a defendant who is bound by a probation order is convicted of an offence constituting a breach of condition of the order and,

(a) the time within which the defendant may appeal or make a motion for leave to appeal against that conviction has expired and the defendant has not taken an appeal or made a motion for leave to appeal;

(b) the defendant has taken an appeal or made a motion for leave to appeal against the conviction and the appeal or motion for leave has been dismissed or abandoned; or

(c) the defendant has given written notice to the court that convicted the defendant that the defendant elects not to appeal, or where the defendant otherwise wilfully fails or refuses to comply with the order, the defendant is guilty of an offence and upon conviction the court may,

(d) impose a fine of not more than $1,000 or imprisonment for a term of not more than thirty days, or both, and in lieu of or in addition to the penalty, continue the probation order with such changes or additions and for such extended term, not exceeding an additional year, as the court considers reasonable; or

(e) where the justice presiding is the justice who made the original order, in lieu of imposing the penalty under clause (d), revoke the probation order and impose the sentence the passing of which was suspended upon the making of the probation order.

PART V GENERAL PROVISIONS

Limitation

76(1) A proceeding shall not be commenced after the expiration of any limitation period prescribed by or under any Act for the offence or, where no limitation period is prescribed, after six months after the date on which the offence was, or is alleged to have been, committed.

Extension

(2) A limitation period may be extended by a justice with the consent of the defendant.

Electronic court documents

76.1(1) A document that is required or authorized to be filed, given or delivered to a court office or the clerk of the court under this Act may, in accordance with the regulations, be filed, given or delivered electronically.

Electronic signature

(2) An electronic document that is filed, given or delivered to a court office or the clerk of the court may be signed electronically in accordance with the regulations.

Electronic copy of paper original

(3) When a document is filed, given or delivered to a court office or the clerk of the court in paper form, the court may create and retain an electronic copyinstead of the paper original.

Duty to ensure integrity

(4) A person who creates, retains or reproduces an electronic copy of a document for the purposes of subsection (3) shall ensure the integrity of the information contained in the electronic copy.

Power to deal with electronic documents

(5) Anything that the court is required or authorized to do with respect to a document may be done with respect to an electronic document.

Delivery in person

(6) Nothing in this section limits the operation of a requirement to deliver a document personally or in person to a court office or the clerk of the court.

Regulations

(7) The Lieutenant Governor in Council may make regulations respecting,

(a) governing the electronic filing, giving and delivery of documents to a court office or the clerk of the court;

(b) respecting the electronic signing of electronic documents that are filed, given or delivered to a court office or the clerk of the court;

(c) governing the storage, retention and disposal of computer-readable media used to file, give or deliver documents to a court office or the clerk of the court

(d) governing the creation, storage, retention, transfer, reproduction, distribution, disposal or use of electronic documents by the court;

(e) respecting the electronic signing or certification of electronic documents by the court.

Parties to offence

77(1) Every person is a party to an offence who,

(a) actually commits it;

(b) does or omits to do anything for the purpose of aiding any person to commit it; or

(c) abets any person in committing it.

Common purpose

(2) Where two or more persons form an intention in common to carry out an unlawful purpose and to assist each other therein and any one of them, in carrying out the common purpose, commits an offence, each of them who knew or ought to have known that the commission of the offence would be a probable consequence of carrying out the common purpose is a party to the offence.

Counselling

78(1) Where a person counsels or procures another person to be a party to an offence and that other person is afterwards a party to the offence, the person who counselled or procured is a party to the offence, even if the offence was committed in a way different from that which was counselled or procured.

Idem

(2) Every person who counsels or procures another person to be a party to an offence is a party to every offence that the other commits in consequence of the counselling or procuring that the person who counselled or procured knew or ought to have known was likely to be committed in consequence of the counselling or procuring.

Computation of age

79. In the absence of other evidence, or by way of corroboration of other evidence, a justice may infer the age of a person from his or her appearance.

Common law defences

80. Every rule and principle of the common law that renders any circumstance a justification or excuse for an act or a defence to a charge continues in force and applies in respect of offences, except in so far as they are altered by or inconsistent with this or any other Act.

Ignorance of the law

81. Ignorance of the law by a person who commits an offence is not an excuse for committing the offence.

Representation

82. A defendant may act by representative.

Evidence, recording and taking

83(1) A proceeding in which evidence is taken shall be recorded.

Evidence under oath or affirmation

(2) Evidence under this Act shall be taken under oath or affirmation, except as otherwise provided by law.

Electronic conferences

Definition

83.1(1) In this section,

"electronic method" means video conference, audio conference, telephone conference or other method determined by the regulations.

Appearance by electronic method

(2) Subject to this section, in any proceeding under this Act or any step in a proceeding under this Act, if the appropriate equipment is available at the courthouse where the proceeding occurs,

(a) a witness may give evidence by electronic method;

(b) a defendant may appear by electronic method;

(c) a prosecutor may appear and prosecute by electronic method; and

(d) an interpreter may interpret by electronic method.

Consent required

(3) A witness may appear by electronic method to give evidence in a proceeding commenced by information under Part III only with the consent of both the prosecutor and the defendant.

Attendance by justice

(3.1) A justice may attend and conduct a sentencing hearing under sections 5.1 and 7 and any other proceeding or any step in a proceeding determined by the regulations, by means of electronic method, if the appropriate equipment is available at the courthouse where the proceeding occurs, and the justice may,

(a) adjourn the sentencing hearing to have the defendant appear in person before the justice for the purpose of ensuring that the defendant understands the plea; and

(b) adjourn any other proceeding or step in a proceeding determined by the regulations if he or she is satisfied that the interests of justice require it or it is necessary for a fair trial.

Limited use of certain electronic methods

(4) Attendance by audio conference or telephone conference may only be used for the purpose of,

(a) attending a pre-trial conference;

(b) attending a meeting between the defendant and the prosecutor under section 5.1; or

(c) attending or appearing at any other proceeding or step in a proceeding determined by the regulations.

Appearance in person

(5) The court may order any person described in subsection (2) to appear in person if it is satisfied that the interests of justice require it or it is necessary for a fair trial.

Oaths

(6) Despite the *Commissioners for taking Affidavits Act*, where evidence is given under oath by electronic method, the oath may be administered by the same electronic method.

Regulations

(7) The Lieutenant Governor in Council may make regulations,

(a) respecting the conditions for using any electronic method, including the degree of any remoteness required;

(b) determining proceedings where attendance or appearance may be made by electronic method;

(c) requiring the payment of fees for using electronic methods, fixing the amounts of the fees, and prescribing the circumstances in which and the conditions under which a justice or another person designated in the regulations may waive the payment of a fee.

Interpreters

84(1) A justice may authorize a person to act as interpreter in a proceeding before the justice where the person swears the prescribed oath and, in the opinion of the justice, is competent.

Idem

(2) A judge may authorize a person to act as interpreter in proceedings under this Act where the person swears the prescribed oath and, in the opinion of the judge is competent and likely to be readily available.

Extension of time

85(1) Subject to this section, the court may extend any time fixed by this Act, by the regulations made under this Act or the rules of court for doing any thing other than commencing or recommencing a proceeding, whether or not the time has expired.

Limit on number of applications

(2) No more than one application for an extension of the time for filing of an appeal may be made in respect of a conviction.

Exception for commencing parking proceeding

(3) A justice may extend the time for commencing a parking proceeding where the court is unable to obtain proof of ownership of the vehicle or to send a notice of impending conviction to the defendant within that time because of extraordinary circumstances, including labour disputes and disruptions of postal services, power services and technological facilities.

Penalty for false statements

86. Every person who makes an assertion of fact in a statement or entry in a document or form for use under this Act knowing that the assertion is false is guilty of an offence and on conviction is liable to a fine of not more than $2,000.

Delivery

87(1) Any notice or document required or authorized to be given or delivered under this Act or the rules of court is given or delivered if,

(a) delivered personally or by mail;

(b) delivered in accordance with a method provided by this Act or the regulations; or

(c) delivered in accordance with a method provided under any other Act or prescribed by the rules of court.

Exception, personal delivery

(1.1) Despite subsection (1), a notice or document shall be delivered personally if this Act or the rules of court require it to be given or delivered personally or in person.

Rebuttable presumption, mail delivery

(2) If a notice or document that is required or authorized to be given or delivered to a person under this Act is mailed to the person at the person's last known address appearing on the records of the court in the proceeding, there is a rebuttable presumption that the notice or document is given or delivered to the person.

Rebuttable presumption, electronic delivery

(2.1) If a notice or document that is to be given or delivered to a person under this Act is delivered electronically, in accordance with a method provided by the regulations, to an email address or phone number that the person has provided for the purpose of receiving electronic notices or documents, there is a rebuttable presumption that the notice or document is given or delivered to the person.

Regulations

(3) The Lieutenant Governor in Council may make regulations respecting the method of delivery for any notice or document, including additional electronic methods, for the purposes of this Act.

Civil remedies preserved

88. No civil remedy for an act or omission is suspended or affected for the reason that the act or omission is an offence.

Process on holidays

89. Any action authorized or required by this Act is not invalid for the reason only that the action was taken on a non-juridical day.

Irregularities in form

90.(1) The validity of any proceeding is not affected by,

(a) any irregularity or defect in the substance or form of the summons, warrant, offence notice, parking infraction notice, undertaking to appear or recognizance; or

(b) any variance between the charge set out in the summons, warrant, parking infraction notice, offence notice, undertaking to appear or recognizance and the charge set out in the information or certificate.

Adjournment to meet irregularities

(2) Where it appears to the court that the defendant has been misled by any irregularity, defect or variance mentioned in subsection (1), the court may adjourn the hearing and may make such order as the court considers appropriate, including an order under section 60 for the payment of costs.

Contempt

91(1) Except as otherwise provided by an Act, every person who commits contempt in the face of a justice of the peace presiding over the Ontario Court of Justice in a proceeding under this Act is on conviction liable to a fine of not more than $1,000 or to imprisonment for a term of not more than thirty days, or to both.

Statement to offender

(2) Before a proceeding is taken for contempt under subsection (1), the justice of the peace shall inform the offender of the conduct complained of and the nature of the contempt and inform him or her of the right to show cause why he or she should not be punished.

Show cause

(3) A punishment for contempt in the face of the court shall not be imposed without giving the offender an opportunity to show cause why he or she should not be punished.

Adjournment for adjudication

(4) Except where, in the opinion of the justice of the peace, it is necessary to deal with the contempt immediately for the preservation of order and control in the courtroom, the justice of the peace shall adjourn the contempt proceeding to another day.

Adjudication by judge

(5) A contempt proceeding that is adjourned to another day under subsection (4) shall be heard and determined by the court presided over by a provincial judge.

Arrest for immediate adjudication

(6) Where the justice of the peace proceeds to deal with a contempt immediately and without adjournment under subsection (4), the justice of the peace may order the offender arrested and detained in the courtroom for the purpose of the hearing and determination.

Barring representative in contempt

(7) Where the offender is appearing before the court as a representative and the offender is not licensed under the *Law Society Act*, the court may order that he or she be barred from acting as representative in the proceeding in addition to any other punishment to which he or she is liable.

Appeals

(8) An order of punishment for contempt under this section is appealable in the same manner as if it were a conviction in a proceeding commenced by certificate under Part I of this Act.

Enforcement

(9) This Act applies for the purpose of enforcing a punishment by way of a fine or imprisonment under this section.

Regulations for purpose of Act

92. The Lieutenant Governor in Council may make regulations,

(a) prescribing any matter referred to in this Act as prescribed by the regulations;

(b) prescribing the form of certificate as to ownership of a motor vehicle given by the Registrar under subsection 210(7) of the *Highway Traffic Act* for the purpose of proceedings under this Act;

(c) providing for the extension of times prescribed by or under this Act or the rules of court in the event of a disruption in postal services;

(d) requiring the payment of fees upon the filing of anything required or permitted to be filed under this Act or the rules and fixing the amounts thereof, and providing for the waiver of the payment of a fee by a justice, or by a judge under Part VII, in such circumstances and under such conditions as are set out in the regulations;

(e) fixing costs payable upon conviction and referred to in subsection 60(1);

(f) fixing the items in respect of which costs may be awarded under subsection 60(2) and prescribing the maximum amounts that may be awarded in respect of each item;

(g) prescribing administrative fees for the purposes of subsection 70(1) for the late payment of fines or classes of fines, and prescribing the classes.

PART VI   YOUNG PERSONS

Definitions, Part VI

93. In this Part,

"parent," when used with reference to a young person, includes an adult with whom the young person ordinarily resides;

"young person" means a person who is or, in the absence of evidence to the contrary, appears to be,

(a) twelve years of age or more, but

(b) under sixteen years of age,

and includes a person sixteen years of age or more charged with having committed an offence while he or she was twelve years of age or more but under sixteen years of age.

Minimum age

94. No person shall be convicted of an offence committed while he or she was under twelve years of age.

Offence notice not to be used

95. A proceeding commenced against a young person by certificate of offence shall not be initiated by an offence notice under clause 3(2)(a).

Notice to parent

96(1) Where a summons is served upon a young person or a young person is released on a recognizance under this Act, the provincial offences officer, in the case of a summons, or the officer in charge, in the case of a recognizance, shall as soon as practicable give notice to a parent of the young person by delivering a copy of the summons or recognizance to the parent.

Where no notice given

(2) Where notice has not been given under subsection (1) and no person to whom notice could have been given appears with the young person, the court may,

(a) adjourn the hearing to another time to permit notice to be given; or

(b) dispense with notice.

Saving

(3) Failure to give notice to a parent under subsection (1) does not in itself invalidate the proceeding against the young person.

Sentence where proceeding commenced by certificate

97(1) Despite subsection 12(1), where a young person is found guilty of an offence in a proceeding commenced by certificate, the court may,

(a) convict the young person and,

(i) order the young person to pay a fine not exceeding the set fine that would be payable for the offence by an adult, the maximum fine prescribed for the offence, or $300, whichever is the least, or

(ii) suspend the passing of sentence and direct that the young person comply with the conditions prescribed in a probation order; or

(b) discharge the young person absolutely.

Term of probation order

(2) Section 72 applies with necessary modifications to a probation order made under subclause (1)(a)(ii), in the same manner as if the proceeding were commenced by information, except that the probation order shall not remain in force for more than ninety days from the date when it takes effect.

s. 12(2) applies where proceeding initiated by summons

(3) Subsection 12(2) applies with necessary modifications where a young person is convicted of an offence in a proceeding initiated by summons, in the same manner as if the proceeding were initiated by offence notice.

Young person to be present at trial

98(1) Subject to subsection 52(1) and subsection (2) of this section, a young person shall be present in court during the whole of his or her trial.

Court may permit absence

(2) The court may permit a young person to be absent during the whole or any part of his or her trial, on such conditions as the court considers proper.

Application of ss. 42, 54

(3) Sections 42 and 54 do not apply to a young person who is a defendant.

Failure of young person to appear

(4) Where a young person who is a defendant does not appear at the time and place appointed for a hearing and it is proved by the prosecutor, having been given a reasonable opportunity to do so, that a summons was served, an undertaking to appear was given or a recognizance to appear was entered into, as the case may be, or where the young person does not appear upon the resumption of a hearing that has been adjourned, the court may adjourn the hearing and issue a summons to appear or issue a warrant in the prescribed form for the arrest of the young person.

Compelling young person's attendance

(5) Where a young person does not attend personally in response to a summons issued under section 51 and it is proved

by the prosecutor, having been given a reasonable opportunity to do so, that the summons was served, the court may adjourn the hearing and issue a further summons or issue a warrant in the prescribed form for the arrest of the young person.

Identity of young person not to be published

99(1) No person shall publish by any means a report,

(a) of an offence committed or alleged to have been committed by a young person; or

(b) of a hearing, adjudication, sentence or appeal concerning a young person who committed or is alleged to have committed an offence,

in which the name of or any information serving to identify the young person is disclosed.

Offence

(2) Every person who contravenes subsection (1) and every director, officer or employee of a corporation who authorizes, permits or acquiesces in a contravention of subsection (1) by the corporation is guilty of an offence and is liable on conviction to a fine of not more than $10,000.

Exceptions

(3) Subsection (1) does not prohibit the following:

1. The disclosure of information by the young person concerned.

2. The disclosure of information by the young person's parent or lawyer, for the purpose of protecting the young person's interests.

3. The disclosure of information by a police officer, for the purpose of investigating an offence which the young person is suspected of having committed.

4. The disclosure of information to an insurer, to enable the insurer to investigate a claim arising out of an offence committed or alleged to have been committed by the young person.

5. The disclosure of information in the course of the administration of justice, but not for the purpose of making the information known in the community.

6. The disclosure of information by a person or member of a class of persons prescribed by the regulations, for a purpose prescribed by the regulations.

Pre-sentence report

100(1) Section 56 applies with necessary modifications where a young person is convicted of an offence in a proceeding commenced by certificate of offence, in the same manner as if the proceeding were commenced by information.

Pre-sentence report mandatory where imprisonment considered

(2) Where a young person who is bound by a probation order is convicted of an offence under section 75 and the court is considering imposing a sentence of imprisonment, the court shall direct a probation officer to prepare and file with the court a report in writing relating to the defendant for the purpose of assisting the court in imposing sentence, and the clerk of the court shall cause a copy of the report to be provided to the defendant or his or her representative and to the prosecutor.

Penalties limited

101(1) Despite the provisions of this or any other Act, no young person shall be sentenced,

(a) to be imprisoned, except under clause 75(d); or

(b) to pay a fine exceeding $1,000.

Sentence where proceeding commenced by information

(2) Where a young person is found guilty of an offence in a proceeding commenced by information, the court may,

(a) convict the young person and,

(i) order the young person to pay a fine not exceeding the maximum prescribed for the offence or $1,000, whichever is less, or

(ii) suspend the passing of sentence and direct that the young person comply with the conditions prescribed in a probation order; or

(b) discharge the young person absolutely.

Term of probation order

(3) A probation order made under subclause (2)(a)(ii) shall not remain in force for more than one year from the date when it takes effect.

No imprisonment for non-payment of fine

102(1) No warrant of committal shall be issued against a young person under section 69.

Probation order in lieu of imprisonment

(2) Where it would be appropriate, but for subsection (1), to issue a warrant against a young person under subsection 69(3) or (4), a judge may direct that the young person comply with the conditions prescribed in a probation order, where the young person has been given fifteen days notice of the intent to make a probation order and has had an opportunity to be heard.

Term of probation order

(3) A probation order made under subsection (2) shall not remain in force for more than ninety days from the date when it takes effect.

Open custody

103. Where a young person is sentenced to a term of imprisonment for breach of probation under clause 75(d), the term of imprisonment shall be served in a place of open custody designated under section 24.1 of the *Young Offenders Act* (Canada), whether in accordance with section 88 of the *Youth Criminal Justice Act* (Canada) or otherwise.

Evidence of young person's age

104. In a proceeding under this Act, a parent's testimony as to a young person's age and any other evidence of a young person's age that the court considers credible or trustworthy in the circumstances are admissible.

Appeal

105. Where the defendant is a young person, an appeal under subsection 135(1) shall be to the Superior Court of Justice, but the procedures and the powers of the court and any appeal from the judgment of the court shall be the same as if the appeal were to the Ontario Court of Justice presided over by a provincial judge.

Arrest without warrant limited

106. No person shall exercise an authority under this or any other Act to arrest a young person without warrant unless the person has reasonable and probable grounds to believe that it is necessary in the public interest to do so in order to,

    (a) establish the young person's identity; or

    (b) prevent the continuation or repetition of an offence that constitutes a serious danger to the young person or to the person or property of another.

Release of young persons after arrest by officer

s. 149 does not apply

107(1) Section 149 does not apply to a young person who has been arrested.

Requirement to release

(2) Where a police officer acting under a warrant or other power of arrest arrests a young person, the police officer shall, as soon as is practicable, release the young person from custody unconditionally or after serving him or her with a summons unless the officer has reasonable and probable grounds to believe that it is necessary in the public interest for the young person to be detained in order to,

    (a) establish the young person's identity; or

    (b) prevent the continuation or repetition of an offence that constitutes a serious danger to the young person or the person or property of another.

Release by officer in charge

(3) Where a young person is not released from custody under subsection (2), the police officer shall deliver the young person to the officer in charge who shall, where in his or her opinion the conditions set out in clause (2)(a) or (b) do not or no longer exist, release the young person,

    (a) unconditionally;

    (b) upon serving the young person with a summons; or

    (c) upon the young person entering into a recognizance in the prescribed form without sureties conditioned for his or her appearance in court.

Notice to parent

(4) Where the officer in charge does not release the young person under subsection (3), the officer in charge shall as soon as possible notify a parent of the young person by advising the parent, orally or in writing, of the young person's arrest, the reason for the arrest and the place of detention.

Release after young person brought before justice

(5) Sections 150 and 151 apply with necessary modifications to the release of a young person from custody under this section.

Place of custody

(6) No young person who is detained under section 150 shall be detained in any part of a place in which an adult who has been charged with or convicted of an offence is detained unless a justice so authorizes, on being satisfied that,

    (a) the young person cannot, having regard to the young person's own safety or the safety of others, be detained in a place of temporary detention for young persons; or

    (b) no place of temporary detention for young persons is available within a reasonable distance.

Idem

(7) Wherever practicable, a young person who is detained in custody shall be detained in a place of temporary detention designated under the *Youth Criminal Justice Act* (Canada).

Functions of a justice of peace limited

108(1) The functions of a justice with respect to a defendant who is a young person shall be performed only by a judge where a defendant is charged with an offence under section 75.

Exception

(2) Subsection (1) does not apply to the functions of a justice under Parts III and VIII.

PART VII   APPEALS AND REVIEW

Definitions, Part VII

109. In this Part,

"court" means the court to which an appeal is or may be taken under this Part;

"judge" means a judge of the court to which an appeal is or may be taken under this Part;

"sentence" includes any order or disposition consequent upon a conviction and an order as to costs.

Custody pending appeal

110. A defendant who appeals shall, if in custody, remain in custody, but a judge may order his or her release upon any of the conditions set out in subsection 150(2).

Payment of fine before appeal

111(1) A notice of appeal by a defendant shall not be accepted for filing if the defendant has not paid in full the fine imposed by the decision appealed from.

Exception with recognizance

(2) A judge may waive compliance with subsection (1) and order that the appellant enter into a recognizance to appear on the appeal, and the recognizance shall be in such amount, with or without sureties, as the judge directs.

Simultaneous applications

(3) A defendant may file an application to waive compliance with subsection (1) at the same time as the notice of appeal.

Role of prosecutor

(4) The defendant shall give the prosecutor notice of any application to waive compliance with subsection (1) and the prosecutor shall have an opportunity to make submissions in the public interest in respect of the application.

Stay

112. The filing of a notice of appeal does not stay the conviction unless a judge so orders.

Fixing of date where appellant in custody

113(1) Where an appellant is in custody pending the hearing of the appeal and the hearing of the appeal has not commenced within thirty days from the day on which notice of the appeal was given, the person having custody of the appellant shall make a motion to a judge to fix a date for the hearing of the appeal.

Idem

(2) Upon receiving a motion under subsection (1), the judge shall, after giving the prosecutor a reasonable opportunity to be heard, fix a date for the hearing of the appeal and give such directions as the judge thinks appropriate for expediting the hearing of the appeal.

Payment of fine not waiver

114. A person does not waive the right of appeal by reason only that the person pays the fine or complies with any order imposed upon conviction.

Transmittal of material

115. Where a notice of appeal has been filed, the clerk or local register of the appeal court shall notify the clerk of the trial court of the appeal and, upon receipt of the notification, the clerk of the trial court shall transmit the order appealed from and transmit or transfer custody of all other material in his or her possession or control relevant to the proceeding to the clerk or local registrar of the appeal court to be kept with the records of the appeal court.

APPEALS UNDER PART III

Appeals, proceedings commenced by information

116(1) Where a proceeding is commenced by information under Part III, the defendant or the prosecutor or the Attorney General by way of intervention may appeal from,

(a) a conviction;

(b) a dismissal;

(c) a finding as to ability, because of mental disorder, to conduct a defence;

(d) a sentence; or

(e) any other order as to costs.

Appeal court

(2) An appeal under subsection (1) shall be,

(a) where the appeal is from the decision of a justice of the peace, to the Ontario Court of Justice presided over by a provincial judge; or

(b) where the appeal is from the decision of a provincial judge, to the Superior Court of Justice.

Notice of appeal

(3) The appellant shall give notice of appeal in such manner and within such period as is provided by the rules of court.

Simultaneous application

(4) Despite subsection (3), the notice of appeal may be filed at the same time as an application under section 85 to extend the time to give notice of appeal.

Conduct of appeal

117(1) The court may, where it considers it to be in the interests of justice,

(a) order the production of any writing, exhibit or other thing relevant to the appeal;

(a.1) amend the information, unless it is of the opinion that the defendant has been misled or prejudiced in his or her defence or appeal;

(b) order any witness who would have been a compellable witness at the trial, whether or not he or she was called at the trial,

(i) to attend and be examined before the court, or

(ii) to be examined in the manner provided by the rules of court before a judge of the court, or before any officer of the court or justice of the peace or other person appointed by the court for the purpose;

(c) admit, as evidence, an examination that is taken under subclause (b)(ii);

(d) receive the evidence, if tendered, of any witness;

(e) order that any question arising on the appeal that,

(i) involves prolonged examination of writings or accounts, or scientific investigation, and

(ii) cannot in the opinion of the court conveniently be inquired into before the court, be referred for inquiry and report, in the manner provided by the rules of court, to a special commissioner appointed by the court; and

(f) act upon the report of a commissioner who is appointed under clause (e) in so far as the court thinks fit to do so.

Rights of parties

(2) Where the court exercises a power under this section, the parties or their representatives are entitled to examine or cross-examine witnesses and, in an inquiry under clause (1)(e), are entitled to be present during the inquiry and to adduce evidence and to be heard.

Right to representation

118(1) An appellant or respondent may appear and act personally or by representative.

Attendance while in custody

(2) An appellant or respondent who is in custody as a result of the decision appealed from is entitled to be present at the hearing of the appeal.

Sentencing in absence

(3) The power of a court to impose sentence may be exercised although the appellant or respondent is not present.

Written argument

119. An appellant or respondent may present the case on appeal and argument in writing instead of orally, and the court shall consider any case or argument so presented.

Orders on appeal against conviction, etc.

120(1) On the hearing of an appeal against a conviction or against a finding as to the ability, because of mental disorder, to conduct a defence, the court by order,

(a) may allow the appeal where it is of the opinion that,

(i) the finding should be set aside on the ground that it is unreasonable or cannot be supported by the evidence,

(ii) the judgment of the trial court should be set aside on the ground of a wrong decision on a question of law, or

(iii) on any ground, there was a miscarriage of justice; or

(b) may dismiss the appeal where,

(i) the court is of the opinion that the appellant, although the appellant was not properly convicted on a count or part of an information, was properly convicted on another count or part of the information,

(ii) the appeal is not decided in favour of the appellant on any ground mentioned in clause (a), or

(iii) although the court is of the opinion that on any ground mentioned in subclause (a)(ii) the appeal might be decided in favour of the appellant, it is of the opinion that no substantial wrong or miscarriage of justice has occurred.

Idem

(2) Where the court allows an appeal under clause (1)(a), it shall,

(a) where the appeal is from a conviction,

(i) direct a finding of acquittal to be entered, or

(ii) order a new trial; or

(b) where the appeal is from a finding as to the ability, because of mental disorder, to conduct a defence, order a new trial, subject to section 44.

Idem

(3) Where the court dismisses an appeal under clause (1)(b), it may substitute the decision that in its opinion should have been made and affirm the sentence passed by the trial court or impose a sentence that is warranted in law.

Orders on appeal against acquittal

121. Where an appeal is from an acquittal, the court may by order,

(a) dismiss the appeal; or

(b) allow the appeal, set aside the finding and,

(i) order a new trial, or

(ii) enter a finding of guilt with respect to the offence of which, in its opinion, the person who has been accused of the offence should have been found guilty, and pass a sentence that is warranted in law.

Orders on appeal against sentence

122(1) Where an appeal is taken against sentence, the court shall consider the fitness of the sentence appealed from and may, upon such evidence, if any, as it thinks fit to require or receive, by order,

(a) dismiss the appeal; or

(b) vary the sentence within the limits prescribed by law for the offence of which the defendant was convicted,

and, in making any order under clause (b), the court may take into account any time spent in custody by the defendant as a result of the offence.

Variance of sentence

(2) A judgment of a court that varies a sentence has the same force and effect as if it were a sentence passed by the trial court.

One sentence on more than one count

123. Where one sentence is passed upon a finding of guilt on two or more counts, the sentence is good if any of the counts would have justified the sentence.

Appeal based on defect in information or process

124(1) Judgment shall not be given in favour of an appellant based on any alleged defect in the substance or form of an information, certificate or process or any variance between the information, certificate or process and the evidence adduced at trial unless it is shown that objection was taken at the trial and that, in the case of a variance, an adjournment of the trial was refused although the variance had misled the appellant.

Idem

(2) Where an appeal is based on a defect in a conviction or an order, judgment shall not be given in favour of the appellant, but the court shall make an order curing the defect.

Additional orders

125. Where a court exercises any of the powers conferred by sections 117 to 124, it may make any order, in addition, that justice requires.

New trial

126(1) Where a court orders a new trial, it shall be held in the Ontario Court of Justice presided over by a justice other than the justice who tried the defendant in the first instance unless the appeal court directs that the new trial be held before the justice who tried the defendant in the first instance.

Order for release

(2) Where a court orders a new trial, it may make such order for the release or detention of the appellant pending such trial as may be made by a justice under subsection 150(2) and the order may be enforced in the same manner as if it had been made by a justice under that subsection.

Appeal by way of new trial

127(1) Where, because of the condition of the record of the trial in the trial court or for any other reason, the court, upon the motion of the appellant or respondent, is of the opinion that the interests of justice would be better served by hearing and determining the appeal by holding a new trial in the court, the court may order that the appeal shall be heard by way of a new trial in the court and for this purpose this Act applies with necessary modifications in the same manner as to a proceeding in the trial court.

Evidence

(2) The court may, for the purpose of hearing and determining an appeal under subsection (1), permit the evidence of any witness taken before the trial court to be read if that evidence has been authenticated and if,

(a) the appellant and respondent consent;

(b) the court is satisfied that the attendance of the witness cannot reasonably be obtained; or

(c) by reason of the formal nature of the evidence or otherwise the court is satisfied that the opposite party will not be prejudiced,

and any evidence that is read under the authority of this subsection has the same force and effect as if the witness had given the evidence before the court.

Dismissal or abandonment

128(1) The court may, upon proof that notice of an appeal has been given and that,

(a) the appellant has failed to comply with any order made under section 110 or 111 or with the conditions of any recognizance entered into under either of those sections; or

(b) the appeal has not been proceeded with or has been abandoned,

order that the appeal be dismissed.

Dismissal by justice

(2) Where the clerk of the court considers that an appeal has not been proceeded with or has been abandoned, the clerk may, after giving notice to the parties to the appeal, have the matter brought before a justice sitting in open court to determine whether the appeal has been abandoned and the appeal should be dismissed.

Motion to restore

(3) A party to an appeal that was dismissed under subsection (2) may apply to have the appeal restored.

Costs

129(1) Where an appeal is heard and determined or is abandoned or is dismissed for want of prosecution, the court may make any order with respect to costs that it considers just and reasonable.

Payment

(2) Where the court orders the appellant or respondent to pay costs, the order shall direct that the costs be paid to the clerk of the trial court, to be paid by the clerk to the person entitled to them, and shall fix the period within which the costs shall be paid.

Enforcement

(3) Costs ordered to be paid under this section by a person other than a prosecutor acting on behalf of the Crown shall be deemed to be a fine for the purpose of enforcing its payment.

Implementation of appeal court order

130. An order or judgment of the appeal court shall be implemented or enforced by the trial court and the clerk or local registrar of the appeal court shall send to the clerk of the trial court the order and all writings relating thereto.

Appeal to Court of Appeal

131(1) A defendant or the prosecutor or the Attorney General by way of intervention may appeal from the judgment of the court to the Court of Appeal, with leave of a judge of the Court of Appeal on special grounds, upon any question of law alone or as to sentence.

Grounds for leave

(2) No leave to appeal shall be granted under subsection (1) unless the judge of the Court of Appeal considers that in the particular circumstances of the case it is essential in the public interest or for the due administration of justice that leave be granted.

Appeal as to leave

(3) No appeal or review lies from a decision on a motion for leave to appeal under subsection (1).

Custody pending appeal

132. A defendant who appeals shall, if the defendant is in custody, remain in custody, but a judge may order his or her release upon any of the conditions set out in subsection 150(2).

Transfer of record

133. Where a motion for leave to appeal is made, the Registrar of the Court of Appeal shall notify the clerk or local registrar of the court appealed from of the motion and, upon receipt of the notification, the clerk or local registrar of the court shall transmit to the Registrar all the material forming the record including any other relevant material requested by a judge of the Court of Appeal.

Application of lower court of appeal procedures, etc.

134. Sections 114, 117, 118, 119, 120, 121, 122, 123, 124, 125 and 126, clause 128(b) and section 129 apply with necessary modifications to appeals to the Court of Appeal under section 131.

APPEALS UNDER PARTS I AND II

Appeals, proceedings commenced by certificate

135(1) A defendant or the prosecutor or the Attorney General by way of intervention is entitled to appeal an acquittal, conviction or sentence in a proceeding commenced by certificate under Part I or II and the appeal shall be to the Ontario Court of Justice presided over by a provincial judge.

Application for appeal

(2) A notice of appeal shall be in the prescribed form and shall state the reasons why the appeal is taken and shall be filed with the clerk of the court within 30 days after the making of the decision appealed from, in accordance with the rules of court.

Simultaneous application

(2.1) Despite subsection (2), the notice of appeal may be filed at the same time as an application under section 85 to extend the time to give notice of appeal.

Notice of hearing

(3) The clerk shall, as soon as is practicable, give a notice to the defendant and prosecutor of the time and place of the hearing of the appeal.

Conduct of appeal

136(1) Upon an appeal, the court shall give the parties an opportunity to be heard for the purpose of determining the issues and may, where the circumstances warrant it, make such inquiries as are necessary to ensure that the issues are fully and effectively defined.

Review

(2) An appeal shall be conducted by means of a review.

Evidence

(3) In determining a review, the court may,

(a) hear or rehear the recorded evidence or any part thereof and may require any party to provide a transcript of the evidence, or any part thereof, or to produce any further exhibit;

(b) receive the evidence of any witness whether or not the witness gave evidence at the trial;

(c) require the justice presiding at the trial to report in writing on any matter specified in the request; or

(d) receive and act upon statements of agreed facts or admissions.

Dismissal on abandonment

137(1) Where an appeal has not been proceeded with or abandoned, the court may order that the appeal be dismissed.

Dismissal by justice

(2) Where the clerk of the court considers that an appeal has not been proceeded with or has been abandoned, the clerk may, after giving notice to the parties to the appeal, have the matter brought before a justice sitting in open court to determine whether the appeal has been abandoned and the appeal should be dismissed.

Motion to restore

(3) A party to an appeal that was dismissed under subsection (2) may apply to have the appeal restored.

Powers of court on appeal

138(1) Upon an appeal, the court may affirm, reverse or vary the decision appealed from or where, in the opinion of the court, it is necessary to do so to satisfy the ends of justice, direct a new trial.

New trial

(2) Where the court directs a new trial, it shall be held in the Ontario Court of Justice presided over by a justice other than the justice who tried the defendant in the first instance, but the appeal court may, with the consent of the parties to the appeal, direct that the new trial be held before the justice who tried the defendant in the first instance or before the judge who directs the new trial.

Costs

(3) Upon an appeal, the court may make an order under section 60 for the payment of costs incurred on the appeal, and subsection (3) thereof applies to the order.

Appeal to Court of Appeal

139(1) An appeal lies from the judgment of the Ontario Court of Justice in an appeal under section 135 to the Court of

Appeal, with leave of a judge of the Court of Appeal, on special grounds, upon any question of law alone.

Grounds for leave

(2) No leave to appeal shall be granted under subsection (1) unless the judge of the Court of Appeal considers that in the particular circumstances of the case it is essential in the public interest or for the due administration of justice that leave be granted.

Costs

(3) Upon an appeal under this section, the Court of Appeal may make any order with respect to costs that it considers just and reasonable.

Appeal as to leave

(4) No appeal or review lies from a decision on a motion for leave to appeal under subsection (1).

REVIEW

Mandamus, prohibition, certiorari

140(1) On application, the Superior Court of Justice may by order grant any relief in respect of matters arising under this Act that the applicant would be entitled to in an application for an order in the nature of mandamus, prohibition or certiorari.

Notice of application

(2) Notice of an application under this section shall be served on,

    (a) the person whose act or omission gives rise to the application;

    (b) any person who is a party to a proceeding that gives rise to the application; and

    (c) the Attorney General.

Appeal

(3) An appeal lies to the Court of Appeal from an order made under this section.

Certiorari

141(1) A notice under section 140 in respect of an application for relief in the nature of certiorari shall be given at least seven days and not more than ten days before the date fixed for the hearing of the application and the notice shall be served within thirty days after the occurrence of the act sought to be quashed.

Filing material

(2) Where a notice referred to in subsection (1) is served on the person making the decision, order or warrant or holding the proceeding giving rise to the application, such person shall forthwith file with the Superior Court of Justice for use on the application, all material concerning the subject-matter of the application.

Motion to continue proceeding

(2.1) Where a notice referred to in subsection (1) is served in respect of an application, a person who is entitled to notice of the application under subsection 140(2) may make a motion to the Superior Court of Justice for an order that a trial in the proceeding giving rise to the application may continue despite the application and the Court may make the order if it is satisfied that it is in the interests of justice to do so.

Where appeal available

(3) No application shall be made to quash a conviction, order or ruling from which an appeal is provided by this Act, whether subject to leave or otherwise.

Substantial wrong

(4) On an application for relief in the nature of certiorari, the Superior Court of Justice shall not grant relief unless the court finds that a substantial wrong or miscarriage of justice has occurred, and the court may amend or validate any decision already made, with effect from such time and on such terms as the court considers proper.

(5) Repealed.

Habeas corpus

142(1) On application, the Superior Court of Justice may by order grant any relief in respect of a matter arising under this Act that the applicant would be entitled to in an application for an order in the nature of *habeas corpus*.

Procedure on application for relief in nature of habeas corpus

(2) Notice of an application under subsection (1) for relief in the nature of *habeas corpus* shall be served upon the person having custody of the person in respect of whom the application is made and upon the Attorney General and upon the hearing of the application the presence before the court of the person in respect of whom the application was made may be dispensed with by consent, in which event the court may proceed to dispose of the matter forthwith as the justice of the case requires.

Idem

(3) Subject to subsections (1) and (2), the *Habeas Corpus Act* applies to applications under this section, but an application for relief in the nature of certiorari may be brought in aid of an application under this section.

Idem

(4) The *Judicial Review Procedure Act* does not apply to matters in respect of which an application may be made under section 140.

Costs

(5) A court to which an application or appeal is made under section 140 or this section may make any order with respect to costs that it considers just and reasonable.

PART VIII ARREST, BAIL AND SEARCH WARRANTS

ARREST

Officer in charge, Part VIII

143. In this Part,
"officer in charge" means the police officer who is in charge of the lock-up or other place to which a person is taken after his or her arrest.

Execution of warrant

144(1) A warrant for the arrest of a person shall be executed by a police officer by arresting the person against whom the warrant is directed wherever he or she is found in Ontario.

Idem

(2) A police officer may arrest without warrant a person for whose arrest he or she has reasonable and probable grounds to believe that a warrant is in force in Ontario.

Arrest without warrant

145. Any person may arrest without warrant a person who he or she has reasonable and probable grounds to believe has committed an offence and is escaping from and freshly pursued by a police officer who has lawful authority to arrest that person, and, where the person who makes the arrest is not a police officer, shall forthwith deliver the person arrested to a police officer.

Use of force

146(1) Every police officer is, if he or she acts on reasonable and probable grounds, justified in using as much force as is necessary to do what the officer is required or authorized by law to do.

Use of force by citizen

(2) Every person upon whom a police officer calls for assistance is justified in using as much force as he or she believes on reasonable and probable grounds is necessary to render such assistance.

Immunity from civil liability

147. Where a person is wrongfully arrested, whether with or without a warrant, no action for damages shall be brought,

   (a) against the police officer making the arrest if he or she believed in good faith and on reasonable and probable grounds that the person arrested was the person named in the warrant or was subject to arrest without warrant under the authority of an Act;

   (b) against any person called upon to assist the police officer if such person believed that the police officer had the right to effect the arrest; or

   (c) against any person required to detain the prisoner in custody if such person believed the arrest was lawfully made.

Production of process and giving of reasons

148(1) It is the duty of every one who executes a process or warrant to have it with him or her, where it is feasible to do so, and to produce it when requested to do so.

Notice of reason for arrest

(2) It is the duty of every one who arrests a person, whether with or without warrant, to give notice to that person, where it is feasible to do so, of the reason for the arrest.

BAIL

Release after arrest by officer

149(1) Where a police officer, acting under a warrant or other power of arrest, arrests a person, the police officer shall, as soon as is practicable, release the person from custody after serving him or her with a summons or offence notice unless the officer has reasonable and probable grounds to believe that,

   (a) it is necessary in the public interest for the person to be detained, having regard to all the circumstances including the need to,

      (i) establish the identity of the person,

      (ii) secure or preserve evidence of or relating to the offence, or

      (iii) prevent the continuation or repetition of the offence or the commission of another offence; or

   (b) the person arrested is ordinarily resident outside Ontario and will not respond to a summons or offence notice.

Release by officer in charge

(2) Where a defendant is not released from custody under subsection (1), the police officer shall deliver him or her to the officer in charge who shall, where in his or her opinion the conditions set out in clauses (1)(a) and (b) do not or no longer exist, release the defendant,

   (a) upon serving the defendant with a summons or offence notice;

   (b) upon the defendant entering into a recognizance in the prescribed form without sureties conditioned for his or her appearance in court.

Cash bail by non-resident

(3) Where the defendant is held for the reason only that he or she is not ordinarily resident in Ontario and it is believed that the defendant will not respond to a summons or offence notice, the officer in charge may, in addition to anything required under subsection (2), require the defendant to deposit cash or other satisfactory negotiable security in an amount not to exceed,

   (a) where the proceeding is commenced by certificate under Part I or II, the amount of the set fine for the offence or, if none, $300; or

   (b) where the proceeding is commenced by information under Part III, $500.

Person in custody to be brought before justice

150(1) Where a defendant is not released from custody under section 149, the officer in charge shall, as soon as is practicable but in any event within twenty-four hours, bring the defendant before a justice and the justice shall, unless a plea of guilty is taken, order that the defendant be released upon giving his or her undertaking to appear unless the prosecutor having been given an opportunity to do so shows cause why the detention of the defendant is justified to ensure his or her appearance in court or why an order under subsection (2) is justified for the same purpose.

Order for conditional release

(2) Subject to subsection (1), the justice may order the release of the defendant,

(a) upon the defendant entering into a recognizance to appear with such conditions as are appropriate to ensure his or her appearance in court;

(b) where the offence is one punishable by imprisonment for twelve months or more, conditional upon the defendant entering into a recognizance before a justice with sureties in such amount and with such conditions, if any, as are appropriate to ensure his or her appearance in court or, with the consent of the prosecutor, upon the defendant depositing with the justice such sum of money or other valuable security as the order directs in an amount not exceeding,

(i) where the proceeding is commenced by certificate under Part I or II, the amount of the set fine for the offence or, if none, $300, or

(ii) where the proceeding is commenced by information under Part III, $1,000; or

(c) if the defendant is not ordinarily resident in Ontario, upon the defendant entering into a recognizance before a justice, with or without sureties, in such amount and with such conditions, if any, as are appropriate to ensure his or her appearance in court, and depositing with the justice such sum of money or other valuable security as the order directs in an amount not exceeding,

(i) where the proceeding is commenced by certificate under Part I or II, the amount of the set fine for the offence or, if none, $300, or

(ii) where the proceeding is commenced by information under Part III, $1,000.

Idem

(3) The justice shall not make an order under clause (2)(b) or (c) unless the prosecutor shows cause why an order under the immediately preceding clause should not be made.

Order for detention

(4) Where the prosecutor shows cause why the detention of the defendant in custody is justified to ensure his or her appearance in court, the justice shall order the defendant to be detained in custody until he or she is dealt with according to law.

Reasons

(5) The justice shall include in the record a statement of the reasons for his or her decision under subsection (1), (2) or (4).

Evidence at hearing

(6) Where a person is brought before a justice under subsection (1), the justice may receive and base his or her decision upon information the justice considers credible or trustworthy in the circumstances of each case except that the defendant shall not be examined or cross-examined in respect of the offence with which he or she is charged.

Adjournments

(7) Where a person is brought before a justice under subsection (1), the matter shall not be adjourned for more than three days without the consent of the defendant.

Expediting trial of person in custody

151(1) Where a defendant is not released from custody under section 149 or 150, he or she shall be brought before the court forthwith and, in any event, within eight days.

Further orders

(2) The justice presiding upon any appearance of the defendant in court may, upon the motion of the defendant or prosecutor, review any order made under section 150 and make such further or other order under section 150 as to the justice seems appropriate in the circumstances.

Appeal, order re release

152. A defendant or the prosecutor may appeal from an order or refusal to make an order under section 150 or 151 and the appeal shall be to the Superior Court of Justice.

Accounting for deposit, recognizance, etc.

Appointment of agent for appearance

153(1) A person who is released upon deposit under subsection 149(3) or clause 150(2)(c) may appoint the clerk of the court to act as the person's agent, in the event that he or she does not appear to answer to the charge, for the purpose of entering a plea of guilty on the person's behalf and authorizing the clerk to apply the amount so deposited toward payment of the fine and costs imposed by the court upon the conviction, and the clerk shall act as agent under this subsection without fee.

Returns to court

(2) An officer in charge or justice who takes a recognizance, money or security under section 149 or 150 shall make a return thereof to the court.

Returns to sureties

(3) The clerk of the court shall, upon the conclusion of a proceeding, make a financial return to every person who deposited money or security under a recognizance and return the surplus, if any.

Recognizance binding

154(1) The recognizance of a person to appear in a proceeding binds the person and the person's sureties in respect of all appearances required in the proceeding at times and places to which the proceeding is adjourned.

Recognizance binds independently of other charges

(2) A recognizance is binding in respect of appearances for the offence to which it relates and is not vacated upon the arrest, discharge or conviction of the defendant upon another charge.

Liability of principal

(3) The principal to a recognizance is bound for the amount of the recognizance due upon forfeiture.

Liability where sureties

(4) The principal and each surety to a recognizance are bound, jointly and severally, for the amount of the recognizance due upon forfeiture for non-appearance.

Relief of surety

155(1) A surety to a recognizance may, on motion in writing to the court at the location where the defendant is required to appear, ask to be relieved of the surety's obligation under the recognizance and the court shall thereupon issue a warrant for the arrest of the defendant.

Certificate of arrest

(2) When a police officer arrests the defendant under a warrant issued under subsection (1), he or she shall bring the defendant before a justice under section 150 and certify the arrest by certificate in the prescribed form and deliver the certificate to the court.

Vacating of recognizance

(3) The receipt of the certificate by the court under subsection (2) vacates the recognizance and discharges the sureties.

Delivery of defendant by surety

156. A surety to a recognizance may discharge the surety's obligation under the recognizance by delivering the defendant into the custody of the court at the location where he or she is required to appear at any time while it is sitting at or before the trial of the defendant.

Default of recognizance

157(1) Where a person who is bound by recognizance does not comply with a condition of the recognizance, a justice having knowledge of the facts shall endorse on the recognizance a certificate in the prescribed form setting out,

(a) the nature of the default;

(b) the reason for the default, if it is known;

(c) whether the ends of justice have been defeated or delayed by reason of the default; and

(d) the names and addresses of the principal and sureties.

Certificate as evidence

(2) A certificate that has been endorsed on a recognizance under subsection (1) is evidence of the default to which it relates.

Motion for forfeiture

(3) The clerk of the court shall transmit the endorsed recognizance to the local registrar of the Superior Court of Justice and, upon its receipt, the endorsed recognizance constitutes a motion for the forfeiture of the recognizance.

Notice of hearing

(4) A judge of the Superior Court of Justice shall fix a time and place for the hearing of the motion by the court and the local registrar of the court shall, not less than ten days before the time fixed for the hearing, deliver notice to the prosecutor and to each principal and, where the motion is for forfeiture for non-appearance, each surety named in the recognizance, of the time and place fixed for the hearing and requiring each principal and surety to show cause why the recognizance should not be forfeited.

Order as to forfeiture

(5) The Superior Court of Justice may, after giving the parties an opportunity to be heard, in its discretion grant or refuse the motion and make any order in respect of the forfeiture of the recognizance that the court considers proper.

Collection on forfeiture

(6) Where an order for forfeiture is made under subsection (5),

(a) any money or security forfeited shall be paid over by the person who has custody of it to the person who is entitled by law to receive it; and

(b) the principal and surety become judgment debtors of the Crown jointly and severally in the amount forfeited under the recognizance and the amount may be collected in the same manner as money owing under a judgment of the Superior Court of Justice.

SEARCH WARRANTS

Search warrant

158(1) A justice may at any time issue a warrant under his or her hand if the justice is satisfied by information upon oath that there are reasonable grounds to believe that there is in any place,

(a) anything on or in respect of which an offence has been or is suspected to have been committed; or

(b) anything that there are reasonable grounds to believe will afford evidence as to the commission of an offence.

Same

(1.1) The search warrant authorizes a police officer or person named in the warrant,

(a) to search the place named in the information for any thing described in clause (1)(a) or (b); and

(b) to seize the thing and deal with it in accordance with section 158.2.

Expiration

(2) Every search warrant shall name a date upon which it expires, which date shall be not later than fifteen days after its issue.

When to be executed

(3) Every search warrant shall be executed between 6 a.m. and 9 p.m. standard time, unless the justice by the warrant otherwise authorizes.

Definition

(4) In this section and in section 158.1,

"place" includes a building and a receptacle.

Telewarrants
Submission of information

158.1(1) Where a provincial offences officer believes that an offence has been committed and that it would be impracticable to appear personally before a justice to make application for a warrant in accordance with section 158, the provincial offences officer may submit an information on oath, by a means of telecommunication that produces a writing, to a justice designated for the purpose by the Chief Justice of the Ontario Court of Justice.

Filing of information

(2) The justice who receives an information submitted under subsection (1) shall, as soon as practicable, cause the information to be filed with the clerk of the court, certified by the justice as to time and date of receipt.

Same, alternative to oath

(3) A provincial offences officer who submits an information under subsection (1) may, instead of swearing an oath, make a statement in writing stating that all matters contained in the information are true to his or her knowledge and belief, and the statement is deemed to be made under oath.

Contents of information

(4) An information submitted under subsection (1) shall include,

(a) a statement of the circumstances that make it impracticable for the provincial offences officer to appear personally before a justice;

(b) a statement of the alleged offence, the place to be searched and the items alleged to be liable to seizure;

(c) a statement of the provincial offences officer's grounds for believing that items liable to seizure in respect of the alleged offence will be found in the place to be searched; and

(d) a statement as to any prior application for a warrant under this section or any other search warrant, in respect of the same matter, of which the provincial offences officer has knowledge.

Issuing warrant

(5) A justice to whom an information is submitted under subsection (1) may, if the conditions set out in subsection (6) are met,

(a) issue a warrant to a provincial offences officer conferring the same authority respecting search and seizure as may be conferred by a warrant issued by a justice before whom the provincial offences officer appears personally under section 158; and

(b) require that the warrant be executed within such time period as the justice may order.

Conditions

(6) The conditions referred to in subsection (5) are that the justice is satisfied that the information,

(a) is in respect of an offence and complies with subsection (4);

(b) discloses reasonable grounds for dispensing with an information presented personally; and

(c) discloses reasonable grounds, in accordance with section 158, for the issuance of a warrant in respect of an offence.

Application of s. 158(2) and (3)

(7) Subsections 158(2) and (3) apply to a warrant issued under this section.

Form, transmission and filing of warrant

(8) A justice who issues a warrant under this section shall,

(a) complete and sign the warrant, noting on its face the time, date and place of issuance;

(b) transmit the warrant by the means of telecommunication to the provincial offences officer who submitted the information; and

(c) as soon as practicable after the warrant has been issued, cause the warrant to be filed with the clerk of the court.

Copies

(9) The copy of the warrant that is transmitted to the provincial offences officer and any copies that are made from the transmitted copy have the same effect as the original for all purposes.

Providing or affixing copy when executing warrant

(10) When a provincial offences officer executes a warrant issued under this section,

(a) if the place to be searched is occupied, the provincial offences officer shall, before entering or as soon as practicable thereafter, give a copy of the warrant to any person present and ostensibly in control of the place; and

(b) if the place to be searched is unoccupied, the provincial offences officer shall, on entering or as soon as practicable thereafter, cause a copy of the warrant to be suitably and prominently affixed within the place.

Proof of authorization

(11) In any proceeding in which it is material for a court to be satisfied that a search or seizure was authorized by a warrant issued under this section, the warrant or the related information shall be produced and the court shall verify,

(a) in the case of the warrant, that it is signed by the justice and bears on its face a notation of the time, date and place of issuance;

(b) in the case of the related information, that it is certified by the justice as to time and date of receipt.

Presumption

(12) If the warrant or related information is not produced or if the matters set out in clause (11)(a) or (b) cannot be verified, it shall be presumed, in the absence of evidence to the contrary, that the search or seizure was not authorized by a warrant issued under this section.

Duty of person who carries out seizure

158.2(1) Subsection (2) applies when,

(a) a person has, under a warrant issued under this or any other Act or otherwise in the performance of his or her duties under an Act, seized any thing,

(i) upon or in respect of which an offence has been or is suspected to have been committed, or

(ii) that there are reasonable grounds to believe will afford evidence as to the commission of an offence; and

(b) no procedure for dealing with the thing is otherwise provided by law.

Same

(2) The person shall, as soon as is practicable, take the following steps:

1. The person shall determine whether the continued detention of the thing is required for the purposes of an investigation or proceeding.

2. If satisfied that continued detention is not required as mentioned in paragraph 1, the person shall,

   i. return the thing, on being given a receipt for it, to the person lawfully entitled to its possession, and

   ii. report to a justice about the seizure and return of the thing.

3. If paragraph 2 does not apply, the person shall,

   i. bring the thing before a justice, or

   ii. report to a justice about the seizure and detention of the thing.

Order of justice re things seized

159(1) When, under paragraph 3 of subsection 158.2(2), a thing that has been seized is brought before a justice or a report in respect of it is made to a justice, he or she shall, by order,

(a) detain the thing or direct it to be detained in the care of a person named in the order; or

(b) direct it to be returned.

Detention pending appeal, etc.

(1.0.1) A direction to return seized items does not take effect for 30 days and does not take effect during any application made or appeal taken in respect of the thing.

Same

(1.1) The justice may, in the order,

(a) authorize the examination, testing, inspection or reproduction of the thing seized, on the conditions that are reasonably necessary and are directed in the order; and

(b) make any other provision that, in his or her opinion, is necessary for the preservation of the thing.

Time limit for detention

(2) Nothing shall be detained under an order made under subsection (1) for a period of more than three months after the time of seizure unless, before the expiration of that period,

(a) upon motion, a justice is satisfied that having regard to the nature of the investigation, its further detention for a specified period is warranted and he or she so orders; or

(b) a proceeding is instituted in which the thing detained may be required.

Motion for examination and copying

(3) Upon the motion of the defendant, prosecutor or person having an interest in a thing detained under subsection (1), a justice may make an order for the examination, testing, inspection or reproduction of any thing detained upon such conditions as are reasonably necessary and directed in the order.

Motion for release

(4) Upon the motion of a person having an interest in a thing detained under subsection (1), and upon notice to the defendant, the person from whom the thing was seized, the person to whom the search warrant was issued and any other person who has an apparent interest in the thing detained, a justice may make an order for the release of any thing detained to the person from whom the thing was seized where it appears that the thing detained is no longer necessary for the purpose of an investigation or proceeding.

Appeal where order by justice of the peace

(5) Where an order or refusal to make an order under subsection (3) or (4) is made by a justice of the peace, an appeal lies therefrom in the same manner as an appeal from a conviction in a proceeding commenced by means of a certificate.

Claim of privilege

160(1) Where under a search warrant a person is about to examine or seize a document that is in the possession of a lawyer and a solicitor-client privilege is claimed on behalf of a named client in respect of the document, the person shall, without examining or making copies of the document,

(a) seize the document and place it, together with any other document seized in respect of which the same claim is made on behalf of the same client, in a package and seal and identify the package; and

(b) place the package in the custody of the clerk of the court or, with the consent of the person and the client, in the custody of another person.

Opportunity to claim privilege

(2) No person shall examine or seize a document that is in the possession of a lawyer without giving him or her a reasonable opportunity to claim the privilege under subsection (1).

Examination of documents in custody

(3) A judge may, upon the motion made without notice of the lawyer, by order authorize the lawyer to examine or make a copy of the document in the presence of its custodian or the judge, and the order shall contain such provisions as are necessary to ensure that the document is repackaged and resealed without alteration or damage.

Motion to determine privilege

(4) Where a document has been seized and placed in custody under subsection (1), the client by or on whose behalf the claim of solicitor-client privilege is made may make a motion to a judge for an order sustaining the privilege and for the return of the document.

Limitation

(5) A motion under subsection (4) shall be by notice of motion naming a hearing date not later than thirty days after the date on which the document was placed in custody.

Attorney General a party

(6) The person who seized the document and the Attorney General are parties to a motion under subsection (4) and entitled to at least three days notice thereof.

Private hearing and scrutiny by judge

(7) A motion under subsection (4) shall be heard in private and, for the purposes of the hearing, the judge may examine the document and, if he or she does so, shall cause it to be resealed.

Order

(8) The judge may by order,

(a) declare that the solicitor-client privilege exists or does not exist in respect of the document;

(b) direct that the document be delivered up to the appropriate person.

Release of document where no motion under subs. (4)

(9) Where it appears to a judge upon the motion of the Attorney General or person who seized the document that no motion has been made under subsection (4) within the time limit prescribed by subsection (5), the judge shall order that the document be delivered to the applicant.

PART IX   ORDERS ON APPLICATION UNDER STATUTES

Orders under statutes

161. Where, by any other Act, a proceeding is authorized to be taken before the Ontario Court of Justice or a justice for an order, including an order for the payment of money, and no other procedure is provided, this Act applies with necessary modifications to the proceeding in the same manner as to a proceeding commenced under Part III, and for the purpose,

(a) in place of an information, the applicant shall complete a statement in the prescribed form under oath attesting, on reasonable and probable grounds, to the existence of facts that would justify the order sought; and

(b) in place of a plea, the defendant shall be asked whether or not the defendant wishes to dispute the making of the order.

PART X   AGREEMENTS WITH MUNICIPALITIES CONCERNING ADMINISTRATIVE FUNCTIONS AND PROSECUTIONS

Definition

161.1 In this Part,

"transfer agreement" means an agreement under subsection 162(1)

Agreements

162(1) The Attorney General and a municipality may enter into an agreement with respect to a specified area, authorizing the municipality to,

(a) perform courts administration and court support functions, including the functions of the clerk of the court, for the purposes of this Act and the *Contraventions Act* (Canada); and

(b) conduct prosecutions,

(i) in proceedings under Parts I and II, and

(ii) in proceedings under the *Contraventions Act* (Canada) that are commenced by ticket under Part I or II of this Act.

Application of cl. (1)(a)

(2) Clause (1)(a) also applies to the functions assigned to the clerk of the court by any other Act.

Performance standards and sanctions

(3) Performance standards and sanctions shall be specified in the agreement; the municipality shall meet the standards and is subject to the sanctions for failure to meet them.

Definition

(4) In subsection (3),

"performance standards" includes standards for the conduct of prosecutions, for the administration of the courts and for the provision of court support services.

Area of application

163. A transfer agreement may specify an area that includes territory outside the municipality.

Evidence and effect of agreement

Deposit with clerk

164(1) When the Attorney General and a municipality have entered into a transfer agreement, a copy of the agreement shall be deposited with the clerk of the municipality and with the clerk of any other municipality that has jurisdiction in the specified area.

Judicial notice

(2) Judicial notice shall be taken of the agreement without the agreement or its deposit being specially pleaded or proved.

Non-compliance

(3) No proceeding is invalidated by reason only of a person's failure to comply with the agreement.

Fair hearing

(4) Without limiting the generality of subsection (3), that subsection does not preserve the validity of the proceeding if the failure to comply with the agreement results in prejudice to the defendant's right to a fair hearing.

Collection and enforcement

165(1) When a transfer agreement is in force, the municipality has power to collect fines levied in respect of proceedings under Parts I, II and III, including costs under section 60, surcharges under section 60.1 and fees referred to in section 66.2, and to enforce their payment; collection and enforcement shall be carried out in the manner specified in the agreement.

Contraventions Act (Canada)

(2) Subsection (1) also applies to fines and fees imposed under the *Contraventions Act* (Canada).

Non-application of subss. 69(6-21)

(3) Subsections 69(6) to (21) do not apply to fines that are governed by the agreement.

Fines, etc., payable to municipality

(4) Fines that are governed by the agreement are payable to the municipality and not to the Minister of Finance.

Payments to Minister of Finance

(5) The municipality shall pay to the Minister of Finance, at the times and in the manner specified in the agreement, amounts calculated in accordance with the agreement, in respect of,

(a) surcharges collected by the municipality under section 60.1;

(b) other fine revenues collected by the municipality that constitute money paid to Ontario for a special purpose within the meaning of the *Financial Administration Act*;

(c) costs the Attorney General incurs for adjudication and prosecution, for monitoring the performance of the agreement and for enforcing the agreement; and

(d) fines and fees imposed under the *Contraventions Act* (Canada) and collected by the municipality.

Exception, federal-municipal agreement re parking fines and fees

(6) Despite clause (5)(d), fines and fees imposed under the *Contraventions Act* (Canada) in relation to the unlawful parking, standing or stopping of a vehicle and collected by the municipality shall be paid in accordance with any agreement made under sections 65.2 and 65.3 of that Act.

Payments to another municipality

(7) The municipality acting under a transfer agreement shall pay to another municipality,

(a) the amount of any fine collected by the municipality that was imposed for a contravention of the other municipality's by-law;

(b) the amount of any fine collected by the municipality that was imposed for a contravention of a provincial statute and that would, except for the agreement, be payable to the other municipality; and

(c) the amount of any allowance retained by the municipality that would, except for the agreement, be payable to the other municipality under a regulation made under clause 20(1)(g).

Retention of balance

(8) Despite the *Fines and Forfeitures Act*, the municipality is entitled to retain, as a fee, the balance remaining after payment under subsections (5) and (7).

No other charge

(9) The municipality shall not collect any other charge for acting under a transfer agreement, except in accordance with section 304 of the *Municipal Act, 2001* or section 240 of the *City of Toronto Act, 2006* or with the Attorney General's advance written consent.

Disclosure to consumer reporting agency

(10) When a transfer agreement applies to a fine, section 69.1 applies to the municipality in the same manner as it applies to the Ministry of the Attorney General.

Exception, transitional period

(11) Despite subsection (4), while a regulation made under clause 174(b) is in effect, fines that are governed by the agreement remain payable to the Minister of Finance, who shall,

(a) calculate and retain the appropriate amounts under subsection (5);

(b) make any payments required by subsection (7); and

(c) pay the balance remaining to the municipality in accordance with subsection (8).

Municipal defendants

165.1(1) In this section,

"local board" has the same meaning as in the *Municipal Affairs Act*, but does not include a school board or a hospital board.

Special rules

(2) When a transfer agreement is in effect, the special rules set out in subsection (3) apply to a proceeding if,

(a) the proceeding is under Part I or III; and

(b) the defendant is a municipality or one of its local boards.

Same

(3) The special rules referred to in subsection (2) are:

1. The fine is payable to the Minister of Finance and not to the municipality, despite subsection 165(4).

2. The prosecutor may elect to collect and enforce the fine instead of the municipality, despite subsection 165(1) and the provisions of the agreement relating to collection and enforcement.

3. Notice of the election shall be given to the municipal representative named in the agreement for the purpose, or if none is named, to the clerk of the court.

Fines imposed before effective date

166. A transfer agreement may,

(a) authorize the municipality to collect and enforce the payment of fines that were imposed before the agreement's effective date; and

(b) provide in what proportions and in what manner the amounts collected are to be shared between the municipality and the Minister of Finance.

Rules under agreements

167(1) When a transfer agreement is in effect, the following rules apply:

1. The clerk of the court may be a municipal employee.

2. Subject to section 29, the court may sit in the location designated by the municipality, which need not be in premises operated by the Province of Ontario for court purposes.

3. The court office shall be in the location designated by the municipality.

4. Despite anything else in this Act, the municipality shall not without the Attorney General's written consent, obtained in advance, assign to a person other than its own employee a function that the agreement gives to the municipality.

Definition: "prosecutor," Part X

(2) For the purposes of this Part,

"prosecutor" means the Attorney General or, where the Attorney General does not intervene, means a person acting on behalf of the municipality in accordance with the agreement or, where no such person intervenes, means the person who issues a certificate or lays an information, and includes an agent acting on behalf of any of them.

Attorney General's right to intervene

168. A transfer agreement does not affect the Attorney General's right to intervene in a proceeding and assume the role of prosecutor at any stage, including on appeal.

Municipality not Crown agent

169. A municipality that acts under a transfer agreement does not do so as an agent of the Crown in right of Ontario or of the Attorney General.

Protection from personal liability

170(1) No proceeding shall be commenced against any person for an act done in good faith in the performance or intended performance of a function under a transfer agreement or for an alleged neglect or default in the performance in good faith of such a function.

Municipality not relieved of liability

(2) Subsection (1) does not relieve a municipality of liability in respect of a tort committed by a person referred to in subsection (1) to which the municipality would otherwise be subject.

Revocation or suspension of agreement

Order for compliance

171(1) When a transfer agreement is in effect, the Attorney General may make an order directing the municipality to comply with the agreement within a specified time.

Revocation or suspension

(2) The Attorney General may revoke or suspend the agreement if the municipality does not comply with the order within the specified time.

Protection from personal liability

(3) No proceeding for damages shall be commenced against the Attorney General or an employee of the Ministry of the Attorney General for anything done or omitted in good

faith in connection with the revocation or suspension of a transfer agreement.

Review committee

172. A transfer agreement may provide for a review committee whose composition and functions are determined by regulation.

Transition: application to all proceedings

173(1) Unless a transfer agreement provides otherwise, the agreement applies in respect of a proceeding whether it was commenced before or after the agreement's effective date.

Exception

(2) However, if one of the following conditions applies to a proceeding, the trial and disposition, including sentencing, shall be conducted as if there were no agreement:

1. The trial is scheduled to begin within seven calendar days after the effective date.

2. The trial began before the effective date and the disposition, including sentencing, is not yet complete on that date.

Regulations re agreements

174. The Attorney General may, by regulation,

(a) impose obligations in connection with a transfer agreement on a person who is not a party to the agreement;

(b) provide that fines governed by a transfer agreement may, for a transitional period after its effective date, be paid to the Minister of Finance;

(c) determine the composition and functions of a review committee for the purposes of section 172;

(d) provide for the effective implementation of transfer agreements.

Municipal powers

174.1(1) A municipality has power to enter into and to perform a transfer agreement.

Employees and others

(2) The functions given to a municipality by a transfer agreement or by an agreement under subsection (3) or (7) may be performed,

(a) by the municipality's employees;

(b) by a combination of the municipality's employees and the employees of another municipality, if the municipalities have an agreement under subsection (3) or (7); or

(c) by any other person, with the Attorney General's consent, as described in subsection 175(2).

Joint performance agreement between municipalities

(3) A municipality that has entered into a transfer agreement may enter into an agreement with one or more other municipalities for the joint performance, by a joint board of management or otherwise, of the functions given to the first municipality by the transfer agreement.

Attorney General's consent

(4) The joint performance agreement requires the Attorney General's written consent, obtained in advance.

Extra-territorial effect

(5) The power to perform an agreement under subsection (3) may be exercised in an area outside the municipality's territorial limits if that area forms part of the area specified in the agreement.

Intermunicipal agreements

(6) Municipalities may enter into and perform intermunicipal agreements to implement a transfer agreement.

Further agreements

(7) A municipality that has entered into a transfer agreement may enter into an agreement with one or more municipalities for the performance by the other municipality or municipalities of any of the functions given to the first municipality by the transfer agreement and the municipalities have the power to enter into and perform the agreement under this subsection.

Consent

(8) An agreement entered into under subsection (7) requires the Attorney General's written consent.

Extra-territorial effect

(9) The power to perform an agreement under subsection (7) may be exercised in an area outside the municipality's territorial limits.

Delegation

175(1) Subject to subsection (2), a municipality has power to assign to any person a function that a transfer agreement gives to the municipality.

Attorney General's consent

(2) An assignment to a person other than the municipality's employee requires the Attorney General's written consent, obtained in advance.

(3) Repealed.

Group of municipalities

176. A transfer agreement may also be made with two or more municipalities, and in that case sections 162 to 175 apply with necessary modifications.

POA Rules

Rules of The Ontario Court (Provincial Division) in Provincial Offences Proceedings

Under *Courts of Justice Act*, RSO 1990, c C.43

RRO 1990, Reg 200

1. In these rules,

"Act" means the *Provincial Offences Act*.

2(1) These rules apply to proceedings under the Act and a word or term in the Act has the same meaning in these rules as it has in the Act.

(2) In these rules any reference to electronic process is a reference to the electronic process in force at the time of the coming into force of the *Provincial Offences Statute Law Amendment Act, 1993*.

3. These rules shall be construed liberally so as to obtain as expeditious a conclusion of every proceeding as is consistent with a just determination of the proceeding.

4. The following apply to the calculation of a period of time prescribed by the Act, section 205.7 or 205.19 of the *Highway Traffic Act*, these rules or an order of a court:

1. The time shall be calculated by excluding the first day and including the last day of the period.

2. Where a period of less than six days is prescribed, a Saturday or holiday shall not be reckoned.

3. Where the last day of the period of time falls on a Saturday or a holiday, the day next following that is not a Saturday or a holiday shall be deemed to be the last day of the period.

4. Where the days are expressed to be clear days or where the term "at least" is added, the time shall be calculated by excluding both the first day and the last day of the period.

5. A notice or document given or delivered by mail shall, unless the contrary is shown, be deemed to be given or delivered on the seventh day following the day on which it was mailed.

6. For the purpose of proceedings under Part I or II of the Act, the amount of fine set by the court for an offence is such amount as may be set by the Chief Judge of the Ontario Court (Provincial Division).

7.(1) An application provided for by the Act or these rules shall be commenced by notice of application.

(2) A motion provided for by the Act or these rules shall be commenced by notice of motion.

(3) There shall be at least three days between the giving of notice of application or notice of motion and the day for hearing the application or motion.

(4) An applicant or moving party shall file notice of application or notice of motion at least two days before the day for hearing the application or motion.

(5) Evidence on an application or motion may be given,

(a) by affidavit;

(b) with the permission of the court, orally; or

(c) in the form of a transcript of the examination of a witness.

(6) Upon the hearing of an application or motion and whether or not other evidence is given on the application or motion, the justice may receive and base his or her decision upon information the justice considers credible or trustworthy in the circumstances.

(7) An application or motion may be heard without notice,

(a) on consent; or

(b) where, having regard to the subject-matter or the circumstances of the application or motion, it would not be unjust to hear the application or motion without notice.

(8) Subrules (2) to (5) do not apply in respect of a motion under section 66 of the Act.

8. (1) Where a certificate of parking infraction has been issued in respect of a parking infraction under a municipal by-law without a reference to the number of the by-law that creates the offence, the number of the by-law shall be affixed or

appended to the court filing document when the certificate is filed in the office of the court.

(2) Where a certificate of parking infraction has been issued alleging a parking infraction against the defendant as owner of a vehicle, evidence of the ownership of the vehicle shall be affixed or appended to the court filing document when the certificate is filed in the office of the court.

(3) A certificate of parking infraction shall be affixed or appended to the court filing document when the certificate is filed in the office of the court.

(4) Where a defendant delivers a parking infraction notice or notice of impending conviction in respect of an alleged parking infraction under a municipal by-law and gives notice of intention to appear in court for the purpose of entering a plea and having a trial of the matter, the parking infraction notice or notice of impending conviction shall be affixed or appended to the court filing document when the certificate of parking infraction is filed in the office of the court.

(5) Where a defendant files a notice of intention to appear under subsection 17.1 (3) or 18.1.1 (3) of the Act, the notice of intention to appear shall be affixed or appended to the court filing document when the certificate of parking infraction is filed in the office of the court.

(6) In this rule and subrule 22 (2),

"court filing document" means a document approved by the clerk of the court.

9. (1) A provincial offences officer who files a certificate of offence in the office of the court shall file with the certificate of offence a certificate control list, in the form that shall be supplied by the clerk of the court, with the certificate recorded on the list.

(2) A provincial offences officer who files a certificate of parking infraction in the office of the court shall file with it a certificate control list in the form approved by the clerk of the court, with the certificate recorded on the list.

(3) A single certificate control list may be filed with as many certificates of offence as can be accounted for on the certificate control list.

(4) A single certificate control list may be filed with as many certificates of parking infraction as can be accounted for on the certificate control list.

(5) The clerk of the court shall endorse on the certificate control list a receipt for the certificates of offence or certificates of parking infraction filed with the certificate control list.

(6) The clerk of the court shall, on request, give a copy of the receipt to the provincial offences officer who filed the certificate control list.

(7) Subrules (1) to (6) do not apply if a certificate of offence or a certificate of parking infraction is filed in an electronic format.

10. A facsimile signature of the person designated by the regulations is sufficient authentication of the certificate requesting a conviction under subsection 18.2 (1.1) of the Act.

11. (1) The clerk of the court shall not accept for filing a certificate of offence more than seven days after the day on which the offence notice or summons was served unless the time is extended by the court.

(2) No certificate of offence, certificate of parking infraction or certificate requesting a conviction shall be accepted for filing by direct electronic transmission after the last day prescribed for its filing, unless the time is extended by the court.

12. (1) The clerk of the court shall endorse the date of filing on every certificate of offence, certificate of parking infraction or certificate requesting conviction filed in the office of the court, except any such certificate filed in an electronic format.

(2) The clerk of the court shall ensure that the date of filing is indicated on any document filed in an electronic format.

(3) A certificate of offence, certificate of parking infraction or certificate requesting a conviction filed by direct electronic transmission shall be deemed to be filed the day on which the transmission concludes, unless the contrary is shown.

12.1 Revoked

13. (1) On the delivery of an offence notice under section 5 of the Act, a parking infraction notice under subsection 17 (1) of the Act or a notice of impending conviction under subsection 18.1 (1) of the Act, giving notice of intention to appear in court for the purpose of entering a plea and having a trial of the matter, the clerk of the court shall, where proceedings have been commenced, set a day and time for trial.

(1.1) On the filing of a notice of intention to appear under section 5.1 of the Act, the clerk of the court shall, where proceedings have been commenced, set a day and time for trial.

(2) Where a parking infraction notice issued in respect of an alleged parking infraction under a municipal by-law is received under subsection 17 (1) of the Act or a notice of impending conviction for such an infraction is received under subsection 18.1 (1) of the Act, the clerk of the court shall give notice of the time and place of trial to the defendant and the prosecutor as soon as practicable after the prosecutor has filed the certificate of parking infraction in the office of the court, together with the corresponding parking infraction notice or notice of impending conviction.

(2.1) Where a notice of intention to appear is filed under subsection 17.1 (3) or 18.1.1 (3) of the Act, the clerk of the court shall give notice of the time and place of trial to the defendant and prosecutor as soon as practicable after the prosecutor has filed the certificate of parking infraction in the office of the court together with the notice of intention to appear.

(3) The clerk of the court shall give notice of the trial to the defendant and prosecutor at least seven days before the day set for trial.

(4) Where a parking infraction is alleged against the defendant as owner of a vehicle, notice of the trial shall be given to the person identified as the holder of the permit, as defined in section 6 of the *Highway Traffic Act*, in the evidence of the ownership of the vehicle affixed or appended to the certificate of parking infraction.

(5) A certificate as to the giving of a notice of trial endorsed on the notice of trial by the clerk of the court shall be received in evidence and, in the absence of evidence to the contrary, is proof of the giving of the notice stated in the certificate.

(6) Where a defendant files a notice of intention to appear under section 5.1 of the Act and it appears that the certificate of offence has not been filed, the clerk of the court shall,

(a) provide the defendant with a receipt for the notice; and

(b) as soon as practicable after the filing of the certificate of offence, set a day and time for trial and issue the notice of trial.

14.(1) A defendant who attends at the time and place specified in an offence notice for the purpose of taking steps under subsection 7 (1) of the Act shall give the offence notice to the office of the court specified in the notice.

(2) The court shall give to a defendant a receipt for an offence notice delivered to the court in accordance with subrule (1).

15.(1) The following matters shall be dealt with only in court:

1. Quashing a proceeding, except under section 9, 18.3 or 18.5 of the Act or under section 205.7 or 205.19 of the *Highway Traffic Act*.

2. Amending an information, a certificate of offence or a certificate of parking infraction.

(2) A justice may dispose of an application under section 18.3 of the Act on the basis of the parking infraction notice and the form of application presented by the applicant.

(3) A justice may dispose of an application under section 18.5 of the Act on the basis of the form of application presented by the applicant, together with any oral submission the applicant wishes to make or the justice wishes to hear.

(4) A justice may dispose of an application under section 19 of the Act on the basis of the notice of fine and due date and the affidavit of the applicant.

16. A justice shall not quash a proceeding or amend a certificate of offence in respect of a defendant who is appearing before the justice for the purposes of section 7 of the Act.

17. Where a defendant appears before a justice under section 7 of the Act and it appears that the certificate of offence has not been filed in the office of the court, the justice may receive the plea of guilty and submissions of the defendant and specify the amount of fine the justice will impose and the time the justice will allow for payment when the certificate of offence is filed and a conviction is entered.

18. Where a defendant appears before a justice under section 7 of the Act and the justice is of the opinion that the certificate of offence is so defective on its face that it cannot be cured under section 33, 34, 35 or 36 of the Act, the justice shall refuse to accept the plea, shall inform the defendant of the reason for the refusal and shall inform the defendant of the provisions of section 5 or 5.1 of the Act, as applicable.

19. Money paid to the office of the court by a defendant who was served with an offence notice shall be refunded to the defendant if the certificate of offence is not filed in the office of the court named therein within seven days after the day on which the offence notice was served or within such extension of time as may be granted by the court.

20. Where notice is given to the clerk by the prosecutor that the prosecutor does not intend to file a certificate requesting conviction or a certificate of parking infraction that has been issued in respect of a parking infraction under an Act of the Legislature or under a regulation made under the authority of an Act, the prosecutor shall furnish the clerk with the name and address of the person to whom the parking infraction notice was issued and money paid to the office of the court in respect of the alleged parking infraction shall be refunded to that person.

21. Every justice shall keep a daily docket, electronically or in the form supplied by the clerk of the court, and shall record the disposition of every proceeding or matter under Part I or II of the Act dealt with by the justice.

22.(1) A justice acting under section 7 of the Act who imposes a fine that is less than the set fine or less than the minimum fine prescribed for the offence by the provision that creates the penalty shall endorse on the certificate of offence or the information, as the case may be, the decision and the reasons for the decision.

(1.1) A justice who quashes a proceeding under section 9 or 9.1 of the Act or under section 205.7, 205.11 or 205.19 of the *Highway Traffic Act* shall endorse on the certificate of offence or the information, as the case may be, the decision and the reasons for the decision.

(2) A justice who quashes a proceeding under section 18.4 of the Act shall endorse on the court filing document to which the certificate of parking infraction is affixed or appended the decision and the reasons for the decision.

(2.1) A justice who strikes out a conviction under section 18.3 or 18.5 of the Act shall endorse on the form of application the decision and the reasons for the decision.

(3) In addition to recording the decision on a daily docket, a justice referred to in subrule (1) or (1.1) shall complete a separate report, in the form that shall be supplied by the clerk of the court, of the decision and the reasons for the decision.

(4) A completed report mentioned in subrule (3) forms part of and shall be kept with the records of the court maintained by the clerk of the court.

22.1 A justice acting under section 9 of the Act or under section 205.7 of the *Highway Traffic Act* may examine by electronic means a certificate of offence that has been filed in an electronic format and may indicate his or her disposition of the proceeding by electronic means.

23. Upon payment of a fine, the administrative officer of the entity receiving the fine shall, upon request, issue to the defendant a receipt for the payment.

24. Revoked.

25. A justice who issues a warrant of committal under subsection 69 (14) of the Act shall enter the reasons for issuing the warrant in the records of the court.

26. Where a person is sentenced to a term of imprisonment and a warrant of committal is issued for custody of the person to commence, under subsection 63 (2) of the Act, on a day that is later than the day of sentencing, the clerk of the court, as soon as practicable after the warrant is issued,

(a) shall cause to be given or delivered to the person a notice stating the warrant has been issued and specifying the place where and the time within which the person is to surrender into custody; and

(b) shall deliver the warrant to the individual who is to accept the custody of the person.

27. (1) The following oath is prescribed for the purpose of subsection 84 (1) of the Act:

I,

………………………………………… ……...………………………………………………………,

do swear (or solemnly affirm) that I am capable of translating and will translate to the best of my skill and ability from

……………………………………….. to……………………………………….

(name of language)   (name of language)

from…………………………………..   to……………………………………….

(name of language)   (name of language)

in this proceeding.

So Help Me God. (Omit this line in an affirmation).

---

(2) The following oath is prescribed for the purpose of subsection 84 (2) of the Act:

I,

....

do swear (or solemnly affirm) that I am capable of translating and will translate to the best of my skill and ability from

....   to.. and

(name of language)   (name of language)

from...   to..

(name of language)   (name of language)

in proceedings under the *Provincial Offences Act.*

So Help Me God. (Omit this line in an affirmation).

---

28. (1) The clerk of the court who receives notice from the clerk of an appeal court that a notice of appeal has been filed shall transmit the order appealed from and transmit or transfer custody of all other material referred to in section 133 of the Act to the clerk of the appeal court within ten days after receiving the notice, to the extent that the clerk of the court receiving notice has the order or the other material in his or her possession.

(1.1) The clerk of the court receiving notice shall direct that any electronic document that has not been previously printed for the purpose of disposing of the charge and that is required as part of an appeal record be printed so as to create an original record, unless the appeal court requests that the document be transmitted to it in an electronic format.

(2) In an appeal from an order made under Part II, if the clerk of the court receiving notice does not have the order or the other material in his or her possession, the clerk may request and the municipality shall provide to the clerk the certificate of parking infraction and proof of ownership of the motor vehicle relating to the prosecution of the matter giving rise to the appeal.

29. Where a transcript of evidence at trial, including reasons for judgment or sentence, is requested from the clerk of the court for the purpose of an appeal, the clerk,

(a) shall complete and deliver to the person making the request a certificate of preparation of transcript in Form 2 of Regulation 196 of the Revised Regulations of Ontario, 1990;

(b) shall ensure that the transcript is prepared with reasonable diligence;

(c) shall obtain and attach to the transcript a certificate by the person who prepared the transcript that it is an accurate transcription of the evidence and reasons recorded at trial; and

(d) shall notify,

(i) the appellant,

(ii) the clerk of the court in which the appeal is taken, and

(iii) if the Crown Attorney is not the appellant or respondent, the Crown Attorney, when the transcript has been completed.

30. The clerk of the court who receives notice of the decision of an appeal court on an appeal from a decision of the court shall give the notice and any written reasons or endorsement included with the notice to the justice whose decision was appealed from.

31. (1) Where, upon an appeal, the appeal court has directed a new trial, upon motion by the prosecutor without notice a justice shall issue a summons to the defendant.

(2) Where a justice issues a summons under subrule (1), the clerk of the court shall, as soon as is practicable, give notice to the prosecutor of the time and place of the trial.

(3) Where the appeal court has directed a new trial and sets a date for the trial with the consent of the parties to the appeal, the defendant shall be deemed to have received notice of trial, and subrules (1) and (2) do not apply.

32. (1) An affidavit of service of an offence notice or summons shall be in Form 101.

(2) An affidavit in support of a request under section 11 or 19 of the Act or section 205.13 or 205.23 of the *Highway Traffic Act* shall be in Form 102.

(3) A certificate under section 11 of the Act or section 205.13 or 205.23 of the *Highway Traffic Act* shall be in Form 103.

(4) A summons under section 22 of the Act shall be in Form 104.

(5) An information under section 23 of the Act shall be in Form 105.

(6) A summons under section 24 of the Act shall be in Form 106.

(7) A warrant for arrest under section 24 of the Act shall be in Form 107.

(8) A notice of cancellation of summons under section 24 of the Act shall be in Form 108.

(9) A summons under section 39 of the Act shall be in Form 109.

(10) A warrant under subsection 40 (1) of the Act shall be in Form 110.

(11) A warrant under subsection 40 (2) of the Act shall be in Form 111.

(12) A recognizance by witness under section 40 of the Act shall be in Form 112.

(13) A warrant under subsection 40 (10) of the Act shall be in Form 113.

(14) An order under subsection 40 (6) of the Act shall be in Form 114.

(15) An order under section 41 of the Act shall be in Form 115.

(16) A certificate under section 42 of the Act shall be in Form 116.

(17) An order to attend for examination under section 44 of the Act shall be in Form 117.

(18) A warrant to take a defendant into custody under section 44 of the Act shall be in Form 118.

(19) A certificate of execution of a warrant issued under subsection 44 (6) of the Act shall be in Form 119.

(20) A summons under section 51 of the Act shall be in Form 120.

(21) An order of dismissal under section 53 of the Act shall be in Form 121.

(22) A summons to a defendant under section 54 of the Act shall be in Form 122.

(23) A warrant under section 54 of the Act shall be in Form 123.

(24) A warrant under subsection 63 (2) of the Act shall be in Form 124.

(25) A motion under subsection 66 (6) of the Act shall be in Form 125.

(26) An order under subsection 66 (6) of the Act extending time for payment of a fine shall be in Form 126.

(27) A certificate of default under section 68 of the Act shall be in Form 127.

(28) Revoked.

(29) Revoked.

(30) Revoked.

(31) An undertaking by a defendant to appear shall be in Form 131.

(32) A probation order under section 72 of the Act shall be in Form 132.

(33) A summons to a defendant where a new trial is ordered by an appeal court shall be in Form 133.

(34) A recognizance under subsection 149 (2) of the Act shall be in Form 134.

(35) A recognizance under section 150 of the Act shall be in Form 135.

(36) An order for detention of a defendant under section 150 of the Act shall be in Form 136.

(37) A warrant under section 155 of the Act for the arrest of a defendant shall be in Form 137.

(38) A certificate of arrest under section 155 of the Act shall be in Form 138.

(39) A certificate under subsection 157 (1) of the Act as to failure to comply with a condition of a recognizance shall be in Form 139.

(40) An information to obtain a search warrant under section 158 of the Act shall be in Form 140.

(41) A search warrant under section 158 of the Act shall be in Form 141.

(42) A statement under section 161 of the Act shall be in Form 142.

(43) A warrant remanding,

(a) a witness under subsection 40 (6) of the Act; or

(b) a defendant under subsection 150 (4) of the Act,

shall be in Form 143.

(44) An order for the release of a defendant under subsection 150 (2) of the Act shall be in Form 144.

(45) An order for the release of a person in custody under subsection 40 (9) of the Act shall be in Form 145.

(46) A warrant of committal the form of which is not otherwise specified in these rules shall be in Form 146.

(47) An order the form of which is not otherwise specified in these rules shall be in Form 147.

(48) A recognizance under subsection 149 (3) of the Act shall be in Form 148.

(49) Revoked.

(50) An application under section 18.3 of the Act shall be in Form?150.

(51) An application under section 18.5 of the Act shall be in Form?151.

(52) An application under subsection 19 (2) of the Act shall be in Form?152.

(53) An order under subsection 69 (21) of the Act shall be in Form 153.

Set Fines from the Provincial Offences Act

Proceedings Commenced by Certificate of Offence

under *Provincial Offences Act*, RSO 1990, c P.33

RRO 1990, Reg 950

Schedule 43

The *Highway Traffic Act*

ITEM	COLUMN 1	COLUMN 2 SECTION	SET FINE
1.	Drive motor vehicle, no permit	7(1)(a)	$85.00
2.	Drive motor vehicle, no currently validated permit	7(1)(a)	$85.00
3.	Drive motor vehicle, no plates	7(1)(b)(i)	$85.00
4.	Drive motor vehicle, fail to display two plates	7(1)(b)(i)	$85.00
5.	Drive motor vehicle, plate improperly displayed	7(1)(b)(i)	$85.00
6.	Drive motor vehicle, no validation on plate	7(1)(c)(i)	$85.00
7.	Drive motor vehicle, validation improperly affixed	7(1)(c)(i)	$85.00
8.	Draw trailer, no permit	7(4)(a)	$85.00
9.	Draw trailer, no plate	7(4)(b)	$85.00

ITEM	COLUMN 1	COLUMN 2 SECTION	SET FINE
10.	Draw trailer, plate improperly displayed	7(4)(b)	$85.00
11.	Fail to surrender permit for motor vehicle	7(5)(a)	$85.00
12.	Fail to surrender permit for trailer	7(5)(b)	$85.00
13.	Have more than one permit	7(15)	$85.00
14.	Drive motor vehicle, not in accordance with permit limitations	8	$140.00
15.	Permit driving of motor vehicle, not in accordance with permit limitations	8	$140.00
16.	REVOKED		
17.	Fail to notify change of address	9(2)	$85.00
18.	Fail to notify change of name	9(2)	$85.00
19.	Fail to notify change of address—lessee	9(3)	$85.00
20.	Fail to notify change of name—lessee	9(3)	$85.00
21.	Drive motor vehicle, no vehicle identification number	10(l)	$85.00
22.	Permit driving of motor vehicle, no vehicle identification number	10(l)	$85.00

ITEM	COLUMN 1	COLUMN 2 SECTION	SET FINE
23.	Draw trailer, no identification number	10(2)(a)	$85.00
24.	Permit drawing of trailer, no identification number	10(2)(a)	$85.00
25.	Draw conversion unit, no identification number	10(2)(b)	$85.00
26.	Permit drawing of conversion unit, no identification number	10(2)(b)	$85.00
27.	Draw converter dolly, no identification number	10(2)(c)	$85.00
28.	Permit drawing of converter dolly, no identification number	10(2)(c)	$85.00
29.	Fail to remove plates on ceasing to be owner	11(1)(a)	$85.00
30.	Fail to remove plates on ceasing to be lessee	11(1)(a)	$85.00
31.	Fail to retain plate portion of permit	11(1)(b)	$85.00
32.	Fail to give vehicle portion of permit to new owner	11(1)(c)(i)	$85.00
33.	Fail to give vehicle portion of permit to lessor	11(1)(c)(ii)	$85.00
34.	Fail to apply for permit on becoming owner	11(2)	$85.00
34.1	Fail to provide valid information package for inspection	11.1(1)	$140.00
34.2	Fail to deliver valid information package at time vehicle transfer	11.1(1)	$140.00
35.	Deface plate	12(1)(a)	N.S.F.
36.	Deface validation	12(1)(a)	N.S.F.
37.	Alter plate	12(1)(a)	N.S.F.
38.	Alter validation	12(1)(a)	N.S.F.
39.	Deface permit	12(1)(a)	N.S.F.
40.	Alter permit	12(1)(a)	N.S.F.

ITEM	COLUMN 1	COLUMN 2 SECTION	SET FINE
41.	Use defaced plate	12(1)(b)	N.S.F.
42.	Use defaced validation	12(1)(b)	N.S.F.
43.	Use altered plate	12(1)(b)	N.S.F.
44.	Use altered validation	12(1)(b)	N.S.F.
45.	Permit use of defaced plate	12(1)(b)	N.S.F.
46.	Permit use of defaced validation	12(1)(b)	N.S.F.
47.	Permit use of altered plate	12(1)(b)	N.S.F.
48.	Permit use of altered validation	12(1)(b)	N.S.F.
49.	Use defaced permit	12(1)(b)	N.S.F.
50.	Permit use of defaced permit	12(1)(b)	N.S.F.
51.	Remove plate without authority	12(1)(c)	N.S.F.
52.	Use plate not authorized for vehicle	12(1)(d)	140.00
53.	Permit use of plate not authorized for vehicle	12(1)(d)	140.00
54.	Use validation not furnished by Ministry	12(1)(e)	140.00
55.	Use validation not furnished for vehicle	12(1)(e)	140.00
56.	Permit use of validation not furnished by Ministry	12(1)(e)	140.00
57.	Permit use of validation not furnished for vehicle	12(1)(e)	140.00
58.	Use plate not in accordance with Act	12(1)(f)	$140.00
59.	Use plate not in accordance with regulations	12(1)(f)	$140.00
60.	Use validation not in accordance with Act	12(1)(f)	$140.00
61.	Use validation not in accordance with regulations	12(1)(f)	$140.00
62.	Permit use of plate not in accordance with Act	12(1)(f)	$140.00

ITEM	COLUMN 1	COLUMN 2 SECTION	SET FINE
63.	Permit use of plate not in accordance with regulations	12(1)(f)	$140.00
64.	Permit use of validation not in accordance with Act	12(1)(f)	$140.00
65.	Permit use of validation not in accordance with regulations	12(1)(f)	$140.00
66.	Confuse identity of plate	13(1)	$85.00
67.	Obstruct plate	13(2)	$85.00
68.	Dirty plate	13(2)	$85.00
69.	Entire plate not plainly visible	13(2)	$85.00
69.0.1	Obstruct plate, preventing accurate photograph by red light camera system	13(3.0.1)	$85.00
69.1	Obstruct plate preventing accurate photograph	13(3)	$85.00
69.2	Obstruct plate preventing identification by toll system	13(3.1)	$85.00
70.	Operate commercial motor vehicle—no valid CVOR certificate	16(2)	$260.00
71.	Drive commercial motor vehicle—no valid CVOR certificate	16(2)	$175.00
72.	Fail to carry fleet limitation certificate	16(3)	$175.00
73.	Fail to carry CVOR certificate	16(3)(a)	$85.00
74.	Fail to carry vehicle lease	16(3)(b)	$85.00
75.	REVOKED		
76.	Fail to surrender CVOR certificate	16(4)	$85.00
77.	Fail to surrender vehicle lease	16(4)	$85.00
78.	REVOKED		
79.	Fail to surrender fleet limitation certificate	16(4)	$175.00

ITEM	COLUMN 1	COLUMN 2 SECTION	SET FINE
80.	Fail to notify change of officer's name	18	$175.00
81.	Fail to notify change of officer's address	18	$175.00
82.	Fail to notify change of officers	18	$175.00
83.	Fail to retain copy of lease	20(1)	$175.00
83.0.1	Provide fictitious, altered or fraudulently obtained CVOR certificate	21(4)	$400.00
83.0.2	Use fictitious, altered or fraudulently obtained CVOR certificate	21(4)	$400.00
83.0.3	Permit the use of fictitious, altered or fraudulently obtained CVOR certificate	21(4)	$400.00
83.0.4	Improperly use CVOR certificate	21(4)	$400.00
83.1	Operate commercial motor vehicle—improper insurance	23(1)	N.S.F.
83.2	Driver of commercial motor vehicle—fail to carry proof of insurance	23(3)	$175.00
83.3	Driver of commercial motor vehicle—fail to surrender proof of insurance	23(3)	$175.00
83.4	Inadequate cargo insurance	23.1	$85.00
83.5	No evidence of cargo insurance in vehicle	23.1	$85.00
84.	Drive motor vehicle—no licence	32(1)	$260.00
84.1	Drive commercial motor vehicle—no licence	32(1)	$310.00
85.	Drive motor vehicle—improper licence	32(1)	$260.00
85.1	Drive commercial motor vehicle—improper licence	32(1)	$310.00

ITEM	COLUMN 1	COLUMN 2 SECTION	SET FINE
86.	Drive streetcar—no licence	32(2)	$260.00
87.	Drive vehicle with air brakes—no endorsement	32(3)	$200.00
87.1	Drive commercial motor vehicle with air brake—no endorsement	32(3)	$310.00
88.	Drive motor vehicle in contravention of conditions	32(9)	$85.00
88.1	Drive commercial motor vehicle in contravention of conditions	32(9)	$310.00
89.	Permit unlicensed person to drive motor vehicle	32(10)	$200.00
89.1	Permit unlicensed person to drive commercial motor vehicle	32(10)	$310.00
90.	Permit person with improper licence to drive motor vehicle	32(10)	$200.00
90.1	Permit person with improper licence to drive commercial motor vehicle	32(10)	$310.00
91.	Permit person to drive motor vehicle in contravention of condition	32(10.1)	$200.00
91.0.1	Permit person to drive commercial motor vehicle in contravention of condition	32(10.1)	$310.00
91.1	Permit operation of vehicles with air brakes—no endorsement on licence	32(11)	$200.00
91.2	Permit novice driver to drive in contravention of condition or restriction	32(11.1)	$200.00

ITEM	COLUMN 1	COLUMN 2 SECTION	SET FINE
92.	Driver fail to surrender licence	33(1)	$85.00
92.1	Accompanying driver fail to surrender licence	33(2)	$85.00
93.	Driver fail to give identification	33(3)	$85.00
93.1	Accompanying driver fail to give identification	33(3)	$85.00
94.	Possess illegal licence	35(1)(a)	N.S.F.
95.	Use illegal licence	35(1)(a)	N.S.F.
96.	Possess non–Photo Card portion of cancelled, revoked or suspended licence	35(1)(b)	N.S.F.
97.	Use non–Photo Card portion of cancelled, revoked or suspended licence	35(1)	N.S.F.
98.	Permit another person to use all or part of licence	35(1)(c)	N.S.F.
98.1	Use other person's licence	35(1)(d)	N.S.F.
98.2	Apply for more than one licence	35(1)(e)	N.S.F.
98.3	Secure more than one licence	35(1)(e)	N.S.F.
98.4	Possess more than one licence	35(1)(e)	N.S.F.
98.5	Fail to surrender suspended, revoked or cancelled licence	35(1)(f)	N.S.F.
99.	Driving under licence of other jurisdiction while suspended in Ontario	36	N.S.F.
100.	Employ person under 16 to drive	37(2)	N.S.F.
101.	Permit person under 16 to drive	37(2)	N.S.F.
101.1	Permit person under 16 on motor-assisted bicycle	38(2)	N.S.F.

ITEM	COLUMN 1	COLUMN 2 SECTION	SET FINE
101.2	Permit person under 16 on power-assisted bicycle	38(2)	N.S.F.
102.	Let unlicensed driver hire vehicle	39(1)	N.S.F.
103.	Fail to produce licence when hiring vehicle	39(3)	$85.00
103.1	Pick up passenger for compensation without authority	39.1(1)	$300.00
103.2	Owner—allow use of vehicle to pick up passenger for compensation without authority	39.1(2)	$300.00
103.3	Arrange for passenger pick-up for compensation without authority	39.1(3)	$300.00
103.4	Offer to arrange for passenger pick-up for compensation without authority	39.1(3)	$300.00
103.5	Fail to carry authority to pick up passengers for compensation	39.1(4)(a)	$300.00
103.6	Fail to surrender authority to pick up passengers for compensation	39.1(4)(b)	$300.00
103.7	Fail to identify self	39.1(6)	N.S.F.
103.8	Novice driver—B.A.C. above zero	44.1(3)	$85.00
103.9	Young driver—B.A.C. above zero	44.1(5)	$85.00
104.	Apply for permit while prohibited	47(5)	N.S.F.
105.	Procure permit while prohibited	47(5)	N.S.F.
106.	Possess permit while prohibited	47(5)	N.S.F.
107.	Apply for licence while prohibited	47(6)	N.S.F.
108.	Procure licence while prohibited	47(6)	N.S.F.
109.	Possess licence while prohibited	47(6)	N.S.F.

ITEM	COLUMN 1	COLUMN 2 SECTION	SET FINE
110.	Procure CVOR certificate while suspended or cancelled	47(7)	$260.00
111.	Apply for CVOR certificate while suspended or cancelled	47(7)	$260.00
112.	Operate commercial motor vehicle—fleet limitation certificate not carried	47(8)(a)	N.S.F.
113.	Operate commercial motor vehicle—CVOR certificate suspended	47(8)(b)	N.S.F.
113.1	Novice driver fail to provide breath sample	48.1(3)	$85.00
113.2	Novice driver refuse to provide breath sample	48.1(4)	$85.00
113.3	Novice driver fail to provide breath sample	48.1(4)	$85.00
113.4	Novice driver refuse to provide breath sample	48.1(4)	$85.00
113.5	Novice driver fail to surrender licence	48.1(5)	$85.00
113.6	Accompanying driver fail to provide breath sample	48.2(2)	$85.00
113.7	Accompanying driver refuse to provide breath sample	48.2(2)	$85.00
114.	Operate vehicle for which permit suspended	51	N.S.F.
115.	Operate vehicle for which permit cancelled	51	N.S.F.
116.	Driving while under suspension	53(1)	N.S.F.
116.1	Passenger fail to identify self	57.1.1(1)	$85.00
116.2	Passenger fail to give required information	57.1.1(2)	$85.00

ITEM	COLUMN 1	COLUMN 2 SECTION	SET FINE
117.	No licence to operate vehicle business	59(1)	N.S.F.
118.	Interfere with officer inspecting vehicle business	59(6)	N.S.F.
119.	Fail to keep records	60(1)	N.S.F.
120.	Deal with vehicle identification number altered	60(2)	N.S.F.
121.	Deface vehicle identification number	60(3)	N.S.F.
122.	Remove vehicle identification number	60(3)	N.S.F.
123.	Fail to notify re vehicle stored more than 2 weeks	60(4)	$60.00
124.	Fail to report damaged vehicle	60(5)	$140.00
124.1	Give false report	60(6)	N.S.F.
125.	Drive without proper headlights—motor vehicle	62(1)	$85.00
125.1	Drive without proper headlights—commercial motor vehicle	62(1)	$200.00
126.	Drive without proper rear light—motor vehicle	62(1)	$85.00
126.1	Drive without proper rear light—commercial motor vehicle	62(1)	$200.00
127.	Drive without proper headlight—motorcycle	62(2)	$85.00
128.	Drive without proper rear light—motorcycle	62(2)	$85.00
129.	Drive without proper headlights—motorcycle with sidecar	62(3)	$85.00
130.	Drive without proper rear light—motorcycle with side car	62(3)	$85.00
131.	Drive with improper headlights	62(6)	$85.00

ITEM	COLUMN 1	COLUMN 2 SECTION	SET FINE
131.1	Drive with improper headlights—commercial motor vehicle	62(6)	$200.00
132.	Drive with headlamp coated	62(7)	$85.00
132.1	Drive with headlight coated—commercial motor vehicle	62(7)	$200.00
133.	Drive with headlamp covered	62(7)	$85.00
133.1	Drive with headlamp covered—commercial motor vehicle	62(7)	$200.00
134.	Drive with headlamp modified	62(7)	$85.00
134.1	Drive with headlamp modified—commercial motor vehicle	62(7)	$200.00
135.	More than 4 lighted headlights	62(9)	$85.00
135.1	More than 4 lighted headlights—commercial motor vehicle	62(9)	$200.00
136.	Improper clearance lights	62(10)	$85.00
136.1	Improper clearance lights—commercial motor vehicle	62(10)	$200.00
137.	Fail to have proper identification lamps	62(11)	$85.00
137.1	Fail to have proper identification lamps—commercial motor vehicle	62(11)	$200.00
138.	Fail to have proper side marker lamps	62(13)	$85.00
138.1	Fail to have proper side marker lamps—commercial motor vehicle	62(13)	$200.00
139.	Use lamp producing intermittent flashes of red light	62(14)	$85.00

ITEM	COLUMN 1	COLUMN 2 SECTION	SET FINE
139.1	Use lamp producing intermittent flashes of red light—commercial motor vehicle	62(14)	$200.00
139.2	Unauthorized red and blue lights at front	62(14.1)	$85.00
139.3	Unauthorized red and blue lights at front—commercial motor vehicle	62(14.1)	$200.00
140	Red light at front	62(15)	$85.00
140.1	Red light at front—commercial motor vehicle	62(15)	$200.00
141.	Improper use of green flashing lights	62(16.1)	$85.00
141.1	Improper use of green flashing lights—commercial motor vehicle	62(16.1)	$200.00
142.	Improper bicycle lighting	62(17)	$85.00
143.	Improper lighting on motor assisted bicycle	62(17)	$85.00
144.	Improper number plate light	62(19)	$85.00
145.	Use parking light while vehicle in motion	62(20)	$85.00
146.	Have more than one spotlamp	62(22)	$85.00
146.1	Have more than one spotlamp—commercial motor vehicle	62(22)	$200.00
147.	Improper use of spotlamp	62(22)	$85.00
147.1	Improper use of spotlamp—commercial motor vehicle	62(22)	$200.00
148.	Improper lights on traction engine	62(23)	$85.00
149.	No red light on rear of trailer	62(24)	$85.00
149.1	No red light on rear of trailer—commercial motor vehicle	62(24)	$200.00

ITEM	COLUMN 1	COLUMN 2 SECTION	SET FINE
150.	No red light on rear of object	62(24)	$85.00
150.1	No red light on rear of object—commercial motor vehicle	62(24)	$200.00
151.	No proper red lights—object over 2.6 metres	62(25)	$85.00
151.1	No proper red light—object over 2.6 m—commercial motor vehicle	62(25)	$200.00
152.	No lamp on left side	62(26)	$85.00
152.1	No lamp on left side—commercial motor vehicle	62(26)	$200.00
153.	Improper lights on farm vehicle	62(27)	$85.00
154.	No directional signals	62(29)	$85.00
154.1	No directional signals—commercial motor vehicle	62(29)	$200.00
155.	No brake lights	62(29)	$85.00
155.1	No brake lights—commercial motor vehicle	62(29)	$200.00
156.	No blue flashing light on snow removal vehicle	62(31)	$85.00
157.	Improper use of blue flashing light	62(32)	$85.00
157.1	Improper use of red and blue flashing lights	62(32)(b)	$85.00
157.2	Improper use of red and blue flashing lights—commercial motor vehicle	62(32)(b)	$200.00
158.	No sign—"right hand drive vehicle"	63	$85.00
159.	Improper braking system	64(1)	$85.00
159.1	Improper braking system—commercial motor vehicle	64(1)	$400.00
160.	Improper brakes on motorcycle	64(2)	$85.00

ITEM	COLUMN 1	COLUMN 2 SECTION	SET FINE
161.	Improper brakes on motor-assisted bicycle	64(2)	$85.00
161.0.1	Improper brakes on power-assisted bicycle	64(2)	$85.00
161.1	Improper brakes on bicycle	64(3)	$85.00
162.1	Improper brakes on trailer—commercial motor vehicle	64(5)	$400.00
162.	Improper brakes on trailer	64(5)	$85.00
163.	Defective brakes	64(7)	$85.00
163.1	Defective brakes—commercial motor vehicle	64(7)	$400.00
164.	Defective braking system	64(7)	$85.00
164.1	Defective braking system—commercial motor vehicle	64(7)	$400.00
165.	Sell improper brake fluid	65(l)(a)	N.S.F.
166.	Offer to sell improper brake fluid	65(l)(a)	N.S.F.
167.	Install improper brake fluid	65(l)(a)	N.S.F.
168.	Sell improper hydraulic oil	65(l)(b)	N.S.F.
169.	Offer to sell improper hydraulic oil	65(1)(b)	N.S.F.
170.	Install improper hydraulic oil	65(l)(b)	N.S.F.
171.	Improper windshield wiper	66(l)(a)	$85.00
171.1	Improper windshield wiper—commercial motor vehicle	66(1)(a)	$200.00
172.	No windshield wiper	66(l)(a)	$85.00
172.1	No windshield wiper—commercial motor vehicle	66(1)(a)	$200.00
173.	Improper mirror	66(l)(b)	$85.00
173.1	Improper mirror—commercial motor vehicle	66(1)(b)	$200.00

ITEM	COLUMN 1	COLUMN 2 SECTION	SET FINE
174.	No mirror	66(l)(b)	$85.00
174.1	No mirror—commercial motor vehicle	66(1)(b)	$200.00
175.	Improper mudguards	66(3)	$85.00
175.1	Improper mudguards—commercial motor vehicle	66(3)	$200.00
176.	No mudguards	66(3)	$85.00
176.1	No mudguards—commercial motor vehicle	66(3)	$200.00
177.	No odometer	66(5)	$85.00
177.1	No odometer—commercial motor vehicle	66(5)	$200.00
178.	Defective odometer	66(5)	$85.00
178.1	Defective odometer—commercial motor vehicle	66(5)	$200.00
179.	Operate motor vehicle—mirrors more than 305 mm	67	$85.00
180.	No speedometer on bus	68	$85.00
181.	Defective speedometer on bus	68	$85.00
181.1	Drive commercial motor vehicle not equipped with working speed-limiting system	68.1(1)	$310.00
181.2	Permit operation of commercial motor vehicle not equipped with working speed-limiting system	68.1(1)	$310.00
181.3	Deactivate speed-limiting system	68.1(2)(a)	$310.00
181.4	Permit person to deactivate speed-limiting system	68.1(2)(a)	$310.00
181.5	Modify speed-limiting system	68.1(2)(b)	$310.00
181.6	Permit person to modify speed-limiting system	68.1(2)(b)	$310.00

ITEM	COLUMN 1	COLUMN 2 SECTION	SET FINE
181.7	Drive commercial motor vehicle with speed-limiting system tampering device	68.1(3)	$310.00
181.8	Permit operation of commercial motor vehicle with speed-limiting system tampering device	68.1(3)	$310.00
181.9	Fail to comply with officer's direction re speed-limiting system	68.1(5)	$310.00
181.10	Sell, offer or advertise speed-limiting system tampering device	68.1(7)	$310.00
182.	Improper tire— damage to highway	69(1)	$85.00
183.	Device on wheels— injure highway	69(2)	$85.00
184.	No lock shoe—animal drawn vehicle	69(3)	$85.00
185.	Improper tires	70(3)(a)	$85.00
185.1	Improper tires— commercial motor vehicle	70(3)(a)	$200.00
186.	Improper tires— drawn vehicle	70(3)(a)	$85.00
186.1	Improper tires— drawn vehicle— commercial motor vehicle	70(3)(a)	$200.00
187.	Improperly installed tires	70(3)(b)	$85.00
187.1	Improperly installed tires—commercial motor vehicle	70(3)(b)	$200.00
188.	Improperly installed tires—drawn vehicle	70(3)(b)	$85.00
188.1	Improperly installed tires—drawn vehicle—commercial motor vehicle	70(3)(b)	$200.00
189.	Fail to mark rebuilt tire	71(2)	N.S.F.
190.	Sell unmarked rebuilt tire	71(3)	N.S.F.

ITEM	COLUMN 1	COLUMN 2 SECTION	SET FINE
191.	Offer to sell unmarked rebuilt tire	71(3)	N.S.F.
192.	Sell new vehicle—no safety glass	72(2)	N.S.F.
193.	Register new vehicle—no safety glass	72(2)	N.S.F.
194.	Install non-safety glass	72(3)	N.S.F.
195.	Window obstructed	73(1)(a)	$85.00
196.	Windshield obstructed	73(1)(a)	$85.00
197.	Have object obstructing view	73(1)(b)	$85.00
198.	Drive with window coated—view obstructed	73(2)	$85.00
199.	Drive with windshield coated—view obstructed	73(2)	$85.00
200.	Colour coating obscuring interior	73(3)	$85.00
201.	No clear view to front	74(1)(a)	$85.00
202.	No clear view to sides	74(1)(a)	$85.00
203.	No clear view to rear	74(1)(b)	$85.00
204.	No muffler—motor vehicle	75(1)	$85.00
205.	No muffler—motor assisted bicycle	75(1)	$85.00
206.	Improper muffler— motor vehicle	75(1)	$85.00
207.	Improper muffler— motor assisted bicycle	75(1)	$85.00
208.	Excessive fumes	75(3)	$85.00
209.	Unreasonable noise—signalling device	75(4)	$85.00
210.	Unreasonable smoke	75(4)	$85.00
211.	Unnecessary noise	75(4)	$85.00
212.	No horn—motor vehicle	75(5)	$85.00
213.	No horn—motor assisted bicycle	75(5)	$85.00
214.	No horn—bicycle	75(5)	$85.00

ITEM	COLUMN 1	COLUMN 2 SECTION	SET FINE
215.	Defective horn—motor vehicle	75(5)	$85.00
216.	Defective horn—motor assisted bicycle	75(5)	$85.00
217.	Defective horn—bicycle	75(5)	$85.00
218.	Have a siren	75(6)	$85.00
219.	No slow moving vehicle sign	76(1)	$85.00
219.1	Slow moving vehicle sign not attached to rear of vehicle or trailer	76(1)	$85.00
219.2	Slow moving vehicle sign not attached in accordance with regulations	76(1)	$85.00
219.3	Slow moving vehicle sign placed on fixed object	76(4)	$85.00
219.4	Prohibited use of slow moving vehicle sign	76(6)	$85.00
219.5	Operate slow moving vehicle over 40 km/h	76(6.1)	$85.00
220.	No sleigh bells	77(1)	$5.00
221.	Drive—display screen visible to driver	78(1)	$400.00
222.	Drive—hand-held communication device	78.1(1)	$40.00
223.	Drive—hand-held entertainment device	78.1(2)	$400.00
224.	REVOKED		
225.	Drive motor vehicle with speed measuring warning device	79(2)	$140.00
225.1	Drive motor vehicle with pre-empting traffic control signal device	79.1(1)	$140.00
226.	Improper means of attachment	80	$85.00
226.1	Improper means of attachment—commercial motor vehicle	80	$200.00

ITEM	COLUMN 1	COLUMN 2 SECTION	SET FINE
227.	Refuse or fail to stop and move vehicle to a safe location	82(9)	$140.00
227.1	Refuse or fail to submit vehicle to examinations and tests	82(9)	$140.00
227.2	Refuse or fail to have vehicle repaired and submitted to further examinations and tests	82(9)	$140.00
227.3	Refuse or fail to have vehicle repaired and submit evidence of compliance	82(9)	$140.00
227.4	Refuse or fail to assist with examinations and tests of vehicle	82(9)	$140.00
227.5	Refuse or fail to place vehicle in safe condition	82(9)	$140.00
227.6	Refuse or fail to remove unsafe vehicle from highway	82(9)	$140.00
227.7	Operate unsafe vehicle on highway contrary to officer's prohibition	82(9)	$140.00
227.8	Permit operation of unsafe vehicle on highway contrary to officer's prohibition	82(9)	$140.00
227.9	Refuse or fail to stop and move vehicle to a safe location—commercial motor vehicle	82(10)	$400.00
227.10	Refuse or fail to submit vehicle to examinations and tests—commercial motor vehicle	82(10)	$400.00
227.11	Refuse or fail to have vehicle repaired and submitted to further examinations and tests—commercial motor vehicle	82(10)	$400.00

ITEM	COLUMN 1	COLUMN 2 SECTION	SET FINE
227.12	Refuse or fail to have vehicle repaired and submit evidence of compliance—commercial motor vehicle	82(10)	$400.00
227.13	Refuse or fail to assist with examinations and tests of vehicle—commercial motor vehicle	82(10)	$400.00
227.14	Refuse or fail to place vehicle in safe condition—commercial motor vehicle	82(10)	$400.00
227.15	Refuse or fail to remove unsafe vehicle from highway—commercial motor vehicle	82(10)	$400.00
227.16	Operate unsafe vehicle on highway contrary to officer's prohibition—commercial motor vehicle	82(10)	$400.00
227.17	Permit operation of unsafe vehicle on highway contrary to officer's prohibition—commercial motor vehicle	82(10)	$400.00
228.	Operate unsafe vehicle	84	N.S.F.
228.1	Operate unsafe vehicle—commercial motor vehicle	84	N.S.F.
229.	Operate unsafe street car	84	N.S.F.
230.	Operate unsafe combination of vehicles	84	N.S.F.
230.1	Operate unsafe combination of vehicles—commercial motor vehicle	84	N.S.F.
231.	Permit operation of unsafe vehicle	84	N.S.F.

ITEM	COLUMN 1	COLUMN 2 SECTION	SET FINE
231.1	Permit operation of unsafe vehicle—commercial motor vehicle	84	N.S.F.
232.	Permit operation of unsafe street car	84	N.S.F.
233.	Permit operation of unsafe combination of vehicles	84	N.S.F.
233.1	Permit operation of unsafe combination of vehicles—commercial motor vehicle	84	N.S.F
234.	Operate vehicle—fail to display device	85(1)	$200.00
235.	Permit operation of vehicle fail to display device	85(1)	$200.00
236.	Issue SSC not provided by Ministry	86	N.S.F.
237.	Affix vehicle inspection sticker not provided by Ministry	86	N.S.F.
238.	Unauthorized person issue SSC	90(1)	N.S.F.
239.	Unauthorized person affix vehicle inspection sticker	90(2)	$200.00
240.	Issue SSC without proper inspection	90(3)(a)	N.S.F.
241.	Affix vehicle inspection certificate without proper inspection	90(3)(a)	N.S.F.
242.	Issue SSC—vehicle not complying	90(3)(a)	N.S.F.
243.	Affix vehicle inspection sticker—vehicle not complying	90(3)(a)	N.S.F.
244.	SSC not made by inspection mechanic	90(3)(b)(i)	N.S.F.
245.	Vehicle inspection record not made by inspection mechanic	90(3)(b)(i)	N.S.F.
246.	SSC not countersigned	90(3)(b)(ii)	N.S.F.

ITEM	COLUMN 1	COLUMN 2 SECTION	SET FINE
247.	Unlicensed inspection station	91(1)	$400.00
248.	Corporation fail to notify change of officer or director	91(7)	N.S.F.
249.	Unregistered mechanic certify SSC	92(1)	N.S.F.
250.	Unregistered mechanic sign vehicle inspection record	92(1)	N.S.F.
251.	Obstruct inspector	98(6)	N.S.F.
252.	False statement in SSC	99(2)	N.S.F.
253.	Sell new vehicle not complying with standards	102(3)	N.S.F.
254.	Offer for sale new vehicle not complying with standards	102(3)	N.S.F.
255.	Expose for sale new vehicle not complying with standards	102(3)	N.S.F.
256.	Sell new vehicle not marked or identified	102(3)	N.S.F.
257.	Offer for sale new vehicle not marked or identified	102(3)	N.S.F.
258.	Expose for sale new vehicle not marked or identified	102(3)	N.S.F.
259.	No name on commercial vehicle	103(1)	$85.00
260.	Less than two reflectors—commercial vehicle	103(2)	$85.00
261.	Less than two reflectors—trailer	103(2)	$85.00
262.	Sell new commercial vehicle without two red rear lights	103(3)(a)	N.S.F.
263.	Offer to sell new commercial vehicle without two red rear lights	103(3)(a)	N.S.F.
264.	Sell trailer without two red rear lights	103(3)(a)	N.S.F.

ITEM	COLUMN 1	COLUMN 2 SECTION	SET FINE
265.	Offer to sell trailer without two red rear lights	103(3)(a)	N.S.F.
266.	Sell new commercial vehicle without two rear red reflectors	103(3)(b)	N.S.F.
267.	Offer to sell new commercial vehicle without two rear red reflectors	103(3)(b)	N.S.F.
268.	Sell trailer without two rear red reflectors	103(3)(b)	N.S.F.
269.	Offer to sell trailer without two rear red reflectors	103(3)(b)	N.S.F.
270.	No name and address on road-building machine	103(4)	$85.00
270.1	Fail to wear proper helmet on power-assisted bicycle	103.1(2)	$85.00
271.	Fail to wear proper helmet on motorcycle	104(1)	$85.00
272.	Fail to wear proper helmet on motor assisted bicycle	104(1)	$85.00
273.	Carry passenger under 16 not wearing proper helmet	104(2)	$85.00
273.1	Fail to wear proper helmet on bicycle	104(2.1)	$60.00
273.2	Permit person under 16 not wearing proper helmet on bicycle	104(2.2)	$60.00
273.3	Equestrian rider—fail to use proper equipment	104.1(1)	$60.00
273.4	Authorize or permit equestrian rider under 16 to ride without proper equipment	104.1(3)	$60.00
274.	Dealing with vehicle not conforming to standard	105(1)	N.S.F.
275.	Dealing with motor assisted bicycle—no document of compliance	105(2)	N.S.F.

ITEM	COLUMN 1	COLUMN 2 SECTION	SET FINE
276.	Drive with seat belt removed	106(1)	$200.00
277.	Drive with seat belt inoperative	106(1)	$200.00
278	Drive with seat belt modified	106(1)	$200.00
279.	Driver—fail to properly wear seat belt	106(2)	$200.00
280.	Passenger—fail to occupy position with seat belt	106(3)(a)	$200.00
281.	Passenger—fail to properly wear seat belt	106(3)(b)	$200.00
282.	Drive while passenger under 16 fails to occupy position with seat belt	106(4)(a)(i)	$200.00
283.	Drive while passenger under 16 fails to properly wear seat belt	106(4)(a)(ii)	$200.00
284.	Drive while child passenger not properly secured	106(4)(b)	$200.00
285.	REVOKED		
286.	REVOKED		
287.	REVOKED		
287.1	REVOKED		
288.	Fail to establish system to periodically inspect and maintain commercial motor vehicles and drawn vehicles	107(1)	$310.00
289.	Fail to keep written record of system to periodically inspect and maintain commercial motor vehicles and drawn vehicles	107(1)	$310.00
290.	Fail to ensure periodic inspections and maintenance are carried out	107(2)	$310.00

ITEM	COLUMN 1	COLUMN 2 SECTION	SET FINE
291.	Fail to ensure performance standards are met	107(3)	$310.00
292.	Fail to supply driver with daily inspection schedule	107(4)(a)	$310.00
293.	Fail to ensure daily inspection is conducted properly	107(4)(b)	$310.00
294.	Fail to ensure under-vehicle inspection is conducted properly	107(4)(c)	$310.00
295.	Fail to ensure daily inspection report is accurately completed	107(4)(d)	$310.00
296.	Fail to ensure under-vehicle inspection report is accurately completed	107(4)(d)	$310.00
297.	Fail to complete daily inspection report forthwith after inspection	107(5)	$200.00
298.	Fail to accurately complete daily inspection report	107(5)	$200.00
299.	Fail to complete under-vehicle inspection report forthwith after inspection	107(5)	$200.00
300.	Fail to accurately complete under-vehicle inspection report	107(5)	$200.00
301.	Fail to carry inspection schedule	107(6)	$85.00
302.	Fail to carry completed daily inspection report	107(6)	$85.00
303.	Fail to carry completed under-vehicle inspection report	107(6)	$85.00
303.1	Fail to surrender inspection schedule	107(7)	$85.00
303.2	Fail to surrender completed daily inspection report	107(7)	$85.00

ITEM	COLUMN 1	COLUMN 2 SECTION	SET FINE
303.3	Fail to surrender completed under-vehicle inspection report	107(7)	$85.00
303.4	Fail to enter defect in daily inspection report	107(8)(a)	$85.00
303.5	Fail to report defect to operator	107(8)(b)	$200.00
303.6	Fail to submit completed daily inspection report to operator	107(8)(c)	$85.00
303.7	Fail to submit completed under-vehicle inspection report to operator	107(8)(c)	$85.00
303.8	Drive commercial motor vehicle without required inspection	107(9)	$200.00
303.9	Drive commercial motor vehicle with a major defect in it or in drawn vehicle	107(11)	$310.00
303.10	Improperly drive commercial motor vehicle with a minor defect in it or in drawn vehicle	107(12)	$200.00
303.11	Fail to maintain books and records	107(13)	$310.00
303.12	Fail to produce books and records	107(13)	$310.00
304.	Overwidth vehicle	109(1)	$310.00
305.	Overwidth load	109(2)	$310.00
306.	Overlength vehicle	109(6)	$310.00
306.1	Overlength full trailer	109(6.2)	$310.00
307.	Overlength combination of vehicles	109(7)	$310.00
307.1	Operate overlength combination of vehicles	109(8)	$310.00
308.	Overlength semi-trailer	109(10)	$310.00
309.	Overlength bus	109(11)	$310.00

ITEM	COLUMN 1	COLUMN 2 SECTION	SET FINE
309.1	Overlength recreational vehicle	109(11)	$310.00
310.	Overheight vehicle	109(14)	$310.00
311.	Fail to carry permit in vehicle	110(6)	$310.00
312.	Fail to produce permit	110(6)	$310.00
313.	Oversize vehicle—violate permit	110(7)	$310.00
314.	Overweight vehicle—violate permit	110(7)	$200.00 + Schedule A
314.1	Fail to comply with condition of permit	110(7)	$310.00
314.2	Violate non-weight condition of special permit	110.2(3)(a)	$310.00
314.3	Violate weight condition of special permit	110.2(3)(b)	Schedule A
314.4	Violate weight condition of special permit—liftable axle lifted	110.2(3)(b)	$200.00 + Schedule A
314.5	Violate weight condition of special permit—liftable axle deployed improperly	110.2(3)(b)	$200.00 + Schedule A
314.6	Violate more than one condition, including a weight condition, of special permit	110.2(3)(c)	$200.00 + Schedule A
314.7	Violate more than one condition, including a weight condition, of special permit—liftable axle lifted	110.2(3)(c)	$400.00 + Schedule A
314.8	Violate more than one condition, including a weight condition, of special permit—liftable axle deployed improperly	110.2(3)(c)	$400.00 + Schedule A
315.	Fail to mark overhanging load	111(1)	$130.00
315.1	Fail to mark overhanging load—commercial motor vehicle	111(1)	$200.00

ITEM	COLUMN 1	COLUMN 2 SECTION	SET FINE
316.	Insecure load	111(2)	$130.00
316.1	Insecure load—commercial motor vehicle	111(2)	$310.00
316.2	Operate vehicle with load not secured as prescribed	111(2.1)	$130.00
316.3	Operate commercial motor vehicle with load not secured as prescribed	111(2.1)	$310.00
316.4	Permit operation of vehicle with load not secured as prescribed	111(2.1)	$130.00
316.5	Permit operation of commercial motor vehicle with load not secured as prescribed	111(2.1)	$310.00
316.6	Drive commercial motor vehicle without conducting inspections	111(2.2)	$310.00
317.	Overweight on tires …kg. … less than 150 mm	115(1)(a)	Schedule A
317.1	Overweight on tires …kg. liftable axle lifted	115(1)(a)	$200.00 + Schedule A
317.2	Overweight on tires …kg.—liftable axle deployed improperly	115(1)(a)	$200.00 + Schedule A
318.	Overweight on tires …kg. … 150 mm or over	115(1)(b)	Schedule A
318.1	Overweight on tires …kg.—liftable axle lifted	115(1)(b)	$200.00 + Schedule A
318.2	Overweight on tires …kg.—liftable axle deployed improperly	115(1)(b)	$200.00 + Schedule A
319.	Overweight single axle (single tires) … kg. Class A Highway	116(1)(a)	Schedule A
319.1	Overweight single axle (single tires) … kg. Class A Highway—liftable axle lifted	116(1)(a)	$200.00 + Schedule A

ITEM	COLUMN 1	COLUMN 2 SECTION	SET FINE
319.2	Overweight single axle (single tires) …kg. Class A Highway—liftable axle deployed improperly	116(1)(a)	$200.00 + Schedule A
320.	Overweight single axle (dual tires) …kg. Class A Highway	116(1)(a)	Schedule A
320.1	Overweight single axle (dual tires) …kg. Class A Highway—liftable axle lifted	116(1)(b)	$200.00 + Schedule A
320.2	Overweight single axle (dual tires) …kg. Class A Highway—liftable axle deployed improperly	116(1)(b)	$200.00 + Schedule A
321.	Overweight dual axle …kg. Class A Highway	116(1)(c)	Schedule A
321.1	Overweight dual axle …kg. Class A Highway—liftable axle lifted	116(1)(c)	$200.00 + Schedule A
321.2	Overweight dual axle …kg. Class A Highway—liftable axle deployed improperly	116(1)(c)	$200.00 + Schedule A
322.	Overweight triple axle …kg. Class A Highway	116(1)(d)	Schedule A
322.1	Overweight triple axle …kg. Class A Highway—liftable axle lifted	116(1)(d)	$200.00 + Schedule A
322.2	Overweight triple axle …kg. Class A Highway—liftable axle deployed improperly	116(1)(d)	$200.00 + Schedule A
323.	Overweight dual axle (single tires) …kg. Class A Highway	116(2)	Schedule A
323.1	Overweight dual axle (single tires) …kg. Class A Highway—liftable axle lifted	116(2)	$200.00 + Schedule A
323.2	Overweight dual axle (single tires) …kg. Class A Highway—liftable axle deployed improperly	116(2)	$200.00 + Schedule A

ITEM	COLUMN 1	COLUMN 2 SECTION	SET FINE
324.	Overweight triple axle (single tires) …kg. Class A Highway	116(3)	Schedule A
324.1	Overweight triple axle (single tires) …kg. Class A Highway—liftable axle lifted	116(3)	$200.00 + Schedule A
324.2	Overweight triple axle (single tires) …kg. Class A Highway—liftable axle deployed improperly	116(3)	$200.00 + Schedule A
325.	Overweight single front axle …kg. No verification. Class A Highway	116(4)	Schedule A
325.1	Overweight single front axle …kg. No verification. Class A Highway —liftable axle lifted	116(4)	$200.00 + Schedule A
325.2	Overweight single front axle …kg. No verification. Class A Highway—liftable axle deployed improperly	116(4)	$200.00 + Schedule A
326.	Overweight single front axle …kg. Exceed rating. Class A Highway	116(4)	Schedule A
326.1	Overweight single front axle …kg. Exceed rating. Class A Highway—liftable axle lifted	116(6)	$200.00 + Schedule A
326.2	Overweight single front axle …kg. Exceed rating. Class A Highway—liftable axle deployed improperly	116(6)	$200.00 + Schedule A
327.	Overweight two axle group …kg. Class A Highway	117(a)	Schedule A
327.1	Overweight two axle group …kg. Class A Highway—liftable axle lifted	117(1)(a)	$200.00 + Schedule A

ITEM	COLUMN 1	COLUMN 2 SECTION	SET FINE
327.2	Overweight two axle group …kg. Class A Highway—liftable axle deployed improperly	117(1)(a)	$200.00 + Schedule A
328.	Overweight three axle group …kg. Class A Highway	117(1)(b)	Schedule A
328.1	Overweight three axle group …kg. Class A Highway—liftable axle lifted	117(1)(b)	$200.00 + Schedule A
328.2	Overweight three axle group …kg. Class A Highway—liftable axle deployed improperly	117(1)(b)	$200.00 + Schedule A
329.	Overweight four axle group …kg. Class A Highway	117(1)(c)	Schedule A
329.1	Overweight four axle group …kg. Class A Highway—liftable axle lifted	117(1)(c)	$200.00 + Schedule A
329.2	Overweight four axle group …kg. Class A Highway—liftable axle deployed improperly	117(1)(c)	$200.00 + Schedule A
330.	Overweight vehicle … kg. Class A Highway	118	Schedule A
330.1	Overweight vehicle … kg. Class A Highway— liftable axle lifted	118	$200.00 + Schedule A
330.2	Overweight vehicle … kg. Class A Highway— liftable axle deployed improperly	118	$200.00 + Schedule A
331.	Overweight during freeze-up …kg.	119(4)	Schedule A
331.1	Overweight vehicle during freeze-up … kg.—liftable axle lifted	119(4)	$200.00 + Schedule A
331.2	Overweight vehicle during freeze-up … kg.—liftable axle deployed improperly	119(4)	$200.00 + Schedule A

ITEM	COLUMN 1	COLUMN 2 SECTION	SET FINE
332.	Overweight on axle … kg. Class B Highway	120	Schedule A
332.1	Overweight on axle … kg. Class B Highway—liftable axle lifted	120	$200.00 + Schedule A
332.2	Overweight on axle … kg. Class B Highway—liftable axle deployed improperly	120	$200.00 + Schedule A
333.	Overweight vehicle—violate permit …kg.	121(1)	Schedule A
334.	Fail to have receipt in vehicle	121(3)	$75.00
335.	Fail to produce receipt	121(3)	$75.00
335.1	Overweight on axle … kg.—reduced load period	122(1)	Schedule A
335.2	Overweight on axle … kg.—reduced load period—liftable axle lifted	122(1)	$200.00 + Schedule A
335.3	Overweight on axle … kg.—reduced load period—liftable axle deployed improperly	122(1)	$200.00 + Schedule A
335.4	Overweight on tire … kg.—reduced load period	122(3)	Schedule A
335.5	Overweight on tire … kg.—reduced load period—liftable axle lifted	122(3)	$200.00 + Schedule A
335.6	Overweight on tire … kg.—reduced load period—liftable axle deployed improperly	122(3)	$200.00 + Schedule A
336.	Fail or refuse to stop	124(3)	$200.00
337.	Fail or refuse to drive vehicle to scale	124(3)	$200.00
338.	Fail or refuse to redistribute or remove load	124(4)(a)	$100.00
338.1	Fail or refuse to stop—commercial motor vehicle	124(5)	$310.00

ITEM	COLUMN 1	COLUMN 2 SECTION	SET FINE
338.2	Fail or refuse to drive vehicle to scale—commercial motor vehicle subsection 124(5)	124(5)	$310.00
338.3	Fail or refuse to redistribute or remove load—commercial motor vehicle	124(6)(a)	$310.00
339.	Cause vehicle to be overloaded	126	Schedule A
340.	Speeding	128	Schedule B
340.1	Speeding—liability of owner where evidence obtained through photo-radar	128	Schedule C
340.2	Speeding—community safety zone	128	Schedule D
340.3	Owner—speeding pursuant to section 207 community safety zone	128	Schedule D
340.4	Speeding—construction zone	128	Schedule E
340.5	Speeding—construction zone—worker present	128	Schedule F
341.	Careless driving	130	$400.00
341.1	REVOKED		
342.	Unnecessary slow driving	132	$85.00
342.1	Unnecessary slow driving—community safety zone	132	$120.00
343.	Disobey officer directing traffic	134(1)	$85.00
343.1	Disobey officer directing traffic—community safety zone	134(1)	$120.00
344.	Drive on closed highway	134(3)	$85.00
344.1	Drive on closed highway—community safety zone	134(3)	$120.00

ITEM	COLUMN 1	COLUMN 2 SECTION	SET FINE
345.	Fail to yield—uncontrolled intersection	135(2)	$85.00
345.1	Fail to yield—uncontrolled intersection—community safety zone	135(2)	$150.00
346.	Fail to yield to vehicle on right	135(3)	$85.00
346.1	Fail to yield to vehicle on right—community safety zone	135(3)	$150.00
347.	Disobey stop sign—stop wrong place	136(1)(a)	$85.00
347.1	Disobey stop sign—stop wrong place—community safety zone	136(1)(a)	$120.00
348.	Disobey stop sign—fail to stop	136(l)(a)	$85.00
348.1	Disobey stop sign—fail to stop—community safety zone	136(1)(a)	$150.00
349.	Fail to yield to traffic on through highway	136(1)(b)	$85.00
349.1	Fail to yield to traffic on through highway—community safety zone	136(1)(b)	$150.00
350.	Traffic on through highway—fail to yield	136(2)	$85.00
350.1	Traffic on through highway—fail to yield—community safety zone	136(2)	$150.00
351.	Fail to yield—yield sign	138(1)	$85.00
351.1	Fail to yield—yield sign—community safety zone	138(1)	$150.00
352.	Fail to yield from private road	139(1)	$85.00
352.1	Fail to yield from private road—community safety zone	139(1)	$150.00

ITEM	COLUMN 1	COLUMN 2 SECTION	SET FINE
353.	Fail to yield from driveway	139(1)	$85.00
353.1	Fail to yield from driveway—community safety zone	139(1)	$150.00
354.	Fail to stop at crossover	140(1)(a)	$150.00
354.1	REVOKED		
355.	Fail to stop at crossover—community safety zone	140(1)(a)	$300.00
355.1	REVOKED		
356.	Pass stopped vehicle at crossover	140(1)(b)	$150.00
356.1	REVOKED		
357.	Pass stopped vehicle at crossover—community safety zone	140(1)(b)	$300.00
357.1	REVOKED		
358.	Fail to yield to pedestrian on roadway	140(1)(c)	$150.00
358.1	REVOKED		
359.	Fail to yield to pedestrian on roadway—community safety zone	140(1)(c)	$300.00
359.1	REVOKED		
360.	REVOKED		
360.1	REVOKED		
361.	REVOKED		
361.1	REVOKED		
362.	REVOKED		
362.1	REVOKED		
363.	REVOKED		
363.1	REVOKED		
364.	REVOKED		
364.1	REVOKED		
365.	REVOKED		
365.1	REVOKED		
366.	REVOKED		

ITEM	COLUMN 1	COLUMN 2 SECTION	SET FINE
366.1	REVOKED		
367.	REVOKED		
367.1	REVOKED		
368.	Pass front of vehicle within 30 m of crossover	140(3)	$150.00
368.1	Pass front of vehicle within 30 m of crossover—community safety zone	140(3)	$300.00
369.	REVOKED		
369.1	REVOKED		
370.	Pedestrian fail to yield at crossover	140(4)	$35.00
371.	Person in wheelchair—fail to yield at crossover	140(4)	$35.00
371.1	Cyclist—ride in crossover	140(6)	$85.00
372.	Improper right turn	141(2)	$85.00
372.1	Improper right turn—community safety zone	141(2)	$120.00
373.	Improper right turn—multi-lane highway	141(3)	$85.00
373.1	Improper right turn—multi-lane highway—community safety zone	141(3)	$120.00
374.	Left turn—fail to afford reasonable opportunity to avoid collision	141(5)	$85.00
374.1	Left turn—fail to afford reasonable opportunity to avoid collision—community safety zone	141(5)	$150.00
375.	Improper left turn	141(6)	$85.00
375.1	1mproper left turn—community safety zone	141(6)	$120.00
376.	Improper left turn—multi-lane highway	141(7)	$85.00

ITEM	COLUMN 1	COLUMN 2 SECTION	SET FINE
376.1	Improper left turn—multi-lane highway—community safety zone	141(7)	$120.00
377.	Turn—not in safety	142(1)	$85.00
377.1	Turn—not in safety—community safety zone	142(1)	$150.00
378.	Change lane—not in safety	142(1)	$85.00
378.1	Change lane—not in safety—community safety zone	142(1)	$150.00
379.	Fail to signal for turn	142(1)	$85.00
379.1	Fail to signal for turn—community safety zone	142(1)	$120.00
380.	Fail to signal—lane change	142(1)	$85.00
380.1	Fail to signal—lane change—community safety zone	142(1)	$120.00
381.	Start from parked position—not in safety	142(2)	$85.00
381.1	Start from parked position—not in safety—community safety zone	142(2)	$150.00
382.	Start from stopped position—not in safety	142(2)	$85.00
382.1	Start from stopped position—not in safety—community safety zone	142(2)	$150.00
383.	Start from parked position—fail to signal	142(2)	$85.00
383.1	Start from parked position—fail to signal—community safety zone	142(2)	$120.00
384.	Start from stopped position—fail to signal	142(2)	$85.00

ITEM	COLUMN 1	COLUMN 2 SECTION	SET FINE
384.1	Start from stopped position—fail to signal—community safety zone	142(2)	$120.00
385.	Improper arm signal	142(4)	$85.00
385.1	Improper arm signal—community safety zone	142(4)	$120.00
386.	Improper signal device	142(6)	$85.00
386.1	Improper signal device—community safety zone	142(6)	$120.00
387.	Use turn signals improperly	142(7)	$85.00
387.1	Use turn signals improperly—community safety zone	142(7)	$120.00
388.	Fail to signal stop	142(8)	$85.00
388.1	Fail to signal stop—community safety zone	142(8)	$120.00
389.	Fail to signal decrease in speed	142(8)	$85.00
389.1	Fail to signal decrease in speed community safety zone	142(8)	$120.00
390.	Improper signal to stop	142(8)	$85.00
390.1	Improper signal to stop—community safety zone	142(8)	$120.00
391.	Improper signal to decrease in speed	142(8)	$85.00
391.1	Improper signal to decrease in speed community safety zone	142(8)	$120.00
392.	Brake lights—improper colour	142(8)(b)	$85.00
392.1	Brake lights—improper colour—community safety zone	142(8)(b)	$120.00
392.2	Fail to yield to bus re-entering lane from bus bay	142.1(1)	$85.00

ITEM	COLUMN 1	COLUMN 2 SECTION	SET FINE
392.3	Fail to yield to bus re-entering lane from bus bay—community safety zone	142.1(1)	$120.00
393.	U-turn on a curve—no clear view	143(a)	$85.00
393.1	U-turn on a curve—no clear view community safety zone	143(a)	$150.00
394.	U-turn—railway crossing	143(b)	$85.00
394.1	U-turn—railway crossing—community safety zone	143(b)	$150.00
395.	U-turn near crest of grade—no clear view	143(c)	$85.00
395.1	U-turn near crest of grade—no clear view—community safety zone	143(c)	$150.00
396.	U-turn—bridge—no clear view	143(d)	$85.00
396.1	U-turn—bridge—no clear view—community safety zone	143(d)	$150.00
397.	U-turn—viaduct—no clear view	143(d)	$85.00
397.1	U-turn—viaduct—no clear view—community safety zone	143(d)	$150.00
398.	U-turn—tunnel—no clear view	143(d)	$85.00
398.1	U-turn—tunnel—no clear view—community safety zone	143(d)	$150.00
399.	Improper stop—traffic signal at intersection	144(5)	$85.00
399.1	Improper stop—traffic signal at intersection community safety zone	144(5)	$120.00
400.	Improper stop—traffic signal not at intersection	144(6)	$85.00

ITEM	COLUMN 1	COLUMN 2 SECTION	SET FINE
400.1	Improper stop—traffic signal not at intersection—community safety zone	144(6)	$120.00
401.	Fail to yield to pedestrian	144(7)	$150.00
401.1	Fail to yield to pedestrian—community safety zone	144(7)	$300.00
402.	Fail to yield to traffic	144(8)	$85.00
402.1	Fail to yield to traffic—community safety zone	144(8)	$150.00
403.	Proceed contrary to sign at intersection	144(9)	$85.00
403.1	Proceed contrary to sign at intersection—community safety zone	144(9)	$120.00
404.	Cyclist — disobey lane light	144(10)(a)	$85.00
404.1	Disobey lane light—community safety zone	144(10)	$120.00
404.2	Disobey lane light	144(10) (b)	$85.00
404.3	Disobey lane light—community safety zone	144 (10) (b)	$120.00
405.	Green light—fail to proceed as directed	144(12)	$85.00
405.1	Green light—fail to proceed as directed—community safety zone	144(12)	$120.00
406.	Flashing green light—fail to proceed as directed	144(13)	$85.00
406.1	Flashing green light—fail to proceed as directed—community safety zone	144(13)	$120.00
407.	Green arrow—fail to proceed as directed	144(14)	$85.00

ITEM	COLUMN 1	COLUMN 2 SECTION	SET FINE
407.1	Green arrow—fail to proceed as directed—community safety zone	144(14)	$120.00
408.	Amber light—fail to stop	144(15)	$150.00
408.1	Amber light—fail to stop—community safety zone	144(15)	$300.00
409.	Amber arrow—fail to stop	144(16)	$85.00
409.1	Amber arrow—fail to stop—community safety zone	144(16)	$120.00
410.	Amber arrow—fail to proceed as directed	144(16)	$85.00
410.1	Amber arrow—fail to proceed as directed—community safety zone	144(16)	$120.00
411.	Flashing amber light—fail to proceed with caution	144(17)	$85.00
411.1	Flashing amber light—fail to proceed with caution—community safety zone	144(17)	$120.00
412.	Red light—fail to stop	144(18)	$260.00
412.1	Red light—fail to stop—community safety zone	144(18)	$400.00
413.	Red light—proceed before green	144(18)	$260.00
413.1	Red light—proceed before green—community safety zone	144(18)	$400.00
413.2	Red light—vehicle owner fails to stop pursuant to section 207	144(18.1)	$260.00
414.	Turn on red light—fail to yield	144(19)	$85.00
414.1	Turn on red light—fail to yield—community safety zone	144(19)	$150.00

ITEM	COLUMN 1	COLUMN 2 SECTION	SET FINE
415.	REVOKED		
416.	Flashing red light—fail to stop	144(21)	$85.00
416.1	Flashing red light—fail to stop community safety zone	144(21)	$150.00
417.	Flashing red light—fail to yield	144(21)	$85.00
417.1	Flashing red light—fail to yield—community safety zone	144(21)	$150.00
418.	Pedestrian fail to use crosswalk	144(22)	$35.00
419.	Pedestrian disobey flashing green light	144(24)	$35.00
420.	Pedestrian disobey red light	144(25)	$35.00
421.	Pedestrian disobey amber light	144(25)	$35.00
422.	Pedestrian disobey "don't walk" signal	144(27)	$35.00
422.1	Cyclist—ride in crosswalk	144(29)	$85.00
423.	Disobey portable amber light—fail to stop	146(3)	$150.00
423.1	Disobey portable amber light—fail to stop—community safety zone	146(3)	$300.00
424.	Disobey portable red light—fail to stop	146(4)	$260.00
424.1	Disobey portable red light—fail to stop—community safety zone	146(4)	$400.00
425.	Disobey portable red light—proceed before green	146(4)	$260.00
425.1	Disobey portable red light—proceed before green—community safety zone	146(4)	$400.00
426.	Disobey portable red light—stop wrong place	146(5)	$85.00

ITEM	COLUMN 1	COLUMN 2 SECTION	SET FINE
426.1	Disobey portable red light—stop wrong place—community safety zone	146(5)	$120.00
427.	Disobey portable amber light—stop wrong place	146(5)	$85.00
427.1	Disobey portable amber light—stop wrong place—community safety zone	146(5)	$120.00
428.	Remove portable lane control signal system	146(6)	$85.00
428.1	Remove portable lane control signal system community safety zone	146(6)	$150.00
429.	Deface portable lane control signal system	146(6)	$85.00
429.1	Deface portable lane control signal system community safety zone	146(6)	$120.00
430.	Interfere with portable lane signal system	146(6)	$85.00
430.1	Interfere with portable lane control signal system—community safety zone	146(6)	$120.00
430.2	Fail to obey traffic control stop sign	146.1(3)	$85.00
430.3	Fail to obey traffic control stop sign—community safety zone	146.1(3)	$120.00
430.4	Fail to obey traffic control slow sign	146.1(4)	$85.00
430.5	Fail to obey traffic control slow sign—Community safety zone	146.1(4)	$120.00
430.6	Display traffic control sign—unauthorized person	146.1(5)	$85.00

ITEM	COLUMN 1	COLUMN 2 SECTION	SET FINE
431.	Fail to keep right when driving at less than normal speed	147(1)	$85.00
431.1	Fail to keep right when driving at less than normal speed—community safety zone	147(1)	$120.00
432.	Fail to share half roadway—meeting vehicle	148(1)	$85.00
432.1	Fail to share half roadway—meeting vehicle—community safety zone	148(1)	$120.00
433.	Fail to turn out to right when overtaken	148(2)	$85.00
433.1	Fail to turn out to right when overtaken—community safety zone	148(2)	$120.00
434.	Fail to share roadway—meeting bicycle	148(4)	$85.00
434.1	Fail to share roadway—meeting bicycle—community safety zone	148(4)	$120.00
435.	Fail to turn out to left to avoid collision	148(5)	$85.00
435.1	Fail to turn out to left to avoid collision—community safety zone	148(5)	$120.00
436.	Bicycle—fail to turn out to right when overtaken	148(6)	$85.00
436.1	Bicycle—fail to turn out to right when overtaken—community safety zone	148(6)	$120.00
437.	Fail to turn out to left to avoid collision with bicycle	148(6)	$85.00
437.1	Fail to turn out to left to avoid collision with bicycle—community safety zone	148(6)	$120.00

ITEM	COLUMN 1	COLUMN 2 SECTION	SET FINE
438.	Motor assisted bicycle—fail to turn out to right when overtaken	148(6)	$85.00
438.1	Motor assisted bicycle—fail to turn out to right when overtaken—community safety zone	148(6)	$120.00
439.	Fail to turn out to left to avoid collision with motor assisted bicycle	148(6)	$85.00
439.1	Fail to turn out to left to avoid collision with motor assisted bicycle—community safety zone	148(6)	$120.00
439.2	Fail to leave one metre while passing bicycle	148(6.1)	$85.00
439.3	Fail to leave one metre while passing bicycle--community safety zone	148(6.1)	$150.00
440.	Fail to stop to facilitate passing	148(7)	$85.00
440.1	Fail to stop to facilitate passing—community safety zone	148(7)	$120.00
441.	Fail to assist in passing	148(7)	$85.00
441.1	Fail to assist in passing— community safety zone	148(7)	$120.00
442.	Pass—roadway not clear—approaching traffic	148(8)(a)	$85.00
442.1	Pass—roadway not clear—approaching traffic—community safety zone	148(8)(a)	$150.00
443.	Attempt to pass—roadway not clear—approaching traffic	148(8)(a)	$85.00
443.1	Attempt to pass—roadway not clear—approaching traffic—community safety zone	148(8)(a)	$150.00

ITEM	COLUMN 1	COLUMN 2 SECTION	SET FINE
444.	Pass—roadway not clear—overtaking traffic	148(8)(b)	$85.00
444.1	Pass—roadway not clear—overtaking traffic—community safety zone	148(8)(b)	$150.00
445.	Attempt to pass—roadway not clear—overtaking traffic	148(8)(b)	$85.00
445.1	Attempt to pass—roadway not clear—overtaking traffic—community safety zone	148(8)(b)	$150.00
446.	Drive left of centre—approaching crest of grade	149(1)(a)	$85.00
446.1	Drive left of centre—approaching crest of grade—community safety zone	149(1)(a)	$150.00
447.	Drive left of centre—on a curve	149(1)(a)	$85.00
447.1	Drive left of centre—on a curve—community safety zone	149(1)(a)	$150.00
448.	Drive left of centre within 30 m of bridge—no clear view	149(1)(a)	$85.00
448.1	Drive left of centre within 30 m of bridge—no clear view—community safety zone	149(1)(a)	$150.00
449.	Drive left of centre within 30 m of viaduct—no clear view	149(1)(a)	$85.00
449.1	Drive left of centre within 30 m of viaduct—no clear view—community safety zone	149(1)(a)	$150.00
450.	Drive left of centre within 30 m of tunnel—no clear view	149(1)(a)	$85.00

ITEM	COLUMN 1	COLUMN 2 SECTION	SET FINE
450.1	Drive left of centre within 30 m of tunnel—no clear view—community safety zone	149(1)(a)	$150.00
451.	Drive left of centre within 30 m of level railway crossing	149(1)(b)	$85.00
452.	Drive left of centre within 30 m of level railway crossing—community safety zone	149(1)(b)	$150.00
453.	Pass on right—not in safety	150(1)	$85.00
453.1	Pass on right—not in safety—community safety zone	150(1)	$150.00
454.	Pass—off roadway	150(2)	$85.00
454.1	Pass—off roadway—community safety zone	150(2)	$150.00
455.	Non-authorized driving on paved shoulder	151(5)	$85.00
455.1	Non-authorized driving on paved shoulder—community safety zone	151(5)	$120.00
456.	Drive wrong way—one way traffic	153	$85.00
456.1	Drive wrong way—one way traffic—community safety zone	153	$150.00
457.	Unsafe move—lane or shoulder	154(1)(a)	$85.00
457.1	REVOKED		
458.	Unsafe move—lane or shoulder—community safety zone	154(1)(a)	$150.00
458.1	REVOKED		
459.	Use centre lane improperly	154(1)(b)	$85.00

ITEM	COLUMN 1	COLUMN 2 SECTION	SET FINE
459.1	Use centre lane improperly—community safety zone	154(1)(b)	$120.00
460.	Fail to obey lane sign	154(1)(c)	$85.00
460.1	Fail to obey lane sign—community safety zone	154(1)(c)	$120.00
460.2	Improper use of high occupancy vehicle lane	154.1(3)	$85.00
460.3	Improper use of border approach lane	154.2(2)	$85.00
460.4	Driver in border approach lane—fail to stop	154.2(4)	$150.00
460.5	Fail to provide required document—driver	154.2(4)	$85.00
460.6	Fail to provide required document—occupant	154.2(4)	$85.00
461.	Drive wrong way—divided highway	156(1)(a)	$85.00
461.1	Drive wrong way—divided highway—community safety zone	156(1)(a)	$150.00
462.	Cross divided highway—no proper crossing provided	156(1)(b)	$85.00
462.0.1	Cross divided highway—no proper crossing provided—community safety zone	156(1)(b)	$120.00
462.1	Backing on roadway—divided highway	157(1)	$85.00
462.1.1	Backing on roadway—divided highway—community safety zone	157(1)	$120.00
462.2	Backing on shoulder—divided highway	157(1)	$85.00
462.3	Backing on shoulder—divided highway—community safety zone	157(1)	$120.00

ITEM	COLUMN 1	COLUMN 2 SECTION	SET FINE
463.	Follow too closely	158(1)	$85.00
463.1	Follow too closely—community safety zone	158(1)	$120.00
464.	Commercial vehicle—follow too closely	158(2)	$85.00
464.1	Commercial vehicle—follow too closely—community safety zone	158(2)	$120.00
465.	Fail to stop on right for emergency vehicle	159(1)(a)	$400.00
465.1	REVOKED		
466.	Fail to stop—nearest curb—for emergency vehicle	159(1)(b)	$400.00
466.1	REVOKED		
467.	Fail to stop—nearest edge of roadway—for emergency vehicle	159(1)(b)	$400.00
467.1	REVOKED		
468.	Fail to slow down and proceed with caution for emergency vehicle or tow truck	159(2)	$400.00
468.1	Fail to move into another lane for emergency vehicle—if safe to do	159(3)	$400.00
468.2	Follow fire department vehicle too closely	159(4)	$400.00
468.3	REVOKED		
469.	Permit attachment to vehicle	160	$85.00
469.1	Permit attachment to vehicle—community safety zone	160	$120.00
470.	Permit attachment to street car	160	$85.00
470.1	Permit attachment to street car community safety zone	160	$120.00
471.	Draw more than one vehicle	161	$85.00

ITEM	COLUMN 1	COLUMN 2 SECTION	SET FINE
471.1	Draw more than one vehicle—community safety zone	161	$120.00
472.	Drive while crowded	162	$85.00
472.1	Drive while crowded—community safety zone	162	$120.00
473.	Disobey railway crossing signal—stop wrong place	163(1)	$85.00
473.1	Disobey railway crossing signal—stop at wrong place—community safety zone	163(1)	$150.00
474.	Disobey railway crossing signal—fail to stop	163(1)	$85.00
474.1	Disobey railway crossing signal—fail to stop—community safety zone	163(1)	$150.00
475.	Disobey railway crossing signal—proceed unsafely	163(1)	$85.00
475.1	Disobey railway crossing signal—proceed unsafely—community safety zone	163(1)	$150.00
475.2	Disobey stop sign at railway crossing—stop at wrong place	163(2)	$85.00
475.3	Disobey stop sign at railway crossing—stop at wrong place—community safety zone	163(2)	$150.00
475.4	Disobey stop sign at railway crossing—fail to stop	163(2)	$85.00
475.5	Disobey stop sign at railway crossing—fail to stop—community safety zone	163(2)	$150.00
475.6	Disobey stop sign at railway crossing—proceed unsafely	163(2)	$85.00

ITEM	COLUMN 1	COLUMN 2 SECTION	SET FINE
475.7	Disobey stop sign at railway crossing—proceed unsafely—community safety zone	163(2)	$150.00
476.	Disobey crossing gate	164	$85.00
476.1	Disobey crossing gate—community safety zone	164	$150.00
477.	Open vehicle door improperly	165(1)(a)	$300.00
478.	Leave vehicle door open	165(1)(b)	$300.00
479.	Pass street car improperly	166(1)	$85.00
479.1	Pass street car improperly—community safety zone	166(1)	$150.00
480.	Approach open street car door too closely	166(1)	$85.00
480.1	Approach open street car door too closely—community safety zone	166(1)	$150.00
481.	Pass street car on the left side	166(2)	$85.00
481.1	Pass street car on the left side—community safety zone	166(2)	$120.00
482.	Frighten animal	167	$85.00
482.1	Frighten animal—community safety zone	167	$120.00
483.	Fail to ensure safety of person in charge of animal	167	$85.00
483.1	Fail to ensure safety of person in charge of animal—community safety zone	167	$120.00
484.	Fail to use lower beam—oncoming	168(a)	$85.00
484.1	Fail to use lower beam—oncoming—community safety zone	168(a)	$120.00

ITEM	COLUMN 1	COLUMN 2 SECTION	SET FINE
485.	Fail to use lower beam—following	168(b)	$85.00
485.0.1	Fail to use lower beam—following—community safety zone	168(b)	$120.00
485.1	Prohibited use of alternating highbeam headlights	169(2)	$85.00
485.2	Prohibited use of alternating highbeam headlights—community safety zone	169(2)	$120.00
486.	Fail to take precaution against vehicle being set in motion	170(9)	$50.00
487.	Fail to have warning lights	170(10)(a)	$50.00
488.	Fail to use warning lights	170(11)	$50.00
489.	Interfere with traffic	170(12)	$50.00
490.	Interfere with snow removal	170(12)	$50.00
490.1	Offer tow truck services in King's Highway within 200 m of accident or apparent accident	171(1)(a)	$200.00
490.2	Offer tow truck services on King's Highway within 200 m of vehicle involved in accident	171(1)(b)	$200.00
490.3	Park tow truck on King's Highway within 200 m of accident or apparent accident—sufficient tow trucks available	171(2)(a)	$200.00
490.4	Stop tow truck on King's Highway within 200 m of accident or apparent accident—sufficient tow trucks available	171(2)(a)	$200.00

ITEM	COLUMN 1	COLUMN 2 SECTION	SET FINE
490.5	Park tow truck on King's Highway within 200 m of vehicle involved in accident—sufficient tow trucks available	171(2)(b)	$200.00
490.6	Stop tow trucks on King's Highway within 200 m of vehicle involved in accident—sufficient tow trucks available	171(2)(b)	$200.00
491.	Race a motor vehicle	172(1)	N.S.F.
491.1	Race a motor vehicle—community safety zone	172(1)	N.S.F.
492.	Race an animal	173	$85.00
493.	Fail to stop at railway crossing—public vehicle	174(1)	$85.00
494.	Stop wrong place at railway crossing—public vehicle	174(1)(a)	$85.00
495.	Fail to look both ways at railway crossing—public vehicle	174(1)(b)	$85.00
496.	Fail to open door at railway crossing—public vehicle	174(1)(c)	$85.00
497.	Cross tracks using gear requiring change public vehicle	174(1)(d)	$85.00
497.1	Change gears while crossing railway track—public vehicle	174(1)(e)	$85.00
497.2	Fail to stop at railway crossing—school bus	174(2)	$85.00
497.3	Stop wrong place at railway crossing—school bus	174(2)(a)	$85.00
497.4	Fail to look both ways at railway crossing—school bus	174(2)(b)	$85.00
497.5	Fail to open door at railway crossing—school bus	174(2)(c)	$85.00

ITEM	COLUMN 1	COLUMN 2 SECTION	SET FINE
497.6	Cross tracks using gear requiring change—school bus	174(2)(d)	$85.00
497.7	Change gears while crossing railway track—school bus	174(2)(e)	$85.00
498.	Bus not used to transport adults with developmental handicaps or children, painted chrome yellow	175(3)	$85.00
498.1	Chrome yellow bus not displaying required markings	175(3.1)	$85.00
499.	Prohibited markings	175(4)	$85.00
499.1	Prohibited equipment—school bus stop arm	175(4)	$85.00
500.	Drive chrome yellow vehicle, not used to transport adults with developmental handicaps or children	175(5)	$85.00
501.	Drive vehicle with prohibited school bus markings	175(5)	$85.00
502.	Drive vehicle with prohibited school bus stop arm	175(5)	$85.00
503.	Fail to actuate school bus signals	175(6)	$85.00
504.	Improperly actuate school bus signals	175(8)	$85.00
505.	Improperly actuate school bus signals at intersection controlled by operating traffic control system	175(9)(a)	$85.00
506.	Improperly actuate school bus signals at location, other than an intersection, controlled by operating traffic control system—at sign or roadway marking indicating stop to be made	175(9)(b)(i)	$85.00

ITEM	COLUMN 1	COLUMN 2 SECTION	SET FINE
507.	Improperly actuate school bus signals at location, other than an intersection, controlled by operating traffic control system—in area immediately before entering crosswalk	175(9)(b)(ii)	$85.00
507.1	Improperly actuate school bus signals at location, other than an intersection, controlled by operating traffic control system—within 5 m of traffic control system	175(9)(b)(iii)	$85.00
507.2	Improperly actuate school bus signals within 60 m of location controlled by operating traffic control system	175(9)(c)	$85.00
507.3	Stop school bus opposite loading zone	175(10)(a)	$85.00
507.5	Fail to stop for school bus—meeting	175(11)	$400.00
507.6	Fail to stop for school bus—overtaking	175(12)	$400.00
507.7	Fail to stop for school bus—owner	175(19)	$400.00
507.8	Fail to stop for school bus—owner	175(20)	$400.00
508.	Guard fail to properly display school crossing stop sign	176(2)	$85.00
509.	Fail to obey school crossing stop sign	176(3)	$150.00
509.1	Fail to obey school crossing stop sign community safety zone	176(3)	$300.00
510.	Improper use of school crossing stop sign	176(4)	$85.00
511.	Unauthorized person display school crossing stop sign	176(5)	$85.00

ITEM	COLUMN 1	COLUMN 2 SECTION	SET FINE
512.	Solicit a ride	177(1)	$50.00
513.	Solicit business	177(2)	$50.00
514.	Attach to vehicle	178(1)	$85.00
515.	Attach to street car	178(1)	$85.00
516.	Ride 2 on a bicycle	178(2)	$85.00
517.	Ride another person on a motor assisted bicycle	178(3)	$85.00
518.	Person—attach to vehicle	178(4)	$35.00
519.	Person—attach to street car	178(4)	$35.00
520.	Pedestrian fail to walk on left side of highway	179	$35.00
521.	Pedestrian on roadway fail to keep to left edge	179	$35.00
522.	Litter highway	180	$85.00
523.	Deposit snow or ice on roadway	181	$85.00
524.	Disobey sign	182(2)	$85.00
524.1	Disobey sign—community safety zone	182(2)	$120.00
525.	Disobey sign at tunnel	183(2)	$85.00
526.	Deface notice	184	N.S.F.
527.	Remove notice	184	N.S.F.
528.	Interfere with notice	184	N.S.F.
529.	Deface obstruction	184	N.S.F.
530.	Remove obstruction	184	N.S.F.
531.	Interfere with obstruction	184	N.S.F.
532.	Fail to remove aircraft	187(1)	N.S.F.
533.	Move aircraft improperly	187(2)	N.S.F.
534.	Aircraft unlawfully take off	187(3)	N.S.F.
535.	Draw occupied trailer	188	$85.00
536.	Operate air cushioned vehicle	189	$85.00
537.	Fail to maintain daily log	190(3)	$320.00
538.	Fail to carry daily log	190(3)	$320.00
539.	Fail to surrender daily log	190(4)	$320.00

ITEM	COLUMN 1	COLUMN 2 SECTION	SET FINE
540.	Driver in possession of more than one daily log	190(5)	$320.00
540.1	Permit person to drive commercial motor vehicle not in accordance with the regulations	190(6)	$320.00
540.2	Fail to produce proof of exemption	191(7)	$85.00
540.3	Drive motor vehicle—toll device improperly affixed	191.2(1)	$85.00
540.4	Drive motor vehicle—no toll device	191.2(1)	$85.00
540.5	Drive motor vehicle—invalid toll device	191.2(1)	$85.00
540.6	Engage in activity to evade toll system	191.3(1)	$85.00
540.7	Engage in activity to obstruct toll system	191.3(1)	$85.00
540.8	Engage in activity to interfere with toll system	191.3(1)	$85.00
540.9	Use device to evade toll system	191.3(1)	$85.00
540.10	Use device to obstruct toll system	191.3(1)	$85.00
540.11	Use device to interfere with toll system	191.3(1)	$85.00
540.12	Sell device designed to interfere with toll system	191.3(4)	$85.00
540.13	Offer to sell device designed to interfere with toll system	191.3(4)	$85.00
540.14	Advertise for sale device designed to interfere with toll system	191.3(4)	$85.00
540.15	Sell device intended to interfere with toll system	191.3(4)	$85.00
540.16	Offer to sell device intended to interfere with toll system	191.3(4)	$85.00

ITEM	COLUMN 1	COLUMN 2 SECTION	SET FINE
540.17	Advertise for sale device intended to interfere with toll system	191.3(4)	$85.00
541.	Fail to report accident	199(1)	$85.00
542.	Fail to furnish required information	199(1)	$85.00
542.1	Fail to report accident—specified location	199(1.1)	$85.00
542.2	Fail to furnish required information	199(1.1)	$85.00
543.	Occupant fail to report accident	199(2)	$85.00
544.	Police officer fail to report accident	199(3)	$85.00
544.1	Insurer fail to notify Registrar as prescribed re irreparable or salvage vehicle	199.1(4)	$400.00
544.2	Specified person fail to notify Registrar as prescribed re irreparable or salvage vehicle	199.1(5)	$400.00
544.3	Misclassify vehicle as irreparable or salvage in notice to Registrar	199.1(7)	$400.00
544.4	Fail to notify permit holder as prescribed re irreparable or salvage vehicle	199.1(8)	$400.00
544.5	Fail to return permit or portion of permit for irreparable or salvage vehicle to Registrar as prescribed	199.1(19)	$400.00
544.6	Drive or draw irreparable or salvage vehicle	199.1(19)	$140.00
544.7	Permit irreparable or salvage vehicle to be driven or drawn	199.1(19)	$140.00
545.	Fail to remain	200(1)(a)	N.S.F.

ITEM	COLUMN 1	COLUMN 2 SECTION	SET FINE
546.	Fail to render assistance	200(1)(b)	N.S.F.
547.	Fail to give required information	200(1)(c)	N.S.F.
548.	Fail to report damage to property on highway	201	$85.00
549.	Fail to report damage to fence bordering highway	201	$85.00
550.	Medical practitioner—fail to report	203(1)	$85.00
551.	Optometrist—fail to report	204(1)	$85.00
552.	Failing to forward suspended licence to Registrar	211(2)	$85.00
553.	Fail to surrender suspended driver's licence	212(2)	$60.00
554.	Refuse to surrender suspended driver's licence	212(2)	$60.00
554.0.1	Fail to assist in examination of commercial vehicle	216.1(1)	$310.00
554.0.2	Fail to stop commercial vehicle for examination	216.1(2)	$310.00
554.0.3	Fail to surrender documents	216.1(3)	$310.00
554.0.4	Fail to furnish information	216.1(3)	$310.00
554.0.5	Fail to comply with direction of officer	216.1(7)	$310.00
554.1	Cyclist—fail to stop	218(2)	$85.00
554.2	Cyclist—fail to identify self	218(2)	$85.00
555.	Obstruct officer	225(5)	$260.00
556.	Withhold record	225(5)	$260.00
557.	Conceal record	225(5)	$260.00
558.	Destroy record	225(5)	$260.00

SCHEDULE	OVERWEIGHT	PENALTY
Schedule A	0-2,499 kg.	$4.00 per 100 kg. or part kg.*
Highway Traffic Act	2,500-4,999 kg.	$5.00 per 100 kg. or part kg.
Set Fine	5,000-7,499 kg.	$6.00 per 100 kg. or part kg.
	Over 7,500 kg.	No Set Fine

* Regardless of the overweight, the penalty will not be less than $100.00.

SCHEDULE	SPEED OVER THE MAXIMUM LIMIT	SET FINES
Schedule B	a) 1-19 kilometres per hour	$2.50 per kilometre
Highway Traffic Act	b) 20-29 kilometres per hour	$3.75 per kilometre
Speeding	c) 30-49 kilometres per hour	$6.00 per kilometre
	d) 50 kilometres per hour or more	No out of court settlement
Schedule C	a) 1-19 kilometres per hour	$2.50 per kilometre
Highway Traffic Act	b) 20-34 kilometres per hour	$3.75 per kilometre
Speeding—Photo radar	c) 35-49 kilometres per hour	$6.00 per kilometre
	d) 50-60 kilometres per hour	$8.00 per kilometre
	e) 61+ kilometres per hour	No Set Fine
Schedule D	a) 1-19 kilometres per hour	$5.00 per kilometre
Highway Traffic Act	b) 20-29 kilometres per hour	$7.50 per kilometre
Speeding—Community Safety Zone	c) 30-49 kilometres per hour	$12.00 per kilometre
	d) 50 kilometres per hour or more	No out of court settlement
Schedule E	a) 1-19 kilometres per hour	$2.50 per kilometre
Highway Traffic Act	b) 20-29 kilometres per hour	$3.75 per kilometre
Speeding—Construction Zone	c) 30-49 kilometres per hour	$6.00 per kilometre
	d) 50 kilometres per hour or more	No out of court settlement
Schedule F	a) 1-19 kilometres per hour	$5.00 per kilometre
Highway Traffic Act	b) 20-29 kilometres per hour	$7.50 per kilometre
Speeding—Construction Zone Worker Present	c) 30-49 kilometres per hour	$12.00 per kilometre
	d) 50 kilometres per hour or more	No out of court settlement

Highway Traffic Act

Demerit Point System

O Reg 339/94

INTERPRETATION

1.(1) In this Regulation,

"accumulated demerit points" means the total demerit points in a person's record acquired as a result of offences committed within any period of two years, less any points deducted for that period under this Regulation.

(2) A reference in this Regulation to a class of driver's licence is a reference to the class of licence as prescribed in Ontario Regulation 340/94.

(3) A reference in this Regulation to "fully licensed driver," "level 1 exit test," "level 2 exit test," "novice driver" and "valid driver's licence" is a reference to those expressions as defined in Ontario Regulation 340/94.

(4) A reference in this Regulation to the surrender of a licence does not include the surrender of a licence card that has been marked by the Ministry as valid only to show the driver's photograph.

(5) The short descriptions in Column 3 of the Table to this Regulation indicate, for convenience of reference only, the general nature of the offences under the provisions in Column 1 of the Table and shall not be construed to limit the offences for which demerit points are imposed.

GENERAL

2. If a person is convicted of an offence under a provision of an Act, regulation or municipal by-law set out in Column 1 of the Table to this Regulation and the penalty imposed by the court for the conviction does not include a period of licence suspension, the Registrar shall record in respect of the person, as of the date of commission of the offence, the number of demerit points set out opposite thereto in Column 2.

3(1) If a person is convicted of an offence or two or more offences arising out of the same circumstances and the penalty imposed by the court includes a period of licence suspension, no demerit points shall be recorded.

(2) If a person is convicted of two or more offences arising out of the same circumstances and the penalty imposed by the court does not include a period of licence suspension, demerit points shall only be recorded for the conviction carrying the greatest number of points.

4(1) If a resident of Ontario is convicted or forfeits bail in another province or territory of Canada or in one of the states of the United States of America for an offence that, in the opinion of the Registrar, is in substance and effect equivalent to an offence for which demerit points would be recorded upon conviction in Ontario, the Registrar may record the demerit points for the conviction as if the conviction had been entered or the bail forfeited in Ontario for the equivalent offence.

(2) For the purposes of subsection (1), "conviction" includes a plea of guilty or a finding of guilt.

(3) Any accumulated demerit points of a new Ontario resident who becomes a fully licensed driver or a novice driver here, including a person classed as a novice driver under subsection 28(1) of Ontario Regulation 340/94 shall be reduced, from the day on which he or she becomes a fully licensed driver or a novice driver,

(a) to seven, if the driver becomes a fully licensed driver and his or her accumulated demerit points total eight or more;

(b) to four, if the driver becomes a novice driver and his or her accumulated demerit points total five or more.

(4) After a reduction under subsection (3), the accumulated demerit points that remain shall be those recorded for the most recently committed offences.

5(1) If a person convicted of an offence set out in Column 1 of the Table appeals the conviction and notice of the appeal is served on the Registrar, the conviction and the demerit points related to it shall not be entered on the person's record unless the conviction is sustained on appeal.

(2) If a conviction referred to in subsection (1) and related demerit points have been recorded prior to service of notice of an appeal on the Registrar, the conviction and demerit points shall be removed from the record, and any suspension imposed as a result of the conviction shall be stayed, as of the date notice is served on the Registrar, unless the conviction is sustained on appeal.

6(1) The notice of suspension sent to a person in respect of a suspension under this Regulation shall state the effective date of the suspension.

(2) Revoked.

(3) The period of licence suspension is concurrent with the unexpired portion of any other licence suspension under this or any other authority.

DEMERIT POINTS: FULLY LICENSED DRIVERS

7(1) If a person who is a fully licensed driver in Ontario in one or more licence classes or a person who is not a resident of Ontario has six, seven or eight accumulated demerit points, the Registrar shall mail a notice setting out the number of points to the person at his or her latest address appearing on the records of the Ministry.

(2) A failure to give notice under subsection (1) does not render any further proceeding under this Regulation ineffective.

8(1) If a person who is a fully licensed driver in Ontario in one or more licence classes or a person who is not a resident of Ontario has 9, 10, 11, 12, 13 or 14 accumulated demerit points, the Registrar may require the person to attend an interview before a Ministry official and to provide information or other evidence to show cause why his or her driver's licence should not be suspended.

(2) The Minister may suspend or cancel the person's driver's licence,

(a) if the person fails to attend the required interview; or

(b) if the person does not comply with the Ministry's requirements as a result of the interview; or

(c) if, in the Minister's opinion, the person has not shown cause at the interview why the licence should not be suspended.

(2.1) The Minister may cancel the person's driver's licence if the person fails to pay a fee required under subsection 56(4) of the Act.

(3) A licence suspended under subsection (2) shall not be reinstated until such period as the Minister considers advisable has elapsed from the date the licence was surrendered on account of the suspension or two years have elapsed from the date of the suspension, whichever occurs first.

9(1) If a person who is a fully licensed driver in Ontario in one or more licence classes or a person who is not a resident of Ontario has 15 or more accumulated demerit points, the Registrar shall, after giving notice, suspend the person's driver's licence.

(2) A licence suspended under subsection (1) shall not be reinstated until,

(a) in the case of a first suspension, 30 days have elapsed from the date the licence was surrendered on account of the suspension or two years have elapsed from the date of the suspension, whichever occurs first; or

(b) in the case of a subsequent suspension, six months have elapsed from the date the licence was surrendered on account of the suspension or two years have elapsed from the date of the suspension, whichever occurs first.

(3) For the purpose of clause (2)(b), a suspension is a subsequent suspension only if it occurs as a result of a conviction for an offence committed within two years after the expiry of a prior suspension under this section.

(4) If a suspension is imposed on a person who, at the time of the suspension, is a fully licensed driver in Ontario in one or more licence classes or a person who is not a resident of Ontario, the person's accumulated demerit points for convictions for offences that occurred prior to the effective date of the suspension shall be reduced to seven on that date and the remaining points shall be those recorded for the most recently committed offences.

10.-14. Revoked.

DEMERIT POINTS: NOVICE DRIVERS

15(1) The Registrar shall mail a notice to a novice driver at his or her latest address on the records of the Ministry setting out the reason for the notice, the circumstances under which his or her licence may be suspended and any other action the Ministry may take if, within any two-year period, the novice driver accumulates two, three, four or five demerit points.

(2) A failure to give notice under subsection (1) does not render any further proceeding under this Regulation ineffective.

16(1) The Registrar may require a novice driver to attend an interview before a Ministry official at a designated time and place if, within any two-year period, the novice driver accumulates six, seven or eight demerit points.

(2) The Minister may suspend or cancel the person's driver's licence,

(a) if the person does not attend the required interview;

(b) if the person does not comply with the Ministry's requirements as a result of the interview; or

(c) if, in the Minister's opinion, the person has not shown cause at the interview why the licence should not be suspended.

(2.1) The Minister may cancel the person's driver's licence if the person fails to pay a fee required under subsection 56(4) of the Act.

(3) A licence suspended under subsection (2) shall not be reinstated until such period as the Registrar considers advisable has elapsed from the date the licence was surrendered on account of the suspension or two years have elapsed from the date of the suspension, whichever occurs first.

17(1) If a novice driver has nine or more accumulated demerit points, the Registrar shall, after giving notice, suspend his or her driver's licence.

(2) A licence suspended under subsection (1) shall not be reinstated until,

(a) in the case of a first suspension, 60 days have elapsed from the date the licence was surrendered on account of the suspension or two years have elapsed from the date of the suspension, whichever occurs first; or

(b) in the case of a subsequent suspension, six months have elapsed from the date the licence was surrendered on account of the suspension or two years have elapsed from the date of the suspension, whichever occurs first.

(3) For the purpose of clause (2)(b), a suspension is a subsequent suspension only if it occurs as a result of a conviction for an offence committed within two years after the expiry of a prior suspension under this section.

(4) If a suspension is imposed on a person who, at the time of the suspension, is a novice driver, the person's accumulated demerit points for convictions for offences that occurred prior to the effective date of the suspension shall be reduced to four on that date and the remaining points shall be those recorded in respect of the most recently committed offences.

(5) If a suspension is imposed on a person who, at the time of the suspension, is no longer a novice driver, the person's accumulated demerit points for convictions for offences that occurred prior to the effective date of the suspension shall be reduced to seven on that date and the remaining points shall be those recorded in respect of the most recently committed offences.

18(1) Sections 7 to 9 apply, and not sections 15, 16 and 17, to a driver who holds a licence that includes more than one licence class, only one of which is novice class, if he or she is a fully licensed driver in the other licence class or classes.

(2) Revoked.

19. Omitted (revokes other Regulations).

20. Omitted (provides for coming into force of provisions of this Regulation).

ITEM	COLUMN 1 PROVISIONS FOR OFFENCES	COLUMN 2 NUMBER OF DEMERIT POINTS	COLUMN 3 SHORT DESCRIPTION OF OFFENCES FOR CONVENIENCE OF REFERENCE ONLY
1	Section 200 of the Highway Traffic Act	7	Failing to remain at scene of accident
1.1	Section 216 of the Highway Traffic Act, except where a suspension order is made under subsection 216(3)	7	Driver failing to stop when signalled or requested to stop by a police officer
2	Section 130 of the Highway Traffic Act	6	Careless driving
3	Section 172 of the Highway Traffic Act	6	Racing
4	Section 128 of the Highway Traffic Act; subsection 13(3) of Regulation 829 of the Revised Regulations of Ontario, 1990; any provision of the National Capital Commission Traffic and Property Regulations CRC 1978, c. 1044 made under the National Capital Act (Canada) fixing maximum rates of speed and any municipal by-law fixing maximum rates of speed where the rate of speed is exceeded by,		
	(a) 50 km/h or more	6	Exceeding speed limit by 50 km/h or more
	(b) 30 km/h or more and less than 50 km/h	4	Exceeding speed limit by 30 to 49 km/h
	(c) more than 15 km/h and less than 30 km/h	3	Exceeding speed limit by 16 to 29 km/h
5	Subsections 174(1) and (2) of the Highway Traffic Act	5	Driver of public vehicle or school bus failing to stop at railway crossings
6	Section 164 of the Highway Traffic Act	3	Driving through, around or under railway crossing barrier
7	Subsections 135(2) and (3), clause 136(1) (b), subsection 136(2), subsection 138(1), subsection 139(1), subsection 141(5) and subsections 144(7), (8) and (21) of the Highway Traffic Act	3	Failing to yield right of way
8	Clause 136(1)(a), subsections 144(14), (15), (16), (17), (18) and (21), subsections 146(3) and (4) and section 163 of the Highway Traffic Act, any municipal by-law requiring a driver to stop for a stop sign or signal light, and the National Capital Commission Traffic and Property Regulations CRC 1978, c. 1044 made under the National Capital Act (Canada) requiring a driver to stop for a stop sign	3	Failing to obey a stop sign, signal light or railway crossing signal
9	Subsection 134(1) of the Highway Traffic Act	3	Failing to obey directions of police constable
10	Subsection 134(3) of the Highway Traffic Act	3	Driving or operating a vehicle on a closed highway
11	Subsections 199(1) and (1.1) of the Highway Traffic Act	3	Failing to report an accident

ITEM	COLUMN 1 PROVISIONS FOR OFFENCES	COLUMN 2 NUMBER OF DEMERIT POINTS	COLUMN 3 SHORT DESCRIPTION OF OFFENCES FOR CONVENIENCE OF REFERENCE ONLY
12	Subsection 148(8), sections 149, 150 and 166 of the Highway Traffic Act	3	Improper passing
13	Section 154 of the Highway Traffic Act	3	Improper driving where highway divided into lanes
14	Subsections 175(11) and (12) of the Highway Traffic Act	6	Failing to stop for school bus
15	Section 158 of the Highway Traffic Act	4	Following too closely
16	Section 162 of the Highway Traffic Act	3	Crowding driver's seat
17	Clause 156(1)(a) of the Highway Traffic Act	3	Drive wrong way—divided highway
18	Clause 156(1)(b) of the Highway Traffic Act	3	Cross divided highway—no proper crossing provided
19	Section 153 of the Highway Traffic Act	3	Wrong way in one way street or highway
20	Subsection 157(1) of the Highway Traffic Act	2	Backing on highway
21	Subsections 140(1), (2) and (3) of the Highway Traffic Act	3	Pedestrian crossover
22	Subsections 148(1), (2), (4), (5), (6) and (7) of the Highway Traffic Act	2	Failing to share road
23	Subsections 141(2) and (3) of the Highway Traffic Act	2	Improper right turn
24	Subsections 141(6) and (7) of the Highway Traffic Act	2	Improper left turn
25	Subsections 142(1), (2) and (8) of the Highway Traffic Act	2	Failing to signal
26	Section 132 of the Highway Traffic Act	2	Unnecessary slow driving
27	Section 168 of the Highway Traffic Act	2	Failing to lower headlamp beam
28	Subsection 165(1) of the Highway Traffic Act	3	Improper opening of vehicle door
29	Section 143 and subsection 144(9) of the Highway Traffic Act and any municipal by-law prohibiting turns	2	Prohibited turns
30	Section 160 of the Highway Traffic Act	2	Towing of persons on toboggans, bicycles, skis, etc., prohibited
31	Subsection 182(2) of the Highway Traffic Act	2	Failing to obey signs prescribed by regulation under subsection 182 (1)
32	Subsection 106(2) of the Highway Traffic Act	2	Driver failing to properly wear seat belt
33	Subclause 106(4)(a)(i) of the Highway Traffic Act	2	Driving while passenger under 16 fails to occupy position with seat belt
33.1	Subclause 106 (4)(a)(ii) of the Highway Traffic Act	2	Driving while passenger under 16 fails to properly wear seat belt

ITEM	COLUMN 1 PROVISIONS FOR OFFENCES	COLUMN 2 NUMBER OF DEMERIT POINTS	COLUMN 3 SHORT DESCRIPTION OF OFFENCES FOR CONVENIENCE OF REFERENCE ONLY
33.2	Clause 106(4)(b) of the Highway Traffic Act	2	Driving while child passenger not properly secured
34	Subsection 8(2) of Regulation 613 of the Revised Regulations of Ontario, 1990	2	Driver failing to ensure infant passenger is secured as prescribed
34.1	Subsection 8(3) of Regulation 613 of the Revised Regulations of Ontario, 1990	2	Driver failing to ensure toddler passenger is secured as prescribed
34.2	Subsection 8(4) of Regulation 613 of the Revised Regulations of Ontario, 1990	2	Driver failing to ensure child passenger is secured as prescribed
35	Clause 159(1)(a) of the Highway Traffic Act	3	Failing to stop on right for emergency vehicle
36	Clause 159(1)(b) of the Highway Traffic Act	3	Failing to stop—nearest curb—for emergency vehicle
36.1	Clause 159(1)(b) of the Highway Traffic Act	3	Failing to stop—nearest edge of roadway—for emergency vehicle
36.2	Subsection 159(2) of the Highway Traffic Act	3	Failing to slow down and proceed with caution for emergency vehicle or tow truck
36.3	Subsection 159(3) of the Highway Traffic Act	3	Failing to move into another lane for emergency vehicle or tow truck—if safe to do so
36.4	Subsection 159(4) of the Highway Traffic Act	3	Following fire department vehicle too closely
37	Subsection 79(2) of the Highway Traffic Act	3	Motor vehicle equipped with or carrying a speed measuring warning device
38	Subsection 154.1(3) of the Highway Traffic Act	3	Improper use of high occupancy vehicle lane
39	Subsection 146.1(3) of the Highway Traffic Act	3	Failing to obey traffic control stop sign
40	Subsection 146.1(4) of the Highway Traffic Act	3	Failing to obey traffic control slow sign
41	Subsection 176(3) of the Highway Traffic Act	3	Failing to obey school crossing stop sign
42	Section 78 of the Highway Traffic Act	3	Driving with display screen visible to driver
43	Section 78.1 of the Highway Traffic Act	3	Driving while holding or using hand-held device
44	Subsection 148(6.1) of the Highway Traffic Act	2	Failing to leave one metre while passing bicycle

AMP Regulation

E

Administrative Penalties

Under *Municipal Act, 2001*, SO 2001, c 25

O REG 333/07

Definitions

1. In this Regulation,

"administrative penalty by-law" means a by-law establishing a system of administrative penalties and described in clause 3 (1) (a)

"designated by-law" means a by-law with respect to parking, standing or stopping of vehicles that is designated by a municipality as a by-law to which the municipality's system of administrative penalties applies and, if only a part of a by-law is designated, includes only the designated part of the by-law.

Application

2. This Regulation applies to administrative penalties that are required by a municipality in respect of the parking, standing or stopping of vehicles and referred to in section 102.1 of the Act.

General condition

3. (1) A municipality shall not exercise the power referred to in section 102.1 of the Act to require a person to pay an administrative penalty unless the municipality,

(a) has passed a by-law establishing a system of administrative penalties that meets the requirements of this Regulation;

(b) has designated the by-laws respecting parking, standing or stopping of vehicles, or the parts of such by-laws, to which the system of administrative penalties applies; and

(c) has met any other requirements of this Regulation.

(2) The purpose of the system of administrative penalties established by the municipality shall be to assist the municipality in regulating the flow of traffic and use of land, including highways, by promoting compliance with its by-laws respecting the parking, standing or stopping of motor vehicles.

(3) REVOKED.

Non-application of *Provincial Offences Act*

4. The *Provincial Offences Act* does not apply to the contravention of a designated by-law.

Liability of owner

5. (1) If a vehicle has been left parked, standing or stopped in contravention of a designated by-law, the owner of the vehicle shall, upon issuance of a penalty notice in accordance with the administrative penalty by-law, be liable to pay an administrative penalty in an amount specified in the administrative penalty by-law.

(2) For the purposes of subsection (1), the owner of a vehicle is deemed to be,

(a) the person whose name appears on the permit for the vehicle; and

(b) if the vehicle permit consists of a vehicle portion and plate portion and different persons are named on each portion, the person whose name appears on the plate portion.

Monetary limit

6. The amount of an administrative penalty established by a municipality,

(a) shall not be punitive in nature; and

(b) shall not exceed the amount reasonably required to promote compliance with a designated by-law.

(c) REVOKED.

Administration of system of administrative penalties

7. A municipality shall develop standards relating to the administration of the system of administrative penalties which shall include,

(a) policies and procedures to prevent political interference in the administration of the system;

(b) guidelines to define what constitutes a conflict of interest in relation to the administration of the system, to prevent such conflicts of interest and to redress such conflicts should they occur;

(c) policies and procedures regarding financial management and reporting; and

(d) procedures for the filing and processing of complaints made by the public with respect to the administration of the system.

Procedural requirements

8. (1) The administrative penalty by-law passed by a municipality shall include the following procedural requirements:

1. The owner of a vehicle must be provided with reasonable notice that an administrative penalty is payable under the administrative penalty by-law.

2. The individual issuing a penalty notice in respect of the contravention of a designated by-law is not allowed to accept payment in respect of the penalty.

3. A person who receives a penalty notice shall be given the right to request a review of the administrative penalty by a screening officer appointed by the municipality for that purpose.

4. The screening officer may cancel, affirm or vary the penalty, including any fee imposed under section 12, upon such grounds as are set out in the administrative penalty by-law.

5. A person who receives notice of the decision of the screening officer shall, in such circumstances as may be specified in the administrative penalty by-law, be given the right to a review of the screening officer's decision by a hearing officer appointed by the municipality for that purpose.

6. The hearing officer shall not make a determination with respect to a review of the screening officer's decision unless he or she has given the person who requested the review an opportunity to be heard.

7. The hearing officer may cancel, affirm or vary the decision of the screening officer upon such grounds as are set out in the administrative penalty by-law.

8. Procedures must be established to allow a person to obtain an extension of time in which to request a review by a screening officer, or a review by a hearing officer, on such grounds as may be specified in the administrative penalty by-law.

9. Procedures must be established to permit persons to obtain an extension of time for payment of the penalty on such conditions as may be specified in the administrative penalty by-law.

10. The procedures established under paragraphs 8 and 9 shall provide for a suspension of the enforcement mechanisms available under sections 9, 10 and 11 in relation to the administrative penalty if an extension of time has been granted.

11. Procedures must be established to permit persons to be excused from paying all or part of the administrative penalty, including any administrative fees referred to in section 12, if requiring them to do so would cause undue hardship.

(2) The appointment of the hearing officer shall be consistent with the conflict of interest guidelines referred to in clause 7 (b) and the hearing officer shall conduct hearings in an impartial manner.

(3) Neither a screening officer nor a hearing officer has jurisdiction to consider questions relating to the validity of a statute, regulation or by-law or the constitutional applicability or operability of any statute, regulation or by-law.

(4) The *Statutory Powers Procedure Act* applies to a review by a hearing officer.

(5) The decision of a hearing officer is final.

Enforcement

9. (1) If an administrative penalty is not paid within 15 days after the date that it becomes due and payable to a municipality, it has the right to enforce payment of the amount in default in accordance with this section.

(2) The municipality may file a certificate of default in a court of competent jurisdiction and, once filed, the certificate is deemed to be an order of the court and may be enforced in the same manner as an order of the court.

(3) A certificate of default shall be in the form approved by the Attorney General.

(4) Costs incurred in obtaining and enforcing the deemed order shall be added to the order and collected under the order.

(5) Revoked.

(6) One certificate of default may be filed with the court in respect of two or more administrative penalties imposed on the same person.

(7) If, after a certificate of default has been filed with the court, every penalty to which the certificate relates is paid in full, the municipality shall,

(a) notify the court in writing; and

(b) if a writ of execution has been filed with the sheriff, notify the sheriff in writing.

Plate denial

10. (1) If an administrative penalty is not paid within 15 days after the date that it becomes due and payable to a municipality, it may notify the Registrar of Motor Vehicles of the default and the Registrar shall not validate the permit of a

person named in the default notice nor issue a new permit to that person until the penalty is paid.

(2) Subsection (1) applies only to the permit related to the vehicle to which the administrative penalty relates.

Other enforcement measures

11. (1) If an administrative penalty is not paid within 15 days after the date that it becomes due and payable to a municipality, it may adopt, in addition to the enforcement measures described in sections 9 and 10, such other enforcement measures as may be permitted under the Act.

(2) The other enforcement measures referred to in subsection (1) shall not be punitive in nature.

Administrative fees

12. (1) Subject to subsection (2), a municipality may charge administrative fees, in the amounts specified in the by-law, as follows:

1. If an administrative penalty is not paid within 15 days after the date that it becomes due and payable to the municipality,

    i. late payment fees, and

    ii. fees in respect of amounts paid by the municipality to obtain documents or information about the vehicle or the owner of the vehicle.

2. A fee in respect of the failure of a person to appear at the time and place scheduled for a hearing by a hearing officer.

3. Any other fee or charge that may be imposed by the municipality in respect of the administration of the administrative penalty system under section 391 of the Act.

(2) No fee may be charged in relation to obtaining a review before a screening officer or a hearing officer.

(3) Revoked.

(4) The fees described in subsection (1) may be added to the administrative penalties in default and the additional amount may be included in the amount to be collected in accordance with the enforcement measures adopted by the municipality under sections 9, 10 and 11.

(5) If a person has paid any of the fees described in subsection (1) in respect of an administrative penalty and the penalty is subsequently cancelled by a screening officer or a hearing officer, the municipality shall refund the fees in full to the person.

Availability of by-laws

13. A municipality shall ensure that its administrative penalty by-law is made available to the public in such manner as it sees fit, at no cost.

14. Omitted (provides for coming into force of provisions of this Regulation).

Glossary

A

absolute liability offence an offence for which the prosecution must prove that the defendant committed the illegal act; the defendant has no opportunity to argue reasonableness or due diligence

adjourn put the trial over to a new date

affidavit a document sworn by a party to attest to the truthfulness of the statements within the document—often used in support of a motion

amending up the practice of having the defendant tried on the actual rate of speed instead of the reduced rate of speed specified by the officer when the charges were laid

appellant the party bringing an appeal, either the defence or the prosecution

arraignment the formal reading of the charges to the defendant or the defendant's representative in anticipation of a plea

B

balance of probabilities a standard of proof where an illegal act must be proven to be more likely than not to have occurred

beyond a reasonable doubt a standard of proof where the prosecution must fully prove that the defendant committed the illegal act (to the extent that a reasonable person would not doubt that the act was committed)

burden of proof the responsibility for proving whether there should be a conviction; primarily rests with the prosecution for provincial offence matters

C

certificate of offence a certificate of a violation prepared by an officer under Part I of the POA and filed with the court to commence proceedings

certificate of parking infraction a notice of a violation issued by an officer under Part II of the POA

charging act a piece of legislation under which a person is charged (e.g., the *Highway Traffic Act*)

charging document the paperwork used to initiate charges against a defendant

contravener a person who has violated an administrative penalty by-law

conviction a final decision by a justice that there is proof that the defendant committed the offence for which he or she was charged

costs a fee added to a court-imposed penalty

court the Ontario Court of Justice, which includes the provincial offences court

court administration staff work within the courthouse providing information and performing various administrative duties

court clerk ensures POA proceedings run smoothly by providing assistance to the judge or justice

court interpreter provides translation services to defendants who do not speak English

court security officer special constables who have been appointed to assist with courthouse security and attend to specific incidents that may arise

cross-examination the prosecution or defence questions the opposing side's witnesses, following examination-in-chief

D

defence of causation the defendant must show that there is no direct link between his or her conduct and the offence

defence of due diligence the defendant must show that he or she took all reasonable steps to avoid committing the offence

defence of involuntariness the defendant must show that his or her actions were not voluntary and not within his or her control

defence of necessity the defendant must show that it was necessary to commit the offence, that no reasonable alternative existed, and that the harm caused by the act was outweighed by the harm that was avoided

defendant has been charged with an offence under a statute governed by the *Provincial Offences Act*

demerit points a penalty administered by the Ministry of Transportation for driving offences

deterrence a principle of sentencing intended to discourage a defendant from reoffending; specific and general are the two types of deterrence

disclosure documentation that the prosecutor will be relying on to prove the charges against the defendant

dismissed a final decision by a justice that there is not enough evidence to support a conviction against the defendant

docket the list of defendants scheduled for trial

driving record a record of convictions against a driver maintained by the Ministry of Transportation

due diligence the standard of care that a reasonable person would be expected to apply to a specific situation

E

elements of the offence the items that have to be proven by the prosecutor to secure a conviction

***ex parte* trial** a trial held in the absence of the defendant or the defendant's representative

examination-in-chief the prosecution or defence questions its own witnesses at the trial

expert witness a person who has specialized knowledge or experience that relates to the charges before the court

F

fatal error a serious mistake on a charging document that will result in the charges being withdrawn, dismissed, or stayed

fresh evidence evidence that was not introduced at trial, but was attempted to be introduced at the appeal

G

guilty with submissions pleading guilty, but providing additional information on why the penalty should be reduced or the time for payment should be extended

H

hearing officer an administrative law judge who provides a final review of a screening officer's decision

hearsay statements that have been made outside of court by someone other than the witness testifying on the stand

held down hearing a matter at a later time

I

included offence an alternative offence that still fits with the facts of the defendant's wrongful behaviour, but carries a lesser penalty

informant a person who commences a Part III proceeding against a defendant

institutional delay the amount of time it takes for a matter to get to trial, minus any delay that was caused by the defendant

J

justice of the peace a magistrate who presides over proceedings in provincial offences court

L

leave to appeal permission from the court to bring an appeal

limitation period the time allowed for an officer to lay a charge against a defendant

M

***mens rea* offence** an offence for which the prosecution must prove that the defendant committed the illegal act and had a guilty mind (i.e., the knowledge, intent, or willingness to commit the act)

mitigating factor favourable information about a defendant that is presented to a justice after conviction which may lead to a lesser penalty

monetary retainer a sum of money paid up front for legal services to be provided in the future

moving party the party who brings a motion

N

non-fatal error a mistake on a charging document that is not serious and will likely be amended in court

Notice of Intention to Appear Form 8, used for the defendant to request a trial

O

offence a violation of a piece of legislation, or of a regulation or a by-law made under a piece of legislation

offence notice a document served on the defendant to inform him/her of the charges (commonly called a "ticket")

onus the burden of proof or responsibility for proving that an allegation, exception, or defence should apply

P

penalty notice the document served on the registered owner of a vehicle under the administrative penalty system

police officer has the authority to lay charges against a defendant

pre-trial motion a motion brought with notice in advance of the trial date

probation order a court order that places conditions on a defendant after conviction, often to control the defendant's movements and require certain action

procedural act a statute that sets out the procedures to be followed when dealing with an offence (e.g., the *Provincial Offences Act*)

procedural stream a category under which an offence can be classified that then determines the procedure for dealing with the charge throughout the provincial offences system

prohibition order a court order that prohibits a defendant from engaging in activities that could lead to a repetition of the offence

proportionality a principle in law that the penalty should be proportional to the offence that was committed

prosecutor an agent of the attorney general who prosecutes the charges against the defendant

provincial court judge a lawyer who has been appointed a judge and typically presides over more serious provincial offences cases and appeals

provincial offences officer has the authority to lay charges against a defendant for specific types of provincial offences (includes a police officer)

public welfare offences offences that are a violation of safety laws that were enacted to protect the public (also known as provincial offences)

Q

quash to nullify or invalidate charges against the defendant such that the charges are thrown out of court

quasi-criminal offences offences that bear a resemblance to criminal matters because the procedure for dealing with them is similar to the criminal process (also known as provincial offences)

R

recognizance an acknowledgment and agreement by the defendant that he or she will attend the next scheduled court appearance

regulations legislation that contains the rules or principles that are enacted under the authority of a statute

regulatory offences offences that are a violation of laws that were enacted to regulate behaviour in society (also known as provincial offences)

representative a lawyer or a paralegal who is authorized to represent a defendant in a proceeding under the POA

responding party the party who does not initiate the motion but will have an opportunity to respond to it

retainer agreement an agreement for legal services between a licensee and a client

reverse-onus the burden of proof shifts to the defendant to prove that he or she did not commit the offence

S

screening officer a municipal employee who provides an initial review of an administrative penalty

set fine the amount of monetary penalty determined by the chief justice of the Ontario Court of Justice for an offence under Part I or Part II

standard of proof the level of certainty needed to establish proof in a provincial offences trial; may apply to the level of certainty needed for the prosecution to obtain a conviction or the level of certainty for the defendant to exonerate himself or herself; can be beyond a reasonable doubt or on a balance of probabilities

staying the proceedings the prosecution of the offence has been halted and a conviction will not be entered against the defendant

strict liability offence an offence for which the prosecution must prove that the defendant committed the illegal act; the defendant then has an opportunity to prove reasonableness or due diligence

summons a document issued to a defendant requiring attendance in court

surety a person who agrees to be responsible for the defendant's appearance in court

T

tier a court session over a specific period of time

U

uncontested adjournment a request by either the prosecution or the defence to move the trial to a new date which is being made with the consent of the other party

V

verdict the decision or ruling of the justice

victim fine surcharge a fee added to a court-imposed penalty that is then transferred to a special fund to assist victims of crime

voir dire a trial within a trial that is conducted to determine whether or not a specific element of evidence should be permitted

W

waive arraignment a legal representative tells the court clerk that it is not necessary to read the charges

withdrawn a decision by the prosecution to remove the charges against the defendant

witness has first-hand knowledge about the matter being prosecuted

Index